ADVANCED PE FOR OCR: A2

Daniel Bonney
John Ireland
Claire Miller
Ken Mackreth
Sarah van Wely

D0538034

Heinemann Educational Publishers
Halley Court, Jordan Hill, Oxford OX2 8EJ
Part of Harcourt Education

Heinemann is the registered trademark of
Harcourt Education Limited

© Daniel Bonney, John Ireland, Claire Miller, Ken Mackreth, Sarah van Wely, 2004

First published 2004

09 08 07 06 05 04
10 9 8 7 6 5 4 3 2 1

British Library Cataloguing in Publication Data is available
from the British Library on request.

ISBN 0 435 50612 9

Typeset by TechType, Abingdon, Oxon

Original illustrations © Harcourt Education Limited, 2004

Illustrated by TechType, Abingdon, Oxon

Printed in Great Britain by Scotprint

Cover photo: © Empics

Picture research by Liz Moore

Acknowledgements
Every effort has been made to contact copyright holders of material reproduced in this book. Any omissions will be
rectified in subsequent printings if notice is given to the publishers.

Photographic acknowledgements
The authors would like to thank the following for permission to reproduce photographs:
(t = top, b = bottom, r = right, L = left, m = middle)

Action Plus p.151, p.318b; Alamy p.125; AP Photo/Greg Baker: p.116; p.34 taken from *Blazers, Badgers and
Boaters: A Pictorial History of the School Uniform*; Bodleian Library, Oxford p.36bl; Bridgeman Art Library/MCC
London p.51; Corbis p.42b, p.52, p.59, p.66, p.84, p.185; Corbis/Duomo p.219; Corbis/Hulton Deutsch p.14, p.61;
Corbis/Layne Kennedy p.178; Corbis/Sygma p.137; Empics p.79, p.102, p.103, p.145, p.146, p.159, p.222, p.226;
Empics/Topham p.141, p.324; Getty News and Sport/AFP p.286; Hulton Archive: p.33; Hulton Getty p.12, p.17b,
p.24, p.58; Illustrated London News p.46b, p.57; Mary Evans Picture Library p.4tr, p.36t, p.48; PA Photos/AAP
p.148; Popperfoto p.49; Popperfoto/Bob Thomas p.19; Popperfoto/Dave Joyner p.131, p.233; Pro
Sport/Topham/Tommy Hindley p.249L; National Portrait Gallery p.26; Rex Features p.258; Sport and the Artist
Volume 1 p.36br; The Governing Body of Charterhouse p.35; Topham p.4bl, p.42t, p.62; Topham/AP p.179;
Topham/British Library/HIP p.45; Topham/Corporation of London/HIP p.13; Topham/Fotomas p.15, p.18, p.20,
p.39; Topham/Image Works p.81, p.83, p.94, p.184, p.239, p.241, p.243, p.249r; Topham/Image Works/Peter
Hzivdak p.161; Topham/PA p.4br, p.170, p.251, p.288r, p.318t; Topham/Pro Sport p.132, p.253, p.314; Topham/Ray
Roberts p.111; Travelsite p.70; Trustees of the British Museum p.4tl; Universal Pictorial Press Photo/Topham p.288L

Websites
There are links to relevant websites in this book. In order to ensure that the links are up to date, that the links work,
and that the sites are not inadvertently linked to sites that could be considered offensive, we have made the links
available on the Heinemann website at www.heinemann.co.uk/hotlinks. When you access the Heinemann website, enter
express code **6129P**, and this will take you to the links you require.

Tel: 01865 888058   www.heinemann.co.uk

Contents

Unit 5: Exercise physiology and the integration of knowledge of principles and concepts across different areas of Physical Education

Unit 6: The improvement of effective performance and critical evaluation of the practical activities with synoptic application

Introduction

This book is designed specifically for students following OCR's A2 Physical Education (PE) course. It will support and reinforce the teaching you receive in your centre following the principle of applying theory to practical performance and relating practical performance to theory. The OCR course also embraces the principle that practical performance is essential to the understanding of theory – students will be assessed in their practical activities with those marks contributing to the overall A2 grade.

The content of the book is presented in a form that is identical to the OCR specification under the same sections and sub-headings. This means that the content will probably be in the same order as you are taught it in your centre. The information is presented in a practical context wherever possible as an aid to your understanding and to prepare you for your examination questions.

ORGANIZATION OF THE BOOK

The book is divided into three units that represent the areas in which you will be examined.

Unit 4 Physical Education: historical, comparative, biomechanical and sport psychology

Unit 5 Exercise physiology and the integration of knowledge and principles and concepts across different areas of Physical Education

Unit 6 The improvement of effective performance and critical evaluation of the practical activities with synoptic application

Wherever possible theory will be applied to practical activities in order that you become accustomed to this approach. This is how you will be taught and examined.

Throughout each unit and chapter you will find a series of tasks which are designed to help you understand, apply and remember the topics they relate to. You will also find that some of the tasks cover work that you will need to include in your Personal Performance Portfolio (PPP).

Important definitions are highlighted in 'KEY WORDS' boxes to make it easier for you to find them. You will also find 'HOT TIPS' included throughout – these are meant to give you guidance as to how to improve your knowledge in order to get better grades in your A2 exams.

At the end of each chapter there will be some sample questions for you to do. In most cases these will be from past examination papers and will not only allow you to test your knowledge and understanding but will also give you an idea of the type and difficulty of the questions you will have to answer in you're A2 examinations.

HOW YOU WILL BE EXAMINED

You have three units to complete, two of which have examination papers with the third being a coursework unit in which your teachers will assess you. Units 4 and 5 are examined in both January and the summer, but Unit 6 can only be taken in the summer.

UNIT 4 (OCR UNIT 2565)

This unit is worth 30% of your A2 marks. It consists of a $1\frac{1}{4}$-hour examination paper consisting of two sections. Section A contains one question on Historical studies in Physical Education and one question on Comparative studies in Physical Education. Section B contains one question on the Biomechanical analysis of human movement and one question on Psychology of sport performance. You must answer two questions, including at least one question from Section A.

UNIT 5 (OCR UNIT 2566)

This unit is worth 40% of your A2 marks. It consists of a $1\frac{1}{2}$-hour examination paper consisting of two sections. Section A consists of a compulsory question on Exercise and sport physiology: the response of the body to performance and training. Section B contains two synoptic questions, one question with a scientific focus and the other question with a socio-cultural focus. One synoptic question must be answered.

UNIT 6 (OCR UNIT 2567)

This unit is worth 30% of your A2 marks. This is the practical (coursework) unit and is split into two parts.

- The selection, application and performance of skills in an open environment (20% of A2).
- Evaluation and appreciation of performance through observation and synopsis of knowledge (10% of A2).

Chapter 1 **Historical studies**

Section 1: *Popular recreation*

Learning objectives

At the end of this section you should be able to:
- understand how the past influences sport and PE today
- start thinking like an historian and asking the right questions
- respond to and interpret visual material
- understand the importance of social class when studying sports history
- identify the characteristics of popular recreation
- explain how these characteristics reflected society
- analyse the extent to which certain sporting examples 'fit' the normally accepted 'model' of popular recreations in Britain
- trace the emergence of certain individual activities and games.

KEY WORDS

Popular recreation

Pre-industrial sports and pastimes mainly associated with the peasant class. This term could also refer to the most popular pastimes at that time.

Public schools

Old, established, fee-paying schools dominated by upper- and upper-middle-class boys (and later girls).

Spartan

A word to describe poor living standards and a situation where young children were treated severely by masters and older boys.

Rational recreation

Civilized and organized sports and pastimes of post-industrial Britain.

Industrial Revolution

The transformation of society from a rural agricultural system to an urban factory system.

State elementary schools

A school for junior-aged children maintained by public spending. State education began in Britain following the Forster Education Act 1870.

Introduction

Our times and our thoughts, our games and our sports are shaped by the past. A study of sports history helps us to appreciate contemporary sport and PE. The 'Historical studies' specification is divided into four sections, which will be covered as follows.

Section 1: Popular recreation focuses on pre-industrial sports and pastimes, particularly of the lower class.

Section 2: Nineteenth century public school developments of athleticism focuses on the English **public schools**, such as Rugby, Eton and Charterhouse, which changed so dramatically during the nineteenth century. Initially they were riotous and **Spartan** institutions. However, by the 1870s they had become highly respected institutions where most boys and many masters regarded team games as more important than academic work.

Section 3: Rational recreation in an urban industrial society is concerned with the emergence of comparatively sophisticated and civilised post-industrial activities. The impact of the **Industrial Revolution** (which shaped late nineteenth-century British sport) and the emergence of the middle class (for whom many of the rational sports were developed) will be key features.

Section 4: The development of drill, physical training and physical education in elementary schools looks at developments in twentieth-century **state elementary** (primary) **schools**. The objectives, contents and ways of teaching military drill,

HOT TIPS

Make sure you are clear about the dates of the eighteenth, nineteenth and twentieth centuries, and remember that anything before 1800 is considered as 'pre-industrial'.

therapeutic drill, physical training and physical education will be studied in relation to changing social attitudes and the impact of war.

Four aspects of sports history

Fig. 1.01 A variety of pre-industrial sports and pastimes.

Fig. 1.02 Public school discipline at the beginning of the nineteenth century.

Fig. 1.03 Rational sport – 'sphairistike' or lawn tennis.

Fig. 1.04 Physical education in the 1950s.

Figure 1.05 helps us to see how the four aspects of sports history fit together. The OCR specification requires you to focus on these aspects.

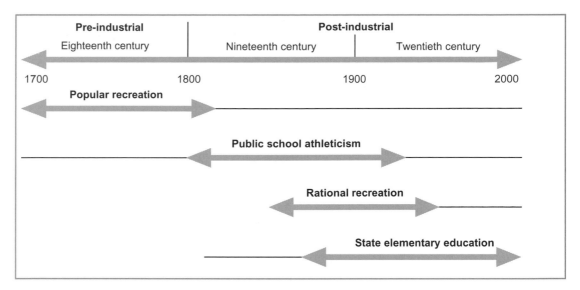

Fig. 1.05 Four aspects of sports history.

Individual activities	Games
Bathing and swimming	Mob football and Association Football
Rowing	Cricket
Athletics	Real tennis and lawn tennis

Case studies of each of the above activities and games will appear as themes in each section. After each case study section (for example, athletics as a popular recreation), page references will be given to the relevant information in the previous and/or next section so that the development of a particular sport can be read as a whole.

Background information

It is useful to set the scene with some of the historical landmarks that had an impact on sport.

![HOT TIPS]

HOT TIPS

You do not have to learn all the background information in this table. Use it for reference and try to have a general overview.

1066	The Norman Conquest – William the Conqueror	Introduction of the feudal system whereby Norman lords ruled over Anglo-Saxon commoners (serfs). The 'Age of Chivalry' – tournaments and jousting.
1200–1485	The Middle Ages or 'medieval period'	Recreation for rural peasants (the majority) limited to annual festivals because of their hard and long working days, lack of time and lack of opportunity. Tournaments continued for the ruling class. Archery compulsory as military training. The Church opposed many popular sports and pastimes.
1485–1603	The Tudor era	Renaissance gentlemen needed to be both sporting (hunting, horsemanship, swordplay, jousting, real tennis, dancing) and cultural (art, poetry).

1509	Henry VIII becomes king	A great lover of sports – hunting, wrestling, real tennis – as well as feasting and partying. Play for the peasants centred on traditional local festivals and fairs, such as Christmas.
1558	Elizabeth I becomes queen	Mob games and animal baiting flourished.
1603	James I becomes king – the start of the Stuart era	Seventeenth century Puritans despised the spontaneity and freedom of traditional sports and pastimes, believing that only the sober, quiet and hard working would be saved. They also opposed animal baiting and cruelty. However, James I's *Book of Sports* (1617) ensured the rights of the people to recreation as long as church attendance was observed.
1649	Execution of Charles I. Oliver Cromwell Protector of Britain	Cromwell was a Parliamentarian and a Puritan. A bleak time for sport.
1660	Charles II – the **Restoration** of the monarchy	Restoration of some previously banned sports and pastimes, saint's days and parish feasts.
1671	**Game Laws**	Prevented ordinary people from hunting and shooting game.
1714–90	The Hanoverian era. The start of the Industrial Revolution	The Church provided frequent feast days and a suitable space for gatherings. First formalisation of cricket (rules in 1727), rowing (Doggett Coat and Badge Race, 1715), horse racing (Jockey Club formed 1752) and prizefighting (Broughton's rules, 1743) as spectator attractions and commercial enterprises.
1790–1830	The Regency period	A time of high fashion. Pedestrianism and prizefighting at their peak of popularity. Church once again against popular recreations, considering them to be of the devil! Pressure to stop Sunday play (Sabbattarianism), traditional festivals, race meetings, prizefights and animal baiting.
1837–1901	The Victorian era	During the nineteenth century, society, education, sports and games changed dramatically. Christianity and the Protestant work ethic became established. Working hours and health provision improved for the working classes in the latter part of the 19th century, while pay and provision of open space increased. A revolution in transport and communications had a massive impact on the development of sport.
1700s–early 1900	The British Empire	Britain 'ruled the waves' in Imperial dominance and spread its systems of government, education, sport, culture and religion abroad.

KEY WORDS

The Restoration

In 1660, the army asked Charles I's son, Charles II, to take the throne, in this way restoring the monarchy to power. Puritanism was in decline, and Church support for sports and recreations increased.

Game Laws

These eighteenth- and nineteenth-century laws gave sole right to kill game to the upper class, and caused deep and lasting hostility in many rural areas.

Thinking like a historian

Part of your task is to imagine your way into the minds of the people who lived in earlier times and try to think about experiences as they did. Social history is about seeing what happened, working out why it happened and putting both continuity and change into societal context.

You can find out what happened by looking at evidence. The most reliable evidence is from a primary source, as it was seen and recorded first hand by eyewitnesses. Primary sources include diaries, newspapers, magazines, pictures taken or painted at the time, and authentic official documents. Libraries, public record offices and archives will help if you are keen and have time to do some primary research.

Interviews are also a primary source, though clearly only the most recent aspects of the specification can still be researched in this way. Primary sources can make the past come alive. For example, we know from primary evidence that many late nineteenth-century public school boys were obsessed by team games and other athletic pursuits, as this 1895 diary of a Charterhouse boy reveals. At the end of one particular day he wrote:

> *I played five games of fives and then tried the high jump. Then we had a shootabout and a kind of runabout. Then we went down to the racquet courts and played racquets. Before tea we played in a football game on Big Ground, I put the weight and went again to shootabout.*

Not surprisingly, he added, 'I was awful tired at the end.' For your A2 sports history study you will mainly use secondary source material – books and articles that either interpret primary sources or re-tell a story originally told by someone else. These are obviously very valuable but should be read with caution. First, different historians can interpret the same information in different ways, and, second, we all know what happens to a story each time it is re-told!

Asking the right questions

Essential information can be established by asking the right questions, the answers to which will provide plenty to think, talk and write about.

HOT TIPS

To be an effective A level sports historian, you must try to combine chronology (the order of dates in which events took place) with causation (the relationship between cause and effect) and continuity with change.

TASK 1

Look at the four pictures in Figures 1.01–1.04. Try to get into the minds of the people shown and think about the experience as they did. Then consider the following questions.

1   What activity is being pursued? Is it an individual activity (for example, swimming, athletics or rowing) or a game (for example, cricket, tennis or football)? Also, what really happened? You need to recognise romantic

myth from historical reality. It might be fun to think that William Webb Ellis simply picked up the football and ran with it while playing one day at Rugby School, so creating a new game (but there is no evidence that he did).

2   Who is taking part? In addition to satisfying curiosity, the 'who' questions can make us think about power, responsibility and who was affected by those who dominated society. The focus here should be on class and gender.

   Class: pre-industrial Britain was mainly a two-class society. The upper class (also called the gentry or aristocracy) dominated the peasant or lower class. There was also a merchant class from whom the middle class later emerged. In post-industrial Britain, this new middle class became a dominant societal and sporting force. Meanwhile, the rural peasants who had migrated to towns to find factory work were called the working class.

   Gender: freedom of opportunity has always been linked with class. In pre-Industrial Britain, upper class women were free to pursue certain elitist pastimes, such as hawking. Lower class women were free to be physical in smock races. The Victorian era brought new attitudes, especially for middle class women for whom physical activity was deemed unsuitable, undignified and even dangerous. Nineteenth century women were later not only constrained by societal attitudes but also by lack of opportunity and provision.

3   When is the sport or pastime being pursued? The 'when' question highlights the fact that historians analyse continuity and change over time. Was the activity pre-industrial or post-industrial, occasional or regular, at an informally organised time or a pre-set specific time?

4   Where is it taking place? Is it in a rural or urban setting? Is it in a simple, natural environment or a purpose-built facility?

5   Why are people taking part or spectating? Is it purely for entertainment or perhaps as their profession? Are they betting on the outcome or is it a social occasion? The 'why' question highlights the importance of cause and effect, which is central to historical study.

6   How sophisticated is the activity? Is it being played in a civilised manner? Is it highly organised with rules, boundaries and a league system?

The development of popular recreation in the United Kingdom

Pre-industrial popular recreation reflected the society, life and time in which it existed. The activities were often colourful and lively and were supported by a strict class system. Different classes sometimes shared activities (for example, cock fighting), sometimes took part in different activities (for example, mob football for the peasants, real tennis for the aristocracy), and sometimes had different roles within the same activity (for example, the bare-knuckle fighter was lower class while his **patron** was upper class).

The Reformation

A movement that started in sixteenth-century Germany, which called for the reform of the Roman Catholic Church. The Reformation led to Protestantism, Puritanism and an attack on the sports and pastimes of the common people.

Puritanism

Puritans believed that idleness and playfulness were sinful and that salvation could only be earned through a life of prayer and restraint in all areas.

The role and attitude of the Church in the development of sport is important, with popular recreations having been subject to periodic interference since medieval times. When Henry VIII broke with Rome, he had no desire to change fundamentally the religious, social or sporting habits of his subjects. Only later, as a result of **the Reformation**, did attitudes change and the powerful force of **Puritanism** emerge. Puritans were fiercely opposed to the excess, unruliness, spontaneity, swearing and drinking associated with contemporary recreations.

This was a bleak time for popular sports and pastimes. The Puritan ethic gave way to the work ethic and spreading of Protestantism, whereby leisure pursuits were acceptable only in that they restored people for work.

The life of the eighteenth-century peasant was tough, and sports and pastimes echoed this harshness. Baiting and blood sports, for example, where trained dogs attacked bears or bulls that were chained up, attracted large crowds. In 'ratting' contests, dogs were released into an enclosed pit and had a set time to kill as many rats as possible. The rowdy crowd, meanwhile, would bet on the outcome. In cock fighting, prize birds had sharp spurs attached to their claws to ensure maximum damage in a dramatic, brutal and relatively well-organised activity, which would often take place in an inn's yard.

The eighteenth-century drinking house was central to village life. It was the place to socialise, do business, find work, receive wages and organise political activity. It was the stopping station for coaches, a place to change horses, and a hotel for travellers. Most importantly for your study, it was the focus for leisure activities for the community. It hosted bear and badger baiting, dog fighting and prizefighting, as well as less barbaric games such as billiards, quoits, bowls and skittles. Landlords often provided prizes for sporting matches and primitive equipment for ball games in order to stimulate interest and, perhaps more importantly, boost profit. The landlord was the promoter of sports, arranged matches and provided prize money, as well as being the bookmaker. Many late eighteenth- and early nineteenth-century sports clubs used the public house as their base – most famously perhaps, the Hambledon Cricket Club at the Bat and Ball Inn, Hampshire, where the game of cricket was developed between 1750 and 1780.

Coursing

The chasing of hares by trained dogs for a wager.

Country pursuits (or field sports) such as hunting, **coursing** and shooting, had functional origins. Hunting grew from the search for food and developed into a status symbol for wealthy landowners whose Game Laws ensured that only the highest social groups had the right to hunt. If the lower classes broke the Game Laws by poaching, they ran the risk of a six-month jail sentence and a public whipping.

Militaristic combat activities such as archery, sparring and fencing, grew from the need to defend and attack, and only when their functional role was removed with the availability of guns did these skills develop into recreational and competitive sports in their own right.

The characteristics and cultural factors of popular recreation

The unsophisticated (even uncivilised) sports and pastimes of the common people were occasional rather than regular. The annual village fair, parish feast or Christmas celebration was an important time of universal merriment. Drinking and play have always been closely associated. Dennis Brailsford, in *British Sports: A Social History* (1997), explains:

> *In ... groups of villages in Wiltshire, the thirteenth-century practice was for the bachelors to have free ale as long as they could stand up, but once they sat down they had to pay!*

On a smaller scale, the weekly market was social and sporting as well as an exchange of goods and services. Other than these occasional gatherings, the peasants had little free time for sports and pastimes.

In the eighteenth century, life was cheap; mortality rates were high and public hangings a spectator attraction, so displays of merciless cruelty in the name of entertainment and sport were common. Some sports developed from the occupation of participants – for example, competitive rowing, which grew from the work of ferrymen taking passengers across the River Thames. As the impact of the Industrial Revolution was not yet felt, life and sports were rurally based using natural or easily accessible equipment and facilities. Organisation was basic with rules being simple, unwritten and passed on by word of mouth. The national governing bodies had not yet been formed (they grew rapidly in the 1860s and 70s), illiteracy was the norm, and primitive transport and communications caused sports to be local in nature. There was no need for widespread agreement about rules. Furthermore, it was not until the arrival of weekly papers such as the *Sporting Magazine* (from 1793), *Bell's Weekly Messenger* (from 1796), and *The Weekly Dispatch* (from 1801) that sport became widely advertised, discussed and promoted to a captive and increasingly literate audience.

A key feature of most popular recreations was wagering or betting on the outcome. From the poorest farm worker to the wealthiest aristocrat, wagering was an eighteenth- and nineteenth-century obsession. The poor focused on the slim chance of a big win, while betting by the wealthy was a social display of financial and social status. The story goes that at the Derby, two gentlemen witnessed a lady fainting: they did not help her, but rather bet on the length of time it would take her to come round!

HOT TIPS

Make certain that you:

• know the characteristics of popular recreation

• understand the social reasons for the characteristics

• can discuss to what extent each of your case study activities 'fits' with these normally accepted characteristics.

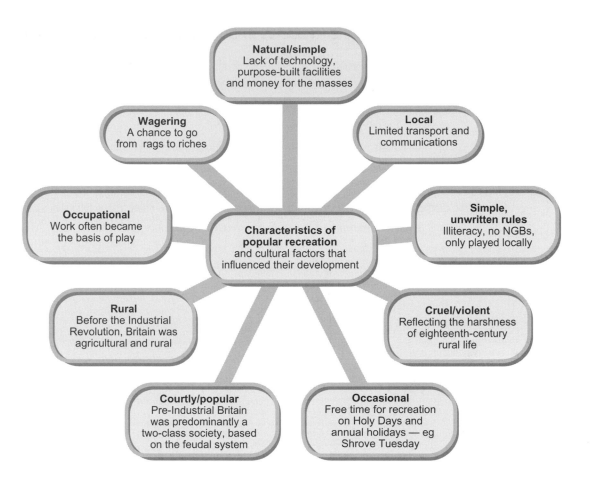

Fig. 1.06 Characteristics of popular recreation

Bathing

In the Middle Ages, towns were built at defensive sites and river crossing points. Bathing for pleasure was an obvious outcome, especially on hot summer days. As well as a natural playground, the river provided a ready supply of food, a means of transport, and a place to wash. It was the commercial centre of the area. With work, play and the river so inter-related, learning to swim for safety also became a necessity. In the natural environment, it was as important to swim as to run! In *Sports and Pastimes of the People of England* (1830), Joseph Strutt quoted a sixteenth-century writer:

> ❛ *Take two strong men and in Temese cast them,*
> *And both naked as a needle, their non sikerer than another;*
> *The one hath cunnynge and can swymme and dyve,*
> *The other is lewd of that laboure, lerned never to swym.*
> *Which trowest of these two in Temese is most in dred,*
> *He that never dyved he nought can of swymmyng,*
> *Or the swimmer that is safe if he himself lyke?* ❜

HOT TIPS

Remember to link bathing with recreation, survival and health.

TASK 2

In pairs, try to interpret the old English writing in the extract on page 11 in order to understand one person's view of swimming in the 1500s.

KEY WORDS

Chivalric code

The courteous, gallant and gentlemanly behaviour associated with the nobility or aristocracy.

Just as the Roman nobility had done, the English aristocracy of the Middle Ages considered the ability to swim as part of their **chivalric code**. They would sometimes sponsor (or 'patronise') outstanding lower-class swimmers to represent them in wager races in the same way that they would sponsor prizefighters, rowers or runners. These swimmers might become swimming 'masters', described by Norman Wymer (in *Sport in England – A History of Two Thousand Years of Games and Pastimes*, 1949):

> *All who dwelt by the river, or earned their living on it, now took out a form of insurance for their own safety, so that wherever there was a river or lake – or indeed, any suitable stretch of water – there would usually be found a band of swimming masters to teach the art to every local child, from the sons of the squire to the lowliest peasant. Many strokes were taught and if the child appeared particularly nervous or lacking in confidence, they would fasten a bundle of bull rushes or a line of corks to his body to give him greater buoyancy.*

Charles II (1660–85) even established a series of fashionable swimming contests on the Thames and the first open-air swimming bath was built in London in 1784.

Throughout history, various other sports and pastimes have centred on the riverside, particularly in river loops and adjoining water meadows. These areas of common land had no trees or agriculture and so provided a large flat space for casual, informal games, athletic sports, horse racing and shooting. They were liable to flooding, so in frozen conditions they also provided a place for sliding and skating. In 1896, *Cassell's Complete Book of Sports and Pastimes* included the advice that 'the boy who had never in his early days enjoyed a good slide is never very likely to enjoy any manly outdoor exercise'. Occasionally, the river itself froze, providing a surface for multi-sports festivals called frost fairs or ice fairs. Pictures of Thames frost fairs in the 1600s show a variety of fairground stalls, bull baiting, prizefighting, sliding, football and feasting. When the Thames froze in 1813, a four-day frost fair was set up (see Figure 1.07).

Fig. 1.07 Thames frost fair, 1813.

See page 32 for swimming in public schools and page 45 for swimming as a rational recreation.

Rowing

Throughout British History, rowing has been a functional activity necessary for warfare, fishing, travel and commerce. Various forms of recreational boating came from these origins. From the early eighteenth century to the mid-nineteenth century, rowing was a major sporting amusement, especially on the Thames, Tees, Tyne and Mersey.

KEY WORDS

Watermen

Men who earned their living on or about boats.

In the days when there were few bridges across the River Thames, ferrymen were in demand. The wealthy employed **watermen,** in the same way as they employed coachmen, and provided them with elaborate uniforms as a show of the patrons' wealth. Other freelance individuals carried passengers across and along the river. Frequently, passengers in neighbouring boats would bet on their waterman winning an impromptu race. The winner would be handsomely rewarded and in this way be motivated to be fit and fast.

The most famous rowing race was the legacy of Thomas Doggett, an Irish comedian. A *Daily Telegraph* report of 1994 said that:

> ❝ *One dark and stormy night, a brave young waterman, fresh out of apprenticeship, agreed to row Doggett home across the choppy waters and the idea of testing such youthful endeavour in an annual race was born.* ❞

When Doggett died he left money for Thames watermen to have a rowing race on 1 August each year, forever. Only watermen who had just completed their first year of apprenticeship could enter. He provided three prizes: a waterman's coat with large silver badge for the winner, and small amounts of money for those in second and third place.

Fig. 1.08 Doggett's coat and badge – the prize rowed for by Thames watermen since 1715.

The route was from the Old Swan Stairs near London Bridge to the White Swan at Chelsea – against the tide. The race became known as The Doggett Coat and Badge Race. It is widely accepted as the root of competitive rowing and over the years it has produced the best-known professionals, including nearly all the British champions and some world champions.

To what extent does early rowing fit with the characteristics of popular recreation? It was neither cruel nor violent, did not lack rules and was not unorganised. However, it was of local importance and is perhaps the best example of an occupation that became a recreation. As Tony Money explains in *Manly and Muscular Diversions: Public Schools and the Nineteenth Century Sporting Revival*, 1997:

> ❝ *As with every sporting event of the time, from the "Fancy" (bare-knuckle boxing) to the "Turf", from "Pedestrianism" (professional running) to the "Canine Fancy" (the public house rat-pit), "Aquatics" attracted widespread betting.* ❞

See page 33 for rowing in public schools and pages 46–7 for rowing as a rational recreation.

The development of sports festivals

Athletics

A large range of popular games and contests were played in Britain before the advent of modern sports, many of which can be viewed as seeds from which rationalised athletics grew. 'Folk sports' associated with annual parish feasts and fairs have already been mentioned (see page 10). Hiring fairs and village wakes must also be noted. Farm labourers and servants could be sacked at a moment's notice and if they had to find a new employer, they could go to the nearest hiring or 'mop' fair. They would stand in line, offering their services as maid, cook, shepherd or ploughman. Wakes originated from the time of paganism, when the fear of evil was great and when superstitions were rife. Wakes were annual religious celebrations in thanksgiving for the harvest and for the presence of Christianity in the community. In harsh times, they were also an opportunity to pray for survival. Praise and worship were always followed by festivity and feasting.

A traditional wake was a great social occasion, bringing all parts of the community together. These local events were associated with all kinds of excess, such as drinking, blood sports and promiscuity. They were also opportunities for men to test their strength and prove their speed and virility in events such as stick fighting, wrestling and running. More playfully, they would try to catch pigs whose tails had been soaped, and compete in whistling matches and grinning contests! Prizes were generally practical – shirts, smocks, hats, cheeses, joints of meat and sometimes more. Free to be athletic and not yet restrained by nineteenth-century Victorian ethics, peasant women would also race and 'nothing is more usual than for a nimble-footed wench to get a husband at the same time as she wins a smock' (Lovesey, *The Official Centenary History of the AAA*, 1979).

Fig. 1.09 Gurning through a horse collar.

> ❛ *Since 1927, there has been a great celebration fair at the end of the harvest in Egremont in Cumbria. Today, the World Gurning Championship is the highlight of the fair. 'To "gurn" meant to "snarl like a dog and distort the countenance". The practice is reputed to have originated from the tradition of mocking the village idiot, when the unfortunate soul would have his head put through a horse's collar and be persuaded to pull strange faces in return for a few tankards of ale.* ❜
> (*The Independent*, 26 January 1997)

The Reformed Church frowned upon traditional wakes and by the mid-nineteenth century, fetes and tea parties were organised as respectable alternatives.

Fig. 1.10 A smock race, early nineteenth century.

The Cotswold Games, revived by Robert Dover in Gloucestershire in 1604, attracted huge crowds to watch contests of leaping, shin-kicking, wrestling, coursing and jousting, in what Holt refers to as 'a kind of proto-national event' (*Sport and the British*, 1989). It attracted both upper- and lower-class participants. These 'Dover' games survived until the mid-nineteenth century, when rowdy Black Country families arrived by train, caused havoc and the event was suspended.

The Much Wenlock Olympian Games emerged from a rural sports festival and when revived by Dr Penny Brookes in 1850, they became a highly respected rival to athletic developments at the Oxford and Cambridge universities. Brookes was keen to add a pure form of athletics to traditional events, so, along with twenty-a-side football matches, an old woman's race for a pound of tea, a blindfold wheelbarrow race and chasing a cornered pig, there were more refined running, jumping and throwing events.

A contemporary observer described the Hungerford Revels of 1826 as follows.

> *It consists of all kinds of rustic sports, which afford capital fun to the spectators.*
> *1st Girls running for "smocks", which is a well-known amusement at country fairs.*
> *2nd Climbing the greasy pole for a piece of bacon, which is placed on the top. This afforded very great amusement, as it is a difficult thing to be accomplished.*
> *3rd Old women drinking hot tea for snuff. Whoever can drink it the quickest and hottest gains the prize.*
> *4th Gurning through horse-collars. Several men stand in a row, each holding a collar; whoever can make the ugliest face through it gains the prize. This feat is also performed by old women and certainly the latter are the most amusing.*
> *5th Racing between twenty and 30 old women for a pound of tea. This occasions much merriment and it is sometimes astonishing to see with what agility the old dames run in order to obtain the prize.*
> *6th Hunting a pig with a soaped tail. This amusement creates much mirth and, in my opinion, is the most laughable.*
> *7th Jumping in sacks for cheese. Ten or eleven candidates are chosen; they are tied in sacks up to their necks and have to jump about 500 yards. It is truly laughable.*

TASK 3

Read the description of the Hungerford Revels. To what extent does this occasion 'fit' with the commonly accepted characteristics of popular recreation? (Local, occasion, cruel, violent, wagering, rural, courtly/popular, lacking in predetermined rules, and so on.)

TASK 4

Hold a whistling match and grinning contest in your class.

- In a whistling match, a number of contestants try to whistle to the end of a selected tune without interruption while a fun-loving 'merry Andrew' tries to make them laugh.

- In grinning or 'gurning' contests, contestants must pull the funniest or ugliest face they can. Instead of holding the customary horse collar, try using hoops.

Judges award prizes to winners.

Pedestrianism

Perhaps the most obvious forerunner to athletics was pedestrianism. Since the late seventeenth century, the gentry employed footmen as messengers and competitive runners. Athletic success was seen as a way of enhancing a gentleman's social status. Such races attracted wagers of up to 1000 guineas, so a good living could be earned by a small number of professional athletes each being promoted and sponsored by the gentry. As these events increased in popularity, large venues, such as Newmarket Racecourse and the Agricultural Hall in Islington, were used. Men of all backgrounds competed. Scottish landowner Robert Barclay Allardice, for example, attracted a crowd of more than 10,000 in 1809 when he walked 1000 miles in 1000 consecutive hours (that is about a month without a night's sleep!). For the next 40 years, pedestrianism grew in popularity. Gambling was central to pedestrianism and for those accustomed to poverty and hardship, winning could mean the difference between starvation and survival.

The largest bets were for one-man challenges against the clock or calendar, though head-to-head matches were also popular. In addition to the more serious races, many novelty races were held, such as walking backwards, pushing wheelbarrows and gathering potatoes.

A thirteen year-old named Mountjoy Jr, twice completed a 64-mile return trip between Swansea and Neath within the space of a few days in 1844. During the challenge he managed one 45-minute period of running half a mile forwards, walking three-quarters of a mile backwards, running and hopping a hundred yards

Fig. 1.11 Billposter for a head-to-head pedestrian contest.

each, picking up a hundred eggs with his mouth, and finally clearing twenty hurdles.

Pedestrianism had its problems. Trickery was commonplace – with fleet-footed amateurs entering races under false names, professionals impersonating unknown amateurs and match-fixing, – while riots among the crowds also brought the sport into disrepute. In the 1860s, the great athlete Deerfoot visited England. This Native American attracted huge crowds and, along with other Victorian professionals, he helped to inspire early amateur athletes.

See page 33 for athletics in public schools and pages 47–9 for athletics as a national recreation.

Games in popular recreation
Mob football

A variety of games involving kicking and throwing a ball were regular features of English pre-industrial society. They were sometimes bizarre, always lively and often tragic. As a rowdy, violent, locally coded, occasional encounter between neighbouring villages, mob football is without doubt the best example of a popular recreation.

Early mob football games were played in restricted city streets as well as in the countryside. They were little more than massive brawls involving brute force between hoards of young men. They caused uproar, damage to property and a perfect setting for anyone attracted to violence. According to one early observer, mob football was:

Fig. 1.12 Street football, 1721.

'… abominable enough, and, in my judgement at least, more common, undignified and worthless than any other kind of game, rarely ending but with some loss, accident or disadvantage to the players themselves.'

Shrove Tuesday became a traditional day for mob games, seen as an opportunity for fun and excitement before the seriousness of Lent. Some of the best known were in Ashbourne and Derby. In Derby, the game between the parishes of St Peter and All Saints resulted in the term a local 'Derby', while in Ashbourne, two teams consisting of anyone who lived in the town, surged between 'goals' three miles apart. You will remember from your Contemporary Studies work that many such games survive today.

Throughout history, kings, governments and local authorities have frowned on mob games because they caused:

- damage to property
- injury to young men (often making them unfit for army training)
- disrespect for the Sabbath
- social unrest (which might lead to riot or even rebellion).

In spite of successive authorities declaring the game illegal, it still survived. Without an effective policing system, laws were fairly easy to ignore.

TASK 5

Research a mob football game looking for evidence of the characteristics of popular recreation.

See pages 34–5 for football in public schools and pages 49–51 for football as a national recreation.

Cricket

Village cricket was played from the early eighteenth century, especially in Kent, Sussex and Hampshire. From the start, the social classes played together reflecting the feudal/class structure of the village. Patrons from the gentry employed estate workers as gardeners and gamekeepers primarily for their cricketing talents. There were also some freelance professionals who played in a servant role to their current employer. Early clubs emerged from these rural village sides.

Fig. 1.13 Cricket, 1743.

TASK 6

What features of the picture in Figure 1.13 confirm that it is an eighteenth-century or early game of cricket?

Interest and patronage by the gentry led to the early standardisation of rules.

- 1727 – the first 'Articles of Agreement' were written.
- 1744 – more extensive rules were produced.
- 1774 – 'New Articles of the Game of Cricket' formalised the size of wicket, stumps and bat, added the third stump, made six balls an over and added the rule that it was illegal to charge fielders attempting to catch a ball!

- 1809 – 'The Laws of the Noble Game of Cricket' were set out by Marylebone Cricket Club (MCC).
- Round-arm bowling was legalised in 1835 and over-arm bowling was legalised in 1864.

There are three main aspects of the story of early cricket.

1 The Bat and Ball Inn

This pub in Hambledon, Hampshire, was nicknamed 'the cradle' of cricket, as it was where the game was encouraged and developed from 1750. Outside the inn on Broadhalfpenny Down, the landlord, Richard Nyren, captained the side that dominated cricket for half a century. At its peak it could take on and beat the rest of England. Large crowds of up to 2000 spectators watched and wagered on the outcome of matches. Stakes of £5000 (approximately £500,000 today) were paid to winning sides.

2 Marylebone Cricket Club

The gentlemen who developed the laws of cricket in 1774 formed the While Conduit Club, which became Marylebone Cricket Club (MCC) in 1788. The rise of MCC forced the decline of Hambledon. Why? First, the gentry now supported the new London club and second, Hambledon players were now employed by MCC as coaches and players. MCC became the main club in England and took on the role of the governing body. It played at the first Lords ground in 1787, moved to Lisson Grove twenty years later, and finally to the present site in St John's Wood around 1811. MCC toured the country and had annual games against public schools.

Fig. 1.14 William Clarke, who captained the All England XI in the 1840s.

3 The William Clarke XI

William Clarke was a cricketer who took advantage of the changing economic and social conditions of the 1840s and helped change cricket from a fragmented localised sport to a national success. By the 1840s, upper-class patronage of cricket declined and professionals looked elsewhere for employment. Some went to the public schools and universities, while others joined professional touring sides, such as the William Clarke XI (established 1847), or the breakaway United XI (formed by unhappy Clarke professionals who complained that they were not being paid enough). These touring sides toured England for many seasons, attracting huge crowds and taking on teams of up to 22 opponents.

Again, you should assess the extent to which early cricket 'fits' the normally accepted model of popular recreation.

Cricket was a popular recreation because:	On the other hand:
• it attracted widespread wagering • it was played by both males and females (it took the restricting ethics of Victorianism to restrict women's sporting pursuits) • it was predominantly rural • it was often associated with feasts and festival days • its rules could be locally adapted.	• it was predominantly non-violent • it had an early rule structure • it had national touring sides from the 1840s.

See pages 35–6 for cricket in public schools and pages 51–2 for cricket as a rational recreation.

KEY WORDS

Civil War

The war was between the Royalists (or Cavaliers), who tended to be gentry, rural and High Church, and the Roundheads (supporters of Parliament), who were largely merchant class, urban and Low Church. The Roundheads were led by Oliver Cromwell. The climax of the Civil War in 1649 was the trial and execution of Charles I. England was declared a republic and the Puritan lifestyle was imposed. This was a very bleak time for sports and games.

HOT TIPS

Be able to compare real tennis with mob football. Think about who played it, where it was played, rule structure, numbers involved, dress, levels of skill or force, regularity of play and so on.

Real tennis

Real or royal tennis originated in France and became popular in Britain during the fourteenth century. It was an exclusive game for kings, nobles and merchants, who played on purpose-built highly sophisticated courts which varied in size and shape.

The one that became standard is shown in Figure 1.15 and shows a side passage for spectators. In keeping with the complicated court, the game had complex rules and required high levels of skill. Henry VIII built the court at Hampton Court Palace, which is still used today, and 'judging by the money he paid out in lost wagers, he was not too skilled' (Money, *Manly and Muscular Diversions*, 1997). Most university colleges had a court and Charles I played at Oxford when the city was his stronghold during the **Civil War**.

Other versions of 'tennis'

A variety of hand and ball or bat and ball games were all called 'tennis'. Those not eligible to play real tennis would copy their social superiors and play their own versions against church or pub walls. Their games were variously called tennis, fives or racquets. They also played field tennis or handball in the street and countryside.

Fig. 1.15 Frontispiece of a book containing the first laws of the game known to exist. The court became a theatre, like most of the courts of the seventeenth century.

Racquets

The story of racquets is one of rags to riches. It originated in Fleet Prison, London, and ended up being played by upper-class public school and university men. Prison inmates were not hardened criminals but debtors, and often gentlemen of high social standing so they were allowed to exercise in the prison yard. In *The Pickwick Papers* (1837), Charles Dickens described the game as follows:

> ❛ *The yard was just wide enough to make a good racket court ... one side, of course, [was formed] by the wall itself and the other by that portion of the prison which looked (or rather would have looked but for the wall) towards St Paul's Cathedral ... sauntering or sitting about, in every possible attitude of listless idleness, were a great number of debtors ... looking on at the racquet players, or watching boys as they tried the game.* ❜

See pages 36–8 for court and racquet games in public schools and pages 52–3 for lawn tennis as national recreation.

Revise as you go! Test your knowledge and understanding

- What are the four main aspects of the OCR specification?
- Which three individual activities and three games do you have to study in depth?
- What is the difference between primary and secondary historical evidence?
- Identify seven characteristics of popular recreation.
- Explain the societal influences on each of the characteristics identified above.
- What is the meaning of each of the following key terms: 'wagering', 'courtly' and 'rural'?
- How was early swimming connected with recreation, survival and health?
- To what extent do pedestrianism and mob football 'fit' the normally accepted characteristics of popular recreation?

Sharpen up your exam technique!

1 How did mob football reflect pre-industrial Britain?   (4 marks)

2 If you were watching an ancient Shrove Tuesday game of mob football, what characteristics of the game would you expect to see?   (4 marks)

3 In pre-industrial Britain, many sports developed in river towns. Identify key features of the Doggett Coat and Badge rowing competition.   (4 marks)

4 Identify key characteristics of popular recreation and explain how accurately three of these characteristics describes early cricket.   (6 marks)

5 Why was real tennis such an exclusive game in pre-industrial Britain?   (4 marks)

6 Compare the rural sporting activities of the gentry with those of the agricultural worker.   (4 marks)

7   What games, based on the courtly game of real tennis, were adapted by the lower classes?   (3 marks)

8   Describe (a) the sort of summer festivals you would expect in a waterfront town, and (b) another type of festival that might have occurred in a cold winter in this town, explaining why the winter activity would have taken place.   (7 marks)

9   Analyse the emergence of pedestrianism as a major popular recreation in the early nineteenth century.   (4 marks)

Section 2: *Nineteenth century public school developments of athleticism*

Learning objectives

At the end of this section you should be able to:
- identify the characteristics of public schools
- explain the significance of these characteristics to the development of sports and games
- understand that nineteenth-century public schools went through three stages of development
- explain how (with reference to technical developments) and why (with reference to social developments) sports and games evolved during the three stages
- identify and explain the significance of the reforms of Dr Thomas Arnold and other liberal headmasters
- understand how the 'cult' of athleticism spread throughout Britain, Europe and the British Empire
- analyse the technical developments, social relationships and character building values evident in selected passages from *Tom Brown's Schooldays*.

 KEY WORDS

Dr Thomas Arnold

The reforming headmaster of Rugby School (1828–42). Like most public school headmasters of the era, he was a Doctor of Divinity and an ordained clergyman.

Introduction

Certain schools were called public schools because they were not privately owned but were controlled by a group of trustees. The riotous games and activities popular at these schools at the beginning of the nineteenth century were vastly different from those played there 100 years later. Your task is to trace and explain this development from 'boy culture' to regulated rationalised activities (with reference to your six case study activities) and to clarify the changing nature and aims of public school sport throughout the nineteenth century.

Winchester	1382
Eton	1440
St Paul's	1509
Shrewsbury	1552
Westminster	1560
Merchant Taylor's	1561
Rugby	1567
Harrow	1571
Charterhouse	1611

Fig. 1.16 The **Clarendon Schools:** foundation dates.

To help you, refer to selected extracts from *Tom Brown's Schooldays*. This novel, written by Thomas Hughes in 1857, is important as it both reflected and influenced life at Rugby School under **Dr Thomas Arnold**. The book was widely read by a whole generation of public school boys who copied the behaviour and activities of the central characters, especially the hero Tom Brown. The important extracts are:

- The football match
- Country pursuits and swimming
- The fight
- The cricket match.

In each case, you need to be aware of:

- the **technical developments** of the activity (such as rule structure, regularity, level of skill over force, quality of facilities and coaching, and so on)
- the **social developments** being displayed (such as friendships, loyalty, respect or disdain)
- the character-building **values** being reinforced (such as teamwork, manliness, loyalty, honour, respect for opponents and so on).

KEY WORDS

Technical developments

Developments related to rule structure, equipment, facilities, spectatorship, level of skilfulness, and so on.

Values

Ethics and morals that build 'character' and become guidelines for living. For example, teamwork, manliness, loyalty, honour, respect for opponents and so on.

Clarendon Schools

The great or 'big nine' public schools investigated by the Earl of Clarendon and his team of Commissioners in 1864 (see Figure 1.16). Queen Victoria appointed the commission to examine all aspects of public school life. The result was two huge volumes, which included criticisms of many aspects of public school life and both general and specific advice for each school.

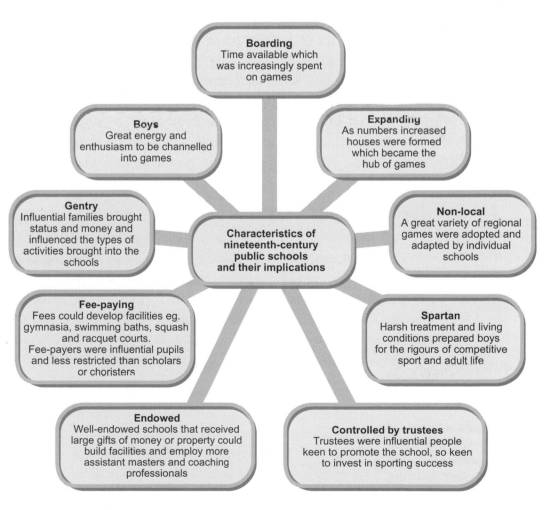

Boarding
Time available which was increasingly spent on games

Boys
Great energy and enthusiasm to be channelled into games

Expanding
As numbers increased houses were formed which became the hub of games

Gentry
Influential families brought status and money and influenced the types of activities brought into the schools

Characteristics of nineteenth-century public schools and their implications

Non-local
A great variety of regional games were adopted and adapted by individual schools

Fee-paying
Fees could develop facilities eg. gymnasia, swimming baths, squash and racquet courts. Fee-payers were influential pupils and less restricted than scholars or choristers

Spartan
Harsh treatment and living conditions prepared boys for the rigours of competitive sport and adult life

Endowed
Well-endowed schools that received large gifts of money or property could build facilities and employ more assistant masters and coaching professionals

Controlled by trustees
Trustees were influential people keen to promote the school, so keen to invest in sporting success

Fig. 1.17 Characteristics of nineteenth-century public schools.

KEY WORDS

Social developments

Influences of social change, for example, improved transport and communications, as well as changing social relationships within the schools, such as level of bullying. Headmasters' attitudes and interaction between boys, masters and locals.

Regency period

A time of high fashion associated with the Prince Regent at the turn of the seventeenth and eighteenth centuries.

Preparatory schools

Junior level schools for younger boys who then advanced to the public schools.

Melting pot

The mixing of games and traditions from various sources resulting in one standardised format.

House system

The system whereby boys lived in individual houses while away at boarding school. The house became the centre of social and sporting life.

Social control

The establishment of order, stability and good behaviour.

Hare and hounds

An adaptation of fox hunting whereby one boy ran ahead of the pack dropping a trail of paper as 'scent', which was then followed by the chasing crowd.

Technical and social developments
Stage one (c. 1790–1828): bullying and brutality

At the end of the eighteenth century, English society contrasted the high culture of **Regency period** fashion with the low culture and apparent brutality of blood sports and bare-knuckle fighting. Both ends of this social spectrum were mirrored in the public schools. This was a time of 'boy culture' when the French and American revolutions were copied by public school boys if things did not go their way. In the absence of a police force, such unrest had to be controlled by the army. All recreational activities were organised by the boys for pure enjoyment and to relieve the boredom of academic work, which consisted solely of the classics (Latin and Greek). Masters 'ruled with the rod' in lessons but had no influence or interest outside of the classroom. Perhaps this is why the boys took part in all sorts of mischief including trespass, truancy, poaching and fighting. In both society at large and in individual public schools, control was lost and tyranny and chaos resulted.

Fig. 1.18 Cricket at Harrow School, 1802.

This was also a time of public school expansion, when increasing numbers of upper-class boys were enrolling from a variety of different **preparatory schools** and bringing with them customs and recreations from all over the country. These customs were mixed and moulded, as in a **melting pot**, into schoolboy games and future traditions. In this way, an inward form of sporting diffusion to the public schools was created along with a need for increased housing (expansion of the **house system**) and **social control**. Games and sports would ultimately provide the medium for social control, but severe, imposed discipline by masters and resentful rebellion and hooligan behaviour by boys shaped the norm at this early stage.

This era was one of 'institutionalised popular recreation' and activities ranging from the childlike to the barbaric. Hoops, marbles and spinning tops took place alongside bare-knuckle fights and mob football. The wall at Eton and the cloisters at Charterhouse were the birthplaces of unique and ferocious mob football games. Cricket, the rural game already organised and played by both classes, was immediately adopted by the schools while fox hunting was adapted to **hare and hounds**. Boys would also hire boats from local boatyards, play

KEY WORDS

Fives

A hand and ball or bat and ball game against a suitable wall or (later) in a purpose-built court. Called 'fives' because of the five digits on the hand. Similar to squash.

'fives' and other ball games against suitable walls, swim in natural bathing places and explore the countryside.

Summary of stage one

- Bullying and brutality.
- A reflection of society.
- Institutionalised popular recreation.
- Activities organised by, and for, the boys themselves.
- Ranged from the childlike to the barbaric.
- No master involvement outside of the classroom.
- Simple, naturally occurring facilities used.

Stage two (1828–42): Dr Thomas Arnold and social control

This was a time of change, both in society at large and in the English public schools. Parliament and criminal laws were changing (for example, laws banning cruelty to animals), transport and communications were dramatically improving (with the introduction of the penny post and the railways), and Queen Victoria was crowned in 1837. With life and society becoming more orderly, the freedom and wild escapades of stage one became more and more out of place.

Dr Thomas Arnold and other liberal headmasters wanted to reform the public schools. They reformed:

- the behaviour of boys
- the severity of punishments imposed by masters
- the role of the Sixth Form
- the academic curriculum.

KEY WORDS

Muscular Christianity

The combination of godliness and manliness – the belief in having a strong and fit body to match a robust and healthy soul.

Their main aim, though, was to produce Christian gentlemen and to preach good moral behaviour. This was all part of **Muscular Christianity** or the belief in having a strong soul within a strong body. It was fine to play sport and to play hard, but always for the glory of God – not for its own sake or for any extrinsic values that could be achieved. That was still to come.

Dr Thomas Arnold

Dr Thomas Arnold is still widely regarded as the man who reformed the English public school system at a time when it was out of control. He was head of Rugby School from 1828 until his death in 1842. He attended Winchester as a boy and showed no real interest in games but a great love of the countryside, which stayed with him throughout his life. Later, he was ordained as a clergyman. On joining Rugby, he grew to be obsessed by what he saw as the immorality and sinfulness of boys and was determined to reform them, their attitudes and their school lives.

Fig. 1.19 Dr Thomas Arnold.

> ❛ *Evil was something positive that Arnold could almost see and feel. When faced with it, he would rise in anger and indeed, on occasion, completely lose his self-control.* ❜
> (T. W. Bamford, *Thomas Arnold on Education*)

Arnold used games as a vehicle for establishing social control. He also made the chapel the school's spiritual and symbolic centre, thereby establishing a new moral code, which was better suited to the increasingly civilised society to which the public schools now belonged. Arnold also established a more trusting and sympathetic relationship with the Sixth Form while his masters gradually adopted roles of mentor and guide, rather than judge and executioner. He then raised the status of the Sixth Form, increased their powers of discipline, and in return required them to be positive role models and his 'police force' around the school. The sixth formers became the link between masters and boys. Arnold's primary objective of delivering the Christian message could then be achieved. As a by-product, the status, regularity and organisation of games also increased.

As schools continued to expand, the house system also grew. Individual houses, run initially as commercial enterprises by a housemaster and his wife, became the focus of boys' personal, social, recreational and sporting existence. Games of inter-house cricket and football kept boys out of trouble in the daytime and sent them to bed exhausted. In this way, the playground became a central feature of public school life.

Summary of stage two
- A time of reform and social control.
- Initiated by Dr Thomas Arnold and copied by other liberal headmasters.
- A reflection of societal change.
- The growth of the house system.
- Regular play on an inter-house basis.
- Technical developments (increasing organisation, structure, regularity of play).

Remember, you need to read and analyse all *four* extracts from *Tom Brown's Schooldays*.

TASK 7
1   Read the extract for the football match in *Tom Brown's Schooldays*.
2   Look at the summary sheet for the football match on page 27.
3   Read extracts
    (a) Country pursuits and swimming
    (b) The fight
    (c) The cricket match.
Prepare a summary sheet for each of the above similar to that on page 27.

The football match

The story/scenario

As a new boy at Rugby, Tom joins in the match between School House and the rest of the school.

Evidence of technical developments

Evidence of popular recreation/primitive organisation	Evidence of technical development
Play in the clothes they are wearing – no special uniforms yet	Some tactics, a captain, halves are timed, oranges at half time, Dr Arnold spectating
Uneven numbers: School House (60) v. the rest of the school (120)	Reference to 'scrummage', 'goal' and some basic positions including goalkeeper
School side 'not organised in any way'	Reference to the ball being driven through 'by force or skill'

Explanation of different social relationships

- A ranking order, with smaller boys playing in certain positions.
- Big Brooke as the paternal and admired captain and role model.
- East looking after Tom, the new boy.

Evidence of values being reinforced

- Solidarity of the group – 'fighting' for the house.
- Courage and bravery needed.
- Reference to transfer of skills from games field to battlefield.

Key quotations

> *This is worth living for; the whole sum of schoolboy existence gathered up into one straining, struggling half hour, a half hour worth a year of common life.*

And when Tom gets injured, Brooke acknowledges:

> *Well, he's a plucky youngster and will make a player.*

Fig. 1.20 Tom helped by Brooke.

KEY WORDS

Athleticism

The combination of physical effort and moral integrity, or playing hard but with sportsmanship. By the late nineteenth century, athleticism had reached 'cult' proportions and some argue that it had got out of hand.

Cult

A craze or obsession. The playing of team games became a cult in stage three.

Clifton

A public school in Bristol built as a copy of Rugby. Clifton, Malvern and Cheltenham are examples of middle-class copies of Clarendon Schools, who took on the **games ethic** and had outstanding facilities.

Games ethic

A belief in the value of team games for the development of character.

Uppingham

The grammar school headed by Thring where games were central to school life. Thring played in the school teams.

Stage three (1842–1914): athleticism – the 'cult'

The conventional image of a late nineteenth-century English public school is of mellowed buildings, magnificent games fields, colours, caps and cricketers. These were all symbols of athleticism – the craze for team games and disinterest in academic work.

Between 1850 and 1870, Britain and its Empire was 'ruling the waves' and military drill became part of public school life. The Football Association was founded and the effects of the publication of *Tom Brown's Schooldays* (1857) and the *Clarendon Report* (1864) were felt. Meanwhile, games became compulsory at Harrow, cricket became compulsory at **Clifton**, and at **Uppingham**, the gymnasium was built and the games committee was formed.

Fig. 1.21 Football at Charterhouse, 1892.

Consider what some academics have said about the emergence of athleticism in this stage.

Money (in *Manly and Muscular Diversions*, 1997) argues that by the 1850s headmasters had accepted team games as voluntary free-time activities, with cricket, football, rowing and various racquet games well established recreationally, though not yet as part of the curriculum.

Holt (in *Sport and the British*, 1989) refers to the 1850s as 'the crucial decade in public school sport'.

Mangan (in *Athleticism in the Victorian and Edwardian Public School*, 1981) adds:

> **❛** *... from 1850 onwards, games were purposefully and deliberately assimilated into the formal curriculum of the public schools: suitable facilities were constructed, headmasters insisted on pupil involvement* [and] *staff participation was increasingly expected ...* **❜**

Newsome (in *Godliness and Good Learning*, 1961) goes further, arguing that 'Between 1860 and 1880, games became compulsory, organised and eulogised at all the leading public schools.'

The ex-public school boy was expected to have a well-rounded character, impeccable manners and enviable personal qualities. Furthermore, having led a team on the games field, it was assumed that he could lead a regiment on the

KEY WORDS

British Empire

The spread of British forms of government, religion and culture to nations considered to be less advanced or civilised. On the positive side, this involvement included the building of roads, schools and hospitals, but usually at a loss of inherent traditions and cultures.

battlefield. According to one observer, public schools created men who would be 'acceptable at a dance and invaluable in the shipwreck!' So, in the space of 60 years, what had been an embarrassment to public school headmasters became their pride – games and athletic pursuits.

On leaving university, these young men would go into adult life taking the 'games ethic' with them.

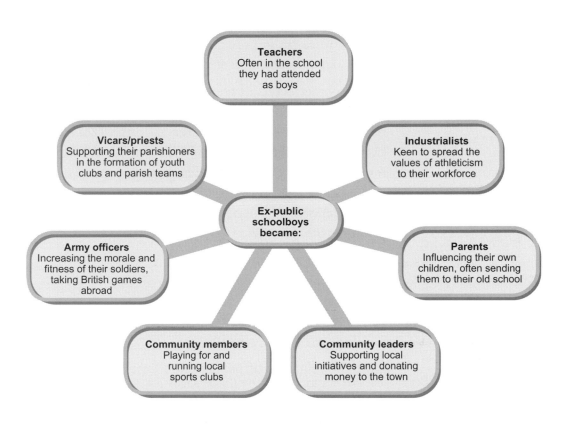

Fig. 1.22 The spread of team games throughout Europe and the **British Empire**.

The development of athleticism in girls' public and private schools

While athleticism was reaching cult proportions in boys' public schools, there was a delay in the development of opportunities for upper- and middle-class girls. The reasons for this were as follows:

- The traditional role of women – education of females was seen as a threat to the behavioural norms of society. There was also anxiety over the wearing of slightly revealing clothing for physical exercise.
- Status of women in society – girls' schools that did exist concentrated mainly on music, dancing and posture. It was not considered necessary to give girls the same opportunities as boys.
- Unladylike – it was thought inappropriate for women to be competitive or lively.

- Medical concerns – it was believed that strenuous physical activity would complicate or even prohibit child bearing.
- Perceived physical inferiority – there were concerns that girls would not be able to cope with strenuous physical activity.

Also, there were fewer prominent personalities to match boys' heads such as Dr Arnold of Rugby or Thring of Uppingham. Three women who should be mentioned, however, are:

- Frances Mary Buss
- Dorothea Beale
- Madame Bergman Osterberg.

These women were all great pioneers of, and for, female physical education in the mid to late nineteenth century. They had to overcome prejudice and sometimes ridicule, but they made a difference. In the 1860s, Frances Buss founded the North London Collegiate School and Camden School for Girls, while Dorothea Beale transformed Cheltenham Ladies College into an esteemed school for upper- and middle-class girls. The Swedish Madame Bergman Osterberg became Lady Superintendent of Physical Education in London in 1881 and soon founded the first full-time specialist PE college for women – Dartford.

Summary of stage three
- Athleticism as a 'cult'.
- Compulsory games for the development of character.
- Influence of ex-public school boys on the spread of games throughout Europe and the British Empire.

Note the influence of public schools on:

- other schools (which copied the Clarendon nine)
- universities (as a 'melting pot' for the standardisation of rules)
- organisations (formation of governing bodies)
- regularity of play (which increased standards of performance)
- building of specialist facilities (for example, swimming baths and gymnasia)
- festival days (for example, sports day, which rivalled speech day in the school calendar)
- fields (extensive playing fields created and proudly maintained).

HOT TIPS

Exam questions could ask you to focus on one stage of development or to assess change over the three stages. Remember to read the question carefully to determine exactly what is being asked of you.

TASK 8
1 Try to think of eight things that increased in the public schools from stage one to stage three (for example, coaching) and others that decreased (for example, mob games).
2 For each of the letters in the word ATHLETICISM, try to think of a character-building value that was thought to be achievable through playing team games in stage three – for example 'H' for honour or 'M' for manliness. Keep a mental list of these 'values' for your examination.

3   Why do you think that most sports organisations and national governing bodies were formed between 1863 and 1888? (Clue: think about the impact of public schools, values associated with games, the impact of improved transport and communications, the needs of a modern industrial society and so on.)

TASK 9

In which of the three stages of development would you place the following (some fit into more than one stage):

- melting pot
- Muscular Christianity
- values
- social control
- Dr Thomas Arnold
- professional coaches
- inter-house
- hooligans
- mob activities
- character development
- recreation.

Stage one 'Bullying and brutality' →	Stage two 'Social control' →	Stage three 'Athleticism'
Informal bathing	More regular and regulated bathing (for hygiene, safety and recreation)	Changing huts, diving boards, purpose-built facilities, galas and attendants for safety
Running, exploring countryside	Hare and hounds, steeple chasing	School sports days as major sporting and social occasions
Casual boating	More organised rowing (beginning of rowing clubs and master involvement)	Rowing clubs, school boats, **Oxbridge 'blues'** and coaches
Mob games	More formalised football rules for individual schools (for example, the running, handling game at Rugby School)	Formal rules (FA, 1863), 'colours', caps, inter-school fixtures
Cricket	Cricket continued (encouraged due to its non-violent nature, rule structure and upper-class involvement)	'Colours', caps, inter-school fixtures (for example, versus the MCC), professional coaches
Informal fives against suitable walls/buildings	Some fives courts built – still an informal boy culture activity. Racquets developing as more formal alternative	Fives continued as recreational game. Racquets as more formal game of higher status. Tennis more in girls' school – low status
Hunting, poaching, trespass	Restricted and banned (gave the school a bad name, annoyed neighbours, against Christian ethics)	Cross-country running, steeple chasing and cadet corps

KEY WORDS

Oxbridge 'blues'

An Oxford or Cambridge student/graduate who has represented their university in a varsity match against the other university. They became sought-after **assistant masters** in public schools.

Assistant masters

Junior masters without the responsibility of a house. Taught an academic subject but was fully involved in the games programme.

Fig. 1.23 Technical developments: the emergence of structured and organised sports and games

Swimming

At the beginning of the nineteenth century, bathing in public schools was spontaneous, unorganised and centred around natural facilities such as local rivers or ponds. Boys had swum in the open at home and brought this culture to school, bathing in their free time and with no master input or supervision. The river was a place to wash and have fun. As the century progressed and athleticism developed, swimming became more structured and regulated with natural facilities such as the River Wey at Charterhouse or the Duck Puddle at Harrow being transformed into major bathing facilities with changing huts, diving boards, swimming instructors and competitive events.

Increasingly, headmasters regarded swimming as a necessary athletic, as well as a safe and hygienic pursuit, and they followed contemporary fashion in believing water immersion to be therapeutic. No doubt the boys also enjoyed the excitement and relative freedom of swimming, especially once organised lessons and regular competitions were established. An article in the Harrow School magazine in the late 1800s explains:

Fig. 1.24 The Harrow Duck Puddle.

' *Ducker lies just across the road and therein swimming, diving and racing of all kinds is practised. Every boy, unless he holds a medical certificate, is compelled to learn to swim, though the distance which qualifies for a pass is not great. On a hot holiday afternoon, boys lounge there for hours, sometimes in the water and sometimes wrapped in their large ducker towels, lying on the warm pavement, eating the 'tuck' they are careful to provide for themselves.* '

Safety was of utmost importance. A well-maintained and safe bathing place gave a good impression at a time of stiff competition between schools. Even more impressive would have been purpose-built swimming baths such as the one built at Charterhouse in 1863.

> **TASK 10**
>
> In pairs, discuss (a) why swimming was considered valuable in late nineteenth-century public schools, and (b) whether it would have had as much status as cricket, rugby or football.

See pages 11–12 for swimming as a popular recreation and pages 45–6 for swimming as a rational recreation.

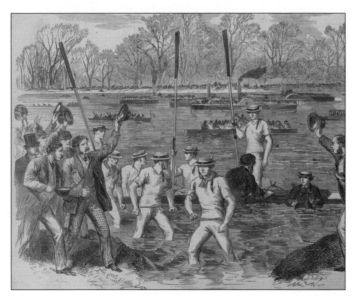

Fig. 1.25 Eton v. Westminster, Putney, 1843.

Rowing

The adoption of rowing by Eton, Shrewsbury, Westminster and the universities of Oxford and Cambridge, dates from around 1800. Other schools that had river access soon followed. The first inter-school race was between Westminster and Eton and the University Boat Race was first rowed at Henley in 1829. Public school boys enjoyed casual boating (simply hiring boats from local yards) long before rowing became either an accepted vehicle for the promotion of desirable values or a major public school sport. Headmasters would turn a blind eye to these casual expeditions as long as lateness, rowdy behaviour and drunkenness was kept to a minimum.

TASK 11

Other than teamwork, what valuable qualities of character were thought to be achieved through rowing?

Fear of drowning caused the sport to become more formalised from the 1840s and participants were required to pass swimming tests. The common practice of having professional watermen (rather than schoolboys) to stroke and steer was also discontinued around this time. This apparently stopped fouling and unsporting behaviour. The phrase 'the harmony of the rowing eight' depicts the teamwork required by successful teams.

See page 13 for rowing as a popular recreation and pages 46–7 for rowing as a rational recreation.

Athletics

Eighteenth-century public school boys took the sports of their local village wakes and fairs back to school after the holidays. They played them for fun and to relieve the boredom of early nineteenth-century school life. With no stabling or kennels at school, fox hunting could not be adopted. Instead it was adapted to 'hare and hounds' where the human 'hare' would run ahead and drop 'scent' (paper) for the 'hounds' (other schoolboys) to follow. *Cassell's Complete Book of Sports and Pastimes* (1896) stresses that:

> *long runs, steady exercise, careful diet, and especially early hours of bedtime are requisite to prepare for a severe hare and hound match … nothing but pluck and stamina combined brings the leaders to their places of honour at the finish.*

HOT TIPS

Initially, headmasters were against hare and hounds as it annoyed neighbouring farmers, led to truancy, and boys would often tear up their textbooks for the 'scent'.

Fig. 1.26 The Rugby School paper chase champion of 1886.

A more refined form of athletics came to public schools from Exeter College, Oxford, in 1850. A group of undergraduates, disappointed by their poor riding in the traditional steeplechase, ran in a 'foot grind' or a cross country race and also staged an Autumn Meeting. The meeting was run on Jockey Club lines even to the weighing of top runners and the inclusion of a consolation stake for beaten 'horses'. In spite of some concern by the school authorities that such events would lead to betting, the idea was soon copied and by the 1870s athletic sports day had become both a major social occasion and a symbol of a more modern age.

School sports day represented an era of technical advancement, more friendly social relationships between boys and masters, and a developing interest in skilfulness over brute force. It was also a useful day for the headmaster to proudly display his school and to tout for financial support. Sports days were highly organised with elaborate ribboned programmes, press coverage, large numbers of spectators and often a military band.

See pages 14–17 for athletics as a popular recreation and pages 47–9 for athletics as a rational recreation.

Football

From the earliest days of public school history, impromptu, natural forms of football were played. Boys brought games from home, which developed into school games dependent on the natural facilities available.

During the second phase of public school development, with rebellion almost over and fighting on the decline, football became the place to settle disputes and to show courage and determination. Ironically, football helped the social class that had traditionally tried to kill it off and for the first time in British history it became respectable.

By the 1860s, transport and communications had greatly improved. School football had also developed and a variety of internal and external contests were organised. Disagreement often occurred in inter-school matches, however, as each school had different rules.

School football variations

Eton College
1   The Wall Game – A ten-a-side static game with the half-sized soccer ball worked along the wall by the 'bully' or scrum. One goal is a door in an end wall, the other a tree. Annual, festival match on St Andrew's Day but other matches also played.
2   The Field Game – played since 1847. Combinations of 'handling' and 'dribbling' rules. Scores made by goals and 'rouges' (similar to rugby tries). Scrummage called a 'ram'.

Fig. 1.27 The cloisters at Charterhouse, home to unique games of mob football.

Charterhouse

1   The Cloister Game – played in the old monastic cloisters at the London site until the school moved to Godalming in 1872. The cloisters had a smooth flagstone floor but sharp jagged flint walls making injuries frequent. The doorways at each end of the cloisters were used as goals and twenty fags (junior pupils) would guard them against violent scrimmages that lasted up to an hour. Bloody noses and broken teeth were accepted as part of the experience.

2   The Association Game – Charterhouse was central to the formation of Association Football.

Harrow

Harrow Football – mainly 'dribbling' rules but if caught and a call of 'yards' was made, a free kick was awarded. Goals called 'bases'.

Rugby

Rugby Football.

Shrewsbury

Douling – played up to around 1880. Similar to rugby. Line out called a 'squash'.

Winchester College

Winchester Football – ten-foot high nets called 'canvases' run along the sides of the 80×25 yard field. Ropes set alongside the 'canvases'. Ends of field marked with furrows called 'worms'. Very complex rules.

Westminster

A game in which trees and rails formed twenty-yard wide goals. Between twelve to fifteen 'duffers' or small boys acted as goalkeepers.

Uppingham

As in most schools up to the 1860s, internal games were concocted from within the school – for example, 'tall v. short' or 'those with an R in their names v. those who have not'. There is a story of Headmaster Thring's anger when he discovered a proposed game between 'those who have been flogged by Mr Thring v. those who have not'. 'If that game goes ahead,' he apparently said, 'all the players will be on the same side!'

See pages 17–18 for football as a popular recreation and pages 49–51 for football as a rational recreation.

Cricket

Already a popular rural game by the mid 1700s, cricket was soon adopted by the public schools. Headmasters were happy to accept the game as its standardised rules, lack of violence and involvement by the gentry made it respectable. It also occupied boys and kept them out of mischief.

Changes that occurred during the three stages of development reflected changes in the game at large. During the 1850s and 60s, cricket grew with William Clarke's All England XI touring the country to entertain and inspire; the Lord's festival week being established as a social display of wealth for the Eton, Harrow and Winchester nobility, and the first England team visiting Australia in 1861.

As a reflection of these developments, cricket in public schools was now associated with:

* regularity as an inter-house and inter-school game
* compulsory participation
* investment in equipment and groundwork
* the employment of professional coaches
* more time spent in training
* the appointment of assistant masters for their cricketing skills
* the hosting of matches as grand social occasions
* the belief that it instilled a range of character building qualities.

Fundamentally though, this was the same game that rural peasants and gentry patrons had played over 100 years before.

See pages 18–20 for cricket as a popular recreation and pages 51–2 for cricket as a rational recreation.

Fig. 1.28 Eton v. Harrow, Lords, 1864.

Court and racquet games
Fives

Fig. 1.29 The chapel steps at Eton.

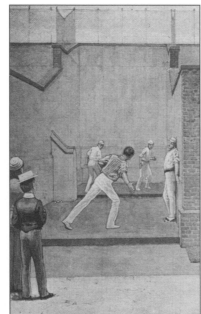

Fig. 1.30 Eton Fives court.

The game of fives is ancient and informal in origin. The best-known structured version is Eton Fives whose odd shaped court is a modification of the space by the Eton Chapel steps. Fives was hugely popular in the public schools but failed to become a national game of any standing. This was because:

* it had a tradition of being played as a recreational game in free time
* there were different versions of the game (for example, Eton Fives and Winchester Fives)
* it had limited scope for developing the character
* the more sophisticated game of racquets was already established.

TASK 12

Try to find a suitable outside wall or corner in your school or college to develop a game of hand or glove fives. What rules will you use?

Racquets and squash

At first, racquets was played informally by schoolboys on naturally occurring 'courts'. By 1850 two standardised courts were built at Harrow at a cost of £850. By the time Old Boys took the game to university and to their private clubs, it had attained a high social status far beyond its beginnings in a prison. As the game became more sophisticated, the court was rationalised with four walls (instead of one) and a roof to guard against bad weather.

Many argue that racquets led to the invention of the more compact and less expensive game of squash. Boys at Harrow who were waiting to play racquets began playing outside. To avoid damage to windows, they used a less hard, more 'squashy' ball than for racquets. By the 1860s, purpose-built squash courts were common and boys took the game on to university and often back to their country homes.

TASK 13

In pairs, discuss how the games of racquets and squash could have developed the character of its public school enthusiasts. What physical or temperamental qualities did it require?

Lawn tennis

Lawn tennis was invented by, and for, the middle classes as a social experience. Importantly, it also became a vehicle for the emancipation (freedom from restrictions) of women. It is not surprising that it was not welcomed by the boys' public schools at a time when manliness and courage were all important.

Why did the boys' public schools reject lawn tennis as anything other than an informal social event often on house courts, but seldom as an inter-school, serious event, and never for the development of character?

* Lawn tennis courts took up a comparatively large space for the number of boys occupied.
* It did not require the courage or physicality of football or cricket.
* It could not rival the contemporary status of cricket or football.
* It did not require the teamwork or co-operation of major games.
* It had a reputation of being 'pat ball' and suitable only for girls.
* As a new invention it was treated with some suspicion.

See pages 20–1 for lawn tennis as a popular recreation and pages 52–3 for lawn tennis as a rational recreation.

Revise as you go! Test your knowledge and understanding

- Identify six characteristics of early nineteenth-century public schools.
- What is meant by the following terms: 'technical development', 'social relationships' and 'values'?
- Identify three aspects of public school life that Dr Arnold wanted to reform.
- What is meant by the term 'Muscular Christianity'?
- Identify three key features of stage one of development in nineteenth-century public schools.
- What was significant about annual athletics sports days?
- Why did headmasters accept cricket but reject poaching?
- Why did fives fail to become a prominent national game?
- Why was lawn tennis considered less valuable than cricket?

Sharpen up your exam technique!

1 In the nineteenth century, English public schools were reformed. Describe the nature of sports and pastimes in public schools in stage one of development (before the reforms of Dr Thomas Arnold). (5 marks)

2 How did rowing reflect the values of athleticism, which had reached cult proportions in public schools by the 1880s (stage three of development)? (4 marks)

3 Identify three characteristics of nineteenth-century public schools and explain how each of these features contributed to the development of the 'cult of athleticism'. (6 marks)

4 Trace the development of athleticism in English public schools. Refer to each of the following stages:

- Stage one: bullying and brutality
- Stage two: the influence of Dr Arnold
- Stage three: athleticism – the 'cult'.

Include discussion on attitudes of headmasters, behaviour of boys and development of facilities. (9 marks)

5 The public schools of the nineteenth century had a profound influence on the emergence and development of sports and games. With reference to the three stages of public school development, discuss the development of either football or swimming. (6 marks)

6 Describe the values to be gained by participation in house and school games at the height of athleticism. (5 marks)

7   Only a small proportion of children went to public schools in the nineteenth century. Explain the rapid spread of athleticism throughout Europe and the British Empire.   (4 marks)

8   Explain the delayed development of athleticism in girls' public schools.   (4 marks)

9   Discuss either (a) Country pursuits and swimming, or (b) The fight from *Tom Brown's Schooldays* in relation to technical developments and social relationships at nineteenth-century public schools.   (4 marks)

Section 3: *Rational recreation in an urban industrial society*

Learning objectives

At the end of this section you should be able to:
- identify the characteristics of rational recreation
- explain how these characteristics reflected societal conditions
- understand the particular significance of the industrial, agrarian and urban revolutions on the development of sport
- compare rational recreation with popular recreation
- trace the development of individual activities (swimming, athletics and rowing) and games (football, cricket and tennis) through the three developmental stages (popular recreation, public school athleticism and rational recreation).

Fig. 1.31 Rational recreation: middle-class ladies playing croquet in the late nineteenth century.

Introduction

The contrast between rationalised croquet and mob football is striking. Remember the 'W' questions? Rational recreation differed from popular recreation in terms of who was playing, where it was played, when it was played and why it was being played (and, of course, how it was being played). These changes reflected societal change. By the mid-nineteenth century, Britain was a fully industrialised society; railways were having a massive impact and ex-public school boys were influencing the development of sport in society.

TASK 14

With reference to figure 1.32, try to answer the 'W' questions (who, what, when, where, why).

It is essential that you know the characteristics of rational recreation and understand the cultural or societal factors that influenced their development. Then, as you did with popular recreation, you can assess the extent to which the three individual activities (swimming, athletics and rowing) and three games (football, cricket and tennis) 'fit' the model. You should also compare the characteristics of rational recreation with those of popular recreation, which changed, of course, because society was changing.

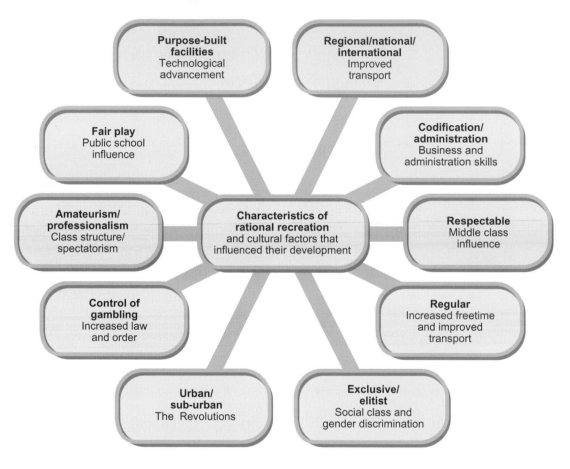

Fig. 1.32 The characteristics of rational recreation and cultural factors that influenced them.

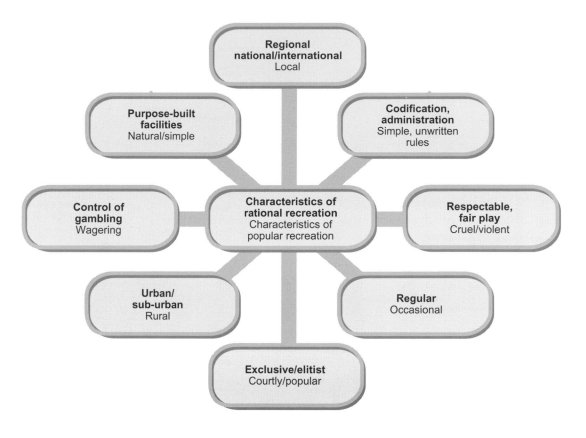

Fig. 1.33 Comparison of characteristics: rational recreation and popular recreation.

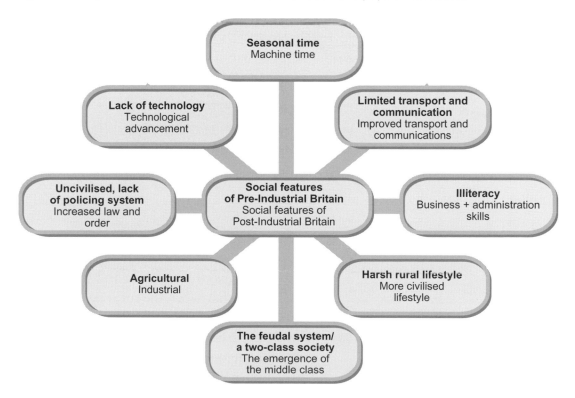

Fig. 1.34 Comparison of pre- and post-industrial societal factors that influenced sport.

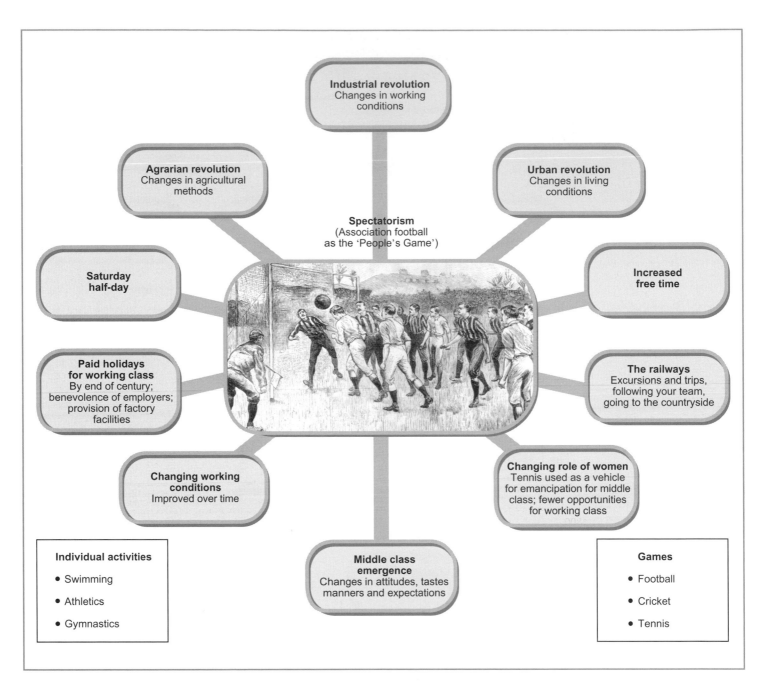

Industrial revolution
Changes in working conditions

Agrarian revolution
Changes in agricultural methods

Urban revolution
Changes in living conditions

Spectatorism
(Association football as the 'People's Game')

Saturday half-day

Increased free time

Paid holidays for working class
By end of century; benevolence of employers; provision of factory facilities

The railways
Excursions and trips, following your team, going to the countryside

Changing working conditions
Improved over time

Changing role of women
Tennis used as a vehicle for emancipation for middle class; fewer opportunities for working class

Individual activities
- Swimming
- Athletics
- Gymnastics

Middle class emergence
Changes in attitudes, tastes manners and expectations

Games
- Football
- Cricket
- Tennis

Fig. 1.35 Urban industrial factors influencing the development of rational recreation.

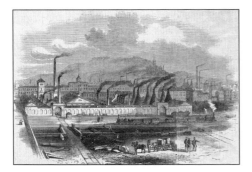

Fig. 1.36 Industrial Britain.

The emergence of sport for the masses, particularly spectator sport, excursion trips to the seaside and paid holidays were hard won. Figure 1.37 shows that when the rural peasants initially migrated to towns and cities in search of regular work opportunities decreased. Life was bleak – the peasants became slaves to the factory system, to machine time and to their employers. It was a time of decay, gloom and even poverty for those out of work who faced life on the streets. The last thing on the minds of this new industrial working class in the first half of the century was sport or recreation. It is important to consider what they had lost:

- **A**cceptance of their traditional activities (due to the 'respectable' middle class)
- **S**pace to play (due to urbanisation/over-crowding)
- **H**ealth/energy (due to slaving in the factories)
- **I**ndependence (due to being controlled by their social superiors)
- **R**ights (due to changes in criminal law/police enforcement/RSPCA)
- **T**ime (due to a 72-hour week/reduction in number of saint's days).

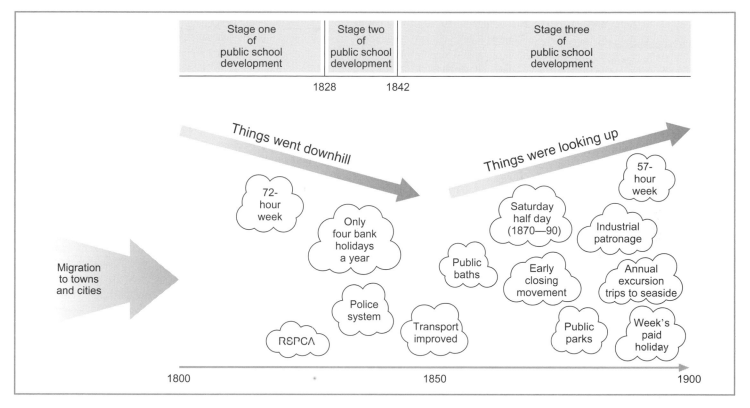

Fig. 1.37 Changes in nineteenth-century working-class opportunity and provision as a parallel process to public school developments.

HOT TIPS

When an exam question asks you to compare or contrast two things (for example, mob football and Association Football), make sure that you make the comparisons or point out the similarities and differences and do not just talk about one or the other. It is best to make the comparisons and points as you go along rather than to talk all about one then all about the other. For example: 'Mob football was occasional whereas Association Football was regular.'

It was only in the second half of the nineteenth century that things began to look up. Various Factory Acts improved working conditions; kind factory owners began to look after their staff in order to win their loyalty and to improve the health and morale of the workforce, and local facilities expanded with the opening of public baths and public parks. By 1890 most workers had won their Saturday half day.

Figure 1.38 shows that a strict class system still underpinned British society. Class determined income, housing, lifestyle and sporting opportunities, and was the basis of amateurism and professionalism, as will be clarified in the following case studies.

TASK 15

Compare mob football in Figure 1.12 (page 17) with Association Football in Figure 1.35 (page 42). Think of the 'W' questions (who, when, where and so on).

HOT TIPS

Remember the importance of improved transport and communications when assessing the development of sport.

• Trains took people further in a shorter time.

• Distant teams could play each other and take supporters with them.

• People could get to the countryside – perhaps taking their (newly acquired) bicycle with them to explore.

• Kindly factory owners could organise and put on excursion trips to the seaside.

• The train journey was often regarded as a pleasurable pastime in its own right.

• Horses no longer had to walk to their next race – so 'the sport of kings' (horse racing) grew too!

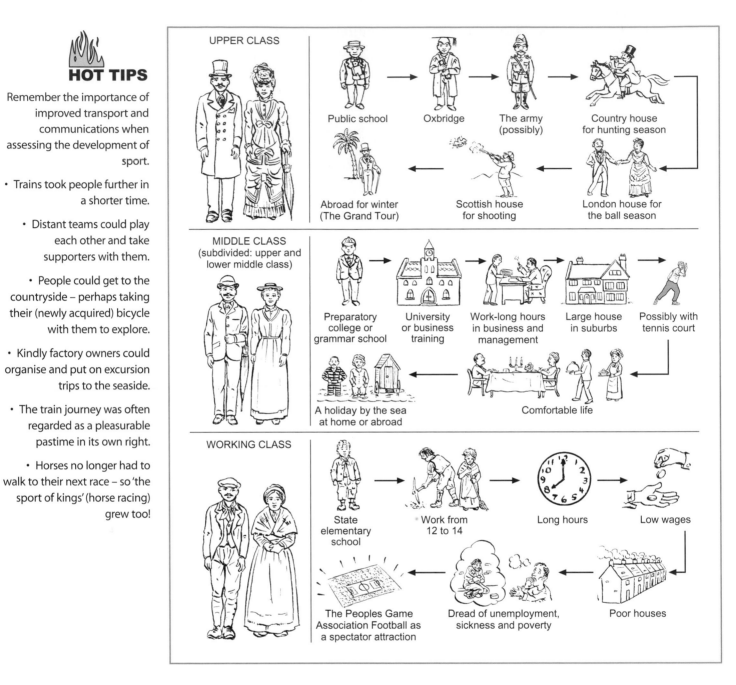

Fig. 1.38 The class system in late nineteenth-century Britain.

TASK 16

In pairs, with reference to Figure 1.37, discuss:

(a) the negative influence (1800–50)

(b) the positive influence (1850–1900)

that each of the identified features would have had on the decline and subsequent rise of sporting opportunities and provision for the industrial working class.

Swimming

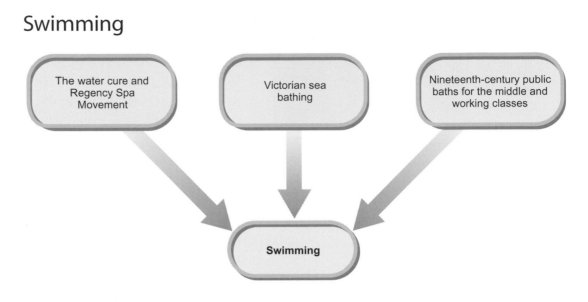

Fig. 1.39 The threads of rational swimming.

KEY WORDS

Water cure

A belief in the therapeutic effects of immersion in water.

Swimming as a rationalised activity has several threads. The **water cure** (the therapeutic effect of immersion in water) existed in inland spas such as Bath and Cheltenham, which grew into large and prestigious resorts for the well off. By the mid-nineteenth century, the newly emerged middle class started to take over these inland spas and chose them as sites for their schools (for example, the colleges of Clifton, Cheltenham and Malvern).

The gentry, meanwhile, had moved on to continental spas and to the English seaside whose cold, salt-water winter cure was now thought to give the most therapeutic effect. With the restrictive ethics of the Victorian era, beaches were designated as socially exclusive and single sexed to ensure modesty and respectability. Bathing machines (wooden changing huts that were towed to the water) gave bathers some privacy, so mixed bathing was eventually allowed. By the 1870s, the new rail network brought the working class to the seaside. They were keen to copy the activities of their social superiors but also sought health and recreation.

Fig. 1.40 Sea bathing in the early nineteenth century, showing a bathing machine.

Meanwhile, bathing facilities in river towns had started to become organised. Floating baths were built (two platforms at right angles to the bank with a chain across the open end), which increased respectability and safety. Swimming became fashionable for the middle class, and amateur swimming as an organised competitive event began with the formation of clubs and the re-establishment of some of the old swimming festivals.

Fig. 1.41 A late nineteenth-century plunge bath.

Eighteenth- and nineteenth-century industrialisation and urbanisation led to overcrowding and disease. In 1846, central government attempted to improve hygiene with its Wash House Acts whereby loans were offered to major towns if they built public baths. These municipal baths had first-class facilities for the fashionable urban middle class (whose plunge pool facilitated the development of indoor amateur swimming clubs and galas) and second-class facilities for the working class who paid 1d (one penny) to wash themselves and their clothes.

In 1869, various middle-class swimming clubs met to establish laws for amateur swimming and in 1874 they were re-named the Swimming Association of Great Britain, which became the Amateur Swimming Association (ASA) in 1884. By 1902, more than 500 clubs were members of the amateur association. While middle-class swimmers (like athletes and rowers) were initially determined to exclude the lower class, by the 1880s, some of this exclusivity had diminished and swimming and water polo clubs were becoming established for the working class with the grudging support from the ASA.

HOT TIPS

Outbreaks of cholera spread rapidly through the country, killing thousands and leaving countless families without a breadwinner. The first Public Health Act in 1848 and the building of public baths sought to reduce such problems.

See pages 11–12 for swimming as a popular recreation and page 32 for swimming in public schools.

Rowing

Two national festivals belong to the sport of rowing – the Boat Race and Henley Regatta. Amateur regattas stem from early river festivals such as the Doggett Coat and Badge Race (1715). Much later, great rowers like Harry Clasper of Tyneside were idolised by locals and were always ready to make money on wager races. Crowds of thousands would line the river for big challenge matches on popular holidays and 130,000 people lined the streets for Clasper's funeral in 1870. Amateur oarsmen could not hope to compete with such stars, nor could they mix socially with them. By now, sport had become as much a matter of socializing with equals after events as competing with equals during them.

HOT TIPS

Remember public baths:

• prevented the spread of disease

• increased work efficiency

• were used for washing, pleasure and sport.

Henley Regatta was a reflection of the Victorian love of combining sport, commercialism and high society. Initially, only amateurs could compete at Henley though there was not yet any formal definition of an amateur. It was understood that men from Oxford and Cambridge and the rowing schools of Eton and Westminster, plus anyone in the household cavalry, could take part.

Fig. 1.42 Oxford v. Cambridge, 1877.

KEY WORDS

Exclusion clause

A device by upper-class administrators to exclude manual workers from the Amateurs Rowing Association in 1882. Abolished in 1890.

In 1861, the handbook for rowing included the famous **exclusion clause** that no mechanic, artisan (skilled craftsman) or labourer was eligible to row at Henley and in 1878 the newly formed Metropolitan Rowing Association formally defined an amateur as follows:

> ' *No person should be considered an amateur who had ever competed in an open competition for a stake, money or entrance fee, who had ever competed with or against a professional for any prize, who had ever taught pursued or assisted in the practice of athletic exercises of any kind as a means of gaining a livelihood, been employed in or about boats for money or wages, or had been by trade or employment for wages, a mechanic, artisan or labourer.* '

In other words, the working class could not join.

Henley stewards then formed the Amateur Rowing Association (ARA) in 1882 and frightened of being beaten by their social inferiors, and in many cases physical superiors, stubbornly clung to their formal exclusion of manual workers. Working-class rowers who wished to compete without turning professional founded their own National Amateur Rowing Association in 1890. The 'mechanics clause' was abolished in 1890 and the Leander Club began to compete against teams such as Thames Tradesmen and the Metropolitan Police. By 1894, a professional was officially classed as someone who made money from rowing, creating three different categories of oarsmen: amateurs, non-amateurs and professionals.

See page 13 for rowing as a popular recreation and page 33 for rowing in public schools.

Athletics

The steady urbanisation of England led first to the end of rural fairs and then to professional athletics becoming established in the big industrial cities. The lower class took to running as a source of income, even though the winnings were small by pre-Victorian standards. Exploitation was common, just as it was with pedestrianism (see pages 16–17). 'Roping' (holding back in order to lose), 'running to the book' (disguising one's form to keep a generous handicap) and 'ringing in' (where promoters conspired to size the handicapping unfairly) were widespread.

The first purpose-built tracks were built in the late 1830s and by 1850 most major cities had a facility. Carefully measured tracks led to more stringent timekeeping and the beginning of record keeping so that by mid century, up to 25,000 people would watch and wager on a single race.

Ex-university gentleman amateurs who wanted to compete against one another without having to mix with professionals formed the Amateur Athletics Club in 1866. They were desperate to dissociate respectable modern athletics from the old corrupted professional form and so adopted the exclusion clause of the Amateur Rowing Association. The Amateur Athletics Association (AAA) was established in 1880. This organisation was responsible for opening up the sport to all levels of society without compromising its upright image. The exclusion clause was withdrawn and a professional became someone who ran for money rather than someone from the lower class.

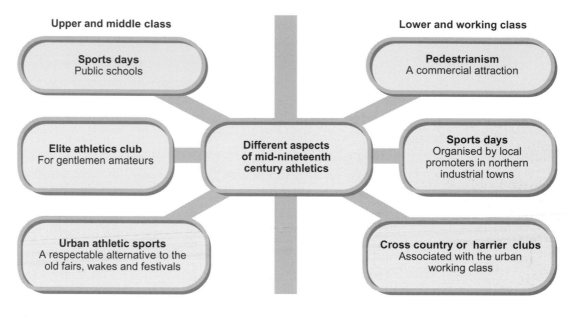

Fig. 1.43 The various aspects of athletics operating by the last quarter of the nineteenth century

TASK 17

With reference to Figure 1.44, try to explain the different motives for participation for both of the athletes.

Fig. 1.44 Six-day pedestrian race, the Royal Agricultural Hall, London, 1870.

The modern Olympic Movement

Inspired by sport in the English public schools of the mid to late nineteenth century, Baron Pierre de Coubertin, a French aristocrat, started the modern Olympic Games in 1896. His aim was to foster patriotism, athleticism and friendship between nations. Unfortunately for de Coubertin, by the time the Games came to London in 1908, those ideals had largely been crushed and international sport had become both an agent of international peace in a world moving towards war and a means of reviving national morale. This move was set against the public school ideal of playing sport honourably and for its own sake. The gentleman amateur did not compete for non-essential rewards, did not train seriously, nor aim to win at all costs.

This conflict was captured in the film *Chariots of Fire* (1981), which follows the preparations and Olympic fortunes of two British athletes in the Paris Games of 1924. Cambridge tutors criticised sprinter Harold Abrahams for being too single minded in his desire to win. Lord Burghley, on the other hand, had the casual attitude of the gentleman amateur. The other main character is the Scot, Eric Liddell, whose need to win was based on a Calvinist belief that 'God made me fast', which meant that he had a duty to use his talent to glorify God in the truest spirit of Muscular Christianity.

Fig. 1.45 The modern Olympic Games, London, 1908.

TASK 18

Try to get hold of a copy of the film *Chariots of Fire* and note:

- the place of university sport in the early twentieth century
- the contrast between amateurism and professionalism and attitudes towards both approaches to sport
- the level of organisation of Olympic teams and the Olympic Games in the early twentieth century.

See pages 14–17 for athletics as a popular recreation and pages 33–4 for athletics in public schools.

Association Football

Ex-public school boys from the universities of Oxford and Cambridge formed the Football Association (FA) in 1863. Prior to this, the dribbling game (soccer) and the handling game (rugby) co-existed. Now, the hackers and handlers moved away to form the Rugby Football Union, and soccer became both an amateur game for gentlemen and a professional game for 'the people' – in other words, the working class. Now, however, football was a regular spectator attraction rather than an annual festival occasion. It soon became clear that the best players could not take unpaid time off work to play and when the Football League was founded in 1888, the FA reluctantly accepted professionalism.

Why did football become so popular so quickly, especially in the northern industrial towns?

- It was simple.
- It fitted the limited space available.
- It fitted perfectly into the newly free Saturday afternoon.

- It provided a focus for community solidarity and comradeship.
- It was affordable.
- It was locally available.
- There was a dense working-class population on hand as spectators.
- Improved transport and communications made travel to away matches and the following of local teams in the press possible.
- Good-hearted factory owners often provided facilities.
- Many teams developed, almost spontaneously, from church and youth movements. Birmingham, Aston Villa, Everton, Fulham, Bolton and Barnsley, for example, were all originally church based.
- For professionals, it offered an improved lifestyle and regular wages (but no security).
- It made the players heroes among the working class.

The first international match between England and Scotland took place in 1870 and by 1885 all the home countries were playing each other. Quite quickly, the working-class dominance of soccer changed the nature of the game. Ex-public school boys fought back with amateur-only leagues, an amateur cup and amateur international fixtures. They criticised the obsession and liveliness of paying spectators, comparing them to pre-industrial mobs who chased pigs' bladders between villages. They also established a team of outstanding amateurs called 'the **Corinthians**' who successfully competed for many years, even against professional sides.

In Rugby Football, meanwhile, there was an increasing need for professional players, particularly in the north of England. Again, players could not afford to take unpaid time from work or be out of action through injury. So the game was split in two and the Northern Football Union (having failed to win **broken-time payments** for players) was formed in 1895. Players could now be paid officially for loss of working time. Effectively, southern clubs excluded manual workers who needed to take time off to train and travel, in this way cementing the tradition that their game was only for gentlemen amateurs – a belief that lasted for

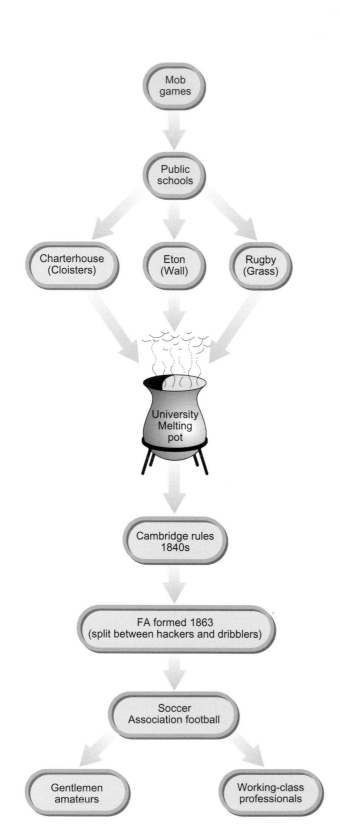

Fig. 1.46 The emergence of Association Football from mob football.

KEY WORDS

Corinthian

An excellent all-round games player who always showed great sportsmanship. The 'Corinthian spirit' is the idea of playing fair.

Broken-time payments

Payments made to working-class players to compensate for loss of earnings. It led to professionalism and was looked down on by gentlemen amateurs.

the next 100 years. With the spread of football across Europe and the Empire, the International Football Federation (FIFA) was formed in 1904 and by 1906 professional football had become the major form of male entertainment in Britain.

See pages 17–18 for mob football as a popular recreation and pages 34–5 for football in public schools.

Cricket

In the 1870s, country cricket took over from the touring XIs (for example, William Clarke's) as a spectator attraction. While county committees needed and respected professionals, they kept them firmly in their social place.

- They had different names – professional v. amateur.
- Their names appeared differently in the programmes – for example, A. Mynn Esq. for a gentleman and Lillywhite for a professional.
- They had different eating arrangements.
- They did not travel together or share a changing room.
- They entered the field of play from a different door.
- The captain was always an amateur.

The university men (amateurs) looked after 'the lads' while 'the lads' arguably respected the gentlemen for their leadership qualities and skills as thinkers and motivators. It was not until 1963 that the distinction between gentlemen and players was finally abolished in English cricket.

Fig. 1.47 England v. Australia, Lords, 1884.

TASK 19

Study the picture of England v. Australia at Lords (Figure 1.47). How do you know that this is a late nineteenth century rational game of cricket rather than a pre-industrial game?

W. G. Grace (1849–1915) was a powerful all-round athlete and the most famous cricketer of his time, who became bigger than the game itself. Once, after an early dismissal at the Oval, he complained to the umpire: 'Nonsense, my man, they have come here to watch me play, not you umpire, play on' – and they did. Grace was a doctor by profession and a gentleman amateur by status, yet he was paid £50 per game. Between 1870 and 1910, he earned £120,000 either directly or indirectly from cricket.

The Ashes

In 1882, an Australian touring party beat England at the Oval. The *Sporting Times* published an obituary for English cricket:

In affectionate remembrance of English Cricket

Which died at the Oval on 19 August 1882,

Deeply lamented by a large circle of sorrowing friends and acquaintances.

R.I.P.

NB the body will be cremated and the ashes taken to Australia.

The next winter, the English team in Australia won a three-match series. Some Australian women supporters burnt a bail, placed the ashes in a small sealed urn and presented them to the English captain. They are now in the Lord's cricket museum.

See pages 18–20 for cricket as a popular recreation and pages 35–6 for cricket in public schools.

Lawn tennis

The game of lawn tennis was patented and popularised by the Army Major Walter Clompton Wingfield in 1874. Wingfield sold the game in a painted box containing pole, pegs and netting for forming the court, four tennis bats, a supply of balls, a mallet and brush, and book of the game. Originally called 'sphairistike', it was played on an hourglass shaped court; but within a few years the name was changed to lawn tennis and the court was modified to become rectangular. Lawn tennis was bought by the most fashionable upper-middle-class families.

In 1877, the All England Croquet Club introduced lawn tennis at Wimbledon. Twenty-two competitors took part and the finals attracted 200 spectators. By 1885, 3500 spectators watched the men's final.

Fig. 1.48 Lawn tennis as a social occasion.

Summary of the development of lawn tennis

*   The middle classes were excluded from real tennis so they looked for their own alternative.

- The game was perfect for upper-middle-class suburban gardens.
- It was patented and became fashionable, almost as a status symbol.
- Tennis clubs were formed, which allowed social gatherings of the same class of people.
- The lower middle class whose gardens were too small for courts also frequented these private clubs.
- The working class were excluded and had to wait for public provision, which delayed their participation.
- The development of tennis reflected the emergence on the urban middle class.

Its role in the emancipation of women

- Lawn tennis helped to remove some stereotypes of earlier Victorian times.
- It was a social occasion and part of family recreation.
- Women could participate but did not have to over do it and were not expected to be good.
- It did not require special dress.
- The true social importance of tennis was that it could be played by men or women or by both together.
- The privacy of the garden, with high hedges or walls, provided an opportunity to invite suitable members of the opposite sex for supervised sports.

Revise as you go! Test your knowledge and understanding

- Compare the characteristics of rational recreation with those of popular recreation.
- With reference to the clue 'A SHIRT', identify what the lower class lost when they migrated to towns and cities in the Industrial Revolution.
- In what ways did improved transport and communications affect the development of sport?
- How did the middle class differ from the working class?
- Identify three different threads from which rational swimming emerged.
- What was the 'water cure'?
- Explain the exclusion clause of the ARA and the AAA.
- Identify six different aspects of athletics in existence between 1870 and 1900.
- With reference to Association Football, explain the terms the 'people's game' and 'broken-time payments'.
- What were/are the Ashes?
- In what year and for what reasons did Baron Pierre de Coubertin start the modern Olympic Games?

Sharpen up your exam technique!

1 Discuss the influence of the Industrial Revolution on the development of rational sport. (5 marks)

2 What was the attraction of Association Football to working-class males in the 1870s? (5 marks)

3 Identify three characteristics of rational recreation and explain how each of these was the result of changing social conditions in post-industrial Britain.

(6 marks)

4 Which features of cricket made it the first widespread and socially acceptable team game? (4 marks)

5 Explain the idea that lawn tennis was invented by, and for, the middle class and comment on the influence of the game on female participation in sport.

(7 marks)

6 Explain the decrease in the leisure opportunities for the industrial working classes as they migrated to towns in the first half of the nineteenth century.

(4 marks)

7 What were the motives behind the provision of public baths and public parks in industrial towns? (4 marks)

8 (a) How did Association Football differ from mob football?

(b) With reference to changes in work conditions, urban expansion and methods of transport, explain why the two games differed so much.

(8 marks)

9 Why did so many public school 'Old Boys' introduce sport to their workers?

(3 marks)

10 Describe the development of public baths in industrial towns in the second half of the nineteenth century and explain their function. (6 marks)

Section 4: *The development of drill, physical training and physical education in elementary schools*

Learning objectives

At the end of this section you should be able to:
- understand that between 1900 and the 1950s physical activity in state elementary schools progressed from military drill to **physical training** and then to physical education
- identify the **content, objectives** and teaching **methods** of each of the above
- explain how war affected the adoption of the different methods
- explain in what ways and why the 'sporting' experiences of working-class children at state elementary schools differed so much from that of middle- and upper-class boys (and girls) at public school.

Introduction

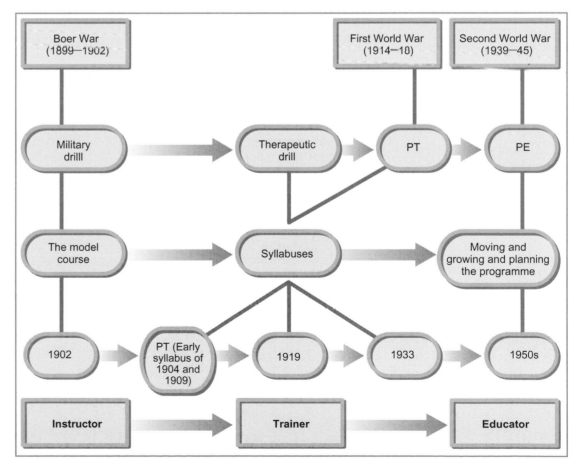

Fig. 1.49 Twentieth-century developments in state elementary schools.

We need to know *how* and *why* the approach to and teaching of physical skills and activities changed throughout the twentieth century. Answers to the 'W' questions will help again. For each stage, identify:

- *what* the emphasis was (for example, drill, training or education)
- *who* did the teaching and learning (that is, class, gender, qualifications of 'teachers')
- *when* it was brought in (you will need to know dates)
- *where* the activity took place (for example, street, playground, purpose-built gymnasium)
- *why* the system was brought in (for example, the effects of war, or due to the influence of particular people).

You must be aware of reasons for change over time, which include:

- change in educational philosophy from instructional to child-centred
- changes from the idealism of the 1950s to increased accountability of teachers today
- changes in the standard of living from poverty to a welfare state system
- social change from a strict class system to an emphasis on equality of opportunity for all
- changes in provision from a playground (at most) to purpose-built facilities and increased availability of equipment
- changes in teacher training from general class teachers to a graduate PE profession
- changes due to the effects of war
- changes in class/group sizes
- imposition of the National Curriculum
- initiatives for sport in schools such as the TOP programmes and specialist sports colleges
- increasing pressures on international sport.

TASK 20
Conduct a five-minute practical role-play of each of the approaches on pages 57–62.

KEY WORDS

Board schools

State schools that opened as a result of the Forster Education Act 1870.

Important points/background information
- In 1866, the army rejected 380 out of each 1000 recruits on physical grounds.
- **Board schools** (state schools) established by the Forster Education Act 1870. Previously, the education of the poor had been a parish responsibility.
- School attendance became compulsory for children aged between five and ten years.
- By 1899, the school leaving age was raised to twelve years.
- By 1900, there had been great progress in terms of provision.
- Restricted space for play and physical exercise.
- Many schools in industrial towns had no playing facilities.

Influences
- The work of European gymnastic teachers, including Guts Muths and Jahn (Germany) and Ling (Sweden), as well as the Briton A. Maclaren.

Elementary school drill
The end of the nineteenth century

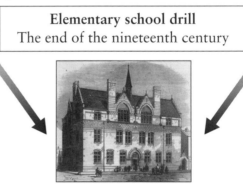

Often built to look like churches, **board schools** had only small playgrounds and no playing fields.

Also note
- Lack of equipment other than staves (sticks) for dummy weapons drill.

Objectives
- Fitness for army recruits
- Discipline
- To do for working-class children what games was doing for public school boys

Content
- 1870 – military drill
- 1890s – Swedish drill
- 1900 – the Board of Education stated that games were a suitable alternative to Swedish drill

Methodology
- Authoritarian/Command-response
- Taught by **army non-commissioned officers** (NCOs) in 1870s
- Taught by qualified class teachers in 1890s

KEY WORDS

Army non-commissioned officers (NCOs)

A low ranking officer who had little interest in or knowledge of child development and whose involvement in presenting the model course lowered the status of the subject.

Fig. 1.50 Elementary school drill at the end of the nineteenth century.

KEY WORDS

Therapeutic

Beneficial, health-giving or remedial.

Boer War

(1899–1902) between the British Empire and Boers of South Africa. Britain lost prestige due to poor performance.

Colonel Fox

A long-serving army officer appointed in 1902, as a result of the Boer War, to establish and ensure the adoption of the model course.

Important points/background information
- Military needs became more powerful than educational theory.
- A backward step educationally with Swedish drill, innovation and a **therapeutic** approach abandoned.
- Condemned by progressives and supporters of the Swedish system.
- Girls and boys instructed together.
- Failed to cater for different ages and/or genders.
- Children treated as soldiers.
- Taught by army NCOs (or teachers who had been trained by them).
- Dull and repetitive – but cheap.
- Large numbers in small spaces.
- Set against backdrop of poor diets, bad housing and other forms of social deprivation.
- It lowered the status of the subject.

Influences
- Imposed as a result of Britain's poor performance in the **Boer War**.
- Produced and imposed by **Colonel Fox** of the War Office (not Education Department).

The Model course 1902

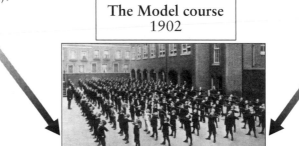

Massed drill in the school yard around 1902.

Also note
❛It is important therefore that the short time claimed for physical training should be devoted wholly to useful exercises. No part of that time should be wasted on what is merely spectacular or entertaining, but every exercise should have its peculiar purpose and value in a complete system framed to develop all parts of the body. (*Model Course of Physical Training*, 1902)❜

Objectives
- Fitness (for military service)
- Training in handling of weapons
- Discipline

Content
- Military drill
- Exercises
- Weapon training
- Deep breathing

Methodology
- Command-response (for example, 'Attention', 'Stand at ease', 'Marching, about turn'.)
- Group response/no individuality
- In ranks

Fig. 1.51 The Model course, 1902.

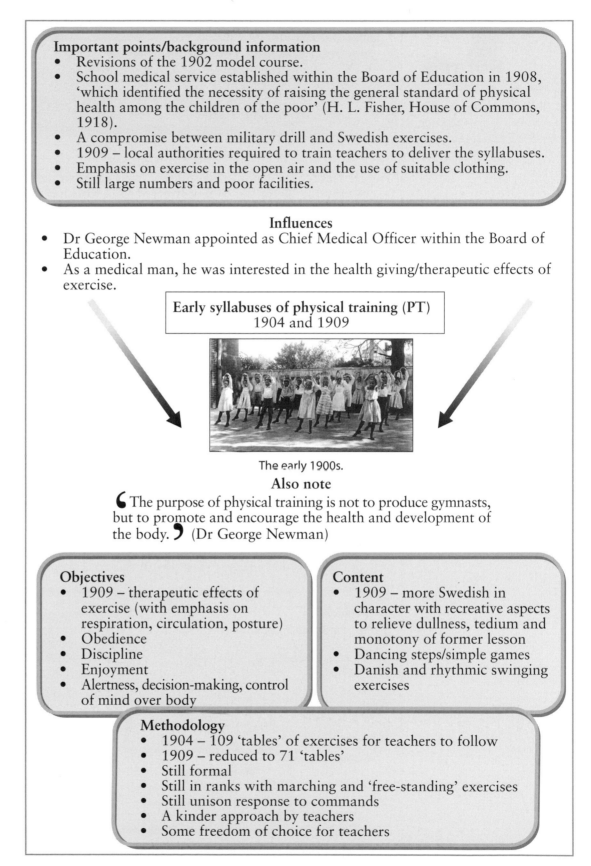

Important points/background information
- Revisions of the 1902 model course.
- School medical service established within the Board of Education in 1908, 'which identified the necessity of raising the general standard of physical health among the children of the poor' (H. L. Fisher, House of Commons, 1918).
- A compromise between military drill and Swedish exercises.
- 1909 – local authorities required to train teachers to deliver the syllabuses.
- Emphasis on exercise in the open air and the use of suitable clothing.
- Still large numbers and poor facilities.

Influences
- Dr George Newman appointed as Chief Medical Officer within the Board of Education.
- As a medical man, he was interested in the health giving/therapeutic effects of exercise.

Early syllabuses of physical training (PT) 1904 and 1909

The early 1900s.

Also note

❛The purpose of physical training is not to produce gymnasts, but to promote and encourage the health and development of the body.❜ (Dr George Newman)

Objectives
- 1909 – therapeutic effects of exercise (with emphasis on respiration, circulation, posture)
- Obedience
- Discipline
- Enjoyment
- Alertness, decision-making, control of mind over body

Content
- 1909 – more Swedish in character with recreative aspects to relieve dullness, tedium and monotony of former lesson
- Dancing steps/simple games
- Danish and rhythmic swinging exercises

Methodology
- 1904 – 109 'tables' of exercises for teachers to follow
- 1909 – reduced to 71 'tables'
- Still formal
- Still in ranks with marching and 'free-standing' exercises
- Still unison response to commands
- A kinder approach by teachers
- Some freedom of choice for teachers

Fig. 1.52 Early syllabuses of physical training (PT), 1904 and 1909.

HOT TIPS

Note the role of Dr George Newman in overseeing the publication of three Board of Education syllabuses between 1909 and 1933.

Important points/background information
- Set against the huge loss of life in World War I and huge loss of life in post-war flu epidemic.
- The syllabus was progressive in terms of its broader content and child-centred appoach.

Influences
- Dr George Newman still influential and eager to fight off accusations that PT was to blame for the lack of fitness of the working class.
- Newman also stressed the benefits of recreative activities for the rehabilitation of injured soldiers.
- The Fisher Education Act 1918 promoted holiday and school camps, school playing fields and school swimming baths.

The syllabus 1919

The style of free standing exercises still recommended in the 1919 syllabus.

Also note
- The first 'child centred' syllabus.
- Broader content than 1902/1904/1909.
- But some older teachers stayed with their old ways.

Objectives
- Enjoyment and play for the under 7s
- Therapeutic work for the over 7s

Content
- The exercises and 'positions' the same as 1909
- Special section of games for the under 7s
- Not less than half the lesson on 'general activity exercises' – active free movement, including small games and dancing

Methodology
- More freedom for teachers and pupils
- Less formality

Fig. 1.53 The syllabus, 1919.

Important points/background information
- The industrial depression of the 1930s left many of the working class unemployed (no state benefits were yet available).
- A watershed between the syllabuses of the past and the physical education of the future.
- This syllabus had one section for the under elevens and one for the over elevens.

Influences
- The Hadow Report of 1926 identified the need to differentiate between ages for physical training.
- Dr George Newman – this was the last syllabus to be published under his direction.

Syllabus of physical training 1933

Emphasis on skills and posture.

Also note
- A detailed, high quality and highly respected syllabus.
- Still set out in a series of 'tables' from which teachers planned their lessons.
- 'The ultimate test by which every system of physical training should be judged [is] to be found in the posture and general carriage of the children' (1933 syllabus).
- Newman stated that good nourishment, effective medical inspection and treatment and hygienic surroundings were all necessary for good health as well as 'a comprehensive system of physical training … for the normal healthy development of the body [and] for the correction of inherent or acquired defects.'

Objectives
- Physical fitness
- Therapeutic results
- Good physique
- Good posture
- Development of mind and body (holistic aims)

Content
- Athletics, gymnastic and games skills
- Group work

Methodology
- Still direct style for the majority of the lesson
- Some **decentralised** parts to the lesson
- Group work/tasks throughout
- Encouragement of special clothing/kit
- 5 × 20-minute lesson a week recommended
- Used many schools' newly built gymnasia
- Outdoor lessons recommended for health benefits

KEY WORDS

Decentralised/ centralised

A centralised lesson has the teacher using an instructional style and the children all answering the same task in unison. A decentralised lesson has the teacher as a guide, with children working at their own pace answering tasks in an individual way.

Fig. 1.54 Syllabus of physical training, 1933.

Important points/background information
- The (Butler) Education Act 1944 aimed to ensure equality of educational opportunity.
- It also required local authorities to provide playing fields for all schools.
- School leaving age was raised to fifteen years.
- These syllabuses should be viewed in the context of overall expansion of physical activities in schools.
- Intended to replace the under elevens section of the 1933 syllabus.

KEY WORDS

Open tasks

Problem-solving tasks that can be solved in many different ways.

Influences
- The Second World War, which required 'thinking' soldiers, and the subsequent perceived need for increasingly 'thinking' children.
- Assault course obstacle equipment, influenced apparatus design.
- Modern educational dance methods influenced the creative/movement approach.
- An experiment in Halifax, which rehabilitated children with disabilities by encouraging individual interpretation of **open tasks**, with no pre-set rhythm or timing. This influenced the problem-solving approach.

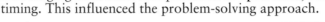

1) Moving and growing; 2) Planning the programme
(1952)　　　　　　　　(1954)

An apparatus lesson in the 1950s.

Also note
- The extensive post-war re-building programme lead to an expansion of facilities.

Objectives
- Physical, social and cognitive skills
- Variety of experiences
- Enjoyment
- Personal satisfaction
- Increased involvement for all

Content
- Agility exercises; gymnastics, dance and games skills
- Swimming
- Movement to music

Methodology
- Child-centred and enjoyment orientated
- Progressive
- Teacher guidance rather than direction
- Problem-solving/creative/exploratory/discovery
- Individual interpretation of tasks
- Using full apparatus (cave, ropes, bars, boxes, mats, and so on)

Fig. 1.55 1 Moving and growing, 1952; 2 Planning the programme, 1954.

TASK 21

1 Fill in an A3 copy of the following table, which will be useful for revision.

	1902	1904/1909	1919	1933	1954	2000
Objective (why)						
Content (what)						
Methodology (how)						
Apparatus						
Other relevant information						

2 Prepare a chart of the positive and/or negative aspects of each syllabus.

Revise as you go! Test your knowledge and understanding

- What is meant by the words 'objectives', 'content' and 'methodology'?
- With which syllabuses would you associate the following words or phrases? (Some may be linked with more than one syllabus.)
  - Child-centred
  - Boer War
  - Dr George Newman
  - Therapeutic
  - Army NCOs
  - Army assault apparatus
  - Play for the under 7s
  - Colonel Fox
- Compare the content of the 1902 model course with that of moving and growing/planning the programme (early 1950s).
- Who was Dr George Newman and how was he influential?
- Identify four things that influenced the development of moving and growing/planning the programme.
- Identify six different reasons for changes in approach to the physical training and/or education of children from 1900 to 2000.

Sharpen up your exam technique!

1   What were the objectives of the physical training of elementary school children during the early years of the twentieth century?   (3 marks)

2   What were the aims of the 1902 model course and why was it replaced by a system of therapeutic physical training?   (5 marks)

3   At the beginning of the twentieth century, state elementary schoolchildren followed a programme of military drill. Why did they not play team games?   (3 marks)

4   Identify key features of the 1933 Board of Education syllabus for state elementary schools.   (4 marks)

5   Outline the effects of World War II on the development of physical education.   (4 marks)

6   Organised physical activity in twentieth-century elementary (primary) schools changed from military drill to physical training and eventually to physical education as we know it today. Explain the objectives underlying each of these three types of approach, giving examples of activities taught and the method used to teach them.   (9 marks)

Chapter 2 **Comparative studies**

Section 1: *Cultural background of the USA*

Learning objectives

At the end of this section you should be able to:
- outline the historical factors that have shaped American society
- understand that ethnic and European games reached America and were played and modified during colonialisation
- account for geographic, demographic and socio-economic influences that have interacted on American society
- explain the mainstream ideologies and counter culture
- relate to the scale of America compared to the United Kingdom.

Ethnic and European games

Prior to the first European settlement, the **indigenous** population of the North American landmass comprised mostly Indian tribes who are now referred to as Native Americans.

It is believed that a primitive form of lacrosse was played among these Native American tribes, usually as a celebration ritual after victory in battle. Lacrosse survived the period of **colonialism** and has emerged today as a sophisticated sport and the only game with roots in the original native culture.

Today, all sports played in America fall into three historical categories.

- Adaptations – modifications to games already in existence. Rugby became American football and baseball developed from an activity played by children called goal ball or rounders.
- Adoptions – games taken directly from European cultures, such as tennis.
- Inventions – the Americans designed new sports to suit the '**New World**' culture, such as basketball.

All of these sports are now multi-million dollar industries, committed to the entertainment market and driven by profit-making motives.

Early foreign settlers were attracted to the country for a number of reasons:

- to escape religious discrimination in Europe
- to establish their own religious communities
- to make fortunes
- to improve the quality of life for themselves and their families.

All settlers found the new land to be drastically different to the countries they had left behind and survival was the priority.

Among the first relocations to the New World were the Jamestown settlers of 1607, many of whom perished in their attempts to set up an English colony.

These early English settlers played a form of football at Jamestown. The rules were unclear and the spectacle resembled a sprawling Shrove Tide mob game directly reflecting the popular culture of England's lower orders. Injuries were common and fatalities occurred in these popular pastimes.

Other sports found their way to new settlements. Polo, hunting and horse racing followed the etiquette and rules laid down in England by the aristocratic class. Races were staged over measured courses and betting was popular.

Fig 2.01 This bare-knuckle fight lasted 75 rounds, or two hours and sixteen minutes, and emphasises the brutality of **popular recreation**.

KEY WORDS

Popular recreation

An unrefined form of recreation that was available to the mass-lower orders of society.

The working classes also had sports and these tended to copy English blood sports by being lawless and violent. Dog fighting and cock fighting were common, while fist fighting and wrestling attracted large crowds and gave further opportunities for gambling. It was common for fighters to grow a long fingernail for eye gouging and biting off the nose of an opponent was a permitted tactic.

Sports and pastimes also took their form from constructive work. Groups of men would arrange to meet to build barns, plough fields and husk corn in the quickest possible time. These activities developed into contests with other groups and the outcomes were productive. These gatherings were called 'bees', reflecting the busy character of the bees' work. Often the work bee ended with dancing and music.

Brutal sports and the activities associated with the bee took place on the **frontier** and reflected the spirit adopted by the early settlers, which enabled this society to survive and later to prosper.

The frontier spirit was epitomised by the way an individual stood up to the harsh environment and its legacy has shaped the ideologies of the USA today. This manly spirit reflected toughness, endeavour and a strong work ethic.

However, by 1750, cricket had become a popular game established by the British, who at that time were the dominant colonists. Other colonies set up by the Dutch, Spanish and French also existed and operated independently. The USA was destined to become a multi-cultural society dominated by **WASPs**.

This domination would later influence the order of society, power distribution and sports development in a country driven by an economy built on **capitalism**.

The Declaration of Independence was signed on 4 July 1776, granting freedom and independence for the American colonies. These colonies became the thirteen original states of America.

The date is recognised as the birth of the American nation, which, with the demise of the Soviet bloc in 1989, became the dominant world super power within a mere 200 years.

Population

The population of the USA is approximately 293 million. The graph below indicates the rapid acceleration from 1850 onwards and this is a continuing trend. In 2003, there were 200 million white people, 38 million Latinos, 35 million African-Americans and 20 million from other races.

The USA is a widely multi-cultural society and claims a policy of **pluralism,** which professes that each culture can co-exist harmoniously. However, the WASPs remain the dominant culture and this is evident in issues concerning ownership and **centrality** in sport. These major issues will be addressed in the section dealing with discrimination in sport (see pages 90–93).

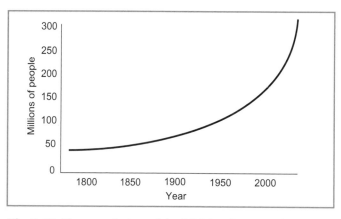

Fig. 2.02 The population of the USA has increased rapidly since 1850.

KEY WORDS

Frontier

An imaginary boundary lying between land occupied by white pioneers and the lands of Native Americans. Such areas had great potential for farming and settlement, which resulted in bitter conflict between the two groups.

Multi-cultural

A society comprising many different cultures.

WASPs

White Anglo-Saxon Protestants.

Capitalism

An economic system that enables private enterprise to accumulate power and wealth.

HOT TIPS

The legacy of the frontier spirit exists in American sport today. This may account for the violence seen in the dominant sports of gridiron football (American football), baseball and ice hockey. Sport is regarded as the 'last frontier'.

KEY WORDS

Pluralism

A view or image of society where each minority culture retains its own traditions and values within the major cultures. Pluralism involves equality and opportunity.

Centrality

WASPs dominate key positions on the sports field. For example, the majority of quarterbacks in gridiron football are white.

TASK 1

Study the following list of sports:

- gridiron football
- basketball
- track and field
- tennis

- baseball
- boxing
- swimming
- golf.

Consider the following.

- Which culture dominates as:
  - a playing participant
  - a coach
  - an owner?
- Does any one culture dominate particular positions in the team?
- To what extent is the trend of one cultural group dominating sport changing?

Size of country

The USA comprises 50 separate states. Figure 2.03 is an attempt to give a picture of the vastness of this continent. The United Kingdom is approximately two-thirds the size of the state of California.

TASK 2

Discuss the influence that a large landmass and a huge population can have on the development of sport in a country such as the USA.

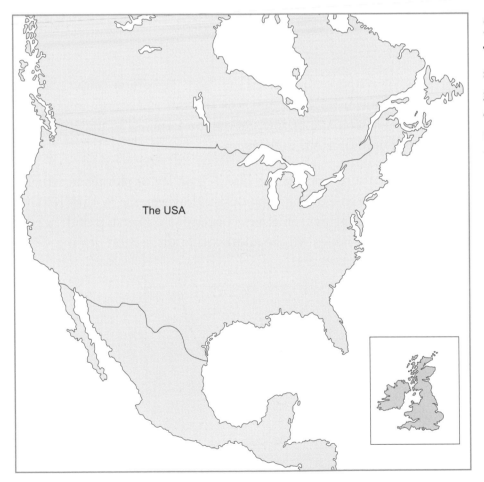

The USA

Fig 2.03 The size of the USA is important to understand but difficult to imagine.

Urbanisation

The population density of America is 70 people per square mile and although some areas constitute **genuine wilderness** and have no population, New York and California have huge urban sprawls, which bring serious congestion and air pollution problems.

Large unpopulated areas of wilderness have helped to stimulate the American passion for the **great outdoors**, while the densely populated settlements have been hotbeds in the development of New World urban sports such as gridiron football, basketball and baseball.

Communications

In contrast to the British, Americans are prepared to travel great distances by car. There is an advanced network of interstate highways and direct urban freeways to accommodate extensive car use. Interstate air travel is essential in such a large country and this mode of transport appears to be more accessible to the individual in the USA than to a person in the UK. Rail links are well established and the network played a key role in the early development of structured competitive sport around 1870.

Climate

North America has huge ranges of latitude and altitude. As a result, the country has a wide range of climatic zones. Terrain also varies markedly from wide plain to desert and high mountain ranges, such as the Western Cordilleras, which contain the Rocky Mountains. These wilderness areas are termed 'frontier country', giving wide opportunity for adventure.

Socio-economic influences

It is important to understand that US society is driven by a form of economic system known as capitalism, which directly influences all that happens in professional sport, sport at **collegiate** and high school level. Capitalism also determines opportunities in physical and outdoor education.

Capitalism allows an individual to accumulate wealth. The important term here is **individualism,** as this powerfully reflects the social history of America.

The USA attracted early settlers because the land was rich and resources were plentiful. However, before resources could be converted into wealth, they had to be won, often single-handedly. This 'every man for himself' **ideology** steered America towards capitalism.

Capitalism has led to the formation of the major American ideologies, which are identified below.

- Provision of opportunity. Opportunity is available and open to all people. Everyone is given the chance to succeed within this system.
- Freedom and liberty. Freedom is given to all individuals to pursue wealth and happiness, which can be gained from capitalism. The popular American slogans that reflect the individual's chance to rise up and prosper in society include 'rags to riches' and 'shoeshine boy to president'.
- The American Dream. It is a strong belief that happiness is secured through the generation of wealth, and the acquisition of both happiness and wealth give the individual the ultimate 'American Dream'. To reach the Dream is the ideal of every American and this ambition drives the machine of capitalism. The Dream can be achieved only at a high price. American society is brutally competitive. Failure in the workplace will result in dismissal. This is directly reflected in sport through the '**hire and fire**' policy.
- Lombardianism. The mainstream competitive culture has acquired the name Lombardianism after coach Vince Lombardi coined the phrase: 'Winning isn't everything – it is the only thing.'

Fig. 2.04 Baseball has been known as the 'national pastime' for over 100 years. It is often said that many American cultural values are displayed through baseball.

Joe Di Maggio, a baseball legend in the 1950s, is quoted as saying: 'Never quit till all bases are uphill.' This means that one can never give up in the American capitalist society. Failure is not an option, as there is always someone waiting to take the place of the unsuccessful person.

It is important to be aware of the existence of counter culture. Counter culture represents a non-competitive approach that states that the process involved in achievement is more important than winning. A minority culture opposes the mainstream

TASK 3

Discus how the ideologies displayed in this model complement each other and fit with the economic system known as capitalism.

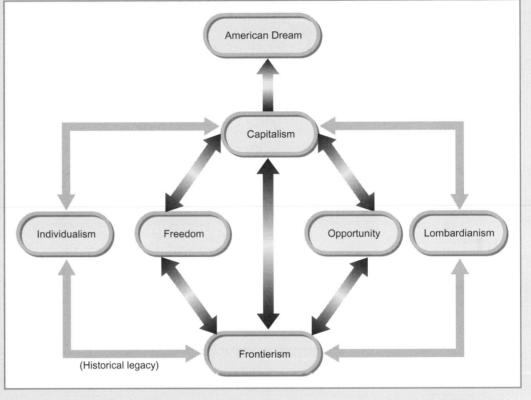

Fig. 2.05 Model of Lombardianism: the slogan 'Nice guys come last' emphasises the spirit of Lombardianism.

Lombardian approach to life in the USA. This alternative attitude will be revisited on page 79.

Pluralistic and hegemonic culture

The USA believes itself to be the 'land of the free' and a 'land of opportunity'; but to what extent are these images accurate?

The USA is a republic with an elected president and, unlike the UK, has never had a monarchy or hereditary privileged class that had the power to determine or influence the opportunity of the people. There is also a tradition of **state autonomy** made possible by the federal administration policy of **decentralisation**.

Decentralisation applies not only in the government of each state but, is also reflected in the administration of business and other institutions. This includes education and sport.

HOT TIPS

Be aware that education in the United States is decentralised (see page 74). Also consider the link between decentralisation and capitalism.

HOT TIPS

It is significant that the wealthiest 1 per cent of Americans directly or indirectly manipulate sport, education and opportunities in the great outdoors for the vast numbers of Americans who have interests in these areas.

The distribution of power gives the opportunity for free enterprise and once again reflects individualism, allowing some institutions to become wealthier than others. This freedom to seek wealth actively is the whole idea of capitalism and is the perfect example of the spirit of the USA.

TASK 4

1   Discuss the reasons why decentralisation is an effective administration system for a country like the USA.

2   Why does the concept of decentralisation link well with the economic system known as capitalism?

There are two images of society in existence in the USA.

Pluralistic	Hegemonic
• No one particular group can be dominant.	• A single group dominates.
• Each culture retains its own identity and is not forced to accept the norms of a dominant culture.	• The dominant group controls the economy and political institutions.
• Each culture has the opportunity to influence the operation of the country.	• The dominant group uses its influence to shape attitudes, values and cultural norms within society.
• Liberty and justice are equally available to all cultures and all individuals.	• Other groups become convinced that the dominant group is right and just. This spreads conformity throughout the whole society.
• There is equality and opportunity for all citizens.	• The dominant group tells everyone else that the country lives by and supports the pluralist image.
• It upholds a government of the people by and for the people.	

The hegemonic group is the dominant group and controls the way of life in the USA. It is the wealthiest group and, like all capitalist countries, wealth is unevenly distributed. Figure 2.06 highlights the uneven distribution of wealth in the USA.

Revise as you go! Test your knowledge and understanding

• Identify the indigenous inhabitants of North America.

• Explain the process of colonialisation.

• Identify the three historical categories that account for the origins of sports played in the USA today.

The bottom 90 per cent of the population owns 29 per cent of wealth

40 per cent of wealth is owned by 1 per cent of the population

31 per cent of wealth is owned by 9 per cent of the population

Fig. 2.06 The distribution of wealth in the USA.

HOT TIPS

The small and wealthy hegemonic group provide the focus for the rest of society. It is they who perpetuate competition through the capitalist system.

HOT TIPS

Make sure you understand the link between sport and commercialism and sport and politics in the United States and United Kingdom. Review page 215 of *Advanced PE for OCR, AS.*

- Outline the reasons why early settlers were attracted to America.
- Describe and account for the sporting experiences of the upper and lower classes during the period of colonialisation.
- Explain the purpose of social gatherings that were called 'the bees'.
- Define the term 'frontier spirit'.
- Describe the status of the group in the USA society known as WASPs.
- Give reasons to explain why the USA experiences such a broad climatic range.
- Explain the term 'genuine wilderness'.
- Describe, briefly, the economic system known as capitalism.
- Outline the differences between hegemony and pluralism.
- Explain the concept of the 'American Dream'.
- Define the term 'Lombardianism'.
- Describe the link between Lombardianism, capitalism and the American Dream.

Sharpen up your exam technique!

1   Describe the features of Lombardianism as they exist in American sport and explain how this ethic can be associated with capitalism.   (4 marks)

2   Explain why sport is called the 'last frontier'.   (3 marks)

3   Describe how the WASP society exerts domination of American sport at professional level.   (4 marks)

4   Outline the wider American cultural values that may be displayed in baseball.   (5 marks)

Section 2: *Physical education and sport in schools (the USA)*

Learning objectives

At the end of this section you should be able to:
- understand the provision made for Physical Education in USA schools
- understand the attitudes shown towards Physical Education in the USA
- describe the policy of co-education and the significance of Title IX legislation
- explain and account for the extra-curricular sport in high schools.

Introduction

The USA has a strong tradition of state autonomy; this is reflected in the education system, which is decentralised, meaning that governance and funding of schools is administered at a local and state level. There is no form of federal (central) government control, although if a national issue arises, the government will provide guidance and funding. In such cases, the US Department of Education, rather than the state administration, will oversee any programmes or initiatives.

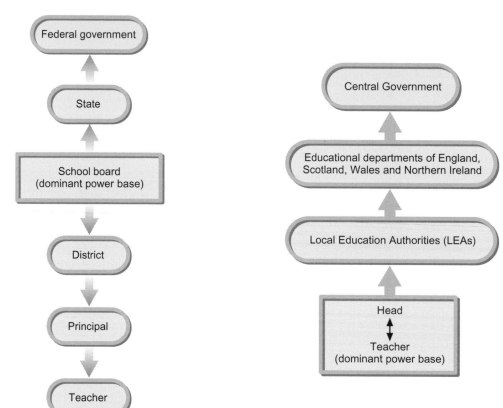

Fig. 2.07 Example of the decentralised structure in the USA.

Fig. 2.08 An example of the decentralised structure in the UK.

American education progression

Age	1	2	3	4	5	6	7	8	9	10	11	12	13	14	15	16	17
	Pre-school kindergarten					Elementary school						Junior high			Senior high		
Grades						1	2	3	4	5	6	7	8	9	10	11	12

Fig. 2.09 American education progression: schools and grades (years).

There are two types of high school.

- Local public schools, where education is free. These schools have a tradition of co-education and are comprehensive.
- Private schools, which are fee-paying schools. These institutions tend to be affiliated to the Church. They may also be single-sex or educate children with special needs.

Seventy-five per cent of all high school students progress to degree courses at college. This has strong implications for sport.

Unlike the UK, the majority of schools in the USA do not train students for externally set examinations, although some states have begun to introduce a high school exit exam. There is a continuous evaluation system and work is marked from grade 'A' (excellent) to 'F' (failure). Completion of studies to pass standard leads to the award of a High School Diploma and this is the accepted requirement for a college degree course.

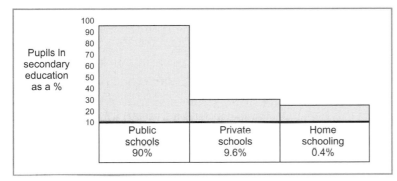

Fig. 2.10 Most children in the USA are educated in state funded schools.

The concept of the National Curriculum does not exist in the USA. A number of compulsory core subjects are taught and physical education is one of these. There is evidence from kindergarten that the **heuristic approach** to teaching physical education has been adopted.

Although there is an element of consultation with the school, the physical education programme is designed and regularly inspected by a Superintendent of the School Board. This means the teacher is accountable and is required to work through the set programme while assessing student performance.

TASK 5

1 What is meant by the term 'accountable'?
2 Discuss why accountability is necessary in a capitalist system.
3 Say why accountability helps to promote a Lombardian ethos.

At high school level, a heavy emphasis is given in the physical education programme to the delivery of fitness and direct skill learning. This system of organisation allows for variations between schools and ensures that the programme is delivered effectively. But while the framework for progression is in place, the nature of this focus restricts the opportunities for creative teaching and virtually prevents the introduction of counter culture activities.

Assessment is essentially practical, and grades are given for effort and attainment in skills and fitness. A written input into the final assessment is required for the purpose of the High School Diploma.

However, physical education is facing a crisis in the USA. After the Nixon administration abolished military conscription in 1970, all states became less vigorous in enforcing compulsory physical education. In 2000, Illinois was the only state enforcing the subject, but since that time it has withdrawn the policy. Chicago officials estimated to save US$16 million a year by making physical education optional in grades eleven and twelve.

Participation in physical education for all students was approximately 70 per cent in the 1980s but fell below 60 per cent by the end of the twentieth century. The greatest decline comes after the sixth grade. The Federal Centre for Disease Control confirms this trend, reporting that while 42 per cent of high school students took daily physical education in 1991, the figure registered at 27 per cent by 1997. The warning given by the National Association for Sport and Physical Education (NASPE) is that the subject is now becoming an expensive luxury.

The decline of physical activities during curriculum time has brought new concerns and accelerated existing problems. Concern regarding an increase in obesity is arising in all affluent countries, although low fitness levels and obesity in teenagers has been an issue in the USA since military recruitment was necessary in 1942. Forty-four million Americans were registered as obese in 2003, reflecting an increase of 74 per cent since 1993.

The Californian Department of Education reported in 2003 that 80 per cent of 1 million pupils in grades 5, 7 and 9 failed to achieve minimum standards in the **fitnessgram** assessment.

Strategies are being put into place to reverse this declining trend and improve the quality of timetabled physical education experiences, which the NASPE believes to be the cornerstone of healthy active lifestyles. Some US$60 million has been invested into a programme entitled 'Physical Education for Progress' (PEP). Local school districts and community organisations can access grant funds to promote activities, develop curriculum, purchase equipment and train teachers.

Addressing equality in physical education and sport
Adaptive physical education

The USA has a very active policy of sports provision, particularly in education for disabled people. Federal law states that physical education must be provided for students with special needs and disabilities. The provision made for these children is called 'adapted physical education'. This involves diverse programmes that have been modified to enable full participation. In order to raise the quality of experience, while at the same time increasing awareness of disability, pupils with special needs are integrated into the mainstream high school curriculum.

Title IX

Title IX was passed as law in 1972 and is an example of central legislation. It addressed the issue of gender inequality in all areas of education and stated:

> *No person in the United States shall on the basis of sex be excluded from participation from any education programme or activity receiving federal assistance.*

In terms of sport, the law was not primarily concerned with opening the traditional physical contact activities like wrestling or gridiron football for female participation. Nor did it state that the exact amount of money granted to men should be invested into women's sports. The focus of Title IX was for women to have equal opportunities.

The situation before Title IX

- Opportunities were severely restricted for female interscholastic and intercollegiate sports fixtures.
- Several states had legislation prohibiting sports fixtures for girls.
- The male-orientated society controlled sport and believed it to be the preserve of men.
- Facilities for women were segregated and inferior to those of men.
- **Athletic** scholarships for women were rare.
- In general, men believed that women would downgrade the status of sport.
- Intense involvement in competitive sport was perceived as unfeminine and lacking in dignity.

Although a general entitlement, the law focused on sports opportunities rather than daily physical education at high school and college, the necessary upgrading of women's facilities has inevitably impacted on the curriculum subject.

KEY WORDS

Athletic

In the USA, the term 'athletic' is used to describe high level competitive sport and is synonymous with the Lombardian ethic.

The table below shows the dramatic increase in female participation since Title IX and makes for an interesting comparison with male involvement.

Year	Boy participants (school level)	Girl participants (school level)
1971	3,666,917	294,015
1987	3,517,829	1,836,256
1997	3,634,052	2,367,936
2002	3,624,500	2,990,836

Fig. 2.11 The growing participation in sport among girls in USA high schools.

Title IX has increased standards in track and field and in 1996 the US national women's soccer team won the first Olympic medal in this sport in front of a crowd of 75,000.

Year	Men				Women			
	Gold	Silver	Bronze	Total	Gold	Silver	Bronze	Total
1972	6	7	6	19	0	1	2	3
1976	6	6	7	19	0	2	1	3
1984	9	8	7	24	7	7	2	16
1988	7	7	5	19	6	2	1	9
1992	8	5	7	20	4	3	3	10
1996	10	4	2	16	3	1	3	7
2000	6	4	3	13	4	0	3	7

Fig. 2.12 The improved performance of American women in Olympic track and field events.

TASK 6

1 Discuss the benefits of increased female participation for USA sport.
2 Discuss why there were outstanding performances by the American team in 1984.
3 Explain why statistics for 1980 do not appear.

KEY WORDS

NCAA

The National College Athletic Association is the major governing association for university sport in the USA.

Fig. 2.13 Florence Griffith Joyner performed successfully during the 1980s. She was a product of increasing opportunity for women in sport.

HOT TIPS

For the exam it is important to know that the USA is in direct contrast to the UK, where Physical Education has high status, whilst extra-curricular inter-school sport is declining in the state sector.

KEY WORDS

Intra-mural

Organised sport programmes within the school or college. Programmes may involve competition but not in the form of organised fixtures with other institutions.

Women are also becoming increasingly prominent in emerging sports such as rowing, water polo and ice hockey. With the creation of the National Collegiate Championships, each has become official **NCAA** sports.

Title IX has its critics. It is claimed that money to support women has been taken directly from men and that minority sports, such as wrestling, are being withdrawn from high schools and colleges for political and financial reasons.

Extra-curricular sport in US high schools

If a crisis exists in the provision of daily physical education, it must be said that interscholastic sport is strong and for several reasons significantly important.

It is important to understand that three ethics co-exist in American sport: Lombardinian, counter culture and radical.

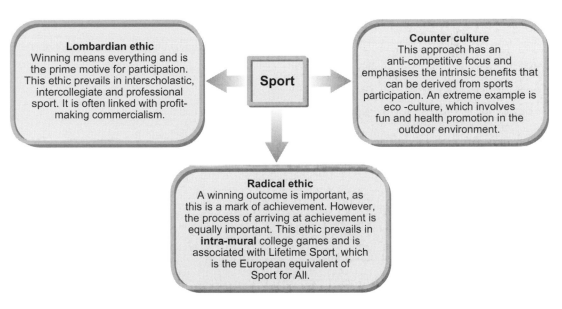

Fig. 2.14 Three ethics of sport in the USA.

Although generalisation is inevitable in such a big country, most major sports are represented in high schools with an emphasis on gridiron football, basketball and baseball. Despite the Title IX legislation, girls tend not to participate in gridiron football but engage in track and field, volleyball, gymnastics and, increasingly, soccer. In districts that are more affluent, opportunities arise to participate in emerging sports. Minneapolis High, for example, has an ice rink, which is used intensively by students and the community for hockey and figure skating.

The State High School Athletic Association (SHSAA), a national advisory body with branches in each state, controls interscholastic athletic competition. An example of a state department is the Arizona Interscholastic Association (AIA). Like

HOT TIPS

Be aware of how school sport is organised in the UK. Review page 181 of *Advanced PE for OCR, AS*. A popular question is to compare the role of the UK PE teacher with the US high school coach.

KEY WORDS

Varsity sport

Organised sport within the education system.

HOT TIPS

High schools in the USA are perceived as centres of sporting excellence.

KEY WORDS

Athletic scholarships

A grant of free education given by a college (university) to only top performers. The student is given an academic course but virtually contracted to play for the college in the sport for which the scholarship has been granted. The student may have a commitment of up to 50 hours per week to the sports team.

all associations, the AIA receives no federal funding, as individual schools finance athletic programmes, but carry the mission that **varsity sport** participation is beneficial to the total education process.

Like all associations throughout the USA, the AIA classifies its schools into five 'conferences' based on the number of enrolled pupils. A 1A conference school would comprise up to 200 pupils, while a school in excess of 1900 would constitute a 5A conference school.

Specialist coaches have charge of the school teams. Assistant coaches work under the leadership of the head coach, who in turn is accountable to the athletic director of the school. The latter manages both physical education and interscholastic sport.

Mission High, in the State of Texas, is a 5A conference school with a strong tradition of gridiron football. Fixtures are played on Friday nights in autumn in the presence of 15,000 spectators. Schools at this standard are perceived as centres of sports excellence and operate as the first progression in the production of elite professional performers.

TASK 7

By using your major sport as an example, describe the routes that could lead a player to professional status.

Matches are played in the school stadium in an atmosphere often enhanced by marching bands and cheerleaders. There is a strong commitment to Lombardianism, not only because the community is a critical presence but also because the coach can be dismissed if the team is unsuccessful. Players also have a powerful incentive to 'win at all cost' as college **athletic scholarships** are on offer.

Fig. 2.15 The American high school coach urges a 'killer instinct'.

TASK 8

1 What is the motive of (a) the coach, and (b) the player, to have a 'killer instinct' on the sports field?

2 Describe how the philosophy of the American coach differs from the physical education teacher in the UK.

KEY WORDS

Alumni

Former pupils or friends of an institution who donate money to the institution.

Interscholastic sport is expensive and the individual school generates finance through gate receipts, sponsorship, media payment and **Alumni** donations. However, the sources of revenue are not always secure and are dependent on the team providing the public with entertainment through attractive play and successful results.

It is evident that American ideologies are reflected in varsity school sports. Opportunity is available for all to play and with it the chance to excel, but only the elite performers of a Lombardian disposition achieve the scholarship honour, bringing professional status and the ultimate dream one step closer.

Revise as you go! Test your knowledge and understanding

- Define the term 'decentralisation'.
- Explain the term 'state autonomy' and say how it relates to decentralised control.
- What is the heuristic approach to physical education teaching?
- Identify the two major activity components of the high school physical education curriculum.
- How is physical education assessed in the USA?
- Describe the crisis that is evident in American physical education.
- Outline three ways in which equality is being addressed in the physical education curriculum.
- Identify the three ethics that co-exist in American sport.
- Describe the function of the State High School Athletic Association (SHSAA).
- Explain how high school sport is funded.
- Why is sport given high status in American high schools?

Sharpen up your exam technique!

1 Give reasons why the number of female participants in sport was low in 1971 and explain the significant increase by 2002. (5 marks)

2 With reference to content and method of assessment, explain how the physical education programme of a typical American high school prepares pupils for competitive sport. (4 marks)

3 Many American high school coaches believe that they are duty bound to inspire a 'killer instinct' in their players prior to competition. Discuss the basis of this belief, referring to American society and possible incentives for the coach and player. (9 marks)

4 Explain how the American education system addresses the issue of equality in physical education. (6 marks)

5 Describe the part played by the American high schools in the production of sports talent. (4 marks)

Section 3: *Ethnic sports and the evolution of new games (the USA)*

Learning objectives

At the end of this section you should be able to:
- explain the game of baggatoway and how it evolved into lacrosse
- understand how the changing American culture felt the need to adapt older games into modern-day games of American football, baseball and ice hockey
- account for the invention of games like basketball and volleyball
- outline the importance of Ivy League colleges during the evolution of American sports

Fig. 2.16 Modern-day lacrosse. The colonials did little to adapt the oldest sport in North America. The game was standardised in 1867.

HOT TIPS

The new emerging culture of USA brought about the adaptation of older games like baggatoway. Review the 'Spread of Imperialism and team games around the world' on page 203 of *Advanced PE for OCR, AS*.

Cultural adaptation of older games

Native Americans played a game known as baggatoway. It was played throughout the country and early explorers called the game 'rackets'. A French Jesuit missionary thought the rackets resembled a bishop's crosier or cross and so renamed the activity lacrosse.

Baggatoway was used to celebrate special religious occasions and served as a preparation for war. Its purpose was also to develop strong virile men. There is evidence to show that matches were played in the 1400s and it is recorded that heavy betting was a characteristic of the occasion.

It was long after the colonial period that modern Americans adapted the original game and changed it from a tribal ritual to a nineteenth-century sport subsequently played at collegiate and professional levels.

By the mid-nineteenth century, American society had changed and was losing its colonial image. This progressive new young culture was ambitious and required a vehicle for expression and identity. Sports of the nineteenth century, which were eventually to become professional and linked to commercial interests, fulfilled this need.

American football, baseball and basketball were heavily promoted, being native to America. These sports were very masculine and used to generate profits, patriotism and national loyalties.

American football

Variants of football were played throughout the colonial period and up until the civil war (1861–5). It was after the civil war that the development of sport was stimulated. Rugby and soccer had evolved through public schools and universities in England and this was the case in America. Sport became an increasingly important feature.

The first intercollegiate match was played between the **Ivy League** universities of Princeton and Rutgers in 1869 in a game more like soccer than rugby.

It was soon evident that rugby was the preferred game. During the period of vast immigration between 1875 and 1895, a soccer tradition gradually came about but was played by the working classes who lacked the power and influence to establish the game. Many European immigrants turned to baseball in an attempt to Americanise themselves and become part of mainstream culture.

Rugby was the forerunner of gridiron football, and the adaptation of the game eventually took place in 1874 when the Ivy League universities of Princeton, Columbia, Harvard and Yale legitimised the forward pass. This new version of rugby was violent and sensational, being in line with a competitive American society, which had inherited a gun culture from the rugged frontier days. The game promoted a masculine ideal and reinforced the American **policy of isolation**.

Fig. 2.17 Gridiron football was first established in the Ivy League colleges. Tackling, blocking and slugging were accepted as fair tactics. Violence caused the death of eighteen players in 1905, prompting intervention from the President.

Baseball

Boys regularly played early forms of baseball, known as goal ball, during the colonial period and the game closely resembled English rounders. However, baseball was to become the 'national game' by the mid-nineteenth century.

Baseball spread quickly to all states and to all classes. Rapid growth was aided by the coming of the railroad, which enabled long-distance fixtures to be played. As a result of growth, the gentlemanly etiquette of the founder clubs was lost and players now contrived to win at all cost.

The National Association of Baseball Players assembled in 1858 to organise leagues and clarify rules. It placed a ban on African-American players and this prevailed until 1947. Black athletes received attention only when it was in the financial interests of the controlling WASP group.

TASK 9

Discuss why baseball is suited to the American culture.

Ice hockey

Ice hockey, as we know it, was adapted from 'ice hurly' by British soldiers serving in Canada in 1850. The rules were unified by McGill University in Montreal and the game was adopted by America in 1893. The speed and collision involved appealed to the quickening pace of American society, and ice hockey became both an Olympic and professional sport by the 1920s. While ice hockey has proven not to be as popular as the 'big three', it parallels their organisation in the present-day business world.

The invention of new games

Basketball

In contrast with gridiron football, baseball and ice hockey, basketball did not evolve through adaptation. It was invented in 1891 by James Naismith at the private Springfield YMCA Training School and was instantly successful in high schools and colleges. Basketball was rooted in white educational institutions and although a few professional teams played to their own rules, early attempts to cash in on the game were unsuccessful.

A century later, this profile had changed drastically. Two female basketball leagues began in 1997 while African-American player Michael Jordan was sports' highest paid athlete at US$33 million per year. Basketball is now called the 'city game' because inner city playgrounds provided an inexpensive sport for millions of poor American youths.

TASK 10

Watch a live game or video recording of a top American basketball match. List five ways the profile of basketball has changed since its invention.

Volleyball

Volleyball was also created in the USA and was promoted initially in the universities. Today, volleyball is an Olympic sport and played professionally. The variation of beach volleyball is an example of a contemporary activity that exists in the USA for a profit-making motive, serving as sport, entertainment and a vehicle for commercial enterprise.

Revise as you go! Test your knowledge and understanding

- What is an Ivy League college?
- Explain why the adapted game of gridiron football was preferred to rugby football.
- Why did baseball rise to become the national game during the period of mass immigration?
- What forms of discrimination were in evidence during the early years of spectator sports?
- Why was cricket rejected in America?
- Explain why baseball grew in popularity at the expense of cricket.
- Identify the 'big four' American sports.
- Explain why these sports have proved to be attractive in American society.
- Describe how the image of basketball has changed since it first appeared on the college scene.

Sharpen up your exam technique!

1. Explain the contribution made by the Ivy League universities to the development of modern American sports. (3 marks)

2. By referring to cultural features, explain why the Americans adapted old colonial games to make their own sports. (4 marks)

3. Describe and explain the social changes that have occurred in basketball since the invention of the game in 1891. (5 marks)

4. Outline features from the present-day 'big four' American sports that reflect the masculine image of the old colonial games. (5 marks)

Section 4: *Sport and the pursuit of excellence (the USA)*

Learning objectives

At the end of this section you should be able to:
- give reasons why sport is regarded as an institution
- describe the close association of professionalism with commercialism
- account for the role of the media in sport
- explain how a high school player can progress to become a professional player
- describe the image of pluralism as it exists in the American society
- understand the significance of stacking and centrality in an unequal society.

HOT TIPS

Academic standards are required for entry to the NCAA although they appear to be below the standard to allow enrolment in the UK..

Introduction

As mentioned on page 80, athletic scholarships are available only to the elite high school performer. Athletic associations govern college athletics and set the rules regarding scholarships. The three major associations comprise the following.

- National Collegiate Athletic Association (NCAA). Classified into three divisions, there are 973 colleges registered with the NCAA, which is the oldest and most prestigious association.
- National Association of Intercollegiate Athletics (NAIA). The colleges in the NAIA tend to be smaller than those in the NCAA and fewer scholarships tend to be given.
- National Junior College Athletic Association (NJCAA). The courses at the colleges in this association last for only two years.

College sport provides the progressive step into professional and international sport. The 'big four' American sports are also successful commercial entertainment businesses at collegiate level on a par with the clubs in the UK Premier Football League. Talented and well-trained players, often fresh from high school, provide amusement and entertainment for audiences who pay large sums of money to watch.

HOT TIPS

Scholarships are available in most major sports. These include the 'big three' American sports, athletics and swimming. Women's hockey, fencing and high diving are recognised, while emerging sports like archery, badminton, bowling, equestrianism and squash carry scholarships for women only. This is to address the Title IX legislation.

TASK 11

Review page 244 of *Advanced PE for OCR, AS*. List the factors that cause English soccer crowds to be violent, then list the factors which prevent USA sports crowds from being violent.

It has been apparent over the years that college administrators have enrolled students who are excellent players but academically under-qualified. Leniency in recruitment enables a college to compete and remain at the highest levels to sustain their commercial viability. The NCAA has stated that 20 per cent of football and basketball players enter university through 'special admit' programmes.

Problems in varsity sport occur when coaches, in their bid for success, exert excessive control onto students and sport loses its value as an educational process. It has also been an issue that when media rights to games are sold, the academic progress of college players are considered less important than profit.

TASK 12

Suggest reasons why Ivy League universities compete successfully with the top sports universities.

Athletic directors, coaches, trainers, publicity directors and support staff can make a good living from collegiate sport. Some athletic directors and coaches earn in excess of US$500,000 per year, and this salary can be further enhanced through sponsorship and television contracts.

In stark contrast, the athlete is not paid and it would be a contravention of association rules if a player received any financial benefits. A scholarship is worth about US$10,000 a year, and this sum is granted by the college to pay for meals, accommodation and tuition fees. The questionable impression given by the university is that a student has been granted a 'free ride' through higher education.

A scholarship is a binding contract to play sport for the college teams. Athletes are no more than labourers who devote in the region of up to 50 hours per week to their sport. In doing so, they generate income for thousands of employers who are directly involved with the collegiate sports industry, the mass media and the corporations that advertise through college sport.

Despite hardship, lack of pay and circumstances verging on exploitation, college athletes do not protest against the system and continue to accept scholarships.

Students remain accepting of this system for the following reasons.
- The opportunity to play major college sports is a dream come true as major events such as the College Rose Bowl attracts in the region of 90,000 spectators.
- There is honour and social status for the athlete at a major university.

- Most athletes have been conditioned from early high school through the domination of sports leadership. They willingly accept the tough-minded disciplined approach and are dependant on the ethos of team conformity.
- The self-esteem of the athlete is dependent on athletic prowess.
- College athletes become single minded in their ambition to be successful. This conforming approach is termed 'pragmatic role acceptance'.
- The **pro-draft system** focuses on selecting the best college players.

Sport	Players participating in high school	Players progressing to college teams	Vacancies in professional sport
American football	928,134	51,162	1400
Basketball	530,068	13,365	405
Baseball	438,846	22,575	700

Fig. 2.18 The highly competitive route to professional status.

TASK 13

Design a table of two columns. In one, list the arguments to support the inclusion of varsity sport at both school and college level. In the other, list any negative issues that could be placed against the inclusion of varsity sport.

Professional sport and commercialism

Professional sport is organised as a commercial industry and operates as a **cartel** for the sole purpose of profit making.

Sports league	Aggregate attendance	Showpiece event
Major League Baseball	71 million	World Series
National Basketball Association (NBA)	19 million	World Championship Finals
National Football League (NFL)	17 million	Super Bowl
National Hockey League (NHL) (ice hockey)	16 million	Stanley Cup Playoffs

Fig. 2.19 Yearly attendance figures for the 'big four' sports in the USA.

Most Americans have contact with professional sport through the medium of television. The major television channels alone transmit 40 hours of sport per week and this figure rises if the cable networks are included. The Super Bowl registers as the highest rated single television programme each year.

KEY WORDS

Franchise

A voting right given to individual teams within the league. This enabled teams to vote for relocation, which would result in increased profit.

Sport space

The theory of sport space states that the success of the dominant four sports has limited the opportunity or closed the space for soccer.

HOT TIPS

Questions often focus on the reasons why high level sports in the USA are often more violent than in the UK. However, the question has arisen as to why UK soccer crowds can be violent whilst crowd violence in the USA 'big four' sports is scarce.

HOT TIPS

Review discrimination in UK sport, page 251, *Advanced PE for OCR, AS*.

Ice hockey joined the 'big three' in the late 1960s when the **franchise** market enabled the major Canadian teams to relocate to the USA. Hockey came of age in 1980 with the unexpected Olympic triumph of the American team. More recently, Quebec Nordiques and Winnipeg Jets, both of the NHL but based in Canada, elected to relocate to the USA.

In the last 50 years there have been about 100 franchise relocations across the four major sports. All moves are undertaken for profit motives and no major American consideration is given to sentiment and community loyalty.

Soccer is striving to become the fifth game and although attendances are rising, the game remains under-developed. One reason given for the lack of popularity is the concept of **sport space**, but in a market of 280 million people, it is difficult to see why soccer is not more prominent. It seems more likely that soccer has lost compatibility with a New World culture, which has long since severed its colonial roots.

Professional sport in the USA tends to be violent. Five factors operate to create this violence (see Figure 2.21).

TASK 14

Use the internet as a resource to find the gross income of one leading team in any one of the USA 'big four' sports. Compare this with a leading UK Premiership soccer club.

Discrimination in American pro-sport

Segregation and inequality have been features of organised sport since the nineteenth century. John L. Sullivan, the first American heavyweight-boxing champion, would accept challenges from white men only. Black players were excluded from Major League Baseball until 1947, but after this time a gradual integration began to take place. To understand the reasons for exclusion it is necessary to be aware that American society is organised not only by wealth but also on the basis of race.

Being the first to become established in the New World, the WASPs (White Anglo Saxon Protestants) have retained domination and contain the controlling hegemonic group.

WASPs
Ethnic Europeans
African-Americans
Mexicans and Puerto Ricans
Vietnamese
Native American Indians

Fig. 2.20 The major ethnic groups listed in order of status.

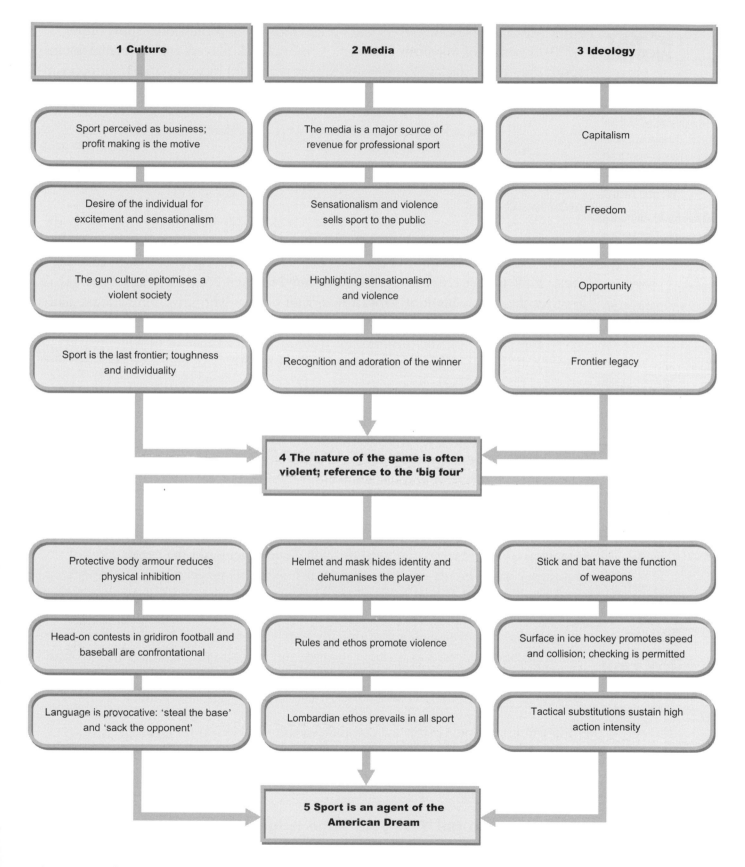

Fig. 2.21 The five major factors that operate to create violence in professional sport in the USA.

HOT TIPS

The concepts of centrality and stacking are popular exam questions.

HOT TIPS

Take note of the reasons why success in sport is important to ethnic minorities.

After African-American players had broken into white professional sport in the 1950s, a period of **tokenism** followed. As more black players entered professional sport, they were 'stacked' into positions that required physical rather than decision-making skills. For example, in baseball, most African-American players were stacked at outfield corner positions, while in gridiron football, the running back, wide receiver and defensive back positions were considered appropriate.

Anglo-Americans tended to occupy decision-making roles in the centre of play. The term given to this central focus is 'centrality' and its occurrence endorsed the social order in society.

Further integration and a more even positional distribution has taken place in the twenty-first century. Major League Baseball now has a 20 per cent black playing staff, while 68 per cent are represented in the National Football League. Basketball receives the largest input of African-American players who now dominate the game on court. Only 20 per cent white players are registered with the NBA and this represents an exit of Anglo-Americans from the game. This exit of white players in basketball is termed **white flight**.

It would appear that American ideologies of having freedom and the opportunity to pursue the American Dream are becoming more available to women and ethnic minorities in sport. The hegemonic group are the providers of opportunity and in so doing have protected their position by establishing **sport as an institution**, endorsing the image of pluralism and ensuring for itself greater financial profit margins.

Success in sport has become significant to ethnic minorities. The ability and potential of the group is endorsed through achievement and the expectation of future success is increased. Role models such as tennis player Venus Williams and basketball player Michael Jordan have emerged, increasing the belief and self-esteem of minority races who now have the confidence and motivation to strive for recognition in sports, which traditionally were the preserve of the dominant white culture group. Success has brought identity and in turn unity to the ethnic groups and with it the chance to dominate and even take over in sports that were formally inaccessible – for example, basketball, track athletics, golf and tennis.

Opportunities now exist in the commercial side of sport in the form of endorsements and sponsorship. On retirement, successful ethnic minority performers are now entering the coaching domain and opportunities are emerging in **stake ownership**.

Revise as you go! Test your knowledge and understanding

- Name the three controlling athletic associations involved in intercollegiate sport.
- Identify the best of these associations and give reasons for your choice.

KEY WORDS

Stake ownership

To have joint or full ownership of a commercial enterprise.

HOT TIPS

The syllabus focuses on increased opportunity provision and esteem as being important to US sub-cultures. Link this to discrimination in sport in the UK, *Advanced PE for OCR, AS*, page 251.

- List the sports for which scholarships can be gained.
- Explain why controversy can arise from the scholarship system.
- Explain why it is misleading to say that an athletic scholarship gives a 'free ride' through the education system.
- Explain the pro-draft system.
- Outline the evidence that would indicate that sport is organised for business purposes.
- Account for the high degree of violence in the 'big four' American sports.
- Explain how racial discrimination has been evident in American sport.
- Outline the reasons why sports success is important to ethnic minority cultures.

Sharpen up your exam technique!

1 With reference to the major American ideologies, discuss the significance of sporting success to potential champions from ethnic minority cultures. (8 marks)

2 Describe the features of commercialism that exist in American professional games. (3 marks)

3 Describe what is meant by the term 'white flight' and explain why this has happened in basketball. (3 marks)

4 Explain the terms 'stacking' and 'centrality' in the context of American sport. (4 marks)

5 Outline the reasons why an outstanding school athlete might take up a college scholarship. (4 marks)

Section 5: *Mass participation in sport (the USA)*

Learning objectives

At the end of this section you should be able to:
*   describe community recreation initiatives in the USA
*   understand the reasons for the lack of tradition of private sports clubs in the USA
*   acknowledge the role of the media in American sport
*   outline the reasons why provision of facilities and opportunity to participate has influenced the self-esteem and belief of ethnic groups.

Introduction

With the exception of the jogging and gym culture, there is little emphasis on mass sport participation for adults in the USA. This is surprising as sport participation was promoted in the late nineteenth century on the belief that it had great personal and social value. The YMCA, for example, used basketball and volleyball to control the behaviour of inner city youth.

The media has played a significant role in making sport accessible to the masses. This has given widespread satisfaction, but there is a danger that the USA is becoming a spectator society.

Fig. 2.22 The attainment of African-Americans in basketball has raised both the self-esteem and belief of the group that success in the mainstream American culture is accessible.

Increasingly, during the last 50 years, television has provided opportunities for commercialism and more recently both terrestrial and sky channels have committed high financial investment for the exclusive rights to televise a sports event. While this has brought increased revenue and attention to emerging sports, it has also forced changes in the presentation of sport. Start times are required to accommodate audience convenience, while matches take place on different days to avoid fixture clashes. The intensity of games has inevitably increased to provide the sensationalism required to make sport entertaining. See the model on page 91 for an overall understanding. Media coverage has promoted the concept of the sports superstar and has given top performers great wealth and social opportunity.

HOT TIPS

Make sure you can compare the policies for increasing sports participation amongst children in the USA with the UK. Look back at pages 220–9 in *Advanced PE for OCR, AS.*

For children and young people there exists a wide base to the participation pyramid.

In addition to the concept of participation and excellence in high school, 'Little League' involvement is very popular and caters for ages seven to sixteen. Sports teams involved in Little League, which forms the foundation of most American sports, are coached and managed by volunteers and, in the main, these tend to be parents.

Examples of Little League sports include:

- Pop Warner Little League Gridiron Football
- Biddy Basketball Little League Basketball
- Pee Wee Baseball Little League Baseball.

Although there is a strong moral philosophy and a great emphasis on safety, the win ethic is strongly evident even at the youngest levels. The parents involved often come from a competitive sports background and are often thought to be living out their own sporting ambitions through their children. The teams play in structured competitions and the format reflects the professional game. Mini 'Super Bowl' finals inspire competition, and Little League attracts both commercial and media attention.

KEY WORDS

Americanised

American strategies and values which are seen to be taking over the sport and system.

Intra mural

Sport within the school or college.

In the UK, provision for state sector interschool sport has declined since 1980 and there has been a growth in organised junior club sport. Although not **Americanised**, junior sport in the UK also relies on active parental involvement, which can become emotive in the pursuit of success. It is the concern of educators that the club ethos focuses on team success at the expense of emphasising personal benefits.

If the promotion of the win ethic is a criticism of Little League, the counter argument is that it prepares children for the competitive nature of American life.

Participation continues with intra-mural sport at high school and college, but there is limited opportunity for those who do not qualify for further education.

Other initiatives, such as those below, have been directed to increase the opportunities for youngsters.

- Time Out for Better Sports for Kids is an initiative of the National Alliance for Youth Sports. Its purpose is to improve the effectiveness of a community youth sports provision and coaches are in charge of teams. Bethel Parks in Connecticut has 2000 participants between the ages of five and eighteen and offers programmes in baseball, softball, soccer and basketball. There are structured competitive leagues and fixtures are organised against other towns.

- Hook a Kid on Golf is a foundation boasting the USA's most comprehensive youth golf programme. The emphasis is not only to develop interest and to teach the fundamentals of the game but also to create career opportunities. Golf is a popular adult recreation but opportunities are not widespread. Clubs tend to be private, expensive and exclusive, and provision does not exist for participation on local courses.

- Start Smart Sports Development Programme is designed to teach fundamental motor skills to children aged between three and six. Parents deliver the non-competitive programme in supervised parent/child groups. The overall purpose of this initiative is to enable children to attain success, which will lead to a lifetime of continued fitness and health.

Although Lifetime Sport and Golden Olympic programmes offer participation to older people, there is a large **post-school gap** in the USA.

Lifetime Sport is the closest equivalent to the UK's Sport for All policy, which is covered in the AS Contemporary studies text. Examples of lifetime sports include tennis, golf and fitness. These tend to be based in private clubs and are expensive. In addition, Golden Olympic programmes include organised sports for older people who still wish to compete in later life.

The post-school gap has been widened by a culture that has established sport as an institution carrying the professional image of competitive elitism.

Revise as you go! Test your knowledge and understanding

- Why have Midnight Basketball Leagues been established in American inner cities?
- Explain why Midnight Basketball Leagues have helped African-American players to dominate the basketball scene.
- Explain why Lifetime Sport as a competitive experience exists only in sports like golf and tennis.
- Identify three American Little Leagues and say which sports are played in each league.
- List the benefits of Little League participation.
- Name three initiatives that have been designed to increase the participation of young people in sport.
- Explain the term 'post-school gap'.
- Describe the Golden Olympic sports programmes.
- Outline the problems of spectatorship.
- Explain why there is a lack of participation opportunities in sport for adults below professional level.

KEY WORDS

Post-school gap

The period when young people drop out of sport upon leaving school to the time when some form of active sport pursuit is resumed.

HOT TIPS

Review 'Sport and Mass Participation in the UK', page 248 of *Advanced PE for OCR, AS*.

HOT TIPS

You need to be aware that the Americans do not have the UK equivalent of the amateur sports club. A lack of provision below professional status means that American spectatorism is quickly replacing participation.

Section 6: *Outdoor recreation and outdoor education (the USA)*

HOT TIPS

Be aware of the organisation and philosophy of outdoor education in the UK (see *Advanced PE for OCR, AS*, pages 179–81).

Learning objectives

At the end of this section you should be able to:
- understand the concept of outdoor recreation
- explain the organisation of national and state parks
- describe the backpacking experience in the wilderness environment
- identify the range of summer camps available to children
- understand the aims of the Outward Bound movement
- describe adventure experiences.

Introduction

This section of the syllabus focuses on physical activities that take place in the natural outdoor environment. Examples of such activities include skiing, rock climbing and canoeing.

KEY WORDS

Self-realisation

The discovery of personal strengths and weaknesses.

The term 'outdoor education' implies a formal process of conveying educational values. This takes the form of teaching physical skills and encouraging personal and social development in the outdoors. Appreciation of the environment would be a priority in an educational experience. Outdoor recreation involves an active leisure experience, which allows choice regarding the activity and the intensity of the undertaking. Outdoor pursuits range from using skills to reach a location or objective, such as route finding on designated cross-country treks, to contests in the natural environment, such as orienteering or scaling classified rock assents. The potential for **self-realisation** is common to all three concepts.

The size, beauty and geographical diversity of North America, coupled with the colonial frontier legacy, has placed the love of the 'outdoors' deep in the tradition of the nation. An association with the natural environment has become part of the American Dream.

HOT TIPS

Link the concept of outdoor education and outdoor recreation in the USA with that in the UK. Refer to page 191 of *Advanced PE for OCR, AS*.

Increasing urbanisation characterised America in the early twentieth century. By this time, the American frontier had vanished and it was recognised that if the natural environment was not protected, it too would disappear. Although the first 'National Forest' was created in 1891, President Roosevelt was the first to establish national parks in 1906.

Today, designated areas of natural beauty include national and state parks, forests, wildlife reserves and historic monuments.

Each American state has national parks and all come under direct federal administration. It is important to convey the scale of these areas. Yellowstone was the first national park, measuring 63 air miles north to south, while the east to west dimension is 54 air miles. The highest point in Yellowstone is Eagle Rock at 11,500 feet. This is four times larger and 8000 feet higher than the English Lake District.

Much of the park acreage is designated wilderness where genuine danger exists from wildlife, weather conditions and rugged high altitude terrain. To protect and advise the public, there are teams of rangers employed by the National Park Service (NPS). The NPS has the responsibility of forming the Nationwide Outdoor Recreation Plan and they are the major planning agency for the federal government. The fundamental mission of the NPS is to develop the facilities and increase the usage of the parks, while preserving its beauty at the same time.

There is a fear that overuse will destroy the natural environment, but it must be remembered that the population density is 70 people per square mile compared with 600 in the UK.

President Bush allocated nearly US$3 million in 2003 to designated national parks as part of his Comprehensive Fitness Agenda. However, the National Parks Conservation Association claims that the parks are US$6 million below budget and that plant and wildlife species are disappearing as a result.

State parks and urban parks are subject to the decentralised control of state and local authorities. Each state is required to maintain a Comprehensive Outdoor Recreation Plan (SCORP) as a condition for receiving acquisition and development grants from federal funds. Within the period 2000–03, 1300 new parks were created at state level, endorsing a national commitment to outdoor recreation.

In addition to federal and state administration, there are fifteen professional and service organisations that have a vested interest in the parks. Examples of these include the National Recreation and Park Association, the Wilderness Society and the Isaac Walton League of America. The purpose of these groups is to promote the conservation and appropriate use of the nation's natural outdoor recreation resources.

TASK 15

Choose three national parks from the USA and three from the UK. Using the Internet as a resource, make comparisons regarding size, topography, demography and service.

Summer camps for children

Several youth agencies, such as the Boy Scouts, YWCA and YMCA, sponsor outdoors activities and some schools offer programmes of low-risk adventure. Outward Bound, Project Adventure and Wilderness Encounter are other examples of packaged adventure programmes that have become popular. By far the largest of these organisations is the Outward Bound Association, which works in collaboration with senior high schools and is an extension of the British Outward Bound Trust. It offers wilderness experiences and proficiency courses in outdoor skills and leadership.

Since the mid-twentieth century, the number of camp schools for young people has increased significantly. These camps take place in the summer holiday for the duration of a few days or up to eight weeks. There are three classifications of camps:

- state-sponsored camps
- camps sponsored by business, ethnic and religious groups
- commercial camps.

State-sponsored camps enable poor children to have a basic outdoor experience, while commercial camps can be very lavish and extremely expensive, and, as a result, are often available only to rich families. This exclusivity reflects once again the discriminatory nature of a capitalist economy.

To ensure the widest opportunity for participation there are 12,000 camps in the USA: 8000 are residential, while 4000 are day camps. A camp is chosen on the basis of the experience required by the child and on what a parent can afford to pay. The most popular specialist activity camps include outdoor adventure and sports. There are also academic camps for gifted children, self-improvement camps offering courses in modelling, weight loss and etiquette, and special needs camps for children with learning difficulties and sensory impairment.

Most camps have a mission to continue a patriotic culture. For example, the bugle sounds the morning waking call, and the stars and stripes flag is formally unfurled and displayed. In the evening, the campfire rituals are a highlight and enjoyed by all children. These features reflect a military ethos and the spirit of frontierism, both of which underpin national pride.

TASK 16
List the types of summer camps available in the USA.

Revise as you go! Test your knowledge and understanding

- Outline the demographical and geographical reasons that give the USA great potential for outdoor recreation.
- Explain how state and national parks are funded.
- Describe the function of the National Park Service and the Land Bureau.
- Name the plan at state level that is in place to promote outdoor activity.
- Give the reason that makes this plan important.
- Outline the role of the ranger service.
- Give examples of professional and service organisations and outline their role in the administration of national parks.
- Identify three classifications of American summer camps.
- Explain how the capitalist system is evident in these classifications.
- Name some of the types of camps available to American children.
- How do summer camps develop patriotism?
- Explain the function of the Outward Bound Association.

Sharpen up your exam technique!

1 Describe an American commercial camp.   (3 marks)

2 Identify two other types of summer camp in the USA and explain how these differ from a commercial camp.   (2 marks)

3 How do the differences between types of summer camp reflect many of the characteristics of American society?   (4 marks)

4 Identify and explain the opportunities for outdoor adventure that exist outside of the camp experience for young people.   (3 marks)

5 Identify the aims of the Outward Bound Association and explain how a young person would benefit from participating in it's courses.   (4 marks)

Section 7: *Cultural background of France*

Learning objectives

At the end of this section you should be able to:
- make a societal analysis and include historical perspectives
- identify and explain the major French ideologies
- understand the significance of climatic, scenic and demographical variables
- explain the centralised administration system and the policy of devolution.

Introduction

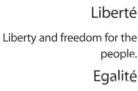

KEY WORDS

Liberté

Liberty and freedom for the people.

Egalité

All people are equal.

Fraternité

Brotherhood of the nation.

Vichy Government

An independent French government set up as an emergency measure during the German occupation of the Second World War.

Joie de vivre, a phrase meaning 'joy of life', captures the spirit of France. An appreciation of style, flair and high culture are common elements in society and are reflected in the national approach to sport.

Historically patriotic, 'joy' has come with achievement while failure has cast national dejection. The victory of the workers over the despotic ruling class in the 1789 Revolution ended the monarchy and marked the beginning of the French Republic in the dawn of passionate nationalism. The mission of the revolution was the patriotic slogan '**Liberté, Egalité et Fraternité**', which remains a significant part of the French ethos today. At this time, the young Republic became known as the 'land of asylum' and so began a long tradition of accommodating 'foreigners'.

In the period following the revolution, the policy under Napoleon's rule was to develop the armed forces. The phrase 'every Frenchman is born a soldier' reflects this priority, and with it came a need for fitness and discipline. Exercise and drill were needed for an effective fighting force and with this militarism came the first move towards organised physical training.

Militaristic France experienced joy as the colonial Empire was consolidated in the late 1800s, but despair when heavy losses in the First World War, then demoralising German occupation in the Second World War, emphasised the geographical vulnerability of France.

During the period of occupation, Germany took over the prosperous commercial and industrial regions of Paris and the north, leaving the French to establish a wartime parliament in the town of Vichy. The **Vichy Government**, as it became known, intended to restore national pride, and not for the last time in the twentieth century sport was used to raise morale and bring control to a dejected and chaotic French society.

In the quest to restore patriotism, sport was to adopt a high moral tone. Payment of players was prohibited, and traditional professional sports like football, cycling and boxing continued as amateur pursuits. A permanent ban was placed on Rugby League, which was perceived as corrupt and detrimental to the cause.

The Vichy government made athletes swear the following oath before participating in sports.

> *I promise to practise sport selflessly with discipline and fairness in order to serve my country better.*

After the Second World War, workers came from Italy, Spain and Portugal to help rebuild and share the prosperity of France. However, the collapse of the empire was to follow, marking another downturn in a chequered history. This event brought the largest increase of immigrants into France. Citizens from former French colonies such as Algeria, Morocco and Tunisia, flowed into the country turning France into one of the world's most cosmopolitan societies.

Fig. 2.23 Zinedine Zidane is an example of a player of ethnic origin from the French colonies. This has enhanced international prowess in sport.

TASK 17

Study a team list of the French National Rugby and/or soccer teams. Identify the number of players from ethnic minorities.

From the late 1950s, France entered a period of stability and optimism as President de Gaulle, who became president in 1958, established the Fifth Republic and set France on its present path to *la grandeur*. He made sport the rallying point for Nationalism.

TASK 18

By listing success at international level, make a case for France being a prominent sporting nation. Include on your list World and European performance, semi-final and final appearances.

Geographic and demographic variables

Despite its proximity to the UK, there are significant differences between the two countries in terms of culture, ideology and geography.

HOT TIPS

Naturalism is the third French ideology and involves participation in outdoor activities. The French have the advantage of extensively diverse natural resources for this purpose.

Although France has the same number of people as the UK, it is more than twice the size. Paris is the central focus of population and the outlying regions are spacious and rural, contrasting with the overcrowded, urban character of the UK.

Three climatic types exist.

- Western Maritime: this climatic type is found on the Atlantic coast of France and is similar to the UK.
- Continental climatic conditions prevail in the French Alps. This is associated with cold winters and high summer temperatures, facilitating year-round mountain walking and skiing at altitudes exceeding 4000 metres. This area is the location of the National Centre of Skiing and Mountaineering. Other mountain areas exist in the Central Massif and Pyrenees. The latter is the venue of the National Altitude Training Centre at Font Romeu (see page 121).
- Mediterranean conditions prevail on the coast of southern France. This climate gives hot dry summers and mild winters. With extensive sandy beaches and calm waters, this is the major region for vacations, with perfect conditions for water skiing, sailing and wind surfing.

Fig. 2.24 The premier European cycling event is the Tour de France. Four major ideologies are embraced by this event:
1. Militarism: the event reflects fitness and organisation
2. Nationalism: it instills national pride
3. Naturalism: the race passes France's best scenery
4. Intellectualism: the event celebrates high culture.

TASK 19

The Tour de France race does much to endorse naturalism. Discuss the reasons why the end of the race may be said to have links with both militaristic and nationalistic ideologies.

Education in France

The fourth major ideology is **intellectualism**. This has an important place in French society, as although there are distinctions between the working and professional classes, intellectual standing tends to determine an individual's status in society.

KEY WORDS

Intellectualism

Indicates learning and the acquisition of knowledge. It is linked with French appreciation of high culture.

It is logical that as the development of intelligence is a societal value, a major government priority is education in schools and universities. The system involves progression through three stages:

- primary school (ages six to eleven)
- colleges (ages eleven to fifteen)
- lycée (ages fifteen to eighteen).

This unified structure has ended the former compartmentalised system based on clear separation between primary and secondary education. Curriculum delivery tends to be formal and teachers and lecturers have high status.

The traditional structure of the education system is similar to the UK in that a private and state sector exists, with the Ministry of Education controlling most schools. The bulk of private schools are Catholic institutions contracted with the state.

Since 1967, school attendance has been compulsory from ages six to sixteen and France has developed an outstanding record in pre-school education since the 1970s. Secondary schooling is divided into two stages. From ages eleven to fifteen, almost all children attend colleges, which, like the British comprehensive system, cater for all abilities. Pupils then divide into an appropriate choice of lycée of which there are three varieties:

KEY WORDS

Baccalaureate

A finishing examination used for entry into university. It is the equivalent of GCE or AVCE taken in the United Kingdom usually in Year 13.

- general – opening a route to prolonged advanced university study
- technical – leading to short college courses
- vocational – allowing the continuation of study, but the major function is to facilitate direct employment.

Each lycée prepares pupils for the corresponding **Baccalaureate** examination, which is usually taken at eighteen.

Decentralisation in education

France had a strong centralised republican tradition and the government consolidated national identity through a school system with the mission to educate future French citizens. For this reason, education is the responsibility of the state. Since the late 1990s, France has engaged in a policy to decentralise administration.

The National Education Ministry has devolved decision-making responsibilities to regional and local authorities. There are now 22 regional departments sub-divided into 96 local departments, which are broken down into communes, being the equivalent of the UK's Local Education Authorities. These have the power to allocate government money.

Increased head teacher autonomy has placed the control of staff appointments, promotions and transfers with the school and curriculum delivery has become more flexible. Decisions are no longer made in Paris and forced upon provinces as unworkable policies. Decentralisation has ensured that the curriculum is directly relevant to the individual school and has brought diversity to an education system that was seen as too uniform in its authoritarian past.

Fig. 2.25 France is divided into 22 regions, which are equivalent to counties in the UK. Each region is divided into communes, which are similar to LEAs. With decentralisation, administrative control has relocated from direct ministerial control in Paris to the outlying regions.

Revise as you go! Test your knowledge and understanding

- Explain why the outcome of the 1789 Revolution marked the beginnings of physical training.
- Define the terms 'Liberté', 'Egalité' and 'Fraternité'.
- How does the spirit of *joie de vivre* display itself in the French approach to sport?
- Outline the four major French ideologies.
- Describe how sport has been used in France to inspire nationalism.
- Explain the significance of intellectualism in French culture.
- What is the French policy of assimilation?
- How has assimilation influenced contemporary French sport?
- Explain why cycling became popular throughout France.
- Describe the features of the Tour de France that reflect naturalism.
- Give one ideological reason why education is a major government priority.
- Explain how the French government has decentralised their education system.
- What is the Baccalaureate?

Sharpen up your exam technique!

1 Identify the natural geographical factors that increase the opportunities for outdoor activities in France. (3 marks)

2 By referring to the cultural background of France, explain why success in sport is of significant national importance. (4 marks)

3 Explain, by giving specific examples, what is meant by the following: 'Sport is a rallying point for French nationalism.' (3 marks)

4 By referring directly to the education system in France, explain the term 'decentralised' and outline the advantages of this system in the delivery of physical education. (3 marks)

Section 8: *Physical education in schools (France)*

Learning objectives

At the end of this section you should be able to:
- assess current attitudes towards physical education
- understand assessment of the subject in schools
- explain the focus of sport study sections
- outline the operation of the UNSS
- explain the meaning and value of the term 'joint provision'
- identify the mission of a primary sports school.

HOT TIPS

The subject of physical education is today timetabled as sport and physical education.

Introduction

The attitude towards physical education in France has reversed significantly since the end of the twentieth century. Formerly, the subject lacked status as a curriculum element and teachers were considered inferior to those delivering 'cultural' subjects.

A lack of status prevailed for five reasons.
- A strong military link existed with the subject. The first physical education teacher training appeared in 1814 when Colonel Amoros established the *Gymnase Normal Militaire*. A primary political requirement was to nurture strong, healthy and well-disciplined youth to defend both country and empire.
- This formal and authoritarian military approach was, in effect, physical training instruction and regarded as non-intellectual.
- For a long period, government legislation came from the Secretary for Youth and Sport while other subjects were controlled by the Minister for Education.
- Centrally controlled programmes were not delivered effectively and a significant **credibility gap** existed. Inspection of programmes occurred rarely and government control appeared less vigorous as distance from Paris increased.
- During the mid 1950s, physical education was recognised as a contributor to health and social values. For this reason, the military connection was severed and by 1975, physical education became a university subject although one of relatively inferior status.

KEY WORDS

Credibility gap

The difference between what is said to be taught and what is actually taught.

HOT TIPS

At present, the subject is perceived to have holistic educative value and control to bring it in line with the values acknowledged in physical education in the UK.

Prior to 1975, teachers trained in special schools known as *Ecoles Nationales du Sport et de l'Education Physique* (ENSEP). However, from 1992, teacher training was undertaken as a postgraduate course and became very selective. *Instituts Universitaires de Formation des Maitres* (IUFM) were designed as specialist academies for teacher education. Teachers tend to study first degrees in sports science faculties, gaining the qualification STAPS (*Sciences et Techniques des Activities Physiques et Sportives*). Later they serve a two-year probationary year in schools after attaining the CAPEPS (*Certificat a Aptitude au Professorat Education Physique et Sportive*).

Sport and physical education continues to move forward in France. In 2002, the government presented a strategy containing long-term plans to ensure the progression of the subject. The plans aim to:

- upgrade teacher training for sport and physical education
- create a new impetus for school sport
- implement the 'Be able to Swim' initiative
- increase student awareness of Olympic values
- undertake a curriculum review from the ages of fourteen to eighteen
- reform the examination of sport and physical education in the Baccalaureate
- introduce the compulsory study of physical education for all teachers during training
- improve provision and quality of sports equipment across the nation.

Attitudes in education tend to be conservative and the public image of physical education depends upon the school, its facilities and the head teacher.

Assessment in schools

Having had successive historical links first with the military then with the development of health, sport and physical education has now entered a phase associated with cognitive and social development.

At primary level, a weekly compulsory commitment is made to physical education but programmes vary in length from one to four hours according to the policy of the school. The teacher tends to be non-specialist and evidence suggests that the programme is taught unwillingly in many schools. Sports instructors, who have the qualification *Brevet d'Etats* (Certificate in Sport), are often engaged to deliver the curriculum.

A legacy of the ***Tier Temps Pedagogique*** lingers but decentralisation enables teachers to deliver a programme that is compatible with the needs and abilities of the pupils. There are no compulsory tests but physical competence is assessed informally.

Five 'families' of sport are now taught at primary level:

- individual
- team
- gymnastic

HOT TIPS

Review physical education in UK schools on page 175 of *Advanced PE for OCR: AS*. Focus on the values of PE in the UK and compare these with France.

KEY WORDS

Tier Temps Pedagogique

A primary school physical education programme that was designed by the government and administered by the former centralised system. It was overly ambitious in terms of content and did not take into account variations in teaching ability, school facilities and regional differences.

- dance
- outdoor education.

In secondary education, sport and physical education is compulsory up to the Baccalaureate. A national curriculum exists in secondary schools outlining content and progression, which is delivered in a three-hour weekly programme. An emphasis is now placed on the development of knowledge, understanding and preparation for continued participation during adulthood.

If the subject is selected by the pupil at Baccalaureate level, a formal practical assessment is required as written tests relate only to safety and rules of the game.

At all levels, schools are inspected every two years and assessment is made of the standard of National Curriculum delivery.

School sport in France

UNSS

HOT TIPS

The UK and France both include PE as part of the National Curriculum.

The UNSS is part of the Multi-Sport Federation and is a government-controlled, centrally organised agency. Its major responsibilities are to implement a Sport for All policy and broaden the participation base by developing the interests of 'non-sporting' pupils. An equal priority is to promote competitive sport and specialist coaches operate to develop excellence. Regular Wednesday afternoon sports fixtures take place and UNSS representation goes up to school international standard. The UNSS uses community facilities and takes the responsibility for sports provision away from schools. Time is not lost from study as French children attend school on Saturday mornings.

HOT TIPS

For the exam, make sure you know that sport has always been regarded favourably in French schools, as it has high status in society. Secondary school children have the benefit of a structured sports programme organised and administered by the *Union Nationale du Sport Scolaire* (UNSS). However, sport is not compulsory at school.

Each school has a sports club called *Association Sportive* (AS), which is affiliated to the UNSS. In theory, the AS is managed by teachers and pupils, and administration and organisation skills are learned. Physical education teachers tend to work alongside coaches.

Sporting sections

Sporting sections, formerly known as sports study sections, have a mission to develop excellence. Sections operate within a conventional school but select children with high sporting potential.

Although the development of sports talent is a priority, academic progress cannot be compromised. Training schedules are arranged around timetabled study and specialist coaches work with children. Sections are located in all regions and, like the UNSS, receive government funding.

Primary sports schools

Primary sports schools extend quality experiences in physical education down to pupils aged six. Such schools occur throughout France. The purpose of sports schools is not to produce champions but to give all children the opportunity to develop talent in a supporting environment. Other specialist schools exist in the disciplines of art, music and circus.

The Sporting Union of the Primary School (USEP) has the responsibility of overseeing the organisation of sport in the primary sector.

Parents elect to send their children to primary sports schools as they are non-selective institutions. It appears that gymnastics is a primary focus but volleyball, basketball and handball are also given priority, indicating a multi-sport approach. Indoor facilities are of a high standard and specialist coaches work alongside physical education teachers.

In one primary school in Chalon, the gymnastic equipment is of Olympic standard matching the provision at Lilleshall Centre of Excellence in the UK. Children in this school follow a daily two-hour physical education programme. The timetabled day begins at 8.30am and extends to 6.30pm, and extra-curricular activities also take place. The facility is also used by the local lycée. This is an example of joint provision in which the community and the school share facilities. Joint provision is a common policy in France.

Revise as you go! Test your knowledge and understanding

- List the reasons why physical education was considered low in status prior to 1975.
- Outline the reasons why physical education is now of equal status to other curriculum subjects.
- Describe how the French physical education teacher becomes qualified.
- Explain what the CAPEPS is.
- Identify the problems with the former *Tier Temps Pedagogique* physical education programme.
- Explain what was meant by the term 'credibility gap'.
- List the five families of sport that are now taught in the primary school.
- Describe the curriculum provision for secondary school physical education.

HOT TIPS

The UNSS and sporting sections have different aims and objectives. You must make distinctions between the two.

HOT TIPS

Review the section on sport in school, page 181 of *Advanced PE for OCR: AS*. Compare the initiatives for broadening participation and developing excellence in the UK and France.

HOT TIPS

Remember the strong commitment to the ideology of intellectualism (see page 103). The head teacher in the example given opposite believed that involvement in physical education shaped positive attitudes, which transferred into the classroom.

- List the long-term government measures to improve sport and physical education in French secondary schools.
- Describe the function of the UNSS.
- What is USEP?
- Explain the operation of the primary sports schools.
- Comment on the facilities of the primary sports schools.
- Explain the meaning of joint provision.

Sharpen up your exam technique!

1 In France, sport for young people is considered important. Describe the features of the UNSS and its connection with the development of youth sport in France. (4 marks)

2 Outline the factors that have changed and positively influenced attitudes towards PE in France during recent times. (4 marks)

3 Describe how sporting study sections operate. (4 marks)

4 Explain the provision made in French primary schools to help develop young sports talent. (4 marks)

Section 9: *Ethnic sports and cultural links (France)*

Learning objectives

At the end of this section you should be able to:
- define an ethnic game
- give examples of ethnic games in France
- identify the structure and function of these games
- make a comparison with traditional ethnic games in the UK
- recognise *la boule* as a nationwide street game.

Introduction

An ethnic game is one that is confined to a small geographical area that is usually rural and remote. Isolation brought about through distance, mountain ranges and obstructing river courses, has prevented the spread of ethnic games and despite their historical roots they often have only local significance.

Games can take place on a daily basis (churn carrying in central France) or as part of a large annual festival (the Basque Games in south western France).

Breton wrestling is confined to the region of Brittany in the north-west of France and dates back to the 1300s. It is bound by its own traditional rules, which were originally enforced by an organiser wielding a whip.

Fig. 2.26 In the UK, bull fighting is generally considered a cruel blood sport. In the Basque Provinces, it has traditionally reflected the working environment and proof of manliness. Today, as with many ethnic games, there is a commercial interest in these activities.

In the south, the six Basque Provinces meet annually for a rural games festival. 'Strongman' sports dominate the programme with events like hay bale raising, log sawing and anvil lifting. Despite the exhausting nature of competing, the winning team claims only the traditional beret as a trophy.

The Basque Provinces also engage in bull fighting. This is an extremely popular festival event, which is a brutal spectacle evoking opposition from the French Animal Rights League and revulsion from the British.

La boule, or boules, is a street game that is popular throughout France. It involves aiming to gain the position closest to the 'jack' or '*crochonnet*' by throwing a ball underarm. It is an ancient game and became popular in France around the fourteenth century. *Petanque* or *boule* is often played in the centre of villages or towns between avenues of trees that give shade. It is a social game, often played late in the evening by groups of men who may also take time to drink the local wine.

HOT TIPS

Comparisons can be made between ethnic games in the UK and France. Review page 200 in *Advanced PE for OCR:AS*.

Revise as you go! Test your knowledge and understanding

- List examples of French ethnic games.
- Define an ethnic game.
- Explain the characteristics and functions that are common to all ethnic games.
- What are the attractions of *la boule*?

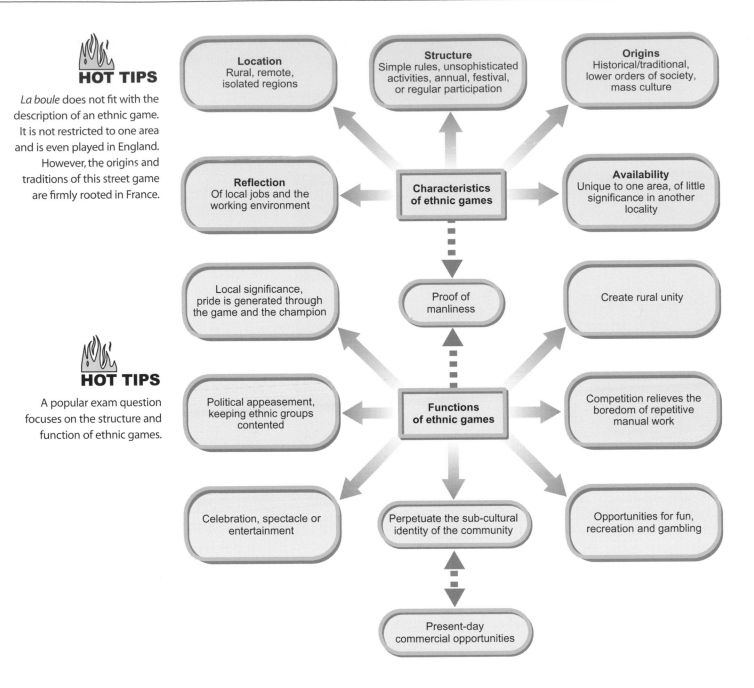

Fig. 2.27 All ethnic games from France and the UK have common features.

Sharpen up your exam technique!

1   Give an example of one ethnic sport from France and explain why it is considered important within the community.   (5 marks)

2   Describe the characteristics and explain the functions of a named French ethnic game.   (7 marks)

Section 10: *Mass participation (Sport for All) (France)*

Learning objectives

At the end of this section you should be able to:
- understand the organisation for the provision of mass sport participation in France
- explain the funding of joint provision
- describe the function of the Ministry for Youth and Sport and the administration of sporting federations
- explain the rise of new sports such as golf and tennis.

HOT TIPS

The beginning of the 40-year period coincides with De Gaulle's plan to use sport as the rallying point for the revival of French nationalism (see page 102).

Government policies relating to sport

Sport has increasing importance in French society and in the 40-year period up to 2003, club membership has risen sixfold.

France was one of the first countries to provide state funding for sport and President de Gaulle's Economic Plan of 1958 did much to stimulate mass participation. At this time, France was still recovering from German occupation during the Second World War (see pages 101 and 102).

De Gaulle made sport the rallying point for the revival of national pride. His motive to invest in sport was compounded by the failure in 1956 of the French Olympic team.

Not only have government policies and investment provided more opportunities for participation but they have also helped to increase French international status in sports such as cycling, soccer, Rugby Union and tennis.

HOT TIPS

These strategies are likely to be the focus of exam questions.

President de Gaulle's Economic Plan for sport comprised seven major strategies. The main aims were to:
- extend the base of the participation pyramid by increasing the opportunity through central funding for active involvement
- build multi-sports facilities in every major settlement
- maximise facility usage by implementing a national policy of joint provision; this meant that facilities were shared by clubs, communities and schools
- develop provision in schools; this eventually led to the operation of the UNSS, sporting sections and primary sports schools (see page 108 and 109)

HOT TIPS

In 2003, 50 per cent of French people say they take part in sport. Although activities included in this statistic are walking, swimming and health club membership, this surpasses the UK's participation figures.

- move towards the decentralisation of resources and involve the whole country in the quest for sporting talent; previously, focus had been given to Paris
- commit to developing Centres of Sporting Excellence in each region
- establish a framework of coaching on a national scale.

Today, government and sporting organisations are committed to increasing the numbers taking part in sport believing that sporting activities not only contribute to the health of the nation but also are fundamental elements of education, culture and social life.

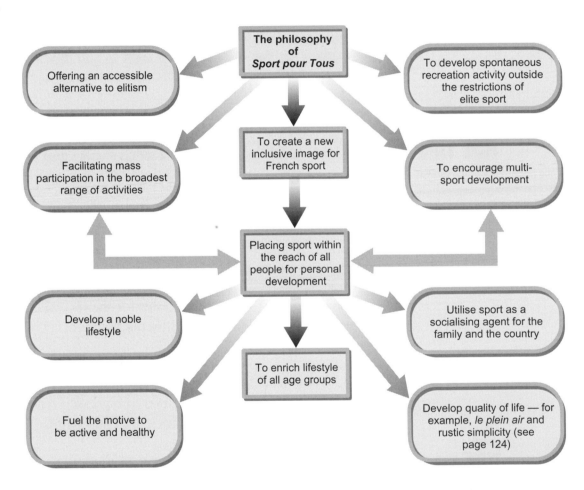

Fig. 2.28 Philosophy of *Sport pour Tous*.

In common with the international Sport for All policy, the French have *Sport pour Tous*.

The organisation for the provision of mass participation is complex. The Ministry for Youth and Sport manage the National Sports Fund. This is the *Fund Nationale pour le Developement du Sport* (FNDS). The FNDS is used to promote growth at grass root level and provide equipment for regional sports clubs. The fund is supported through taxation and a small percentage of profits made by public companies. In addition, the French National Lottery has provided a significant financial contribution since 1985.

Finance is distributed through four separate sporting federations.

- *Sports Olympiques* (Olympic Federation)
- *Sports Non-Olympiques* (Non-Olympic Federation)
- Multi-Sports Federation (associated federations)
- *Scholaires et Universitaires* (School and University Federation).

Each is responsible for the organisation and development of its sports at a regional level and requires the accreditation of the Ministry for Youth and Sport.

In 2000, 86 different federation sports were registered comprising 172,000 clubs and 14 million playing members. All federations answer to the French National Olympic and Sports Committee (CNOSF), and the Ministry of Education also monitors the school and university federations.

HOT TIPS

Review the policy for sport section on pages 220–9 of *Advanced PE for OCR: AS*. Compare the funding mechanism for sport in France with that of the UK.

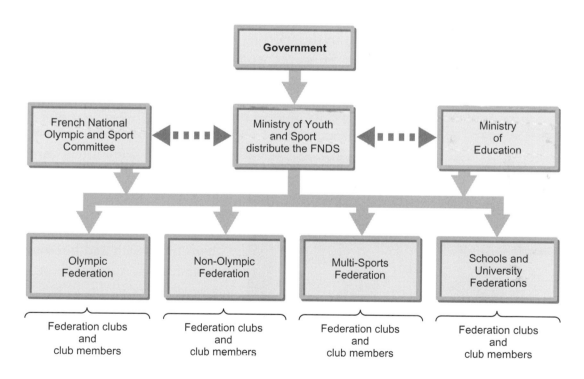

Fig. 2.29 The structure for the allocation of funding to sport.

France has experienced problems similar to the UK in making sport accessible to all people of society. Over the last 30 years, women have become much more involved in sport. The rate of those who regularly participate has increased from

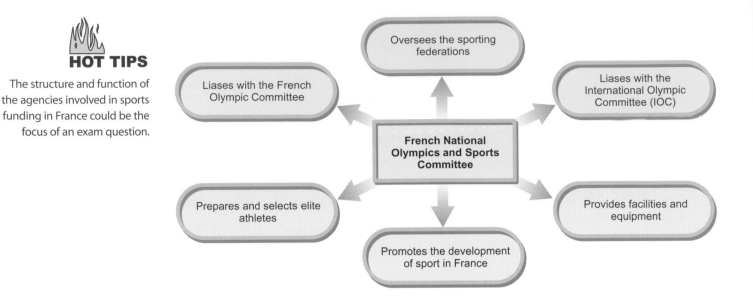

Fig. 2.30 The function of the French National Olympic and Sports Committee (CNOSF).

below 10 per cent in 1970 to 34 per cent in 2001. This increased involvement is reflected in the sporting achievements of women, particularly in tennis and athletics. However, women's sports do not receive the same media attention as men's and participation rates remain considerably lower.

France has a vigorous policy relating to disability and sports participation and this is headed by the *Federation Francaise Handisports* (FFH). The Federation has department committees throughout France and covers a broad range of sports registering more than 500 clubs and 25,000 athletes.

The FFH is primarily a public unity but is a member of both the French and International Paralympic Committees. At the highest level, France attained seventh place in the 2000 Games in Sydney, while in the Winter Paralympics of 2002 in Salt Lake City, the team achieved fifth ranking.

Fig. 2.31 Government commitment to helping athletes with disabilities first came about in 1958.

The rise of 'new' sports

Of the ten most popular games in France, golf ranks as the ninth. It was first played in the country during the sixteenth century but has a new profile due to a recent rise in popularity brought about through increased provision and accessibility.

HOT TIPS

Be aware that in a steadily growing European golf market, France follows the UK, Germany and Spain, but is recognised as belonging to the 'big four' continental golfing nations.

The United Kingdom alone has almost 2000 courses compared with 500 in France. However, as golf is becoming a significant tourist attraction, the potential for expansion is considerable.

Many geographical and cultural advantages could make France a chief player in this market. France occupies a relatively large landmass and being essentially rural there is space for course construction. There are good networks in place to facilitate travel and France is easily accessible from the rest of Europe. There are favourable climatic conditions and a reputation of high renown for food and drink.

Fig. 2.32 Ownership of European golf courses by percentage.

Fig. 2.33 Numbers of participants by percentage.

Increases in leisure time, education, affluence and the age of the population are factors that have stimulated the growth of participation in French golf, while successful role models make golf more attractive to young people.

It is predicted that there will be a significant increase in golf participation on a worldwide scale by 2010. Importantly, the most prolific development will take place in Europe.

Tennis is the second most popular game in France with a registration of more than 1 million players. There is an abundance of courts throughout the country and the fact that even the smallest villages have high-class tennis facilities endorses the success of government investment.

Tennis has historical roots in France but its present form was imported from England at the end of the nineteenth century.

Initially, the best overseas players were not attracted by French championships, but public interest surged when, in 1925, France was designated an international venue. International influence has stimulated the game more recently and although there have been few chances to celebrate home success, the French Open Tournament always attracts large audiences.

At grass roots level, national affluence, facility provision and favourable climatic conditions have accelerated, as with golf, the growth of tennis' popularity.

Revise as you go! Test your knowledge and understanding

- Outline the major strategies of de Gaulle's Economic Plan for sports development.

- Identify the term used by the French for Sport for All.
- List the key words that shape the philosophy of the French Sport for All policy.
- What is the National Sports Fund?
- Describe how the funds are distributed to the sports clubs and organisations.
- List the sports federations.
- What is meant by the term 'grass roots level'?
- Outline the role played by the French National Olympic and Sports Committee.
- Describe the measures taken to make sport accessible to disabled participants.
- List the factors that might account for the growth of golf.
- Explain why France has the potential to become a major European centre for golf.
- Outline the factors that have contributed to the popularity of tennis in France.

Sharpen up your exam technique!

1 Describe the role of the Ministry for Youth and Sport.   (3 marks)

2 Explain the function of the French National Olympic and Sports Committee.

3 Sport for All is an international concept and *Sport pour Tous* is the French equivalent. Outline the major aims of *Sport pour Tous*.   (4 marks)

4 By referring to commercial and cultural factors, explain why golf is becoming increasingly popular in France.   (4 marks)

5 The French government invest money into sport. Describe the strategies made possible by government investment designed to increase sports provision at all standards.   (6 marks)

Section 11: *Sport and the pursuit of excellence (France)*

Learning objectives

At the end of this section you should be able to:
- explain the funding and policies that assist elite performers
- understand the role of INSEP and its change from ENSEP
- describe the nature of professionalism with particular reference to the Tour de France, soccer and Rugby League
- explain the operation of Font Romeu
- consolidate the connection between amateur sport and nationalism.

INSEP

In 1975, ENSEP (*L'Ecole Normale Superieure d'Education Physique*), a teacher training institute with origins dating from the 1817 Amoros Military Gymnasium at Joinville, merged with INS (National Institute of Sport). This created the National Institute of Sport and Physical Education (INSEP).

Located in 34 hectares of ground in the Vincennes Forest on the outskirts of Paris, INSEP operates under the guidance of the Ministry for Youth and Sport, although some autonomy is granted to this multi-purpose institute.

- INSEP is a multi-sport Centre of Excellence for elite performers, catering for 25 different sports and providing facilities for aqua, aesthetic, combat and invasion activities.
- It is also the major sports education centre in France.
- In addition, it makes decisions concerning funding allocations to the sports federations.
- It decides which sports qualify for elite status and selects the athletes who will attend for training.
- INSEP is ultimately responsible for the development of French sport.

In addition to INSEP, there are six national state-run sporting institutes in France specializing in their own field.

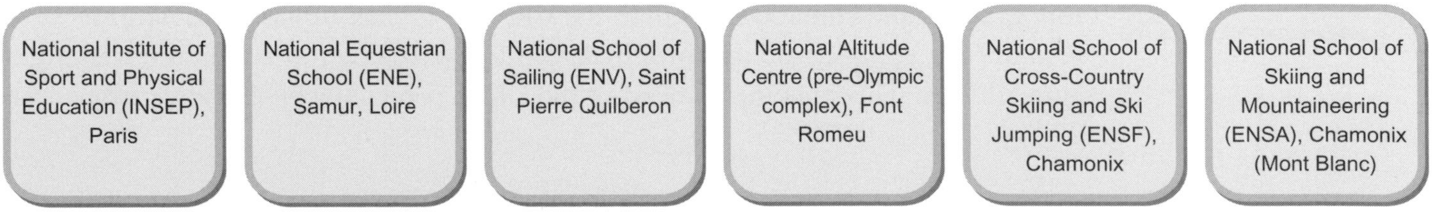

| National Institute of Sport and Physical Education (INSEP), Paris | National Equestrian School (ENE), Samur, Loire | National School of Sailing (ENV), Saint Pierre Quilberon | National Altitude Centre (pre-Olympic complex), Font Romeu | National School of Cross-Country Skiing and Ski Jumping (ENSF), Chamonix | National School of Skiing and Mountaineering (ENSA), Chamonix (Mont Blanc) |

Fig. 2.34 Six National Sports Institutes of France.

KEY WORDS

CREPS (*Centres d'Education Physique et Sporting*)

Centres of Excellence, which are distributed throughout the regions. The sporting federations select the young athletes who may attend these centres.

Approximately 25 per cent of the 3000 elite French athletes can be resident in these institutions at any one time. The remainder attend one of the 22 regional sporting centres (**CREPS**).

In collaboration with laboratories across France, INSEP has developed a specialism in sports-specific science and is currently evolving high level research programmes in:

- biomechanics and physiology
- movement action and performance
- sport psychology
- computer sciences
- sociology.

HOT TIPS

The network of sporting centres of excellence in France may provide the focus of an exam question.

INSEP also delivers academic and professional training to prevent young athletes being disadvantaged in the fields of education and employment. While engaged in high level sports training, a residential athlete may study at a centre for education in Paris. Coaching and study schedules are adapted and education is financed through public and federation loans.

French sports managers also graduate through this educational branch of INSEP. Potential managers contribute to the conferences and seminars, which fall into the annual cycle of INSEP conferences (*Entreties de l'INSEP*).

A further priority for INSEP is to maintain the good health of their elite performers. Athletes undergo frequent physical examinations and tests from a team comprising physicians, general practitioners and sports medicine specialists.

Contemporary France is increasingly seeking to establish European community links and INSEP has a central position in the development of international prestige. The institute is popular throughout the world, having a network exchange with 40 different countries, and is respected as an exemplary sporting Centre of Excellence.

HOT TIPS

Consider the structures that are in place in the UK to develop excellence in sport. Look back at the issues analyisi on page 219 of *Advanced PE for OCR: AS*.

There is no doubt that sports success on the world stage is an important focus of French national values and prestige. However, unlike that of the centrally operated regimes of the former Eastern Bloc countries, the development of sporting excellence controlled by the French government is ethical.

It must be remembered that France is a country with a far greater range of topographic and climatic types than the UK. The French utilise these natural resources to enhance the opportunities for mass participation and in the training of elite athletes. This puts them ahead of the UK in producing elite performers.

Location	Year	Gold	Silver	Bronze	Total	World ranking
Albertville (Winter Olympics)	1992	3	5	1	9	7
Barcelona	1992	8	5	16	29	9
Lillehammer (Winter Olympics)	1994	0	1	4	5	17
Atlanta	1996	15	7	15	37	5
Nagano (Winter Olympics)	1998	2	1	5	8	13
Sydney	2000	13	14	11	38	6
Salt Lake City (Winter Olympics)	2002	4	5	2	11	6

Fig. 2.35 Medals won by France in the winter and summer Olympic Games since 1992.

TASK 20

Using information from the Internet, compare the performance of the British Olympic teams with the French in the Olympic games listed in Figure 2.35. Discuss the reasons why there are significant differences in the results.

Font Romeu

Font Romeu, situated at 1850 metres in the French Pyrennes Mountains, is the National High Altitude Centre. It was built as a facility for athletes to prepare for the Mexico Olympic Games (1968) and is a multi-sports centre with sports hall, track, pool and equestrian facilities of international standard. The centre is used by national teams in most sports including the French Rugby Union and soccer teams.

In keeping with the policy of joint provision (see page 109), Font Romeu is used by students as an altitude school and by the public when facilities are available. A recent building programme has upgraded the complex and today the centre is described as a 'City of Sports and Culture'.

As Figure 2.35 indicates, France has emerged as a successful Olympic nation and sport has become the showpiece of de Gaulle's prosperous Fifth Republic, emphasising the link between sport and the ideology of nationalism.

Amateur sport and nationalism

Historically, France is an enigma in terms of its stance on amateurism and professionalism. Baron de Coubertin resurrected the modern Olympic Games in 1896 as a strictly amateur enterprise and the Vichy Government of 1942 abolished all professional sport. In both cases, the amateur ethic supported the mission of nationalism.

Cycling

The Tour de France, first organised in 1903, is the world's best-known professional cycle race and it is clear that the motives underlying the event are not wholly nationalistic.

The Tour de France covers 3000km in the most picturesque French mountains and countryside, commanding intense media interest and bringing the country to a standstill for three weeks.

The original prize was 2000 gold francs divided between 60 riders and today the winner claims more than 300,000 euros.

Since 1969, although national teams have periodically appeared, representation has increasingly been organised on the basis of brand name sponsorship. In the formerly exclusive professional race, amateurs were permitted to ride during the 1980s and women were given the opportunity to 'tour' on a shorter course.

Each year the starting location varies, with Dublin having the honour in 1998. Today, the race detours through some of France's neighbouring countries as one illustration of European solidarity. However, the finish in Paris is always the traditional sprint along the historic Champs Elysees.

Rugby

Rugby has its roots in middle class England, in the Home Nations and the British Empire. So why would the French, of a vastly different culture, embrace the game? Rugby was played throughout France but with a Latin-tinged passion in the south-west of the country, which remains as the game's heartland today.

Violence, and particularly the open payment of players, conflicted strongly with the amateur ethics laid down by the English Rugby Union and, as a result, France was suspended from the Five Nations Championship in 1931. The popularity of the established code declined and Rugby League emerged as a serious rival.

The 'new code' could make legitimate payments and was never to be popular with the middle classes who accused Rugby League of being the 'upstart cousin of Rugby Union'. Further to its detriment, Rugby League had associations with the left wing Popular Front government. This lack of favour in high society ultimately led to the demise of Rugby League in 1942 at the hands of the Vichy Government.

The sport, always called *Jeu a Treize* (the game for thirteen), as the name Rugby League was forbidden, had a brief revival in the 1950s but today the game is marginalised, being played by approximately only 20,000 people.

HOT TIPS

Review page 234 of *Advanced PE for OCR: AS*, on the Real Issue. Compare commercialism in French sport with that in UK sport.

In 2003, France won the Victory Cup (a World Cup for emerging rugby league nations) defeating the British amateur team in the final.

Despite investment from Rupert Murdoch's Sky channel and financial input from the English Rugby League, France cannot sustain a 'super league' club. In historical terms, this is ironic, as the best athletes are now turning towards Rugby Union, which has an increasingly professional orientation.

French law impedes the growth of an extravagant American style sports business by preventing clubs from making profits for shareholders and by inflicting heavy taxation on high earning players. This is a serious problem for the top professional soccer clubs, which in other European countries are operating as public limited companies. As a result, players are seeking contracts outside France. However, dominant soccer clubs like Paris St Germain, now owned by the TV channel Channel Plus, are trying to modify the law to allow them to compete at European level.

This disadvantage did not prevent France from winning the soccer World Cup in 1998. This is because the state funds sport at grass roots level to provide good facilities and coaching progression. However, politicians would like to see more French soccer stars playing at home rather than for Manchester United or Real Madrid.

Revise as you go! Test your knowledge and understanding

- Outline the mergers that took place to create INSEP in 1975.
- Describe how INSEP is funded.
- Explain the function of INSEP.
- List the state-controlled sporting institutes of France.
- What purpose is served by Font Romeu?
- How is the joint provision policy served by Font Romeu?
- Define the term 'CREPS'.
- Explain the function of the regional CREPS.
- What is the Tour de France?
- Explain how France benefits from the Tour de France.
- Explain why it might be considered unusual for rugby to have gained a foothold in France.
- Describe why Rugby League was unpopular with the French middle classes.
- Explain why French soccer players choose to play abroad.
- Why did this trend not prevent France winning the soccer World Cup in 1998?
- Indicate why soccer players may be attracted back into domestic French leagues before 2006.

Sharpen up your exam technique!

1 Explain why the modern Tour de France does not wholly endorse French nationalism. (3 marks)

2 Explain why French soccer players elect to play outside the country and why this did not prevent the nation's World Cup victory in 1998. (3 marks)

3 Explain the policies undertaken by the French government to bring about the country's sporting success since the 1956 Olympic failure. (5 marks)

Section 12: *Outdoor education and outdoor recreation (France)*

HOT TIPS

Outdoor education is teacher led and part of curriculum design. It is a formal education process. Outdoor recreation is a leisure time experience, which inevitably involves learning. While activities provide fun and personal enrichment, the process of formal education is not a priority.

HOT TIPS

Activity holidays involving recreation activities in the outdoors are the fastest growing element of the French tourist industry.

🔑 KEY WORDS

Le plein air

The open air (see page 114).

Rustic simplicity

Basic activities in the outdoors – for example, hiking or camping.

Learning objectives

At the end of this section you should be able to:
*   understand the concept of *le plein air*
*   identify the features of French national parks
*   describe the holiday patterns of the French
*   explain the provision for outdoor activities
*   describe the operation of *Les Classes Transplantees*.

Introduction

Outdoor education and outdoor recreation have common elements. They both involve participation in activities taking place in the outdoor natural environment. However, clear differences exist between the concepts of outdoor education and outdoor recreation. One is a medium for learning, while the other is a leisure experience.

Outdoor recreation has the broadest definition as activities can be carried out alone completely voluntarily and controlled totally by the individual, or undertaken in a group as part of a highly structured itinerary.

The whole concept of outdoor activities in the natural environment in France is expressed in the phrase **le plein air**, which reflects the ideology of naturalism. Associated with the open air is the notion of '**rustic simplicity**'.

There is immense scope for outdoor activities as France is a large scenic country with favourable climatic types.

National parks

There are seven national parks in France: Les Cévennes, Les Ecrins, La Guadeloupe, Le Mercantour, Port-Cros, Les Pyrénées and La Vanoise. Each of these national parks is under strict state control, and of the seven only the Cevennes is permanently inhabited. There are zones within the parks that do not permit cars and the conservation of beauty is of highest priority. In addition, 40 regional parks are distributed evenly throughout France and these are subject to local authorisation. Regional parks are extremely popular tourist venues and, in common with conservation areas in the UK, experience problems of overuse resulting in erosion and pollution. A further sixteen regional parks are planned to be in operation before 2010.

France	4.5%
Europe as a whole	7.0%
North America	9.0%
Australia	2.0%

Fig. 2.36 Percentage of total land area protected as nature reserves or parks.

Holiday patterns and tourism

There is a worldwide trend in all affluent countries to spend more time and money on leisure activities and holidays and the French are no exception. With an average of five weeks paid leave per year, more than 60 per cent of French people take at least one holiday. Due to increased provision of winter sports facilities, vacations in this market have doubled in popularity since 1985.

Summer holidays retain the highest seasonal figures with one-third of all vacations taken between 1 July and 15 August. The Mediterranean resorts are the major attractions and camping is a very popular choice of holiday experience.

Fig. 2.37 A privately run *Centre de Vacances* in rural Franches-Martagnes, where activities such as rock climbing, riding, cross-country skiing and mountain biking, are offered to all ages.

Centres de Vacances

General opportunities for outdoor activity participation are increasing for all ages. The state and some industrial companies continue to fund some activities for children but the private holiday businesses have experienced most significant growth since the 1980s.

Centres de Vacances are holiday recreation centres offering activities and sports to all age groups. They have rural locations and tend to be self-catering with chalet accommodation to provide comfort in a **rustic setting**.

Village camps

Village camps specialise in outdoor education for school children between the ages of six and sixteen. Teachers accompany the pupils but all activities are led by camp instructors. Emphasis is placed on team work in the outdoors and encouraging children to venture out of their 'comfort zones' in order to develop self-esteem and confidence. The educational philosophy of the camp is that nature and the environment can best be studied by being part of it.

Summer camps

Vacances sans Frontieres is one example of a large holiday business group that specialises in summer camps and outdoors activity provisions. The ethos of this recreation experience parallels the American camp system. Children of primary and secondary school age spend part of their summer break at the camp. Activities are led and supervised by counsellors who must be qualified and hold a government licence (Certificate of Professional Aptitude Educational Counsellor, or PAEC).

These activity camps also incorporate a cultural experience as every evening there is a traditional 'veillee' of song, dance and story telling. This is similar to the American campfire ritual.

Sports camps

The sports camp is an alternative summer residential experience. Soulac, near Bordeaux, is the venue of a soccer camp offering high standards in coaching and facilities. A medical team staffs the centre and children also experience *le plein air* in the forest and on the beach.

All the previously mentioned residential camps are paid for by parents, which highlights a new societal trend. The concept of the French family vacation is changing, as some parents are now taking holidays alone while children attend summer camps.

Outdoor pursuits

Although the term 'outdoor pursuits' can be used in connection with outdoor education and recreation, it is also associated with competitive and high-risk activities and has a definition of its own. Ski jumping and mountaineering in severe and often uncharted Alpine or Himalayan terrain fit into the outdoor pursuit category.

Outdoor pursuits are coached to a high standard at the Chamonix Mountain Centre of Excellence and *Le Centre Nationale des Sports de Plein Air*. This is located at Vallon-Pont-D'Arc and is similar to the UK's *Plas y Brenin*. Although these facilities offer programmes to the public, Olympic athletes and high altitude mountaineers also train here.

With more extreme levels of participation in mind, the French constructed their first centre as a base for the Outward Bound movement at Banassac in southern France in 1993. As in the UK, this enterprise issues challenge and adventure opportunities to young people, but the French version, named *Hors Limites*, is driven by their own national philosophy.

Les Classes Transplantees

The first experience for young children of the outdoor environment is likely to be at school through the government subsidised *Classes Transplantees* programme. This curriculum innovation was implemented in the 1960s and the key to understanding this concept is in the word 'transplanting'. Children, predominantly of primary school age, are taken out of the classroom and taught in an area of natural beauty. The snow class is one of many options. Children engage in classroom lessons in the morning and activities in the afternoon

There are many programmes or classes and some are unusual. For example, classes with the GRAAL involve lessons in scuba diving, while *Classe de Decouverte* relates to discovery learning in the outdoors.

HOT TIPS

Look back at the section on outdoor education in the UK, *Advanced PE for OCR: AS*, page 179. Compare the provision for outdoor education in France with that in the UK.

The major and most relevant *Classes Transplantees* to outdoor education are:
- *Classe de Neige*: downhill and cross-country skiing
- *Classe de Vert*: orienteering, hiking and expeditions in the forest
- *Classe de Mer*: sailing and other aquatic activities in the sea.

Classes can take place at any time of the year and extend from one to three weeks. Teachers accompany children on at least a 1:10 ratio and the pattern is for morning schoolwork followed by afternoon activities. The quality of education is never compromised as the concept of the programme supports the notion of intellectualism, naturalism and the promotion of national culture.

It is a desire of all residential experiences that children should take away not only memories of happiness, achievement and friendship, but also a strong sense of French culture, which underlies nationalism and the irrepressible spirit of *joie de vivre*.

Revise as you go! Test your knowledge and understanding
- Outline the differences between outdoor education and outdoor recreation.
- Explain why France has great potential to develop outdoor activities.

- What is the meaning of the term '*le plein air*'?
- Explain the term 'rustic simplicity'.
- Highlight the similarities and differences between national and regional parks.
- List the trends that are currently appearing in the French tourist industry.
- Explain the function of a *Centre de Vacances*.
- Identify the types of opportunities available to young people who wish to have activity experiences during summer holidays.
- What is meant by *Hors Limites*?
- Identify the provisions made for outdoor education.
- List the major classes in the *Classes Transplantees* programme.
- Explain the *Classes Transplantees* programme.

Sharpen up your exam technique!

1 Identify the types of outdoor experience available to all French children during curriculum time. (3 marks)

2 Give reasons why outdoor education has such a high status in French schools. (4 marks)

3 Outline the differences between French summer camps and *Les Classes Transplantees*. (6 marks)

Section 13: *Cultural background of Australia*

Learning objectives

HOT TIPS

In the exam, you will not be required to make comparisons between the USA, Australia and France. All comparisons will link one country of study with the UK.

At the end of this section you should be able to:
- explain the demography and population distribution in Australia
- describe the tribal origins with an emphasis on native Aborigines
- appreciate the influence of Melanesian and Polynesian cultures on Australian sport
- understand the Anglo-Celt domination of society and the colonial influence
- identify the major ideologies of the Australian nation
- outline the organisation of federal government
- identify the regional focus of Australian football and rugby football.

KEY WORDS

Motherland

A reference to England.

Introduction

After gaining independence from the UK in 1901, Australia has now entered its second century of nationhood with a confident sense of international place and identity. Unlike the USA, Australia has maintained its links with the former

'**Motherland**' and throughout the country there is evidence of colonial roots. For example, the education and judicial systems, sports ethos and general traditions are very similar to those found in the UK today.

Although it is part of the Commonwealth and has elected to retain the monarch of England as the Chief of State, Australia has a federal parliament based in the capital city Canberra. An elected prime minister who in turn selects a ministerial cabinet heads the parliament. There are three levels of government:

- central government operating at a federal level
- six states and two territories
- local government.

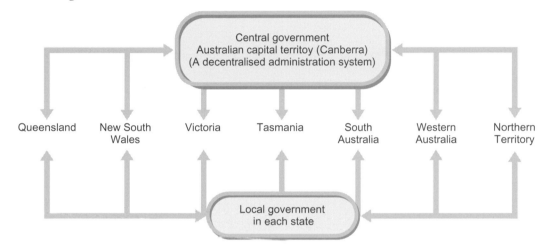

Fig. 2.38 The diagram indicates the decentralised system of government.

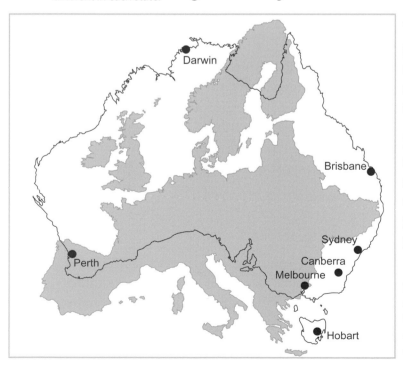

The constitution of Australia places local government outside federal jurisdiction, therefore a decentralised system of control is in place giving autonomy to each state. Local government differs significantly between the states and territories.

It is essential to comprehend the size of Australia, for example, a flight from Sydney to Perth takes six hours. The tyranny of distance presented a difficulty for the development of sport in all populated areas in the nineteenth century (see page 130).

Fig. 2.39 The population of Australia is small and largely settled around eight cities. A large percentage of Australia is uninhabitable and the bulk of the population is centred on the southern and eastern seaboards. Australia is considered urban.

State or territory	Number of authorities	Population	Principal city
Australian capital territory		311,200	Canberra
New South Wales	180	6,451,700	Sydney
Northern territory	70	194,000	Darwin
Queensland	156	3,539,500	Brisbane
South Australia	75	1,495,800	Adelaide
Tasmania	29	469,900	Hobart
Victoria	78	4,741,500	Melbourne
Western Australia	142	1,873,800	Perth
Total	730	19,080,800	

Fig. 2.40 Distribution of local government authorities and population.

From 1945 until the mid 1960s, the Australian government sponsored emigration from the UK. Assistance was given on the condition that males were skilled workers and the entire family had to have passed a rigorous medical examination. This explains in part why 95 per cent of the population is white and principally of British descent, making the Anglo-Celts the dominant societal group.

Now, 22 per cent of the population has European origins and the principal ethnic groups include Italians, Croats, Greeks, Maltese, Germans and Dutch. The influx of these European settlers after 1945 brought a tradition of soccer to Australia and, despite early problems, this sport is presently increasing in popularity.

Indigenous peoples

The Aborigines are the indigenous people of Australia and Tasmania. Prior to European settlement in the late eighteenth century, the Aboriginal population of 350,000 was divided into 500 groups each with variations in language and dialect. The Aborigines adopted a close association with nature through 'dreamtime' meditation and have complex systems to determine family and marriage rites. The many separate tribes formed a richly unique culture displayed through art, ritual and sports (see page 140).

The first settlers

In 1788, around 1000 men and women landed by ship at Port Jackson, the present site of Sydney. The majority of these people were convicted criminals under sentence of 'transportation' from England. Consequently, Australia became a penal colony under the governance of Philip Arthur who had the vision to develop the settlement 'for the good of the British Empire'.

HOT TIPS

The Australian nation was not built upon convict settlement. Fortune hunters with a frontier ethos similar to the American pioneers later came to farm the land and dig for gold. Among these migrants was an aspiring middle-class element from England who played sports and did much to shape the culture of Australia.

The Aborigines did not display hostility and kept a distance from the 'white invaders'. The settlers would later persecute the native population, taking over their territories in a fictional claim of 'terra nullius', which denied that lands were previously occupied by Aborigines.

Over 150 nationalities can now be found in Australia and it is one of the most diverse nations. Today its economic ties are increasingly with the Asian-Pacific region; however, Australia has not always shown friendship toward Pacific Island people.

Between 1862 and 1904, more than 60,000 Melanesian and Polynesian natives were transferred, often forcibly, to work as cheap labour on Queensland farms and plantations. The importation of the new immigrant labour force contravened the 'white Australia policy' and resentment was shown by the existing white labour force who referred to the island people as the Kanakas.

Although exploited and confined by strict terms of employment, the Pacific Islanders were instrumental in the development of swimming and surfing in Australia. Furthermore, due to the laws that restricted bathing until the late nineteenth century, the colonists had not been innovative swimmers. Alick Wickham, a native of the Soloman Islands, revolutionised swimming and is credited with the invention of the Australian crawl stroke.

In addition, the Pacific Islanders earned success as professional boxers and although their status in society prevented entry into Rugby Union, they were recruited readily by professional Rugby League clubs after 1907. The tradition of Melanesian and Polynesian representation in Rugby League, both in Australia and New Zealand, has remained up to the present day.

Australia of the twenty-first century desires an inclusive pluralistic society and this is reflected in some major sports. This has not always been the policy (see page 140).

The ideologies of Australia focus on a capitalist democratic society of the western model. A strong egalitarian ethos is present and pluralism is valued in society. There is also a powerful sense of nationalism. Historically, patriotic unity was achieved through:

Fig. 2.41 Cathy Freeman (of Aboriginal origin) was a gold medallist and the central figure in the 2000 Olympic Games opening ceremony in Sydney. She has done much to unite the Aboriginal and Australian cultures.

HOT TIPS

Australia is considered a land of opportunity and this is epitomised in the phrase 'land of fair go'. This means that everyone has a chance to succeed.

- desire for self-government
- allied unity with the UK in two world wars
- sport.

Australia has a reputation for community participation in all forms of sport and a national sports obsession has been nurtured in a continent where favourable climatic conditions support outdoor activities in all seasons. It is one of only three countries to take part in every modern Olympic Games.

Fig. 2.42 Melbourne claims to be the sports capital of the world. Its venues include the world-famous Melbourne cricket ground (pictured here), the Telstra dome, and the Rod Laver International Tennis Centre.

The widest range of international sports exists throughout Australia, although some remain focused in particular states.

Australian football, formerly called 'Aussie Rules', developed in Victoria and emerged as a professional sport in the exclusive Victoria Football League (VFL). Although the hotbed remains in this southern state, Australian football is now played nationally with professional teams in Adelaide, Sydney, Perth and Brisbane. If junior participants are included, half a million players were registered in 2003 to play one of the country's most popular games.

Rugby League and Rugby Union have existed in all states and territories, but outside New South Wales, Queensland and the Capital Territory, they have never rivalled the supremacy of Australian football. The

KEY WORDS

State of Origin

This is a series of three games played between Queensland and New South Wales. These states were the first to play rugby in Australia.

Rugby League stages a test series called **State of Origin**. Rivalry between the foundling states means little to the rest of Australia and is said to have impeded the growth of the game.

Revise as you go! Test your knowledge and understanding

- Explain the process of colonialism.
- What is meant by the term 'Motherland'?
- How does the organisation of government impact on sport and physical education?
- List Australia's dominant ideologies.
- Identify the factors that have created patriotic unity.

Sharpen up your exam technique!

1   Explain the term 'sports obsession' and outline the cultural factors that are responsible for its existence.   (4 marks)

2 Describe the population distribution in Australia and outline the initial problems this caused during the development of organised sport.   (3 marks)

3 Explain why Australia has adopted most of its sports from the UK.

(3 marks)

Section 14: *Physical education in schools and colleges (Australia)*

Learning objectives

At the end of this section you should be able to:
- give a detailed account of physical education and sport education in schools with reference to Victoria in the context of the 2003 review
- understand the context of the SEPEP model
- explain PASE as a professional development programme for teachers in Victoria
- comprehend the significance of 'fair play'
- understand one function of the Australian Sports Commission (ASC) and the introduction of Aussie Sport
- explain the method of assessment in physical education.

HOT TIPS

Government school education is the responsibility of the state and not the federal government (see page 129 on decentralisation).

KEY WORDS

Senate

A senate enquiry is a government examination.

Curriculum Standards Framework (CSF)

Comprises eight compulsory key learning areas, which are delivered to pupils up to Year 10.

Introduction

Following a **senate** enquiry in 1992 into declining standards of skill and fitness levels, changes have taken place in the delivery of sport and physical education in schools.

Victoria State responded to the enquiry by implementing the recommendations of the 1993 Monaghetti Review. The Victoria School Sports Unit was established to introduce strategies and ensure that programmes were being delivered effectively. The unit operates within the Department of Education and is controlled by the state government.

Physical education and sport education programmes were made compulsory for pupils up to Year 10 and included in the **Curriculum Standards Framework (CSF)**. Each programme has an allocated time of 100 minutes per week, and both have different but related aims and objectives.

Australian Sports Commission (ASC)

A government committee with responsibility for sport. Its purpose is to administer and fund sport nationally on behalf of the federal government.

Active Australia

The slogan for Australia's Sport for All policy. This policy has recently been updated and is now termed 'More Active Australia'.

Fundamental skills programme

A compulsory physical education programme for primary school children.

HOT TIPS

SEPEP is not a definitive model. It is a suggested framework and available for adaptation.

HOT TIPS

Unlike the UK, there is no National Curriculum or inspection service. Teachers are granted professional autonomy.

HOT TIPS

Be aware that the ASC withdrew funding for Aussie Sport in 1996 and the programme no longer exists. However, many modified games remain in use in sport education programmes and in junior club initiatives.

Edith Cowan University in Western Australia presented a model as a suggested guide to the teaching of physical activities and this was entitled the Sport Education and Physical Education Project (SEPEP). The **Australian Sports Commission (ASC)** funded the initial research.

Although SEPEP provides a framework and is available to all throughout the Australian physical education system, it forms only a small part of curriculum delivery. Teachers are free to adapt and innovate their own programmes to accommodate variations in abilities of pupils, teaching environment and department expertise.

TASK 22

List the advantages and possible drawbacks of a system that grants autonomy to teachers and does not prescribe a National Curriculum.

The overriding emphasis in Australian schools is on enjoyment and maximum participation. This ethos is at the grass roots of '**Active Australia**' and has foundations in the teacher-delivered skill-based physical education programme.

In primary schools (Years 1–6), the focus is to increase competence in eleven fundamental motor skills and not to be overly concerned with teaching games strategies. The logic of this approach is that if skill levels are high, children will enjoy participation and are less likely to withdraw from sports in later years.

TASK 23

Discuss the advantages of implementing a fundamental skills programme at primary level.

Aussie Sport

An emphasis on primary age participation and on making physical activity more appealing to youngsters is not new. In 1982, the ASC saw a need to reinvigorate junior sport and designed a programme of modified sports and mini-games played with adapted 'child friendly' equipment. The initiative, named 'Aussie Sport', was funded by the ASC and initiated by each state in co-operation with the education departments. Aussie Sport grew to be a generic programme covering a range of initiatives from school and club links to leadership programmes for students. It was similar to the Top Sport and Top Play participation schemes introduced in the UK by the Youth Sport Trust.

Operating alongside physical education in the secondary school is the sports education programme with an aim to develop '**game sense**', enjoyment and the spirit of fair play.

School Sport Australia (SSA, formerly the Australian School Sports Council) is the overarching controlling body for school sport and an advisory council for the whole country. Although each state school sport association (for example, Victoria's VSSSA) needs to affiliate to the SSA, it operates its own programmes independently. The SSA is also responsible for inter-state championships.

The organisation of inter-school sport for Victoria

Sports in Years 7 and 8 tend to be traditional – for example, cricket, football, netball and hockey. Pupils experience a different activity in each of the four ten-week terms that make up the academic year. To facilitate rudimentary learning, sports are initially played on an intra-school basis and progress during the final three weeks of term into inter-schools competition. Matches between local schools include all children and are played on a 'round robin' basis, with the most successful schools qualifying for the state finals. The six school sports associations – for example, VSSSA (Victoria), QSSS (Queensland) – organise intra-state competitions.

This model (Figure 2.44 on page 136) indicates that participation is maximised while good teams and individuals can progress to a higher level. Pupils are released from normal school commitments on days of inter-school competition. Selection for state teams begins at inter-school level.

Fig. 2.43 The opening ceremony of the Pacific School Games.

TASK 24

Consider the framework into which your school or college would fit. Compared with the Australian model, does your framework maximise participation and give similar progressive competitive opportunities?

A further incentive for promising school performers is the possibility of selection for the Pacific School Games (PSG). These games take place every four years and the Victoria Department of Education, on behalf of SSA, hosts the event in Melbourne. The games involve

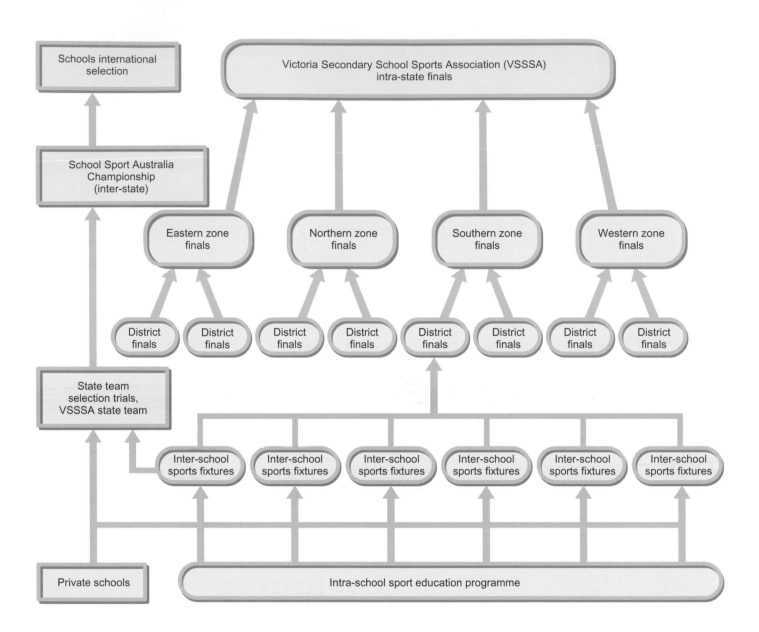

Fig. 2.44 Model of sport education inter-school competition in the state of Victoria.

KEY
WORDS

Elective

Activity options. They broaden experience and prepare older pupils for active pursuits after leaving school – for example, aerobics, surfing and racquet sports.

in excess of 3000 abled and disabled primary and secondary school pupils representing all state and territory education systems and are drawn from 30 Pacific Island countries. Among many positive outcomes, the mission of the enterprise is to improve participation and achievement in education.

Inter-school sport continues during Years 9–10, but traditional sports give way on the timetable to **elective** activities. Sports practice continues an extra-curricular commitment as it does for Years 11–12.

Senior pupils can elect to become sports leaders and become involved in administration, refereeing and coaching. In this capacity, they may help a senior coach to deliver a sport education lesson enabling the teacher to take a co-ordinator's role.

Fig. 2.45 Although sport education has a common purpose, programme delivery across schools will vary. There is not a single model of administration. Sports coaches may be employed on a part-time basis from a club or may be a subject teacher who also specialises in sport at the school.

HOT TIPS

For exam purposes it is important to be aware of the changing emphasis of Sports Search. Collating information is time consuming for a minimal return; therefore, the system has not been pursued in schools since 2000. However, in connection with the 'More Active Australia' policy, students can enter their own scores and obtain advice about the sports in which they are likely to achieve success.

Selection policies

Sport education in Australian schools is non-elitist. Pupils who demonstrate a high level of talent are directed towards club participation. In addition, the Department of Education has implemented a 'sports linkage' policy involving the school and club sharing facilities to benefit the wider community.

Assessment in physical education from Years 7–10 is based on practical competence and attitude. Some schools incorporate health studies into the programme.

Fitness standards are tested in secondary schools leading to the Australian Fitness Education Award. The tests, designed by the Australian Council for Health, Physical Education and Recreation (ACHPER), apply to the whole of Australia and although they give a percentile reading, they are concerned with personal improvement and not direct comparisons. The major justification for testing is to promote a healthy lifestyle and to educate pupils in ways of achieving fitness.

Fitness statistics were at one time monitored by the Australian Institute of Sport (AIS) and if readings were exceptional, individuals were selected for special training. This process, named Sports or Talent Search, operated well for endurance events like rowing but could not predict games potential.

In Years 11 and 12, students throughout Australia take the High School Certificate (HSC) examination. Each state has a version of the HSC – for example, the Victoria Certificate of Education (VCE). As the Australian school year begins at the end of January, most students take the final examination when they are seventeen. Hence Year 12 marks the end of secondary education for students in Australian schools. It is usual to take five HSC subjects, which accumulate a points score to give a Tertiary Entrance Rank (TER) to determine university eligibility.

At VCE level, physical education is an elective subject and is assessed entirely on theoretical knowledge. Practical periods are used occasionally to endorse academic principles.

The Victoria School Sports Unit also commits to the training of non-specialist teachers. Primary teachers tend to take courses in physical education, while secondary teachers focus on sport education. Courses are intensive and are placed under the all-embracing title of Physical and Sport Education **professional development programme** (**PASE**). All professional development is financed by the government and delivered by ACHPER. Through high quality on-line resources, good teaching practice is shared and further support is given.

Head teachers have the authority to operate elitist programmes in single sports and engage specialist coaches to work with students who elect to enrol at the school. In New South Wales, some principals have created sports schools incorporating timetable concessions and employing specialist staff to develop excellence. One such example is Westfield Sports High School in New South Wales.

Forty schools in Victoria have earned the status of government exemplary schools. Teachers from these schools deliver professional development and share good practice with neighbouring institutions. Grants are given to cover the cost of teacher release and considerable prestige is associated with the exemplary title. However, these schools are required to be exceptional and make significant contributions to '**cluster schools**' as exemplary status can be withdrawn.

Victoria has committed to raising the profile of physical education and sport. A 'sports person in school' project now exists to bring emerging, established, abled and disabled athletes regularly into schools to advise and act as role models. Athletes must plan talks and workshops, as these engagements are part of the programme called Athletes Career Education (ACE), and for this reason, the government, through the **Victoria Institute of Sport** (**VIS**), pays the athletes for their commitment. The role of the athlete is to supplement curriculum delivery and schools must state how the contribution will integrate with their programme.

Teachers raise their own profiles as role models by engaging in the 'Teachers Games'. These residential competitive sports experiences provide network opportunities and endorse the participation ethic, which is the prime mover in Australian physical and sports education.

Youngsters who are high achievers in sport are acknowledged in Victoria. The government offers regional awards for attainment and fair play, and nominations are submitted for state awards. The latter not only recognises the achievements of pupils but those of outstanding staff and schools. The de Coubertin awards are presented to students who have made outstanding contributions to administration, coaching and other important non-playing roles. The reward reflects the original spirit of the modern Olympics that taking part is more important than victory.

TASK 25

Discuss the reasons why is it essential for a country like Australia to have the widest possible participation base.

Revise as you go! Test your knowledge and understanding

- Identify the role of the Victoria School Sports Unit.
- Describe the SEPEP curriculum initiative.
- State the purpose of the PASE professional development programme.
- Explain the fundamental motor skills programme.
- Define 'Aussie Sport' and explain the legacy it has left.
- Describe the sport linkage policy.
- Outline the functions of ACHPER.

Sharpen up your exam technique!

1 Describe the structure and function of the exemplary schools initiative. (4 marks)

2 Outline the measures taken in Australian schools to increase sports participation amongst young people. (5 marks)

3 Explain how physical education is assessed in Australian schools. (3 marks)

Section 15: *Ethnic sports and new games (Australia)*

Learning objectives

At the end of this section you should be able to:
- describe the nature and purpose of the sports and pastimes of the Aborigine people
- explain the status of the Aborigines from the period of colonialism to the present day
- understand the development of Australian football (formally Aussie Rules).

Introduction

As with the Pacific Island tribal people of Melanesia and Polynesia (see page 131), games played by Aboriginal societies were functional, often focusing on survival. Sports also reflected the economic and cultural concerns in society, served to unite the people and improved fitness necessary for a hunter-gatherer existence.

Aborigines also played games for fun. With a ball made of possum skin, the Gunditmara tribe played marn-grook. It is thought that the leaping tactic employed in play was copied as a marking strategy in what was to become Aussie Rules.

The early British settlers regarded Aborigines as sub-human. They were excluded from the colonial expansion policies, being at best marginalised and at worst killed. Many died because of a lack of resistance to mild infections brought to Australia by the settlers. Through this time of geographical isolation, rampant disease and death, it is surprising that Aborigines played such good cricket. Between two massacres, an Aboriginal team became the first to tour England in 1868 in what was called a 'dignified episode in race relations'. In reality, this tour was more like a circus in which the Aborigines were good but novel performers.

KEY WORDS

Multi-culturalism

Acknowledgement of and equality shown to all cultures.

HOT TIPS

Be aware that like the Aborigines in Australia, ethnic minorities in the UK are represented in top flight sport.

The Aboriginal issue became a source of embarrassment, particularly as a commitment to **multi-culturalism** in 1971 had ended the 'white Australian policy' (see page 130). By the 1990s, the government had granted land rights to the Aborigines and restored a degree of autonomy. More recently, an official expression of regret for the past mistreatment of the native population has been issued and equality is now acknowledged.

Policies and attitudes regarding the inclusion of ethnic minorities in all levels of sport have changed significantly in the UK during the last 25 years. A policy of racial inclusion has been an important focus of Britain's long standing Sport for All

HOT TIPS

As in Australia, over representation of athletes from ethnic backgrounds occurs in some national sports in the UK. Look back at page 256 in *Advanced PE for OCR: PE*.

initiative. However, ethnic minorities are only slowly emerging into international sport.

Today in Australia, native Aborigines make up less than 2 per cent of inhabitants and despite under-representation in many sports they have been disproportionately successful at a high level in the major sports of Aussie Rules, Rugby League and boxing. However, standards of living and life expectancy remain incomparable with Australian people.

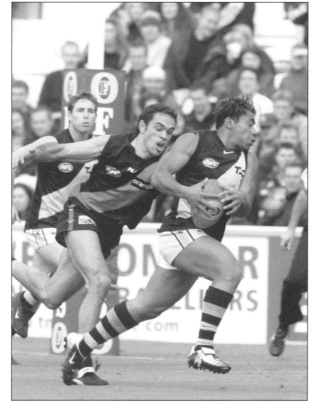

Fig. 2.46 *Populi ludos populo*, Australian football is the game of the people for the people.

KEY WORDS

Cornstalks

Second- and third-generation Australians. Due to improved diets and a superior climate, they had grown taller than the original British settlers from whom they were descended.

Larrikin

A mischievous Australian character.

The development of Australian football (Aussie Rules)

Although Australian football is not an international game, it has grown beyond its Melbourne origins and of Victoria State development to become a popular national game.

There is strong evidence to suggest that the game is genuinely Australian. Allegedly, English-born Tom Wills witnessed Aborigines playing a leaping game with an animal skin in Queensland. He combined this ethnic activity with the basic principles of the ball sports he had experienced in the English public schools and as a result codified the sport of Melbourne Rules in 1858. It is significant that this date precedes the codification of Association Rugby and Gaelic Football, dispelling the myth that the Australian game was an adaptation from a British origin.

Several cultural factors shaped Melbourne Rules, which was originally designed to maintain the fitness of cricketers in winter. The Aborigines contributed athleticism, the Irish strength and ruggedness, while the '**cornstalks**' brought to the sport the new manly image of 'frontier' Australia. Spectators also brought influence. From cabinet ministers to **larrikins**, the game appealed to all classes, endorsing the egalitarian nature of society.

TASK 26

Watch an extract from an Australian football game. Consider how the frontier ethos shows itself during play.

HOT TIPS

Australian football approaches the level of commercialism found in professional soccer in the UK.

In a country where space is boundless, the game developed to be played on huge cricket ovals with dimensions far in excess of the largest soccer grounds in the UK. Today, teams comprise eighteen players with half forwards running 25 kilometres during the course of a highly skilled game requiring six officials to cover the pitch. Australian football has blossomed on twenty-first century commercialism. Sky Television, sponsorship and advertisements occupying breaks in play are lucrative sources of revenue, while features and chat shows market the sport.

'Footy' has evolved rules, skills and tactics of its own and is now the game of the cosmopolitan Australian people moulded by the cultural, social and economic environment of the nation. Despite the physical nature, fair play is a high priority. The Brownlow medal is presented to the best and fairest player each year.

Revise as you go! Test your knowledge and understanding

- What is the function of games and sports in tribal societies?
- Identify the modern sports in which the Aborigines have succeeded.
- Explain the term 'multi-culturalism'.
- Explain why Australian Rules 'footy' is believed to be a genuine Australian game.
- Describe the frontier image.
- List the factors that have shaped Australian football.
- Identify the measures taken by the federal government to give the Aborigines equal rights.

Sharpen up your exam technique!

1   Describe the purpose of the ethnic sports played by the Aboriginal people.

(3 marks)

2   With reference to the culture and the nature of the game, outline why Australian football is a reflection of 'frontierism'. (6 marks)

3   Explain why, in the twenty-first century, a person of Aborigine descent would wish to excel in the national sports of Australia. (4 marks)

Section 16: *Mass participation in sport (Australia)*

Learning objectives

At the end of this section you should be able to:
- understand the state policies and programmes
- explain the development and renewal of the active sport policy
- identify the popularity of colonial games
- understand the issues that have held back the development of soccer.

HOT TIPS

The failure of the Australian team at the Montreal Olympic Games in 1976 (one silver and four bronze medals) emphasised the need to develop a national sports policy.

HOT TIPS

As in the UK, community involvement in sport both widens the base of the participation pyramid and serves to increase national standards in health.

Introduction

The need for federal involvement in sport was emphasised following the failure of the Australia team in the 1976 Montreal Olympic Games. A master plan for sport led to the establishment of the Australian Sports Commission (ASC) (see page 152). The purpose of the ASC is to administer and fund sport nationally on behalf of the federal government. It is also central to an integrated national sports system that encourages sport and physical activity for all Australians. The principal aim is to develop sports excellence and to increase community participation.

The ASC has two 'delivery units' to ensure that sports participation is accessible for the benefit of the whole population.

- The Australian Institute of Sport (AIS) is responsible for the training and emergence of elite teams and athletes.
- The Sport Development Group has responsibility to increase sports participation through the More Active Australia and Active Australia policies. These initiatives aim to increase numbers in the long term through physical education and self-initiated sport.

The initiative of Active Australia has now moved on. Following a review entitled 'Backing Australia's Sporting Ability' in 2000, a new policy was introduced called More Active Australia, which demands a new and purposeful direction. Previous Active Australia initiatives were successful in educating the community about the importance of physical activity in improving health and general well-being; however, the new focus more directly aims to increase the active membership of sports clubs across the country through national and state sporting associations.

The government will invest AU$550 million into the scheme over a four-year period between 2000–04 and the National Sports Organisation will be held responsible for achieving participation growth, business budgets and high performance outcomes.

Popularity of colonial games

The colonial elite established the hunt, golf and later tennis clubs as places in which people of high social status could socialise. Unlike in England, where the boundaries between social classes are preserved, exclusivity was never a national Australian characteristic. In Australia, lower orders were not servile nor was deference shown to people in higher places. Similarly, snobbery was less evident in the society of a 'young country' when survival and prosperity have depended on people working together.

Hard working respectable immigrant settlers of the nineteenth century bettered themselves through self-help and contributed to the positive image of Australia as a workingman's paradise, earning the country the name the 'land of the fair go'.

These people believed that true sportsmanship in competitive situations demanded moral effort and that sport was good for society. This philosophy already existed in English public schools and universities and was called Athleticism.

Athleticism in Australia professed three distinct purposes:
- The elite private schools – for example, Brisbane Grammar (Queensland) and Melbourne Grammar (Victoria) – believed that athleticism prepared boys for leadership, government and business professions.
- Athleticism gave a chance to a rapidly evolving newspaper industry to foster national pride through sport.
- Organised sport was an agent of social control during the rough 'frontier' days of the colonial period when early settlers arrived.

Cricket was the first sport to come to Australia from the UK and the first game was played in Sydney around 1825. It has remained a mass spectator sport and has done much to unite and build the confidence of the nation. Cricket was imported without adaptation but was never seen as the preserve of any one class. Unlike the UK, there was no reference to gentleman and players and no privilege given to the 'school tie' (e.g. the school you attended).

A home victory for Australia in what is recognised as the first cricket test match in 1876 and success in England in 1882 created the 'Ashes' mythology (see page 146). Cricket matches against the 'old masters' then became a benchmark against which the general progress of the young nation was measured.

Rugby was also imported during the period of colonial settlement. As in the UK, educational institutions were foremost in introducing rugby and Sydney University played the first game in 1863. Parallels between the two countries can also be drawn in the fact that games on both sides of the world were strictly amateur and catered for the middle classes.

The sport of soccer did not transfer well to Australia. In the period of colonialisation, played initially by only British immigrants, soccer was called the 'Pommie Game' and was characterised by physical play. However, with the influx of European settlers after 1945, a new style of soccer involving control and skilful touches emerged. This continental style also introduced dissent toward officials, shirt pulling and foul tactics. Australians could not tolerate this approach and the 'land of the fair go' labelled soccer as a foreign game.

Furthermore, new working-class immigrants remained in their ethnic groups and settled in different areas of cities forming 'ghetto cultures'. Each community reflected the country of origin in the name of its soccer team. Names like Melbourne Croatia and St George Budapest stimulated racial rivalry and crowd violence.

The situation has changed and the popularity of soccer is increasing. Sponsors have been attracted because of a stronger administration of the governing body who defused racial problems by withdrawing ethnic team names – for example, Hellas (Greek origin) has become Sydney Knights. As a result, the media has grown less hostile and a television channel now gives extensive soccer coverage promoting it as the main game of Australia.

Youth soccer was one of the sports to benefit from the AIS and it is becoming a very popular elective in school sport education programmes.

Fig. 2.47 Soccer is losing its ethnic image and is emerging as a national sport.

HOT TIPS

Soccer still needs to be cautious as, while other minority groups are encouraged to demonstrate their culture, soccer is forced to hide its ethnicity.

Revise as you go! Test your knowledge and understanding

- Name the Australian Sport for All policy.
- Explain the focus of this policy.
- Explain why sport transcended class boundaries in colonial days.
- Describe why sport was important to the colonial settlers.
- Give reasons to suggest why the result of cricket matches against England became a measure of Australia's general development.
- Account for soccer's lack of popularity in the period between 1945 and 1990.
- What measures have been taken to improve the image of soccer in recent years?

Sharpen up your exam technique!

1   With reference to population, size and national ambition, explain why Australia has adopted a vigorous 'Sport for All' policy.   (4 marks)

2 Explain why settlers believed that sports adopted from the UK would benefit Australian society. Use examples to illustrate your answer.

(5 marks)

3 Explain the cultural problems that have held back the development of soccer and describe the measures taken to overcome them. (5 marks)

Section 17: *Sport and the pursuit of excellence (Australia)*

Learning objectives

HOT TIPS

It is important to be aware of the cultural factors that underpin Australia's national motivation to pursue sporting excellence.

At the end of this section you should be able to:
- understand Australian football, cricket and Rugby League in the context of professional sports
- demonstrate knowledge of traditions in swimming, athletics and tennis
- indicate the influence of ethnic groups in Australian sport
- comprehend issues relating to gender equality
- understand the development of talent through youth sport programmes with reference to the ASC and the AIS.

Fig. 2.48 Cricket has always been taken seriously in Australia. If Bradman had been struck by the English 'bodyline' bowlers in 1932, diplomatic relations between the two countries would have been compromised.

Cricket, Aussie Rules and Rugby League as professional games

Cricket is a little different in Australia compared to the version seen in England. The light is brighter and the pitches harder with more bounce to encourage attack. There are variations in terminology: 'extras' are 'sundries' and the 'googly' is the 'wrong un'.

The development of Australian cricket during the twentieth century has not been without controversy. In 1932, during the infamous 'bodyline' tour, England's tactics were deemed unfair and both sporting and diplomatic relations became strained.

In 1977, the Australian television magnate, Kerry Packer, introduced 'World Series' cricket, which took power away from the traditional International Cricket Board, and this had a direct impact on the modern game. World Series cricket offered lucrative financial contracts to the world's best players to form what was described as a cricket circus. Players who signed up to the circus were subsequently banned from playing for their countries. Australia hosted this series, which, for the first time, involved floodlit cricket, imported pitches and modifications to dress and rules. A limit on overs ensured that a

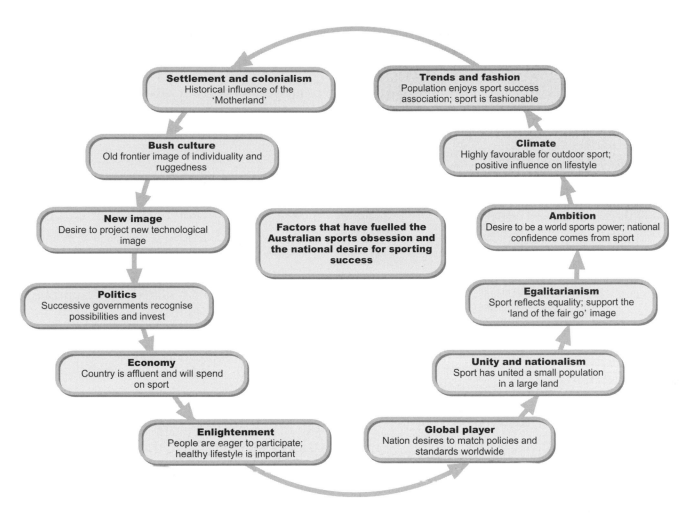

Settlement and colonialism
Historical influence of the 'Motherland'

Trends and fashion
Population enjoys sport success association; sport is fashionable

Bush culture
Old frontier image of individuality and ruggedness

Climate
Highly favourable for outdoor sport; positive influence on lifestyle

New image
Desire to project new technological image

Factors that have fuelled the Australian sports obsession and the national desire for sporting success

Ambition
Desire to be a world sports power; national confidence comes from sport

Politics
Successive governments recognise possibilities and invest

Egalitarianism
Sport reflects equality; support the 'land of the fair go' image

Economy
Country is affluent and will spend on sport

Unity and nationalism
Sport has united a small population in a large land

Enlightenment
People are eager to participate; healthy lifestyle is important

Global player
Nation desires to match policies and standards worldwide

Fig. 2.49 The cultural factors that influence the Australian national desire to achieve sports excellence.

HOT TIPS

Professional sports such as rugby, cricket and Australian football are required to be increasingly entertaining to make them commercially viable.

HOT TIPS

Review pages 234–9 from *Advanced PE for OCR: AS*. Consider the impact of commercialism on sport in the UK and Australia.

game could be finished in one day and guaranteed a result. The spectacle became popular, changing the image of cricket forever. For the first time, television royalties brought wealth to the prominent players and, in effect, World Series cricket had increased the professional intensity of the game.

Rugby League and Rugby Union

The focus of both Rugby League and Rugby Union remains in New South Wales and Queensland, and, unlike the UK, Rugby League tends to be the more popular version.

The breakaway movement to Rugby League came to Australia in 1907 and this allowed professionalism to develop as players could be paid for time spent away from work when playing. Rugby League needed to be a superior spectacle as a paying public provided the players' wages.

In general terms, rugby provides social acceptance and integration for players and supporters of non-British heritage; however, the Rugby League code still displays evidence of its working-class origins.

Fig. 2.50 Polynesian players are now impacting on Rugby Union. The code has always accepted ethnic cultures into its playing ranks.

The 1950s were progressive periods for both Rugby League and Rugby Union, but during the 1970s Rugby League attendances declined necessitating major modifications. A five-team semi-final series, changes in scoring and the six-tackle rule were implemented to increase spectator appeal. Eastern suburbs became the first team to display sponsorship on club jerseys and the inaugural State of Origin match was played in 1980 (see page 132). The contemporary professional game has salary-capped all players and looks increasingly to commercial needs in a competitive market. Although a draft system does not operate, each professional 'club' has an 'academy' team, which has a mission to nurture young local talent. It is significant that the British Rugby League is following the Australian lead.

Rugby Union and the change from amateur to professional status

A major boost for Rugby Union proved to be the inauguration of the World Cup in 1987. Success in this competition has increased the sponsorship for the Australian Rugby Union and has attracted greater television coverage on a commercial network. This was taken further in the 2003 World Cup, despite losing to England in the final. As with Rugby League, this has stimulated rule changes and advances in athleticism and skilfulness to secure spectator interest. The game at top level is no longer amateur, having become professional during the 1990s. International competitions throughout the southern hemisphere have become increasingly intense and great rivalry with European rugby nations has been generated, attracting a wider audience. High quality club competitions like the prestigious 'Super 12's' have raised the profile and television revenue in both New Zealand and Australia.

The growth of Australian football into full-time professionalism has previously been mentioned (see page 141). It is significant to outline how the media have more recently impacted on the game.

- Games are played at strategic times throughout the weekend to attract large television audiences.
- Fixtures are organised in collusion with the television companies to ensure the most even distribution of 'star fixtures'.
- After goals are scored during matches, the referee will restart play only when a light on the scoreboard indicates that the commercial television break has ended.

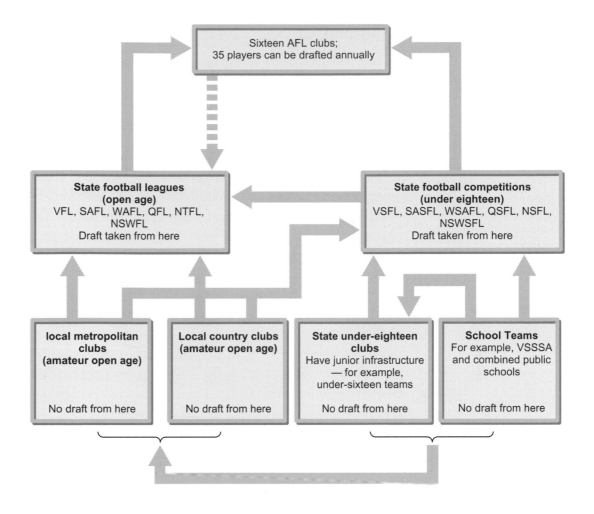

Fig. 2.51 Australian Football League (AFL) Player Pathway.

A draft system operates to spread talent more evenly through the clubs. The route of progression through to top-level Australian football is called a 'pathway'. There are many pathways and some incorporate youth sports programmes in schools and clubs up to state level. The various pathways can be identified from Figure 2.51.

TASK 27

1 Identify a 'pathway' to take a talented schoolboy to professional registration.
2 What measure could be taken if an AFL player loses form or is returning after injury?

Traditions of swimming and athletics

As well as the sports mentioned on pages 141–6, Australia also has traditions in the sports of swimming and athletics.

HOT TIPS

Great role models have been evident throughout Australia's Olympic history. Dawn Frazer and Shane Gould were outstanding swimmers in the 1960s and 70s, while more recently, Ian Thorpe and Michael Klim continued the great tradition into the twenty-first century.

Swimming

Bathing was described as the favourite recreation in Sydney around the 1830s and it was popular across the whole of Australia during the colonial period. The middle classes, with an 'obsession' for health and cleanliness, set the trend that led to the beginnings of a 'beach culture' (see the influence of Melanesian and Polynesian cultures on page 131).

Swimming competitions were common for men, but society believed that for women exertion in sport was unfeminine. The first female carnival took place in 1902. Later, Australian women, such as Sarah Durack and Wilhelmina Wylie, won gold and silver medals at the Stockholm Olympics of 1912 only after special concessions were made allowing them to swim publicly. This is just one episode in the struggle for equal rights for women in sport.

Athletics

A tradition of athletics is deeply rooted in Australian sports and social history. In the early nineteenth century, the lower classes engaged in boxing and foot racing involving running or walking. These events were often organised by colonial tavern keepers who saw the chance to make money.

HOT TIPS

Note in the example opposite the absence of other states. At the time, it was easier to travel from New Zealand to Melbourne, for example, than from Western Australia to Melbourne. Vast distances impeded the growth of nineteenth-century competitive sport and this was referred to as the 'tyranny of distance' (see page129).

The Adelaide Amateur Athletics club was formed in 1864 by a middle-class colonial group who both wished to end the vices of professionalism and promote health, morality and manliness through athletics (see Athleticism on page 144). The amateur ethos of 'sport for sports' sake' was quickly embraced by private schools and universities, lending stability to the Australian athletics movement.

The first Australian track and field competition was held in Melbourne in 1893 and attended by Victoria, New South Wales and New Zealand. The event was successful and widely reported across Australia.

Despite the initial philosophy of Pierre de Coubertin that the Olympic Games must be reserved for men, women were included in the 1924 games in Amsterdam. This stimulated growth in women's athletics (see sport and gender, page 153), but such was the prejudice against female participation that even in the 1938 Empire Games only six women were allowed to represent Australia.

HOT TIPS

Few Aborigines were encouraged to compete as amateurs and have had limited opportunities to represent Australia. Look back at page 140 and the white Australia policy.

Currently, women have won 75 per cent of gold medals for Australia in track and field events and represent great role models for contemporary female athletes. Cathy Freeman (of Aboriginal descent) won gold medals in Atlanta (1996) and Sydney (2000), and represented all people of Australia with distinction.

Although women have dominated gold medal achievement, Australia has produced a wealth of male track stars. In 2003, Patrick Johnson became the first Australian to break ten seconds for 100 metres. After a disappointing team performance in track and field at Sydney 2000, Johnson, who is based at the AIS in Canberra, is expected to lead a revival in the 2004 Olympic Games in Greece. Other outstanding performers include Ron Clarke, who held seventeen world records in the 1960s, and John Landy, now governor of Victoria and author of the report that established the AIS, who was a central figure in the race to break the four-minute mile in the 1950s.

From the 1950s, national interest in athletics was at its height and for the first time the methods of several leading Australian sports coaches became significant. These included track coach Percy Cerutty who trained Herb Elliot, the Olympic champion of 1960. Cerutty's approach was revolutionary as it avoided work on the racetrack and focused on training in the forests and sand dunes. By contrast, fellow Victoria coach Franz Stampfl adopted a more conventional routine. Both men were successful and helped to establish the Australian ambition for success in track and field.

HOT TIPS

Review sport and mass participation on page 248 of *Advanced PE for OCR: AS*. Compare the areas of discrimination in sport in the UK with those in Australia.

Sport and gender

'Frontier' and bush attitudes of early colonialism laid down male domination and led to serious discrimination towards women in sport. The concepts of feminism and fertility were thought to be threatened by participation in all but the most genteel sports.

During the 1950s and early 60s, female sports champions emerged. In athletics (see page 151), gold medallists Betty Cuthbertson and Marjorie Jackson were nationally accepted because the press portrayed them as feminine, but the sprinter Shirley Strickland was criticised as too aggressive and competitive. Similarly, Dawn Fraser had her sexuality questioned after a gold medal performance in swimming in the 1960 Olympic games in Rome. All risked the stigma of being labelled 'butch'.

After this period the male view was challenged and women adapted male styles and strategies. Female representation was earned in horseracing, long-distance running, bodybuilding and latterly triathlon. In a country where women are in the majority, sports representation is still disproportionately low.

Today there is strong desire to address the issue. In 1995, the medical profession urged women to train and 'work out' like their male counterparts to achieve fitness. In schools, sport education programmes are mixed whenever possible. Female role models are used frequently in the 'sports person in schools' project (see page 138) and national heroes like Cathy Freeman are given a high profile.

Fig. 2.52 Australia's women's cricket team elected to play in culottes. They felt that cricket trousers would give the wrong image.

Revise as you go! Test your knowledge and understanding

- Describe the measures taken by the National Rugby League (NRL) to address falling popularity.
- List the reasons for the development of athletics and swimming.
- Explain why women have experienced discrimination in sport.
- Explain how finance is generated in contemporary Australian professional sport.
- Outline the function of the ASC.
- Describe the purpose of the AIS.
- Describe the operation of the national network of sports institutes.
- List the benefits that an institute can provide to an athlete.

Sharpen up your exam technique!

1. Describe the strategies that have been put in place by the Australian government to develop excellence in sport. (4 marks)

2. Explain the cultural factors that inspire Australian success in world sport. (6 marks)

3. Outline the reasons why discrimination against women existed in Australian sport and explain why social prejudices have now changed. (6 marks)

Section 18: *Outdoor education and outdoor recreation (Australia)*

Learning objectives

HOT TIPS

The terms 'outdoor education' and 'outdoor recreation' have the same meaning in Australia as in the UK. They relate to physical experiences in the natural environment.

At the end of this section you should be able to:
- understand the possibilities for outdoor adventure in the context of climate, demography and natural resources
- explain how national and regional parks are organised and regulated
- identify the possibilities for frontier experiences in the outback
- explain the role and opportunities for outdoor education in schools.

HOT TIPS

Review outdoor education (page 179) and outdoor recreation (page 191) in *Advanced PE for OCR:AS.*

Introduction

Australia has the advantage of wonderful natural resources. As a large landmass supporting a small percentage of urban dwellers, there exists the impression of limitless space. The interior provides the opportunity of genuine wilderness experiences in the world's most hostile environments. Australia also has tropically forested areas, high mountains and extensive coastal areas. In sharp contrast, the

UK has no areas of genuine wilderness, nor does it have a comparable diversity of geographical features.

An outdoor lifestyle is an Australian characteristic and this is made possible by a perennially favourable climate in the populated coastal areas. In general, Australian beach culture, with traditions of swimming, surfing and lifesaving clubs, is the focus of a significant fitness cult prevailing alongside an urban sports obsession.

HOT TIPS

The Australian government is promoting international tourism on a large scale but, unlike the American system of federal administration, organisation and stringent regulation of the natural environment is the responsibility of state departments.

The organisation of national and regional parks

There are more than 500 national parks in Australia. Three well-known examples are:

- Kakadu Park, northern territory, approximately 250km east of Darwin
- Uluru Park, central northern territory
- Great Barrier Reef, north-east coast.

Large numbers of smaller regional parks have been designated providing picnic sites that are accessible to the urban population. Despite these geographical assets, the concept of bush walking – an example of a frontier experience – is not as popular as hiking and back packing in the traditional American or British style.

HOT TIPS

A large majority of the Australian population are urban dwellers who have a preference for urban sports as opposed to outdoor adventure experiences.

The role of outdoor education

Primary schools offer outdoor adventure activities as part of a balanced physical education programme. From the age of seven, there is a tradition of the 'school camp', which is strictly supervised.

Each state offers a Youth Development Programme (YDP). For example, the government-funded Victoria Youth Development Programme (VYDP) is a voluntary elective from Year 9. The programme must be linked with any one of four services:

- army cadets
- ambulance
- fire service
- surf lifesaving.

Frankston High School in Victoria has an association with Mount Alisa Lifesaving Club and specialists from this service help to deliver the course. The Frankston VYDP has four components:

- surf lifesaving techniques (a choice from four electives)
- cardiac pulmonary resuscitation (CPR) qualification
- first aid qualification
- Duke of Edinburgh expedition.

The Duke of Edinburgh Award scheme also operates as it does in the UK as a 'stand-alone' elective.

Skiing

Skiing is a sport not often associated with Australia, but for the past 40 years, Camp Big Foot on Mount Buller has been the venue for the Victoria state inter-schools skiing championships. In common with all Australian schools sports policies, a non-elitist participation ethic is central to the mission of this state government subsidised enterprise. More than 4000 primary and secondary pupils and teachers attend this annual event and all categories of skiing are experienced.

Outward Bound

HOT TIPS

As in the UK, outdoor activities in Australia provide challenges and teach people to work effectively with and depend on each other. They also give a sense of adventure.

The Outward Bound Trust also facilitates adventure opportunities. Based on the UK's model, the trust has existed in Australia since the 1960's. There is an Outward Bound school at Tharwa in Australia's capital territories.

In common with schools in the UK, enterprising teachers plan outdoor adventure packages in activities like bush walking, horse riding, canoeing and skiing. It is common for schools to travel overseas for adventure experiences, and Nepal and the South Island Peaks of New Zealand are examples of some locations visited.

Outdoor education as an examination subject

During Years 11 and 12, outdoor education can be taken as a High School Certificate (HSC) course and validated for Tertiary Entrance Rank (TER). The subject has a large theoretical input, but involves practical assessment in a number of options. It is a popular examination elective and the subject is given high status.

Residential experiences

The character-building concept relating to the outdoors pioneered by British public schools has continued in Australian independent schools. Timbertop is a residential upland forested adventure centre belonging to Geelong Grammar School in Victoria and is used to provide students with outdoor residential experiences.

The Alpine School is the Victoria State schools equivalent. In this venue, courses in outdoor leadership and skills are delivered. The centre has a transient Year 9 population, as students are resident for ten weeks or one term.

Revise as you go! Test your knowledge and understanding

- Explain why Australia has great potential to facilitate outdoor education.
- Explain the meaning of the term 'beach culture'.
- Describe how the national parks are managed.
- Why can bush walking in the outback provide a 'frontier' experience?
- Outline the structure of a youth development programme in the context of outdoor education.

- Describe the function of the Alpine School.
- Explain how outdoor education can be continued in Years 9 and 10.

Sharpen up your exam technique!

1 Outline the reasons why outdoor education is significant in Australia and describe how schools undertake to deliver related programmes. (6 marks)

2 Describe what is meant by a 'frontier experience' and explain how the government is trying to develop outdoor recreation. (4 marks)

3 Give examples to indicate how outdoor experiences are incorporated into primary schools. (3 marks)

Chapter 3 **Biomechanics**

Section 1: *Linear motion*

Learning objectives

At the end of this section you should be able to:
- describe and explain Newton's Laws of Motion
- apply your knowledge of Newton's Laws of Motion to sporting examples
- appreciate that there can never be motion without force but that there can be force without motion
- understand the quantities of mass and inertia and their relevance to sporting techniques
- distinguish between scalar and vector quantities, distance and displacement, speed and velocity
- define and use equations to calculate speed, velocity and acceleration
- plot and interpret information from distance/time and velocity/time graphs
- appreciate the relevance of momentum to sporting techniques.

Introduction

In Sections 1–4, the mechanics of motion will be revisited and the field of biomechanics will be looked at in detail. Some of the concepts involved were introduced to you in Chapter 3 of *Advanced PE for OCR, AS* and it may be beneficial to review this chapter before reading further.

Biomechanics is often thought of as the science underlying technique; knowledge in this area helps athletes and coaches to develop efficient techniques and correct errors in performance. Most of today's top performers will use biomechanical analysis to improve their technique and take it one step closer to perfection. Leonardo da Vinci summed up the importance of sports science hundreds of years ago when he wrote:

> *Those who are enamoured of practice without science are like a pilot who goes into a ship without a rudder or compass and never has any certainty where he is going.*

It is hoped that by reading through the following four sections you will develop an appreciation for this area of the specification and use its principles to enhance your own and other's performances.

KEY WORDS

Linear motion

When a body moves in a straight or curved line with all its parts moving the same distance, in the same direction, and at the same speed.

Fig. 3.01 Linear motion of a tobogganist in a straight line.

Velocity

Rate of motion in a particular direction (see pages 164–5).

Acceleration

The rate of change of velocity. Acceleration = change in velocity/time taken
As a body does not change its mass, acceleration = change in momentum.

Momentum

The quantity of motion possessed by a moving body. Momentum = mass × velocity, therefore a stationary body has no momentum.

Force

A push or a pull that alters, or tends to alter, the state of motion of a body.

KEY WORDS

Inertia

The resistance of a body to change its state of rest or motion. See pages 162–3 and 213–17 for more about inertia.

Some of the mechanical concepts involved with **linear motion** are examined in this section.

The first of these mechanical concepts is Newton's Laws of Motion. These three well-known laws govern motion and an understanding of them enables a performer to improve the efficiency of their movement. The section goes on to explain how the linear motion of a performer can be quantified in terms of linear measurements, and the quantities of distance, displacement, speed, **velocity** and **acceleration** are considered. Analysis of linear motion in this way is useful because many movements in sport happen so quickly that techniques are difficult to analyse by visual observation alone. This is particularly notable in the 100m sprint event. You will learn how to present the data collected in graphical form and how to interpret the shape of such graphs. The section concludes with a look at the relevance of **momentum** to sporting techniques.

Newton's Laws of Motion

Newton's Laws of Motion play an important role in explaining the close relationship between motion and **force**.

Newton's First Law of Motion

❛ *A body continues in a state of rest or of uniform velocity unless acted upon by an external force.* ❜

Newton's first law is often referred to as the 'Law of **Inertia**'.

In Latin, 'inertia' means laziness and one famous biomechanics scientist, while trying to explain inertia, has written:

❛ *Everything in the universe is lazy; so lazy that force is necessary to get it on the move, when it then travels in a straight line with constant speed; so lazy that, once in motion, further force must be applied to slow it down, stop it, speed it up or change its direction.* ❜

As with all of Newton's laws, Newton's first law can be applied to any sporting activity. As an example, however, consider the free throw in basketball awarded after a foul or violation (see Figure 3.02) The basketball remains in the hands of the player until he or she generates and applies a force to the ball causing it to move in the direction of the basket. The ball continues

Fig. 3.02 Basketball player at the beginning of a free throw. The ball will remain at rest until a force is imparted on it, when it will travel towards the basket.

to travel in this direction until the force caused by contact with the backboard causes it to change direction and drop down into the net for one point.

Newton's Second Law of Motion

‘ *When a force acts on an object, the rate of change of momentum experienced by the object is proportional to the size of the force and takes place in the direction in which the force acts.* ’

Newton's second law is often referred to as the 'Law of Acceleration'. It is very closely related to Newton's first law. From the first law it is understood that the velocity of a body remains constant until a force acts upon it. Newton's second law explains that any change in velocity will be directly proportional to the amount of force used and will take place in the direction in which the force acts. Again, there are endless examples, but the game of basketball is once again used here. A player who wishes to pass the ball to a team mate who is standing close by will only need to impart a small amount of force in the direction of his or her team mate. This might occur while chest passing to team mates around the 'key'.

A player who wishes to pass the ball to a team mate who is further away will need to impart a much larger force in the direction of his or her team mate. This might occur while javelin passing to a team mate at halfway to initiate a fast break after rebounding.

Newton's Third Law of Motion

‘ *For every force that is exerted by one body on another there is an equal and opposite force exerted by the second body on the first.* ’

Newton's third law is often referred to as the 'Law of Reaction'. It states that for every action there is an equal and opposite reaction. It is usual to call one of the forces involved the **action force** and the other the **reaction force**. There are no strict rules that govern which force is which, but for the purpose of sports mechanics, it is presumed that the athlete exerts the action force.

To return to the sport of basketball, Newton's third law can be clearly explained by a player who is dribbling the ball down the court. The player exerts an action force on the ball in the downward direction. At the same time, the ball exerts a reaction force in the upward direction on the player, felt by a slight increase in pressure on the fingers. The ball then travels down towards the floor and, on contact, the ball exerts a downward action force on the ground that in turn exerts an upward reaction force on the ball and the ball returns to the player's hand.

Newton's third law states that not only does every force have an opposite, but also that this second force is equal in size to the first. Does it not therefore follow that

HOT TIPS

For AS level study of sports mechanics, it was sufficient to give different sporting examples for each of Newton's three laws. At A2 level, you will be expected to state each of Newton's laws and be able to apply all three to one particular sport. It is good advice to practise applying each of Newton's laws to a number of sporting activities.

HOT TIPS

Newton's second law expressed and simplified in algebraic form gives us the equation:

Force = mass × velocity or F = ma.

This tells us that, assuming a body's mass remains constant through a particular amount of time, the acceleration of the body is equal to the size of force causing it.

KEY WORDS

Action force

A force exerted by an athlete on another body. For example, the backward and downward force of a 100m sprinter on the blocks on the 'B' of the bang.

Reaction force

An equal and opposite force to the action force exerted by another body on the athlete. For example, the forward and upward force of the blocks exerted on a 100m sprinter on the 'B' of the bang.

Fig. 3.03 Basketball player imparting a small force to the ball to pass to a team mate in close proximity.

these two forces will cancel each other out and there will be no external force and thus no movement (Newton's first law)? It is agreed that this is a difficult concept to understand but can be explained by the difference in mass of the two bodies concerned. The larger the mass, the smaller the effect of the force and the less the acceleration. As an extreme example, take a table tennis ball bouncing on a table tennis table. At the moment of impact, the table tennis ball exerts an action force on the table and the table surface exerts a reaction force on the ball. The fact that the earth supports the table means it has a colossal mass compared to the mass of the table tennis ball. It follows that the reaction force on the ball is great, but the action force on the table is negligible compared to its mass.

A final thought on Newton's laws

At this stage, it is important to point out that Newton's First Law of Motion explains that motion in sport can only be produced when an external force is applied. However, it also explains that it is possible to have force without motion when all opposite forces are balanced. Take, for example, a gymnast performing a handstand. From our knowledge of gravity and Newton's third law, we know that the gymnast exerts a downward force on the ground that in turn exerts an upward reaction force on the gymnast. These forces are both opposite and equal, meaning there can be no movement and the gymnast remains balanced and still. This difficult concept is explained further on pages 174–5.

Weight due to gravity

Reaction force

Action force

Fig. 3.04 A gymnast in a balanced position showing that there can be force without motion.

TASK 1

1   Copy the following into your file and complete the missing information.
    Newton's First Law of Motion is sometimes called:
    It states that:
    Newton's Second Law of Motion is sometimes called:
    It states that:
    Newton's Third Law of Motion is sometimes called:
    It states that:
2   Learn each of Newton's laws word for word so that you are able to recite them when asked.

HOT TIPS

For each of the linear measurements listed you will need to know:

• a simple definition

• the relevant equation, where appropriate, for numerical calculation

• the unit of measurement, where appropriate.

Measurements used in linear motion

The following quantities are measurements that are commonly used to describe the linear motion of a body. Their values tell us how far a body moves, how fast it moves and how consistent or inconsistent its motion.

For the purpose of the specification, you need to be familiar with the following quantities:

- mass
- distance
- speed
- acceleration

- inertia
- displacement
- velocity

- deceleration
- scalar quantity
- vector quantity.

TASK 2

As you read through the following section, copy this table onto a sheet of A4 paper and complete it as a revision aid for linear motion.

Measurement	Definition	Relevant equation	Unit of measurement
Mass		✗	
Inertia		✗	✗
Distance		✗	
Displacement		✗	
Speed			
Velocity			
Acceleration			
Deceleration			
Scalar quantity		Examples	
Vector quantity		Examples	

KEY WORDS

Mass

The amount of matter or substance in a body. An athlete's mass is made from muscle, bone, fat, tissue and fluid. Mass is measured in kilograms (kg).

Inertia

The resistance of a body to change its state of rest or motion. It is directly related to the body's mass: the greater the mass, the greater the body's inertia and the greater its resistance to change its state of motion.

Mass

Mass is a relatively easy concept because if a body occupies a space, it has mass. It is made up from 'substance' or 'matter'. The more matter from which it is made, the greater the mass. A racing horse has a larger mass than a greyhound; a hammer thrower has a greater mass than a long-distance runner.

Inertia

Inertia is the reluctance of a body to change whatever it is doing. All bodies want to remain at rest when still and want to continue moving in the same direction at the same speed if moving. From Newton's First Law of Motion, we know that a force is required to change this state of motion. The bigger the mass, the larger the inertia of a body and the bigger the force must be to change its state of motion. Think about the different weights of bowling balls at ten pin bowling alleys. It is considerably easier to send a lighter ball towards the pins than it is a bigger and heavier ball. Similarly, if equal force is applied to a javelin and a shot put, the acceleration of the javelin will be greater.

The concept of inertia is the reason behind having different weight categories in contact sports. For example, in judo, it would be very difficult for a lighter competitor with less mass and less inertia to throw a heavier competitor with greater mass and greater inertia.

Inertia may be a hindrance when trying to get an object moving, but it can be of benefit to an athlete who is already moving. Consider a rugby prop forward and a rugby inside centre who are both running at the same speed towards their try line. Although the prop forward would have required a greater force to get him (or her) moving in the first instance, once moving he will be very difficult to stop due to his large inertia. It will take a strong and brave tackle to stop him from scoring!

Distance v. displacement

KEY WORDS

Distance

The path taken in moving from the first position to the second. Distance is measured in metres (m).

Displacement

The shortest straight-line route between two positions in a stated direction. Displacement is measured in metres (m).

The measurements of **distance** and **displacement** are used to describe the extent of a body's motion.

Distance is simply the length of the path taken by a body in moving from one position to another and examples from sport are easy to give:

- the distance run by a London marathon runner is approx 42.2km (26.2 miles) (see Figure 3.05)

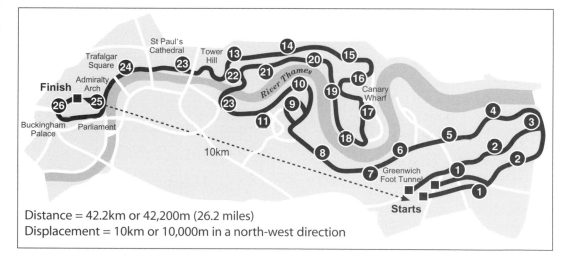

Distance = 42.2km or 42,200m (26.2 miles)
Displacement = 10km or 10,000m in a north-west direction

Fig. 3.05 The route of the London Marathon

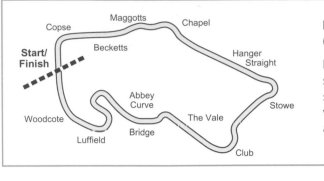

Distance = 303,360m or 303.36km (188.5 miles)

Displacement = 0m (the start is in the same position as the finish, ignoring any small differences in the positions at which the cars cross the line at the start and finish)

Fig. 3.06 The Silverstone motor racing circuit. The British Grand Prix circuit is 5056m in length and the race is over 60 laps.

- the distance covered by a Formula One racing driver in the British Grand Prix at Silverstone is 303,360m or 303.36km (188.5 miles) (see Figure 3.06).

Displacement is a measurement from start to finish 'as the crow flies': the shortest route from the first position to the second. It is important to give a direction when describing displacement. Figures 3.05 and 3.06 show the difference between distance and displacement.

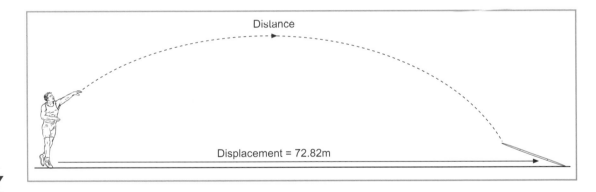

Fig. 3.07 Jan Zelezny did not set a world record distance of 98.48m in the javelin event in 1996, but a world record displacement.

Speed v. velocity

The measurements of **speed** and **velocity** are used to describe the rate at which a body moves from one position to the next.

Speed is the rate of change of distance and its value is calculated by dividing the distance covered in metres by the time taken in seconds.

$$\text{Speed (m/s)} = \frac{\text{distance (m)}}{\text{time taken (s)}}$$

Velocity is the rate of change of displacement and its value is calculated by dividing the displacement covered in metres by the time taken in seconds.

$$\text{Velocity} = \frac{\text{displacement (m)}}{\text{time taken (s)}}$$

TASK 3

In the 50m swimming pool at the Sydney Olympics in 2000, Dutch swimmer Inge de Bruijn set a new world record of 56.61s for the 100m butterfly.

1 Calculate her average speed during the race.
2 Calculate her average velocity during the race.

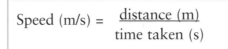

Acceleration

The measurement of **acceleration** is used to describe the rate at which a body changes its velocity. Just like displacement and velocity, direction is important to acceleration. This is the reason why deceleration is often termed negative acceleration and a minus sign is found in front of its value.

$$\text{Acceleration (m/s}^2) = \frac{\text{change in velocity (m/s)}}{\text{time taken (s)}} = \frac{v_f - v_i}{t}$$

V_f = final velocity (m/s)
V_i = initial velocity (m/s)
t = time taken (s)

Acceleration is a very important quantity in sport because the success in many activities is directly related to an athlete's ability to rapidly increase or decrease their velocity. Consider, for example, a netball player who sprints away quickly to lose his or her defender and who then needs to stop abruptly on receiving the ball to avoid breaking the footwork rule.

HOT TIPS

- Remember to give the correct units with your answers. In an examination 'no units = no marks'.

- Remember to write out the equation you are using for your calculations and show all your working. There will be marks available for these stages in your examination questions.

KEY WORDS

Scalar quantity

A quantity that gives an indication of size but not direction. For example, the marathon runner in Figure 3.05 ran a distance of 42.2km.

Vector quantity

A quantity that gives an indication of both size and direction. For example, the marathon runner in Figure 3.05 ran a displacement of 10km in a north-west direction.

TASK 4

The following table gives the 20m split times for the men's 100m final at the Barcelona Olympics in 1992.

Athlete	Country	Time at 0m	Time at 20m	Time at 40m	Time at 60m	Time at 80m	Time at 100m
Linford Christie	UK	0.00s	2.93s	4.74s	6.48s	8.22s	9.96s
Frankie Fredericks	NAM	0.00s	2.91s	4.74s	6.50s	8.26s	10.02s

1. Calculate Christie's velocity at 20m.
2. Calculate Christie's velocity at 80m.
3. Calculate Christie's acceleration between 20m and 80m.
4. State Frederick's velocity at 0m.
5. Calculate Frederick's velocity at 20m.
6. Calculate Frederick's acceleration over the first 20m of the race.

Scalar quantity v. vector quantity

The quantities that have been explained in this section can be split into two groups: those measurements that can be completely described in terms of size (mass, inertia, distance and speed) called **scalar quantity** and those measurements that require describing in terms of size *and* direction (displacement, velocity and acceleration) called **vector quantity**.

Graphs of motion

Graphs help us to make sense of motion as they are a useful means of presenting information. By using graphs, changes and patterns in motion can be recognised and graphs are often used when data is presented very quickly to the naked eye such as the 100m or 200m sprint events.

In Paris in 2003, Tim Montgomery became the fastest man on earth. He ran 100m in 9.78 seconds. From this his average speed can be calculated as approximately 10.2m/s. However, this is the speed that Tim *averaged* over the 100m. At different stages of the race, he would have been running slower than this and at other stages faster. Immediately after the starting gun fires, Tim is gaining speed and running considerably slower than 10.2m/s. It follows that he must have run faster than 10.2m/s elsewhere in the race to average this speed over the whole 100m. To know his speed at different stages of the race requires the use of specific video analysis or radar guns and marker points; the data collected can than be analysed using graphs of motion.

There are two types of graph that need to be examined:

- distance/time graphs
- velocity/time graphs, or speed/time graphs.

For the purpose of sports mechanics at A2 level, velocity/time graphs and speed/time graphs can be treated as practically the same. The shape of the curve plotted on these graphs will enable you to know the pattern of motion occurring at a particular moment at time.

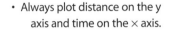

HOT TIPS

- Always plot distance on the y axis and time on the × axis.
- Always label the axes and identify the units.
- You will get marks for this in an examination answer.

KEY WORDS

Gradient of graph

The slope of a graph at a particular moment in time. It is calculated from:

Gradient of graph =

$$\frac{\text{changes in y axis}}{\text{changes in × axis}}$$

Distance/time graphs

A distance/time graph indicates the distance travelled by an object after a certain time.

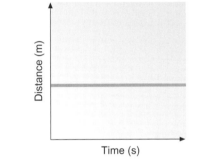

Fig. 3.08 Body stationary.

The body remains at the same distance over a period of time; it is not moving. For example, a hockey goalkeeper who is stationary before the penalty stroke is struck.

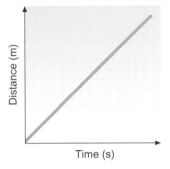

Fig. 3.09 Body moving with constant speed.

The body is moving the same amount of distance at a steady rate.

Gradient of graph = $\dfrac{\text{distance}}{\text{time}}$ = speed

Gradient of graphs remains constant, therefore speed remains constant, for example, a middle distance runner in the intermediate stages of the 1500m race.

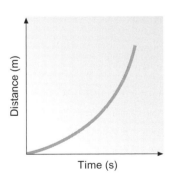

Fig. 3.10 Body is accelerating.

The distance travelled is increasing per unit of time. The gradient of the graph is increasing, therefore the speed is increasing and the body is accelerating – for example, a sprinter who is accelerating from the blocks over the first 20m of the race.

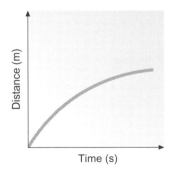

Fig. 3.11 Body is decelerating.

The distance travelled is decreasing per unit of time. The gradient of the graph is decreasing, therefore the speed is decreasing and the body is decelerating – for example, a downhill skier after the finish line who digs his or her edges into the softer snow to bring him or her to a standstill.

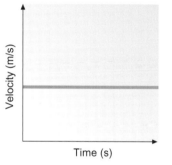

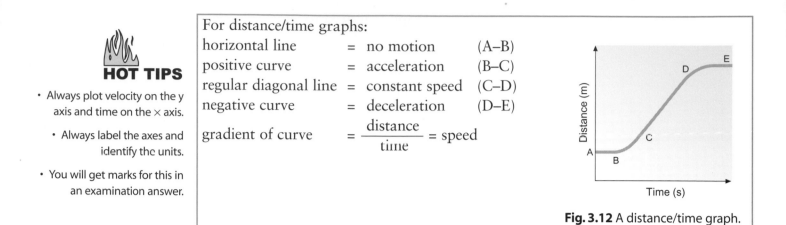

For distance/time graphs:

horizontal line	= no motion	(A–B)
positive curve	= acceleration	(B–C)
regular diagonal line	= constant speed	(C–D)
negative curve	= deceleration	(D–E)

$$\text{gradient of curve} = \frac{\text{distance}}{\text{time}} = \text{speed}$$

Fig. 3.12 A distance/time graph.

Velocity/time graphs

A velocity/time graph indicates the velocity of an object after a certain time.

Fig. 3.13 Body moving with constant velocity.

The body moves with the same velocity during regular time intervals – for example, a golfer walking towards his (or her) ball after his or her drive.

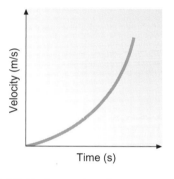

Fig. 3.14 Body accelerating.

The body is moving with increasing velocity. Gradient of graph =

$$\frac{\text{change in velocity}}{\text{time}} = \text{acceleration}$$

Gradient of graph increases – for example, a football accelerating from the spot at a penalty kick.

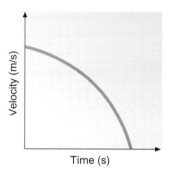

Fig. 3.15 Body decelerating.

The body is moving with decreasing velocity; gradient of graph decreases – for example, a cricket ball being caught by a wicket keeper.

TASK 5

For each of the graphs of motion plotted below:

1 state the pattern of motion taking place between the points identified
2 give an example from sport when a curve of this shape might be plotted.

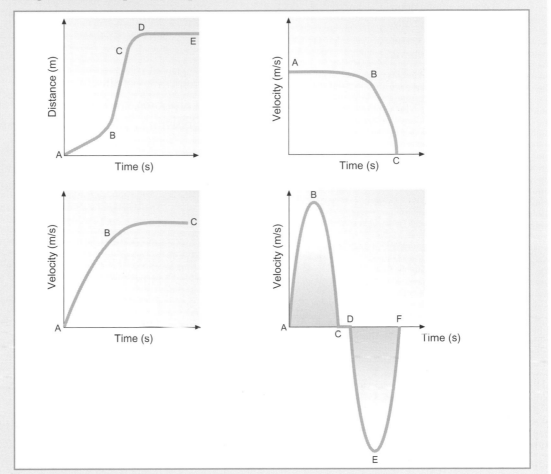

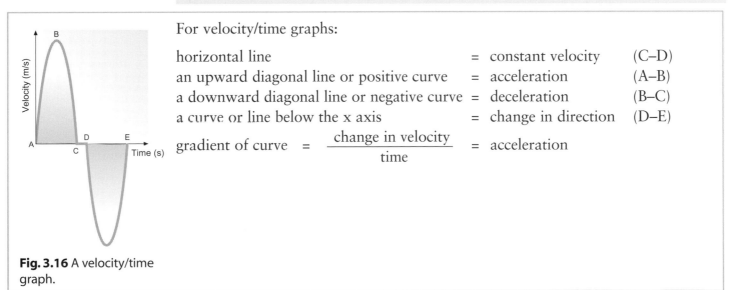

For velocity/time graphs:

horizontal line	= constant velocity	(C–D)
an upward diagonal line or positive curve	= acceleration	(A–B)
a downward diagonal line or negative curve	= deceleration	(B–C)
a curve or line below the x axis	= change in direction	(D–E)

$$\text{gradient of curve} = \frac{\text{change in velocity}}{\text{time}} = \text{acceleration}$$

Fig. 3.16 A velocity/time graph.

Momentum

KEY WORDS

Momentum

The amount of motion possessed by a moving body. Momentum is a vector quantity. Momentum is measured in kgm/s, as it is the product of mass in kg and velocity in m/s.

Momentum is the quantity of motion possessed by a body. It is the product of the body's mass and velocity. If the mass or the velocity increases, the momentum increases and vice versa.

$$\text{Momentum} = \text{mass} \times \text{velocity}$$
$$\text{Mo} = \text{m} \times \text{v}$$

From the equation for momentum, it follows that a stationary body with zero velocity has no momentum and only bodies that move have momentum. In sports movements there is little opportunity to increase or decrease mass and changes in momentum are entirely due to changes in velocity. For example, a 100m sprinter will have a greater momentum at 70m than at 10m because his velocity is greater (mass has remained unchanged).

Momentum plays a more important role in sports involving collisions or impacts. The result of the impact depends on the momentum of each of the colliding bodies just before impact. The greater the momentum of the body, the more pronounced the effect it has on the other body in its path. A good example here is in rugby: the legendary All Black winger Jonah Lomu has a large mass and the ability to run at a very high velocity. His momentum when at full speed is considerable and his opponents find it very difficult to stop or slow his forward momentum.

Fig. 3.17 The considerable momentum of Jonah Lomu has enabled him to charge through many tackles in his career.

HOT TIPS

Remember to show all your working and give the units of measurement.

TASK 6

1 Calculate the momentum of a downhill skier who has a mass of 69kg and is travelling with a velocity of 39m/s.

2 What is the momentum of athlete A whose mass is 65kg and who is running at 8.7m/s?

3 With what velocity would athlete B of mass 58kg need to run to have the same momentum as athlete A?

4 Explain the relevance of momentum to Newton's First and Second Laws of Motion.

Revise as you go! Test your knowledge and understanding

- Explain the following statement giving examples from sport: 'There can be no motion without force but there can be force without motion.'
- Explain the benefits for a rugby team having a heavier pack in the scrum.
- State the distance and the displacement travelled in each of the following examples: a 400m sprint on a 400m track; a 400m sprint on a 200m track; a 100m swim in a 50m pool; a 50m swim in a 25m pool; a 25m swim in a 25m pool.
- What is the difference between a scalar quantity and a vector quantity? List and define all vector quantities used in describing linear motion.
- Why does a bobsleigh take longer to stop at the end of its run than a luge?

Sharpen up your exam technique!

The table below gives data obtained from the IAAF Biomechanical Analysis Programme of the Seoul Olympic 100m finals.

Event Subject	Men's 100m final Ben Johnson	Event Subject	Women's 100m final Florence Griffiths Joyner
Time (s)	*Speed (m/s)*	*Time (s)*	*Speed (m/s)*
0.0	0.00	0.00	0.00
1.8	5.5	2.0	5.0
2.9	9.6	3.1	5.2
3.8	10.8	4.1	10.0
4.7	11.6	5.1	10.3
5.5	11.9	6.0	11.0
6.3	12.1	6.9	10.9
7.1	11.9	7.8	11.0
8.0	11.8	8.7	11.0
8.9	11.5	9.6	11.0
9.8	11.1	10.5	10.9

1 Draw a graph plotting speed against time for both sprinters. (5 marks)

2 Using the information from the graph answer the following.
   (a) Establish Johnson's speed at 0.5 seconds and 2.5 seconds.
      Calculate his average acceleration between 0.5 seconds and 2.5 seconds.
      (4 marks)
   (b) Establish Griffiths Joyner's speed at 0.5 seconds and 2.5 seconds.
      Calculate her average acceleration between 0.5 seconds and 2.5 seconds.
      (4 marks)

Section 2: *Force*

Learning objectives

At the end of this section you should be able to:
- give a definition and measurement of force and explain the effects of a force on a performer or object
- understand the concept of net force and balanced and unbalanced forces
- identify the nature of the forces acting on a sports performer: weight force, reaction force, friction force and air resistance force, and appreciate the effect that they have on the resulting motion of a performer
- sketch free body diagrams to identify the type and size of the forces acting on a sports performer at a particular moment in time
- understand impulse and how it relates to acceleration
- define work and power and give their units of measurement.

KEY WORDS

Force

A push or a pull that alters, or tends to alter, the state of motion of a body. Force is a vector quantity. Force is measured in Newtons (N).

Internal force

A force generated through contraction of skeletal muscle – for example, the force in the biceps brachii caused by concentric contraction to flex the elbow.

External force

A force that comes from outside the body – for example, weight, reaction, friction and air resistance.

Introduction

At AS level, you learned the effects that a **force** has on a body and applied these to different sporting situations. At A2 level, you will need to take your understanding of force considerably further and look at the specific forces that act on sports performers.

There are two types of force: **internal force** and **external force**. This section is concerned with external forces. Internal forces will be considered in Section 4, when we look at lever systems.

More about force

From Newton's laws we know that a body will not change its state of motion unless an external force acts on it and the larger the force, the greater the change in this state of motion. For example, the large force caused by the contact of the golf club head on a golf ball at a drive causes the ball to change from being stationary to moving very quickly.

It can be, however, that a force is not large enough to overcome the inertia of a body and change its state of motion. Think about a training session for rugby forwards who are practising their scrummaging technique against a scrummage machine. The pack is exerting a force, but it is not sufficient to move the machine.

When describing a force, three things need to be considered:

- the point of application of the force
- the size of the force
- the direction of the force.

Due to size and direction being important, force is a vector quantity. It can be calculated using the equation derived from Newton's second law:

$$\text{Force} = \text{mass} \times \text{acceleration}$$
$$F = m \times a$$

HOT TIPS

Remember to show all your working and give the units of measurement.

HOT TIPS

Refer to *Advanced PE for OCR, AS,* chapter 3, page 45.

TASK 7

1 A sprinter of mass 80kg accelerates at 6.8m/s^2 over the first 20m of the 100m sprint. Calculate the force required to achieve this.

2 Copy and complete the following table by stating the five effects that a force can have and give an example from your assessed practical activity for each.

Effect of force	Example from
1	
2	
3	
4	
5	

The fact that force is a vector quantity means that an arrow can represent it. Consider the example of the club head on the golf ball at a drive; the force being exerted can be represented by an arrow.

HOT TIPS

All forces must initiate from somewhere on the body in question. A force cannot be initiated from thin air.

Fig. 3.18 The force of the club head on the golf ball can be represented by an arrow.

It is vital that before drawing an arrow to represent a force, three important questions are answered.

• From where is the force applied?

• In what direction is the force applied?

• How big is the force applied?

Whenever an arrow is drawn to represent a force, three very important things need to be considered.

• *The point of application of the force* – shown by the point at which the arrow begins.
• *The direction of the force* – shown by the direction of the arrow.
• *The size of the force* – shown by the length of the arrow. The larger the force, the longer the arrow.

The force arrow must be accurate in terms of its point of application, its direction and its length to gain marks in an examination question.

Fig. 3.19a Question: From where is the force applied?
Answer: The point of application of the force is at the point of contact of the racket head with the ball.

Fig. 3.19b Question: In what direction is the force applied?
Answer: The force is applied in a forward direction.

Fig. 3.19c Question: How big is the force applied?
Answer: The force of the racket on a ball at a serve is large, therefore the arrow needs to be quite long.

An introduction to net force

KEY WORDS

Net force

The overall force acting on a body when all the individual forces have been considered. Net force is also termed 'resultant force'.

The concept of **net force** is sometimes a tricky one and will be more easily understood when the free body diagrams on pages 180–3 and 190–1 are examined. However, a quick introduction at this point is useful. The fact that force is a vector quantity and has both size and direction is very important as it means that a body can have two forces acting on it that are equal in size but opposite in direction. Consider the stalk stand, where the weight of the body acts vertically downwards but the reaction force from the ground, due to Newton's third law, acts vertically upwards. Both of these forces are equal in size but opposite in direction. There is

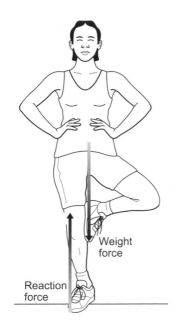

Fig. 3.20 In a balanced and stationary position there are at least two forces acting on a body. These forces are equal in size but opposite in direction. The net force = 0 and there is no change in the state of motion.

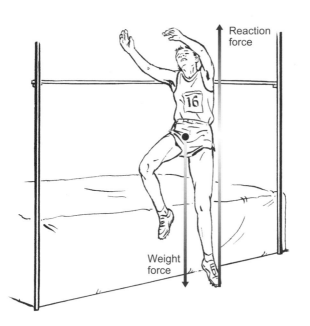

Fig. 3.21 The upward reaction force of the high jumper is greater than the downward weight force. There is a net force in the upward direction and the high jumper is able to leave the ground.

no net force, and from Newton's first law we know that there will be no change to the state of motion of the body and it remains stationary (Figure 3.20).

In the case of a high jumper at take off, the upward reaction force is bigger than the downward weight force. There is a net force in the upward direction. From Newton's first and second laws, we know that there will be a change in the state of motion of the high jumper in an upward direction (Figure 3.21).

Balanced forces

This is when two or more forces acting on a body are equal in size but opposite in direction. This can be true of forces in a vertical direction or forces in a horizontal direction, or both. In all cases the net force = 0 and there will be no change in the state of motion of the body; it will either remain stationary or moving with a constant velocity – for example, the stork stand shown in Figure 3.20.

Unbalanced forces

This is when a force acting in one direction on a body is greater in size than a force acting in the opposite direction. There will be a net force and the body will start to move or accelerate in the direction of the larger force – for example, the high jumper accelerating upwards in Figure 3.21.

TASK 8

Using arrows to represent forces, and being careful about their point of application, direction and size, draw the forces acting on the following bodies. Label each force with F (at this stage do not worry about their correct names). At the bottom of each diagram, make a comment about the net force and whether the forces are balanced or unbalanced.

A gymnast in an arabesque balance

A trampolinist at take off

A middle distance runner with constant speed

A sprinter accelerating from the blocks

Types of force acting on a sports performer

The external forces that act on a sports performer on the ground are best divided into vertical forces and horizontal forces.

Vertical forces: weight and reaction force
Horizontal forces: friction and air resistance

Forces acting on a body in water, such as a swimmer or a kayak, need to have different names.

Vertical forces: weight and buoyancy
Horizontal forces: forward force or thrust and drag (or fluid friction)

Vertical forces

Weight

Weight is the **gravitational force** that the Earth exerts on a body and that tends to pull the body towards the centre of the Earth – that is, downwards. The degree of pull between a body and the earth depends on the mass of the body.

Weight = mass × acceleration due to gravity
$$W = m \times g$$

For our purposes, gravitational acceleration (g) is approximated to 10m/s^2. The larger the mass of a body, the greater its weight.

Weight is always acting on all bodies on the Earth's surface.

TASK 9

1   Calculate the weight of a shot putter of mass 90kg.
2   Calculate the weight of a jockey of mass 55kg.

Remember to show your working and give the correct units of measurement.

Mass and weight are not the same. The mass of an athlete stays the same, but the weight of the athlete can change depending on his (or her) distance from the Earth's core. The further from the Earth's core an athlete stands, the less the Earth's pull on that athlete and the smaller the weight force acting on him. Consider two athletes of equal mass – one performing at the equator and the other performing at the North Pole. Due to the Earth not being perfectly round, the equator is further from the Earth's core than the North Pole and despite the athletes having the same mass, the athlete at the equator will have less weight to overcome than the athlete at the North Pole.

Fig. 3.22 Reaction forces occur whenever two bodies are in contact with each other.

Reaction force

Reaction forces come about because of Newton's Third Law of Motion. A reaction force will always act whenever two bodies are in contact with each other – for example, a sports performer in contact with the ground or a tennis ball in contact with the racket (Figure 3.22).

Horizontal forces

Friction force

Friction force occurs when a solid surface of a body moves or tends to move while in contact with the solid surface of another body. For example, it occurs between the soles of a runner's shoes and the running track, and to a lesser extent between the surface of the skis of a downhill skier and the snow. The confusing aspect of friction force is that it resists the slipping or sliding motion of the two surfaces. Consider Figure 3.23.

The amount of friction force an athlete requires varies dramatically from one sport to another. A runner will want to generate a large friction force to prevent his (or her) feet from slipping and slowing (his or her) forward acceleration. Track athletes wear spiked shoes to increase friction with the ground, whereas the skier in Figure 3.23 will want to minimise the friction force. Because it acts to slow his forward acceleration, he will wax his skis to ensure he glides smoothly over the snow's surface.

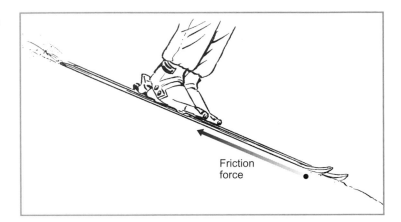

Fig. 3.23 The skis of the downhill skier slide downwards over the snow. Friction force acts against this motion and acts in the backward direction.

Fig. 3.24 Downhill ski racers minimise friction by waxing their skis according to the snow conditions.

TASK 10

1 Think of three examples from sport where an athlete will want to maximise friction. How does he or she achieve this?

2 Think of three examples from sport where an athlete will want to minimise friction. How does he or she achieve this?

KEY WORDS

Air resistance

The force acting in the opposite direction to the motion of a body travelling through air.

Drag

The force produced by the motion of a body in fluid (water or air).

HOT TIPS

The term 'drag force' is used to describe the force that acts in the opposite direction to motion of a body travelling through a fluid – that is, water or air. For the purposes of this book and to differentiate between air and water, the force opposing motion in air is referred to as 'air resistance' and the force opposing motion in water referred to as 'drag'.

Air resistance

Air resistance depends on the shape and surface characteristics of the body, the cross-sectional area of the body and the velocity of the body.

The size of the **drag** force not only depends on the shape, size and velocity of the moving body, but also on the type of fluid environment through which the body is travelling. Water has a greater density than air and is harder to push through. An athlete who runs from the beach into the sea, such as at the start of a triathlon competition, will encounter a greater drag force from the water than from the air.

Air resistance always acts in the opposite direction to the motion of the body. Air resistance opposes the acceleration of a body by pushing, pulling or tugging on an athlete. Consider a time when you may have been on a games field on a windy day and have tried to run into a strong headwind. You may have felt the force of air resistance pushing you back in the opposite direction.

There are a number of factors that affect the size of the air resistance force experienced by a body. These are:

- shape, surface characteristics and position of the body
- cross-sectional area of the body
- velocity of the body.

Factors 1 and 2 are related to streamlining. The more streamlined the body, the less air resistance it will encounter. A more aerodynamic shape and a smooth surface over which air can flow will reduce air resistance and allow greater acceleration.

Speed skiers keep air resistance to a minimum by crouching down low to present as small a cross-sectional area as possible to the oncoming wind. They also wear helmets that extend down to their shoulders, transforming the head and shoulders into a more streamlined shape. These factors, coupled with the smooth surface of their specially designed suits and boots, allow them to reach speeds in excess of 200km/hr

The greater the velocity of a body travelling through air, the greater the air resistance it will encounter. It is because of this fact that athletes try their utmost to use shape, surface characteristics and streamlining to keep air resistance to a minimum in an attempt to optimise forward acceleration.

Fig. 3.25 One of Britain's most successful cyclists ever, Chris Boardman won Olympic gold in Barcelona and set a new world record with the help of a revolutionary new aerodynamic bicycle. He also wore an aerodynamic helmet and lycra body suit.

HOT TIPS

The same factors affect the drag forces on swimmers. The more streamlined the swimmer and the smoother they can make the surface over which the water flows, the less affected by drag they will be. This is the reason behind the development of the full body 'shark suits' worn by many of today's top swimmers.

KEY WORDS

Free body diagram

A clearly labelled sketch showing all of the forces acting on an object at a particular moment in time. Figure 3.26 shows a free body diagram drawn to represent a runner who is accelerating.

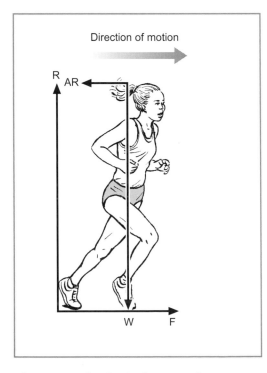

Direction of motion

Fig. 3.26 A free body diagram of a runner accelerating.

TASK 11

Consider the 100m sprint. Give two reasons why air resistance increases during the race. Try to relate your answer to the forward acceleration of the athlete at the start and end of the race.

Free body diagrams

Free body diagrams are used to show the forces acting on a body. The fact that a force is a vector quantity means that an arrow is used to represent it, and the position, direction and length of this arrow must be carefully considered to ensure that each force is represented as accurately as possible.

The four forces of weight, reaction, friction and air resistance can also be shown on a free body diagram in the form of an arrow. To help gain maximum marks in an examination question that requires a sketch of a free body diagram, insert the arrows to represent the forces in a specific order. First, consider the vertical forces.

- Draw on the weight force, as this will always be present.
- Draw on the reaction force(s) wherever there are two bodies in contact with each other, such as the athlete's foot with the ground or the hockey stick with the ball.

Second, consider the horizontal forces.

- Draw on the friction force(s) whenever there are two bodies in contact with each other that may have a tendency to slip or slide over each other, such as a swimmer's foot on the starting blocks.
- Draw on the air resistance force only if the body is moving. Remember that this force will be acting in the opposite direction to motion.

Figure 3.27 summarises the importance of the origin, direction and length of the arrows used to represent the four external forces discussed above.

	1 Weight (W)	2 Reaction (R)	3 Friction (F)	4 Air resistance (AR)
Origin of arrow	From the centre of mass	From the point(s) of contact of two bodies	From the point(s) of contact of two bodies	From the centre of mass
Direction of arrow	Vertically downward	Perpendicular to the surface of contact, usually vertically upward. (For the purposes of A2 biomechanics, it is easier to consider the **normal reaction** force that is drawn at right angles to the ground)	Opposite to the direction of the intended slipping action between the two bodies. This is usually in the same direction as motion	Opposite to the direction of motion of the body
Length of arrow	Dependent on the mass. Bodies with larger masses will have longer weight arrows than bodies with smaller masses	Dependent on the resulting motion and the length of the weight arrow. As a result of Newton's first and second laws: If R = W, net force = 0. If R > W, the body will accelerate upwards. If R < W, the body will. accelerate downwards	Dependent on the resulting motion and the length of the air resistance arrow	Dependent on the resulting motion and the length of the friction arrow. As a result of Newton's first and second laws: If F = AR, net force = 0. If F > AR, the body will accelerate. If F < AR, the body will decelerate
Label	W	R	F	AR
Diagram				

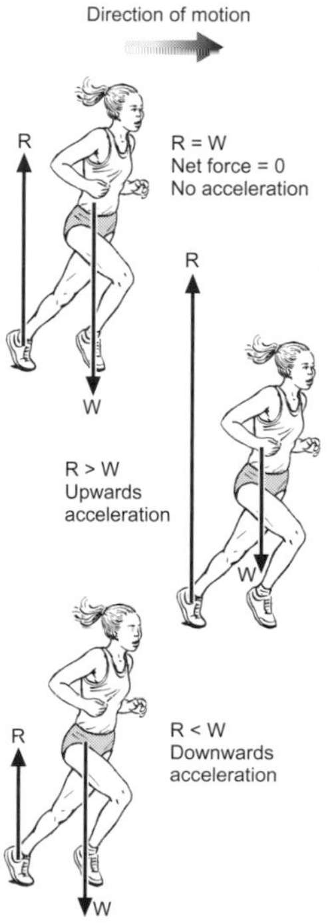

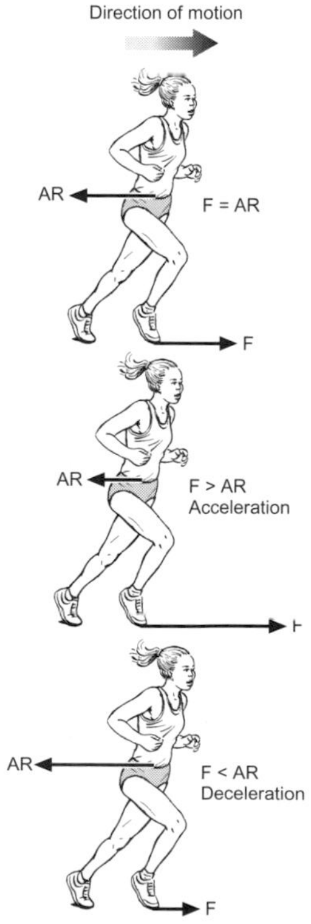

	1 **Weight (W)**	**2** **Reaction (R)**	**3** **Friction (F)**	**4** **Air resistance (AR)**
Notes	• Draw this arrow first • Weight will always act • There will only ever be one weight force per body	• Draw this arrow second • There will be no reaction force if there are no two bodies in contact • There could be more than one reaction arrow	• Draw this arrow third • There will be no friction force if there are no two bodies in contact • There could be more than one friction arrow	• Draw this arrow last • There will be no air resistance arrow if there is no motion • The greater the velocity of the body and the larger its cross-sectional area, the greater the air resistance and the longer the arrow

Fig. 3.27 A summary to show the accurate placement of arrows used to represent forces on free body diagrams.

HOT TIPS

To gain maximum marks in an examination question, a force arrow must be accurate in terms of:

• its point of application
• its direction
• its length.

KEY WORDS

Normal reaction force

The force between two bodies in contact with each other, in a direction perpendicular to the surface of contact.

Figure 3.28 shows three sketches of complete free body diagrams for a runner, showing all the forces acting on her at a particular moment in time: (a) shows the forces acting on her at the start of the race when she is accelerating; (b) shows the forces acting during the middle section of race as she travels with constant velocity; and (c) shows the forces acting on completion of the race when she is decelerating.

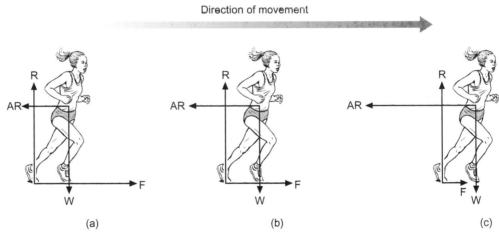

(a) Vertical forces: W = R, net force = 0, no acceleration
Horizontal forces: F > AR, forward acceleration

(b) Vertical forces: W = R, net force = 0, no acceleration
Horizontal forces: F = AR, net force = 0, no acceleration
Runner continues with constant velocity

(c) Vertical forces: W = R, net force = 0, no acceleration
Horizontal forces: F < AR, deceleration

Fig. 3.28 Free body diagram to show the forces acting on a runner during (a) acceleration, (b) constant speed, and (c) deceleration.

HOT TIPS

Three tips for sketching your own free body diagrams:

• use stick men or women
• draw a direction of motion arrow
• it is always a good idea to make a comment about the net force in the vertical direction and the net force in the horizontal direction below or beside your sketch – this will clarify to the examiner the relative sizes of the forces acting and will help you to gain maximum marks.

For example, in an examination question, if you were asked to sketch a free body diagram to show a swimmer on the blocks at the moment of take, your answer should be as follows:

Vertical forces: R > W, upward acceleration

Horizontal forces: F > AR, forward acceleration

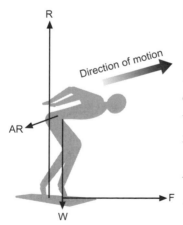

Therefore the swimmer accelerates upwards and forwards into the water.

In situations where there is more than one point of contact such as shown in Figure 3.29, you will need to be extra careful of the length to make the reaction arrows compared to the weight arrow, and the friction arrows compared to the air resistance arrow. Always remember that according to Newton's First Law, if there is no change to the state of motion of the body, there is no net force and all forces are balanced.

Vertical forces: R1 + R2 = W,
net force = 0, no acceleration
Horizontal forces: F1 + F2 = AR,
net force = 0, no acceleration

All forces are balanced; therefore there is no change in the state of motion and the skier travels with constant velocity.

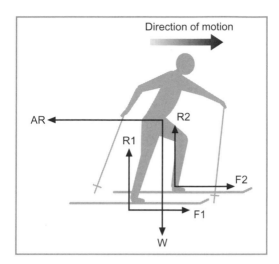

Fig. 3.29 Free body diagram of cross-country skier travelling at constant velocity.

TASK 12

Carefully cut out some action pictures from the sports pages of newspapers or magazines. Stick them onto sheets of plain paper and use them to draw on the forces that are acting. Remember to be very careful in terms of origin, direction and length of arrows, and do not forget to label your arrows clearly.

Impulse

From Newton's Laws we are familiar with the fact that force must be exerted to change the state of motion of a body. It also seems logical that the application of this force will take a certain amount of time. The term given to the product of the force and the time for which it acts is **impulse**.

Athletes can increase impulse in two ways.

• By increasing the amount of muscular force they apply. The greater the force, the greater the impulse. Consider the force that needs to be generated by a high jumper in the early rounds of a competition when the bar is relatively low compared to the force he or she will need to impart in the final stages of the competition when the bar is considerably higher.

KEY WORDS

Impulse

The product of force multiplied by the time for which the force acts.

$$\text{Impulse} = \text{force} \times \text{time}$$
$$I = Ft$$

The units of measurement for impulse are Newton seconds (Ns).

Fig. 3.30 A high jumper can increase impulse by generating a larger force at take off in order to clear a greater bar height.

• By increasing the amount of time over which they apply the force. The longer the time over which the force is applied, the greater the impulse. Consider the greater time for which the force is applied to a discus during a one-and-three-quarter turn compared to a standing throw.

The relative contributions of the size of the force and the time for which it acts will depend on the type of skill being performed. Some skills require a very large force to be applied over a short period of time, while other techniques require a smaller force to be applied for a longer period of time. Consider the force and time applied to a hockey ball during a hitting action compared to a pushing action.

Fig. 3.31 Elite throwers use a turning action across the throwing circle to increase the time over which the force is imparted to the shot/discus. This increases impulse and causes a greater outgoing velocity at the point of release.

TASK 13

1 Name two sporting skills that require a large force to be generated over a short period of time.

2 Name two sporting skills that require a smaller force to be applied over a

An increase in impulse will result in an increase in the rate of change of momentum, causing a larger outgoing velocity. Athletes are always looking to develop sports techniques to achieve a greater impulse.

All good high jumpers also use a technique to maximise impulse at take off. They lean backwards as they plant their take-off foot. This allows them to apply a force to the ground over a longer period of time as their body passes over the planted foot. This increased impulse causes a greater upward acceleration to help clear the bar.

TASK 14

Describe one sporting technique where it is important to optimise impulse, then explain how this is achieved.

Fig. 3.32 Ski jumpers flex at the hip, knee and ankle on landing to extend the time over which the force of impact with the snow acts.

Knowledge of impulse can also be used to slow down or stop a body safely. There are many sports in which athletes are taught specific techniques so that they extend the time that forces act on their bodies to avoid injury. Consider the significant forces that are imparted to the body of a ski jumper on landing. By flexing at the hip, knee and ankle on contact with the snow, the time during which the forces are applied to the jumper on landing is increased and the impact on the body at this moment in time is significantly decreased. This is the reason why all children are coached always to bend their knees on landing.

Graphical representation of impulse

Impulse can be represented by the area under a force/time graph. Figure 3.33 shows a force/time graph that can be sketched during a tennis forehand ground stroke.

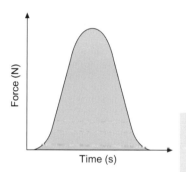

Fig. 3.33 A force/time graph for a forehand drive. The shaded area represents impulse.

TASK 15

1 Sketch a force/time graph for the following situations:
   (a) a hockey ball being hit without follow through
   (b) a hockey ball being hit with follow through.
2 Discuss the advantages of using a follow through in sporting techniques where a large outgoing velocity is required.

KEY WORDS

Work

Work is the product of force multiplied by the distance through which the resistance is moved.

Work done = force × distance moved

W = F × d

The units of measurement for work are joules (j).

Work and power

Work is done when a force is applied to a body to move it over a certain distance. For example, work is performed by a right wing in hockey who dribbles the ball from the half-way line into his or her attacking twenty-five.

Power refers to the amount of work done in a particular period of time. Power is tremendously important in all sports as they rely on the ability to perform work at very high speeds. For example, consider the speed at which a gymnast performs a tumbling routine in the floor exercise or the speed demonstrated during the turn of a hammer during the build up to release.

KEY WORDS

Power

Power is the rate at which work is done.

$$\text{Power} = \frac{\text{work done}}{\text{time taken}}$$
$$= \frac{\text{force} \times \text{distance}}{\text{time taken}}$$

The units of measurement for power are watts (w).

HOT TIPS

If there is no movement resulting from the application of a force, no work is done. For example, an athlete who tries to lift a weight that is too heavy and fail, has not performed work because the weight has not moved and no distance has been covered.

• Remember to show all your working and give the units of measurement.

TASK 16

Figure 3.34 shows two powerful athletes exerting a force of 1250N to move a barbell a distance of 0.7m.

1   Calculate the work done by one of the athletes.
2   Athlete A lifts the weight in 0.04 seconds, while athlete B lifts the weight in 0.08 seconds. Calculate the power outputs of athletes A and B.

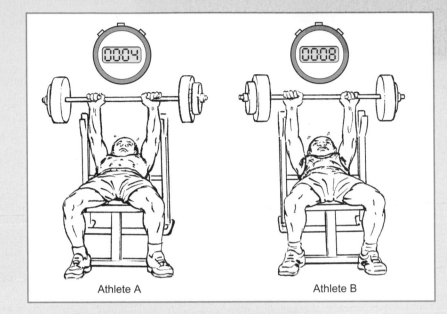

Athlete A   Athlete B

Fig. 3.34 Athletes exerting force to move a barbell.

Revise as you go! Test your knowledge and understanding

• What is meant by the following words?
   a) Force   b) Net force   c) Balance force   d) Unbalanced force
• List the forces that act on a sports performer on the ground.
• List the forces that act on a swimmer in the pool.
• Using examples from a sport of your choice:
   a) give one example of how friction is increased
   b) give one example of how friction is decreased
   c) give one example of how air resistance is increased
   d) give one example of how air resistance is decreased.
• Sketch a free body diagram of a sports person of your choice showing all the forces acting on them at a particular moment in time.
• A female athlete is performing a series of bench presses in the gym using a weight of 500N.
   a) If her arms are 0.6m in length, how much work does she do in a single bench press?
   b) If she performs sets of 15 reps, how much work does she do in one set?

c) If a set of bench presses takes her 40 seconds, calculate the power exerted to perform a single set.

Sharpen up your exam technique!

1   One of the highlights for Great Britain in the Nagano Winter Olympics of 1998 was their bronze medal in the four-man bobsleigh. This particular event involves the generation of an extremely large momentum.
   (a) (i)   Define the term momentum and explain why a downhill skier travelling at 30m/s has a different momentum to a four-man bobsleigh travelling with the same velocity.   (2 marks)
       (ii)   If the total force generated by the team at the start of the run is 5000N over 30m in 5.4 seconds, calculate the work done and the power output of the team for this section of the run.   (4 marks)
   (b)   Once in motion a form of fluid friction will be acting on the bobsleigh and its team members.
       (i)   Identify the nature of this fluid friction force and describe the factors that will determine its size.   (3 marks)
       (ii)   How does the bobsleigh minimise the effect of fluid friction during the run?   (2 marks)

2   The follow through is an important aspect of a ground stroke in tennis.
   (i)   Sketch a graph of force against time to show the force applied by the racket on the ball during a forehand ground stroke in tennis.   (2 marks)
   (ii)   Explain how the use of follow through would affect the motion of the ball.   (4 marks)

Section 3: *Projectile motion*

Learning objectives

At the end of this section you should be able to:
*   identify the factors before take off that determine the trajectory of the flight path of a projectile and appreciate how these factors can be optimised
*   sketch free body diagrams to identify the type and size of the forces acting on a projectile during flight
*   determine the resultant or net force acting on the projectile and explain its effect on the shape of the flight path
*   understand the Bernoulli Principle and apply its concepts to sporting situations

KEY WORDS

Projectiles

Human bodies or objects launched into the air that are subject only to the forces of weight and air resistance.

- describe the four types of spin commonly observed in sporting activities: top spin, back spin, hook and slice
- sketch detailed diagrams to help explain how the Magnus effect causes spinning projectiles to deviate from their non-spinning flight paths.

Introduction

In sport there are a considerable number of events in which bodies are projected into the air to follow a certain flight path. These bodies can either be an athlete who propels him or herself into the air (such as a high jumper or a long jumper in athletics), or can be an object that an athlete hits, kicks or throws into the air (such as a shot put or badminton shuttle). Whenever athletes break contact with the ground or objects are released, they become **projectiles**.

This section will look at the types of projectile that are observed in sporting events and will consider the factors that affect their flight paths before and after take off. This analysis will lead on to looking at the effect of spin on the flight path of a projectile.

The release of projectiles

In sports events that incorporate flight, several factors associated with the release of a projectile influence the flight path followed by the projectile. The horizontal distance that a projectile travels during its flight depends on a combination of three factors:

- the angle of release
- the velocity of the projectile at the moment of release
- the height at which the projectile is released.

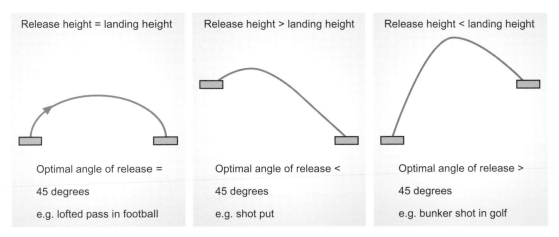

Fig. 3.35 Optimal angles of release depending on the relative heights of release and landing.

Angle of release

To achieve maximum horizontal distance, the optimum angle of release for a projectile is 45 degrees. However, this is only true where the release height is equal to the landing height, such as a footballer executing a lofted pass to the foot of another team mate. This situation is not very common in sporting techniques. It is more common for the release height to be greater than the landing height. When this situation occurs, such as in the shot put event, the optimum angle of release is less than 45 degrees. In a situation where the release height is below the landing height, such as executing a bunker shot in golf, the optimum angle of release needs to be greater than 45 degrees.

TASK 17

For the activities listed, decide whether the optimum angle of release is 45 degrees, less than 45 degrees or greater than 45 degrees.

- Racing dive in swimming
- High jump
- Ski jump
- Under-arm serve in volleyball
- Long jump
- Tennis serve

Velocity of release

Increasing the release velocity of a projectile will increase the horizontal distance travelled. Athletes work very hard to optimise their take off or release velocity. Consider the importance of speed during the run up to the long jump event: the greater the velocity of the athlete at take off, the greater the horizontal distance covered. Another example is the considerable speed of rotation achieved by a hammer thrower as he or she travels across the circle prior to release.

Height of release

In a simplified statement, it can be said that as height of release is increased, horizontal distance travelled is increased for a given angle and velocity of release. Consider two shot put athletes, one taller than the other. Providing the angle and velocity of release are the same for both the athletes, the taller athlete will achieve a greater distance than the shorter athlete because his (or her) height of release is greater.

Fig. 3.36 With angle and velocity of release equal, greater horizontal distance is achieved by increasing the height of release.

Projectiles and forces in flight

Once propelled into the air, projectiles are acted upon by two forces: weight and air resistance. The relative sizes of these forces will affect the flight path.

Projectiles that have a large weight force and small air resistance force, such as a shot put, follow paths close to a true **parabola**. As the effect of air resistance increases, the more a projectile will deviate from a true parabola. Objects that travel at very high speeds (for example, golf balls) objects that have a large cross-

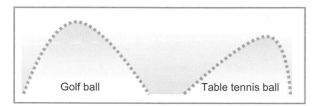

Fig. 3.37 Objects with larger masses are least affected by the force of air resistance.

sectional area (for example, footballs) and objects that do not have a smooth outer surface (for example, shuttle cocks) are most affected by air resistance and therefore follow flight paths that deviate from a true parabola. It is also true that the relative contribution of air resistance compared to weight increases as the mass of an object decreases. Consider a golf ball and a table tennis ball being projected into the air with the same angle, height and velocity of release. The golf ball will follow a flight path closer to a true parabola than the table tennis ball because it is heavier.

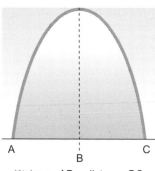

A   C

B

Distance AB = distance BC

HOT TIPS

The flight paths of a javelin and discus are slightly different in that they are affected by a third force of lift due to the Bernoulli Principle. This is explained further on pages 193–4.

TASK 18

Presuming that the following projectiles are launched into the air with the same angle, velocity and height of release, estimate whether their flight paths will be a true parabola or a distorted parabola.

- Cricket ball
- Football
- Hockey ball
- Shot put
- Discus

- Javelin
- Basketball
- Tennis ball
- Badminton shuttle

Projectiles and free body diagrams

The forces acting on a projectile in flight can be represented using a free body diagram. The importance of the origin, direction and length of the arrow used to represent weight and air resistance still holds true. The greater the mass of the projectile, the longer the weight force arrow needs to be. The greater the velocity or cross-sectional area of the projectile, the longer you must make the air resistance arrow.

HOT TIPS

Once in flight, the projectile is not in contact with another body and so projectiles are never affected by reaction or friction forces. The only two forces acting on the projectile are weight and air resistance.

To look at the effect of varying contributions of weight compared to air resistance on flight paths, consider two extremes of projectile: the shot put and the badminton

HOT TIPS

When drawing free body diagrams of projectiles, always remember to include the direction of motion arrow.

shuttle. Looking at the forces acting on the shot put, the weight force will be greater than the air resistance force. The shot put is heavy and has a relatively small cross-sectional area compared to its mass. It also has a reasonably smooth outer surface and is normally projected into the air at a lesser velocity than a badminton shuttle that has been hit by a fast-moving racket. These three factors mean that the air resistance force acting on a shot put is relatively small. A free body diagram for the shot put during flight is shown in Figure 3.38.

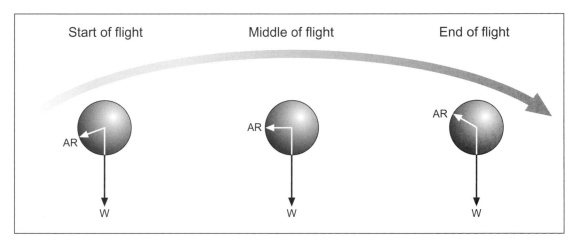

Fig. 3.38 Free body diagram to show the forces acting on a shot put during various stages of flight.

On the other hand, the shuttle is very light and has a feathery outer surface that will affect the airflow over it quite considerably. Consider a shuttle that has been high served: its outgoing velocity is very high, as it has been struck with a large force by the head of the racket. For these reasons, it is greatly affected by air resistance at the start of its flight. The effect of air resistance reduces during flight as the shuttle slows down. A free body diagram for the shuttle during flight is shown in Figure 3.39.

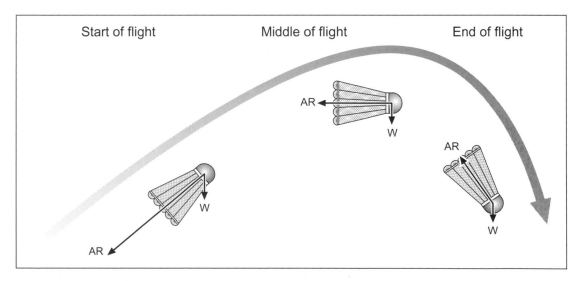

Fig. 3.39 Free body diagram to show the forces acting on a shuttle during various stages of flight.

Resultant force

A single force that represents the sum of all the forces acting on a body.

Parallelogram of forces

A single **resultant force** can represent the two forces of weight and air resistance that act on a projectile.

The direction and length of the resultant force is determined by sketching a parallelogram of forces. Figure 3.40, (a) and (b), shows how sketching a parallelogram of forces on a shot put and a shuttle in flight enables the two forces of weight and air resistance to be replaced by a single resultant force.

HOT TIPS

To ensure the correct direction and size of a resultant force, use the force arrows of weight and air resistance as two sides of a parallelogram and construct the missing sides geometrically. Draw in a diagonal from the origin of the forces to the opposite corner of the parallelogram. This arrow is the resultant force.

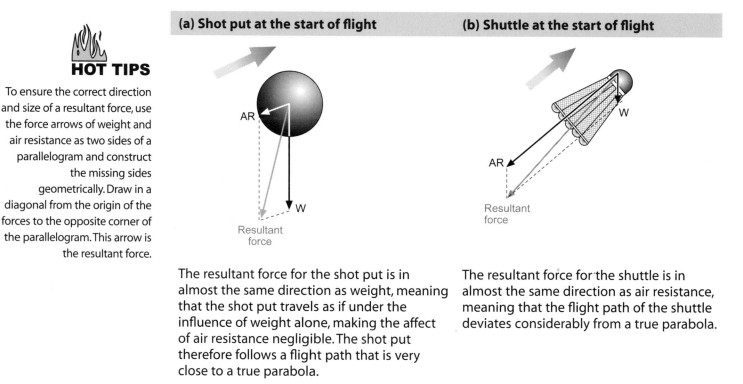

(a) Shot put at the start of flight

(b) Shuttle at the start of flight

The resultant force for the shot put is in almost the same direction as weight, meaning that the shot put travels as if under the influence of weight alone, making the affect of air resistance negligible. The shot put therefore follows a flight path that is very close to a true parabola.

The resultant force for the shuttle is in almost the same direction as air resistance, meaning that the flight path of the shuttle deviates considerably from a true parabola.

HOT TIPS

Remember to:

• include a direction of motion arrow
• be careful of the origin, direction and length of your arrows
• consider the mass, velocity and cross-sectional area of the projectile when deciding on the relative lengths of your arrows.

Fig. 3.40 Using the parallelogram of forces to show the resultant force acting on a shot put and a shuttle at the start of flight.

TASK 19

Sketch a free body diagram for each of the projectiles listed below. Construct a parallelogram of forces to show the resultant force acting on each body and comment on the type of flight path the projectile will follow.

• Long jumper • Tennis ball • Football • Golf ball

Projectiles and lift

If a projectile can gain some lift during flight, it will stay in the air for a longer time and achieve a greater horizontal distance. This is the concept behind the flight path of the discus and the javelin. To be able to fully appreciate the principle that causes a lift effect on these projectiles, it helps to understand how the wing of an aeroplane works.

KEY WORDS

Bernoulli Principle

Named after the Swiss mathematician, Daniel Bernoulli, this principle states that air or water molecules exert less pressure the faster they travel and more pressure the slower they travel. Bernoulli showed that:

• where flow is slow, pressure is high
• where flow is fast, pressure is low.

The wing of an aeroplane is shaped like an aerofoil with a curved upper surface and a flat lower surface. As the aerofoil travels through the air, the curved upper surface pushes air up over the wing and makes it travel further than the air that is deflected underneath the wing's flatter lower surface. The air above the wing travels at a faster velocity than the air below the wing. Faster air has a lower pressure than slower air and this pressure differential works to suck the wing upwards creating lift. The principle behind this is the **Bernoulli Principle**. Figure 3.41 shows the Bernoulli Principle working on an aerofoil.

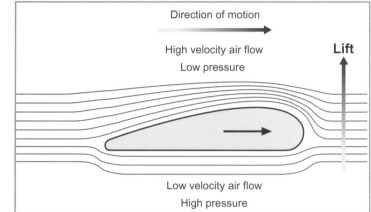

Fig. 3.41 Lift produced by airflow over an aerofoil. High pressure below the wing and low pressure above it causes a lift effect.

From your understanding of respiration, it is straightforward to remember that all gases will flow from areas of high pressure to areas of low pressure. Whenever the Bernoulli Principle is relevant to a projectile, it will be pushed from areas of high pressure to areas of low pressure as the air molecules try to move across the pressure differential.

HOT TIPS

To help remember the Bernoulli Principle, it is quite useful to learn a little rhyme:
Fast flow
Pressure low.

Task 20

Cut a sheet of A4 paper in half. Grip the end corners of the paper in both hands between finger and thumb. Hold the paper so that it is just touching the bottom of your lower lip and blow hard over the top of the paper. Observe what happens.

It is the Bernoulli Principle that explains the lift force imparted to the discus during flight. At the point of release, a good discus thrower will present the discus at such

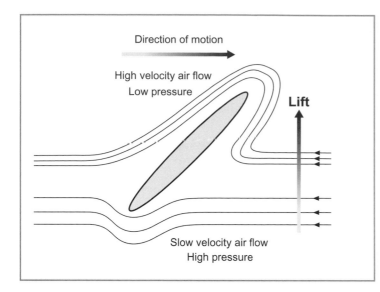

Fig. 3.42 The airflow patterns created by a discus flying at the correct angle produce a lift force that increases the horizontal distance covered.

an angle that the air that travels over the top of the discus has to travel a longer distance than the air that travels underneath. The air above the discus travels faster than the air below, creating a lower pressure above the discus than below. This creates a lift force on the discus that allows it to stay in the air for longer and achieve a greater horizontal distance. This principle is illustrated in Figure 3.42.

TASK 21
Sketch a similar diagram to Figure 3.42 to show the Bernoulli Principle working during the flight of a javelin.

It is important to appreciate that the term 'lift' does not need to imply a force in an upward direction. Motor racing cars have spoilers attached to them that are angled in such a way that the lift force created by the Bernoulli Principle acts in a downward direction. This pushes the car into the track, creating a greater frictional force to enable the tyres to stick to the track better, making it safer to turn corners at speeds in excess of 200km/h.

Projectiles and spin

Magnus effect

Named after a German scientist, Gustav Magnus, this principle explains the deviation of the flight path of a spinning projectile towards the direction of spin. For example, if a golf ball is spinning to the right, the Magnus effect causes the flight path of the golf ball to deviate to the right. For a right-handed golfer, this is slice.

Imparting spin to a projectile at the point of release will affect the flight path. The spin changes the airflow patterns around the projectile to cause it to deviate from its original flight path. The principle causing this deviation in flight direction is called the **Magnus effect**.

Before a full explanation of the Magnus effect and its application to sporting techniques, it is important to familiarise ourselves with the types if spin that are observed in sporting activities. We need to be familiar with the effects of four types of spin:

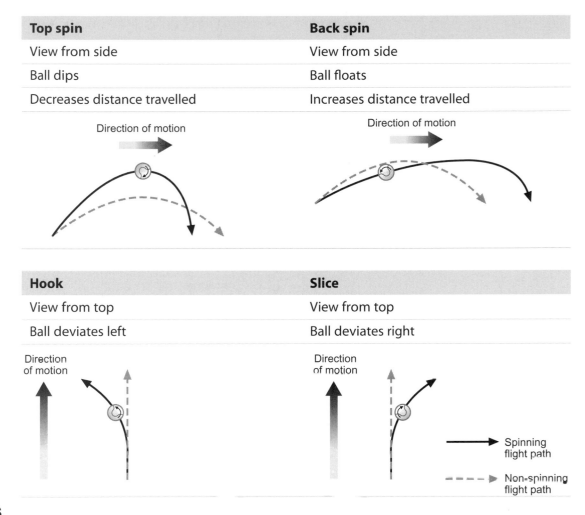

Fig. 3.43 The deviations in flight path caused by imparting spin to a projectile at the point of release.

HOT TIPS

The direction in which a projectile deviates having been imparted with side spin depends on whether it has been struck by a right-handed or left-handed person. To simplify matters for the purposes of this book, all explanations of side spin will be applied to a right-handed person. You will be able to score maximum marks in an examination question on this topic if you do the same. However, it is a good idea to state that your explanations refer to a right-handed person somewhere in your answer.

To ensure you score maximum marks when sketching diagrams to show the deviation in flight path caused by spin, do the following.

- Correctly label your sketch with the type of spin being shown.
- State whether the sketch is viewed from the side (for top and back spin) or the top (for side spin).
- Use an arrow to indicate the direction of motion.
- Show the direction of spin of the projectile using an arrow inside the object.
- Sketch the non-spinning flight path as well as the spinning flight path so that the deviation is obvious.
- State the effect of the spin, that is, top spin (dips), back spin (floats), hook (deviates left), slice (deviates right).

The Magnus effect

The Magnus effect is important in all sports in which sports performers want to bend the flight of a ball. We commonly see the Magnus effect at work in soccer, tennis, golf and table tennis. David Beckham is one footballer who is internationally renowned for his magical ability to curve free kicks around a wall of defenders and into the top corners of the goal. Tennis players also utilise the Magnus effect by hitting balls with considerable top spin. Due to the dipping effect of this type of spin, it allows them to hit the ball extremely hard while ensuring it still bounces before the base line.

Task 22

Without repeating the information given above, identify examples from the following sports of when the Magnus effect is utilised:

- Soccer
- Golf
- Tennis
- Table tennis

The Magnus effect affects the flight path of spinning balls in the following manner. As a spinning ball moves through the air, its spinning surfaces will affect the airflow around it. As an initial explanation, let us consider a tennis ball that has been hit with top spin.

Top spin

To understand Figure 3.44 it is useful to consider the two surfaces of the ball that affect the air flow separately.

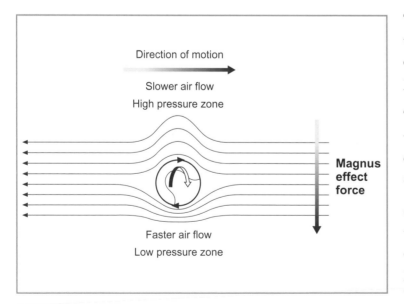

Fig. 3.44 Top spin: view from the side.

The top of the ball: the surface of the ball is travelling in the opposite direction to airflow. This causes the air to decelerate and creates a high pressure (the Bernoulli effect).

The bottom of the ball: the surface of the ball is travelling in the same direction as the airflow. This causes the air to accelerate and the faster moving air sets up a lower pressure (the Bernoulli effect).

Consequence: this pressure differential, high on the top surface and low on the bottom surface, causes the ball to deviate towards the area of low pressure. In the case of top spin, the ball dips and the distance travelled is decreased from the non-spinning flight path.

Back spin

The same explanation can be given for back spin.

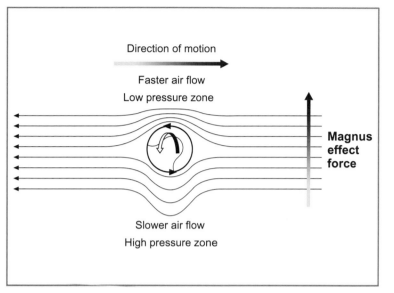

Fig. 3.45 Back spin: view from the side.

The top of the ball: the surface of the ball is travelling in the same direction as the airflow. This causes the air to accelerate and the faster moving air sets up a lower pressure (the Bernoulli effect).

The bottom of the ball: the surface of the ball is travelling in the opposite direction to airflow. This causes the air to decelerate and creates a high pressure (the Bernoulli effect).

Consequence: this pressure differential, low on the top surface and high on the bottom surface, causes the ball to deviate towards the area of low pressure. In the case of back spin, the ball floats and the distance travelled is increased from its non-spinning flight path.

To ensure you score maximum marks when sketching and explaining Magnus effect diagrams, follow these eleven stages.

1 Label the type of spin to be sketched (top/back/hook/slice).
2 Identify the best way to view the diagram (side view/top view).
3 Show clearly the direction of motion arrow.
4 Draw the projectile.
5 Insert an arrow inside the projectile to show the direction of spin.
6 Place an arrow on the affected surfaces of the projectile to show their direction of travel (that is, opposite to or in the same direction as the airflow).
7 Draw in the airflow lines.
8 State where airflow velocity is fast and where airflow velocity is slow.
9 Using your knowledge of the Bernoulli principle, state where pressure is high and where pressure is low.
10 Insert the overall Magnus effect force arrow.
11 Explain your diagram by taking each surface in turn and writing the consequence.

Task 23

Copy and complete the following table for the two types of side spin. Remember to ensure that you have included the eleven stages listed above.

Type of spin	Hook	Slice
Diagram		
	Explanation	Explanation
At the left-hand surface		
At the right-hand surface		
Consequence		

The effect of spin on bouncing

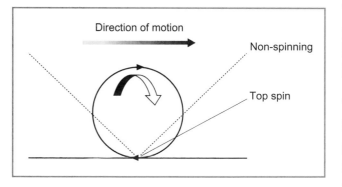

Fig. 3.46 The effect of top spin on bounce.

When spin is imparted to a ball, it not only affects its flight path but also its bounce. Our understanding of friction will help to explain the effect of spin on bounce. Again, let us begin with top spin.

The bottom surface of the ball that hits the ground on the bounce wants to slide backwards along the surface of the ground. Friction will oppose this sliding motion and therefore act in a forward direction, causing the ball to skim off the surface quickly at a low angle from the ground. Tennis players like to hit the ball with top spin as

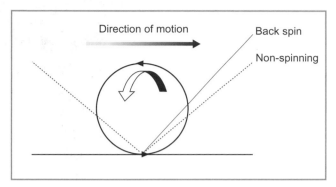

Fig. 3.47 The effect of back spin on bounce.

it causes the ball to increase speed on bouncing, giving their opponent less time to play their shot.

The opposite is true for back spin. The bouncing surface of the ball wants to slide forwards along the ground. Friction will oppose this sliding motion and act in the backward direction causing the ball to kick up from the surface at a large angle from the ground. Some table tennis players can impart so much back spin that they make the ball land on their opponent's side of the table, then jump back across the net. Back spin is also paramount to successful shooting in basketball. A basketball shot with back spin will help the ball sink into the net after rebounding from the backboard. The surface of the basketball that hit the backboard wants to slide upwards. Therefore, the opposing friction force will act downwards to direct the ball into the ring.

Knowledge of the effect of spin on bouncing is also important to golfers. In golf, back spin imparted to the golf ball by the club head not only helps to float the ball a further distance, but also helps to control its landing.

Revise as you go! Test your knowledge and understanding

- Explain how the following factors affect the flight path of a projectile: angle of release; weight of the projectile; air resistance.
- State simply the principle behind the Bernoulli effect. Explain how the Bernoulli principle can be applied to ski jumpers.
- Name the type of spin that has been imparted to produce the effects in the following examples:
  a) a golf drive where the ball has curved to the right
  b) a table tennis shot where the ball has floated over the net to land deep on the other side of the table.
- Name the type of spin not described in the question above. Describe its effect on the flight path and the bounce of the ball. Using a sporting example of your choice, explain the advantages of using this type of spin.

Sharpen up your exam technique!

1 When a goalkeeper in soccer takes a goal kick, certain factors at the point of release will affect the horizontal distance covered by the football. Name these factors and explain how the goalkeeper can achieve maximum horizontal range.
(6 marks)

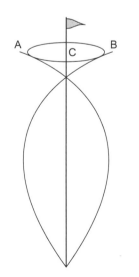

2 A right-handed golfer drives the ball from the tee. The diagram on the left shows the bird's eye view of three possible flight paths.
  a) The flight path labelled C shows a straight and accurate shot that has been hit with backspin. Sketch the same flight path from a side view and

comment on its shape. Name the effect that produces this flight path.

(4 marks)

b) Flight paths A and B show the direction the ball will follow when hit with side spin. Identify the type of spin acting in B and draw a detailed diagram to show the air flow patterns around the ball. Show and explain the resulting motion that this type of spin will cause. (5 marks)

c) Name the forces that act on the golf ball during flight and sketch two diagrams showing the relative sizes of these forces for: (i) a match golf ball (ii) a plastic air flow golf ball. Draw the resultant force on each diagram and use this to explain how the flight paths differ. (10 marks)

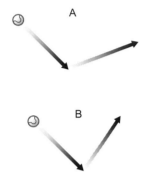

3 Spin will affect the bounce of a ball. The diagrams on the left show the effect of two types of spin on the bounce of a tennis ball.

Identify the type of spin used in A and B and sketch their flight paths prior to bouncing. (4 marks)

Section 4: *Angular motion*

Learning objectives

At the end of this section you should be able to:
- review your understanding of centre of mass and its relationship to balance and rotation
- appreciate that a change in body position causes a change in the position of the centre of mass and that the centre of mass can lie outside the body
- classify the three types of lever system and give specific anatomical examples of where each class of lever can be located in the human body
- define, calculate and give the units of measurement for the moment of a force
- understand the principle of moments and use this to calculate a balancing force for a particular lever system
- identify the three major axes of rotation and give examples of sporting movements that occur around them
- define and give units of measurement for angular motion terminology: angular distance, angular displacement, angular speed, angular velocity and angular acceleration
- understand the relevance of moment of inertia and angular momentum to rotating bodies
- explain the law of conservation of angular momentum and give examples of how athletes use this principle in sports such as trampolining, diving, slalom skiing and running.

Angular motion

When a body or part of a body moves in a circle or part of a circle about a particular point called the axis of rotation – for example, the giant circle on the high bar in men's' Olympic gymnastics.

HOT TIPS

When answering examination questions on biomechanics, the examiners will be looking for your ability to use the correct scientific terminology, so it is important that you understand the meaning behind the key words given in this section and that you try to use them in your answers. This is particularly true if you chose to answer the scientific question in the Synoptic paper. Be warned, however, that you will need to show you understand the meaning of the terminology you use. You will not be credited marks for simply writing a key word that is out of context.

HOT TIPS

Information on numbers 1, 2, 3 and 4 above can be obtained by revising centre of mass in Chapter 3, *Advanced PE for OCR AS*, pages 47–51. To ensure you have a good understanding of this knowledge, complete Task 24.

Introduction

In this section we will revise centre of mass and look at how the human body uses leverage during sporting activities and discuss the advantages and disadvantages of the three classes of lever system used by the body.

This leads on to rotation. Most movements in sport involve some form of rotation. Effective performance in any sporting activity that requires an athlete to somersault, twist, spin, turn, swing or circle will be reliant on an understanding of the principles behind **angular motion**. As you read through this section, you will be able to see the similarities between the principles governing angular motion and the principles governing linear motion that we looked at in Section 1 of this chapter. You will recognise words from Section 1 such as displacement or velocity, but in this section these quantities are preceded by the word 'angular', so you should become accustomed to using the terms 'angular displacement' or 'angular velocity'.

Centre of mass

In an A2 biomechanics question on centre of mass you could be asked about any of the following.

1 Definition and explanation of centre of mass.
2 How the position of the centre of mass, the size of the base of support and the position of the line of gravity relate to stability.
3 How the position of the application of force in relation to the centre of mass affects whether the resulting motion is linear or angular.
4 How the position of the centre of mass can change with alterations in body position.
5 How the centre of mass can lie outside the body and how this can benefit sporting techniques such as the Fosbury flop technique in the high jump.

Task 24

Having read Chapter 3 in *Advanced PE for OCR AS* (pages 47–51), answer the following questions.

1 Give a brief explanation of the following key words, using diagrams where helpful:
   (a) centre of mass
   (b) stability
   (c) line of gravity
   (d) base of support
   (e) direct force
   (f) eccentric force.

2   Using your knowledge of stability, copy and complete the following table.

Contributing factor	Stable body	Unstable body
Position of centre of mass		
Size of base of support		
Position of line of gravity		

3   Complete the following sentence.
    A body becomes unstable when _____

4   Give one example from sport when a body needs to be stable.

5   Give one example from sport when a body needs to be unstable.

6   Explain the relationship between the position of the centre of mass and the line of action of a force when applied to producing:
    a) linear motion
    b) angular motion.

7   Explain briefly how an athlete can manipulate the position of his or her centre of mass.

8   Give an example of a body position in which the position of the centre of mass will move outside the body.

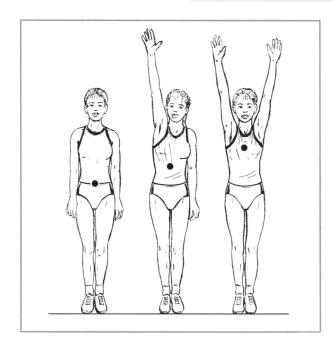

Fig. 3.48 A change in body position causes a shift in the position of the centre of mass. The amount of shift is dependent on the mass of the body parts moved and the distance they have moved.

The final element of centre of mass to be discussed relates to altering its position within or outside the body to produce more efficient sporting techniques. An athlete's centre of mass rarely stays in the same place for very long, as a change in body position will cause a shift in the position of the centre of mass. The distance moved by the centre of mass will depend on the amount of body mass moved and how far it has moved. For example, raising both arms above the head will cause a greater upward shift in the centre of mass than raising just one arm.

Flexible athletes are able to move their body parts through such a large range that they can shift their centre of mass a considerable distance. A gymnast performing a bridge has the majority of mass below her hips. This causes a large shift in the position of the centre of mass, so that it moves outside her body.

The body position of a high jumper using the Fosbury flop is very similar to that of a bridge in gymnastics. In this

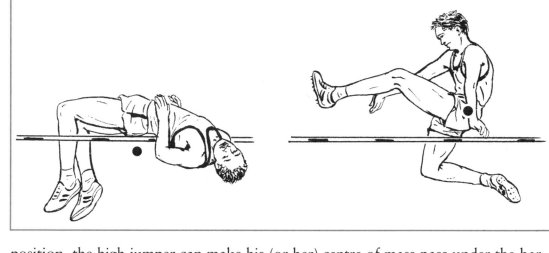

Fig. 3.49 A high jumper using the Fosbury flop technique does not need to lift his (or her) centre of mass 2.10m to clear the height, whereas for the scissors technique the jumper must lift his centre of mass more than 2.10m.

position, the high jumper can make his (or her) centre of mass pass under the bar while his body clears it. Compare this to the scissors technique, where the high jumper must lift his centre of mass over the bar in order to clear the same height. A jumper using the Fosbury flop technique does not have to lift his centre of mass such a great distance in order to clear the bar and therefore does not need to perform so much work. This makes the Fosbury flop a far more efficient technique than the scissors.

KEY WORDS

Lever

A rigid structure, hinged at one point and to which two forces are applied at two other points.

HOT TIPS

In the human body:

• Fulcrum (F) = joint

• Load (L) = weight of limb plus object to be moved

• Effort (E) = agonist muscle responsible for joint movement.

Levers

The use of **levers** occurs in all sports because an athlete's muscles, bones and joints work together as lever systems to produce angular motion. A lever system is a simple structure that consists of a rigid object that rotates around a fixed axis when two unequal forces are applied to it.

A lever has three components:

- the fulcrum (F) = the fixed point
- the load (L) = the weight to be moved
- the effort (E) = the source of energy.

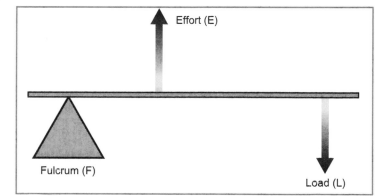

Fig. 3.50 The three components of a lever.

HOT TIPS

When looking at leverage in the human body always isolate one joint in a single phase of a discrete skill (that is, the knee joint in the execution phase of kicking a football) otherwise the process can become very complicated.

KEY WORDS

First class lever

In a first class lever, the fulcrum is located between the load and the effort.

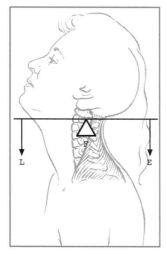

Fig. 3.53 Extension of the neck is a first class lever system.

Classification of levers

Lever systems are classified into three groups according to the arrangement of the fulcrum, the load and the effort. Athletes use all three classes of lever, although the third class lever system is by far the most common.

First class lever system

An example of a **first class lever** system in the human body is found in extension of the neck. The fulcrum (F) is the joint between the atlas and the skull. The load (L) is the weight of the head being tilted backwards. The effort (E) is the force applied by the trapezius muscle as it contracts to pull the head backwards.

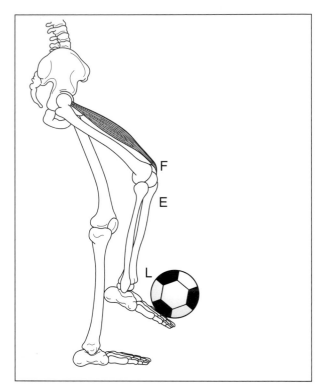

Fig. 3.51 The knee joint as a lever system:
- fulcrum (F) – knee joint
- load (L) = weight of lower leg and football
- effort (E) = rectus femoris and vasti muscles (the quadriceps group).

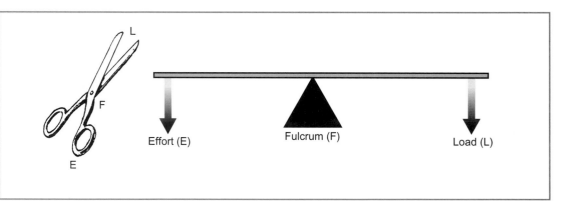

Fig. 3.52 The fulcrum is located between the load and the effort, making the scissors an example of a first class lever system.

Second class lever

In a second class lever, the load is located between the fulcrum and the effort.

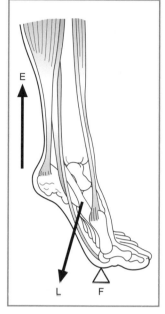

Fig. 3.55 Standing on tiptoe gives a second class lever system at the metatarsals/ phalanges joint.

HOT TIPS

A second class lever system can only be used at this joint complex if the performer is standing. If the performer sits down and plantar flexes his/her ankle a different class of lever system is used.

KEY WORDS

Third class lever

In a third class lever, the effort is located between the fulcrum and the load.

Second class lever system

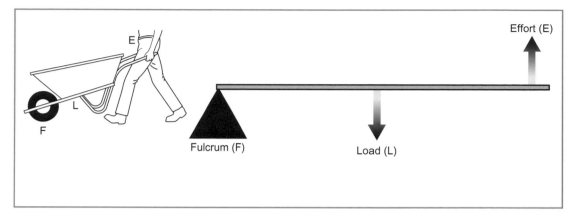

Fig. 3.54 The load is located between the fulcrum and the effort making the wheelbarrow a second class lever.

An example of a second class lever system in the human body is found in the toe joints when an athlete stands on tiptoe. The load (L) is the weight of the body being lifted. The fulcrum (F) is the joint between the metatarsals and the phalanges. The effort (E) is the force applied by the gastrocnemius muscle as it contracts to pull the heel upwards.

Task 25
Working with a partner, take it in turns to sit down with your legs outstretched. Starting with your ankles relaxed, point your toes as far towards the ground as you can. Identify the class of lever system being used as the toes are pointed. Discuss your thoughts with the rest of the class.

The advantage of second class lever systems is that they are able to produce considerable force and are therefore very strong. This is at the expense of speed and range of movement. Second class lever systems are efficient at moving a heavy load over a small distance – for example, when standing on tiptoe an athlete shifts the entire weight of their body a small distance upwards.

Third class lever system

There are many examples of **third class lever** systems in the human body. One straightforward example is found in flexion of the elbow joint. The effort (E) is the force applied by the biceps brachii muscle as it contracts to flex the elbow. The fulcrum (F) is the elbow joint. The load (L) is the weight of the lower arm and the dumbbell being lifted.

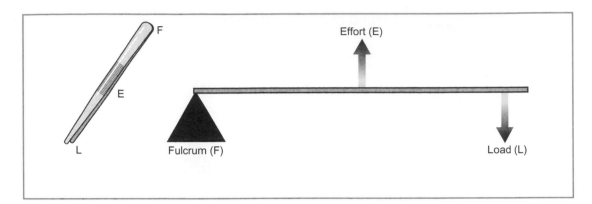

Fig. 3.56 The effort is located between the fulcrum and the load making the tweezers a third class lever.

Third class lever systems are efficient at accelerating a load through a large range of movement. This is at the expense of strength. For example, in the upward phase of the biceps curl the distance moved by the insertion of the biceps brachii (the effort) need only be small to ensure that the dumbbell (the load) is moved through far greater range. If you consider that both distances are achieved in the same time, the speed of the load is faster than the speed of the effort.

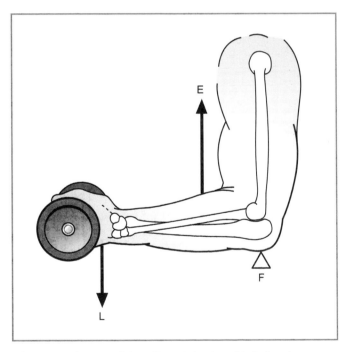

Fig. 3.57 Flexion of the elbow joint is a third class lever system.

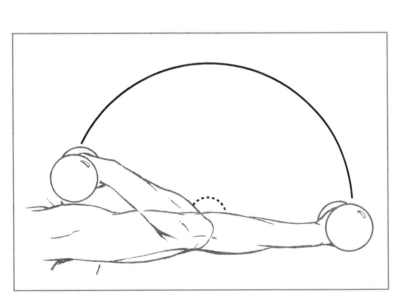

Fig. 3.58 Third class lever systems are able to shift the load at speed through a large range of movement.

Task 26

Using a named activity of your choice, give two examples of when you would make use of a third class lever system.

In many sporting events, longer levers are an advantage because they can generate a greater acceleration of the object to be thrown or hit. Take tennis as an example. The presence of a racket in the hand increases the length of the lever used to hit the ball.

In Figure 3.59, the time taken for the hand to move from A to B is the same as that for the racket head to move from X to Y. The speed of the racket head is considerably greater than the speed of the hand. The presence of the racket ensures a greater acceleration of the ball. The same principle is applied in cricket, hockey, golf and the discus and javelin events in athletics. Athletes with longer arms are at an advantage.

Fig. 3.59 The longer the lever, the greater the range of movement and the outgoing acceleration of the ball.

Task 27

1 Identify three sports in which long levers that allow for a greater range of movement or larger speed would be an advantage.
2 Identify three sports in which short levers that allow for considerable strength would be an advantage.
3 Why do you think that in a set of golf clubs, the driver has a longer shaft than the pitching wedge?

Moment of force or torque

The **moment of a force** or **torque** is the turning effect produced by the force as the lever rotates about the fulcrum. Generating a larger force or increasing the distance of the point of application of the force from the fulcrum can increase the moment of a force. It is calculated using the following equation.

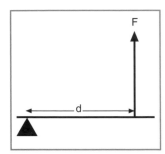

Fig. 3.60 The distance of the force from the fulcrum influences the turning effect.

HOT TIPS

From an understanding of moment of force, it is clear that the further the distance of the force from the fulcrum, the greater the turning effect. This is another explanation as to the advantages of long levers in sports such as discus throwing and tennis.

HOT TIPS

It is sometimes difficult to see which is the clockwise moment and which is the anticlockwise moment. The best way to determine this is to cover one of the arrows with your hand and decide which way the lever system would rotate about the fulcrum if pulled by the remaining force. For the above example:

• by covering the effort (E), we can see that the load (L) would rotate the lever system in a clockwise direction, therefore L × b is the clockwise moment.

• by covering the load (L), we can see that the effort (E) would rotate the lever system in an anticlockwise direction, therefore E × a is the anticlockwise moment.

Moment of force = force × perpendicular distance from fulcrum

Moment of force = F × d

Unit of measurement: Nm

Task 28

Calculate the moment of the force (F) as an athlete lowers a dumbbell in the final stages of the downward phase of a biceps curl. Remember to show all your working and give the units of measurement.

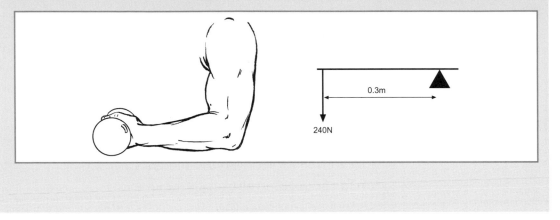

Principle of moments

The principle of moments can be applied to any lever system that is balanced. This means that the moment of force acting in a clockwise direction is equal to the moment of force acting in an anticlockwise direction. The lever system is stationary and there is no rotation about the fulcrum – for example, when a gymnast holds the tuck position at the top of a tuck jump. He/she creates a balanced lever system about the hip joint as shown in Figure 3.61.

For lever system to be balanced:

Clockwise moment of force = anticlockwise moment of force

$$L \times b = E \times a$$

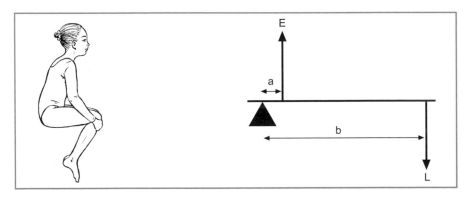

Fig. 3.61 A gymnast creating a balanced lever system about the hip joint.

Task 29

Using the principle of moments, calculate the effort required to be generated by the hip flexor muscles for a gymnast to hold the tuck position shown in the diagram below. Remember to show all your working and give the units of measurement.

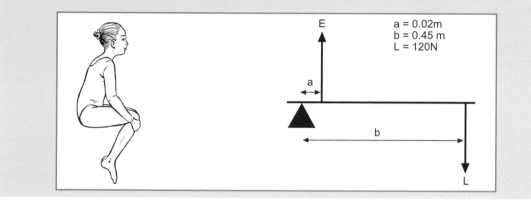

Principle axes of rotation

 KEY WORDS

Axis of rotation

An imaginary line or point about which a body rotates. For example, the leg rotates about the hip joint when kicking a football.

Principle axis of rotation

An axis that is directed through a body's centre of mass. The body has three principle axes of rotation: the longitudinal axis, the transverse axis and the frontal axis.

The rotation of a body is commonly described with reference to the **principle axes of rotation**. The human body has three principle axes of rotation, which all pass through the centre of mass. Lines drawn through the centre of mass can identify these axes.

- The line passing from head to foot is the longitudinal axis.
- The line passing from left to right is the transverse axis.
- The line passing from front to back is the frontal axis.

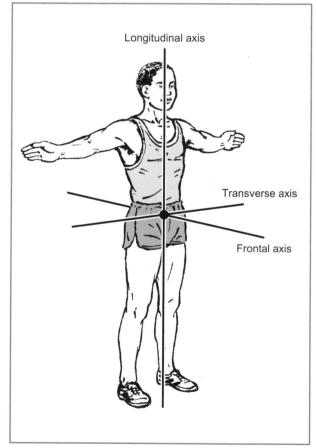

Fig. 3.62 The principle axes of the body pass through the centre of mass.

Task 30

Identify the principle axis of rotation for the following movements.

1 Diver performing a backward somersault.
2 Gymnast executing a side somersault.
3 Trampolinist completing a full turn jump.

Measurements used in angular motion

The following quantities are terminology used to describe the angular motion of a body.

Angular distance   Angular displacement   Degree   Radian
Angular speed   Angular velocity   Angular acceleration

For each of the angular quantities listed you will need to know:

- a simple definition
- the relevant equation (where appropriate) for numerical calculation
- the unit of measurement where appropriate.

HOT TIPS

All of the quantities that you need to know for angular motion have linear equivalents. Therefore this section is relatively straight forward to learn as the quantities are the same you learned in Section 1, except they have the word 'angular' preceding them.

KEY WORDS

Angular distance

The angle through which a body has rotated about an axis in moving from the first position to the second. It is a scalar quantity, which means that it expresses size only. Angular distance is measured in degrees, °, or radians, rad.

Angular displacement

The shortest change in angular position. It is the smallest angle through which a body has rotated about an axis in moving from the first position to the second. It is a vector quantity, which means that it expresses both size and direction. Angular displacement is measured in degrees, °, or radians, rad.

Radian

The unit of an angle.
1 radian = 57.3 degrees

Task 31

As you read through pages 210–12, copy this table onto a sheet of A4 and complete it as a revision aid for angular motion.

Measurement	Definition	Relevant equation	Unit of measurement
Angular distance		✗	
Angular displacement		✗	
Degree		✗	
Radian		✗	
Angular speed			
Angular velocity			
Angular acceleration			

Angular distance and angular displacement

The measurements of **angular distance** and **angular displacement** are used to describe the extent of a body's rotation.

Angular distance is the angle through which a body has rotated in moving from one position to another. Consider the gymnast performing on the asymmetric bars in Figure 3.63. The gymnast mounts the high bar in position A and completes her swing in position B. The angular distance covered is the angle though which she has rotated; in this example angular distance is 4.7 **radians** (270 degrees).

Angular displacement is the smallest angular change between the starting and finishing positions.

HOT TIPS

You will be familiar with using degrees to measure angles. Radians are another unit that can be used to measure angles. They are in fact the Standard International unit for measuring angular speed, angular velocity and angular acceleration and you will come across them in examination questions on angular motion. Try to become familiar with using radians as a measurement for angles.

Task 32

Consider Figure 3.63 and imagine the gymnast now completes a full revolution on the bar – that is, her starting and finishing position is at position B.

State the angular distance and the angular displacement for this revolution in:

1 radians

2 degrees.

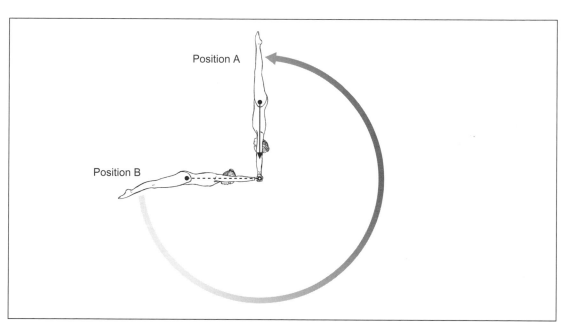

Figure 3.63 In rotating from position A to position B, the gymnast has an angular distance of 4.7rad (270º), but an angular displacement of 1.5rad (90º).

KEY WORDS

Angular speed

The angular distance travelled in a certain time. It is a scalar quantity. Angular speed is measured in radians per second, rad/s.

Angular velocity

The angular displacement travelled in a certain time. It is a vector quantity. Angular velocity is measured in radians per second, rad/s.

Angular speed and angular velocity

The measurements of **angular speed** and **angular velocity** describe the rate at which a body is rotating.

$$\text{angular speed (rad/s)} = \frac{\text{angular distance (rad)}}{\text{time taken (s)}}$$

$$\text{angular velocity (rad/s)} = \frac{\text{angular displacement (rad)}}{\text{time takes (s)}}$$

Task 33

1   The legs of a trampolinist performing a seat drop rotate 1.5 radians in 0.6 seconds. Calculate the angular velocity of the trampolinist's legs in radians/second.

2   During a drive from the tee, a golf club head rotates 9.2 radians in 0.8 seconds. Calculate the angular velocity of the club head in radians/second.

Angular acceleration

The measurement of **angular acceleration** is used to describe the rate at which a body changes its angular velocity.

$$\text{angular acceleration (rad/s}^2) = \frac{\text{change in angular velocity (rad/s)}}{\text{time taken (s)}}$$

KEY WORDS

Angular acceleration

The rate of change of angular velocity. It is a vector quantity. Angular acceleration is measured in radians per second per second, rad/s^2.

Moment of inertia

The resistance of a rotating body to change its state of angular motion.

Angular momentum

The quantity of angular motion possessed by a rotating body. Angular momentum is a vector quantity (see page 166).

Angular analogues of Newton's Laws

In Section 1 of this chapter, we discussed how Newton's Laws of Motion are fundamental to linear motion. They also govern angular motion. The difference in Newton's laws when applied to rotating bodies lies only in the terminology used. The principle behind each law corresponds to our linear understanding of the law. Using the terminology in Figure 3.64, it is possible to write angular analogues for each of Newton's laws.

Angular motion terminology	Linear motion terminology
Torque/moment of force	Force
Angular distance	Distance
Angular displacement	Displacement
Radian	Metre
Angular speed	Speed
Angular velocity	Velocity
Angular acceleration	Acceleration
Moment of inertia	Inertia
Angular momentum	Momentum

Fig. 3.64 Angular terminology and its linear equivalent.

Fig. 3.65 The dancer continues to turn with constant angular momentum until an external torque from the ground acts when the dancer lands.

Task 34

Test yourself on all the measurements shown in Figure 3.64, by stating a definition or equation for each quantity.

Angular analogue of Newton's First Law of Motion

A rotating body continues to turn about its axis of rotation with constant angular momentum unless acted upon by an external torque.

Compare this to the linear equivalent to see the similarity. A dancer who jumps to perform a full turn is a sporting application of this law. The dancer continues to turn until they land when the ground exerts an external torque on them to change their state of angular momentum.

Newton's First Law of Motion has considerable implication to the study of angular motion and is discussed in more detail on page 00.

Angular analogue of Newton's Second Law of Motion

When a torque acts on a body, the rate of change of angular momentum experienced by the body is proportional to the size of the torque and takes place in the direction in which the torque acts.

Compare this to the linear equivalent to see the similarity. Consider a trampolinist who exerts a torque at the take off for a front somersault. The larger the torque the faster the trampolinist will rotate and the greater the change in angular momentum.

Angular analogue of Newton's Third Law of Motion

For every torque that is exerted by one body on another there is an equal and opposite torque exerted by the second body on the first.

Compare this to the linear equivalent to see the similarity. A high diver wishing to generate a left-hand twist at take off is a good sporting application of this law. The diver will apply a downward and right-hand torque to the diving board, which in turn will generate an upward and left-hand torque on the diver allowing him to take off from the board and twist to his left.

Moment of inertia

Moment of inertia is the linear equivalent of inertia and applies to the tendency of a body to initially resist angular motion and the tendency of a body to want to continue rotating once undergoing angular motion.

There are two factors that determine the size of the moment of inertia of a rotating body.

- **The mass of the body:** the larger the mass, the greater the moment of inertia. The smaller the mass, the smaller the moment of inertia. For example, if a shot put and a football are rolled along the ground, the shot put has a higher moment of inertia because it has a greater mass.

- **The distribution of the mass of the body from the axis of rotation:** the further the distribution of mass from the axis of rotation, the greater the moment of inertia. The closer the distribution of mass from the axis of rotation, the smaller the moment of inertia. For example, a gymnast performs two consecutive somersaults about the transverse axis. For the first somersault the gymnast is in a tucked position and for the second she or he is in a straight position. The gymnast has a higher moment of inertia when performing the straight somersault because in this position his/her mass is distributed further from the axis of rotation.

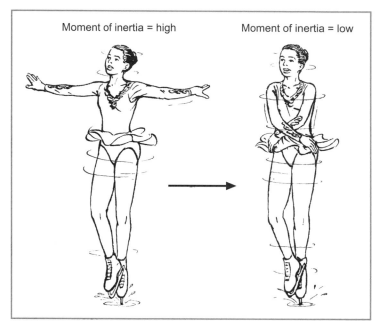

Fig. 3.66 Athletes can change their moment of inertia during rotation by manipulating the distribution of mass from the axis of rotation.

Once a body is rotating, it is possible to change its moment of inertia. This is commonly observed in figure skating when a skater begins a spin with his (or her) arms stretched out to the side and during the spin brings his arms into his body. The skater is rotating about the longitudinal axis. When he brings his arms into his body the distribution of mass from the axis of rotation is reduced and the moment of inertia becomes smaller.

The same principle can be applied to the action of the leg during sprinting where the leg rotates about the hip joint. In the drive phase of the leg action, the sprinter's leg is extended. The mass is distributed away from the hip joint (the axis of rotation) and the leg has a high moment of inertia. During recovery, flexion of the knee brings the mass of the leg closer to the hip joint and reduces moment of inertia. Reducing moment of inertia makes rotation faster and easier and the sprinter is able to bring the leg through quickly to begin another drive phase. This partly explains why a high knee lift is important to efficient sprinting

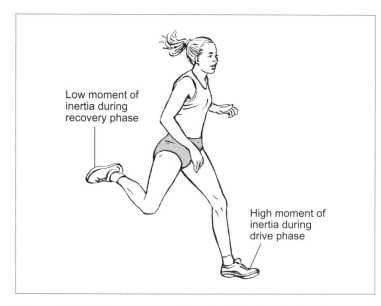

Figure 3.67 A low moment of inertia of the leg during the recovery phase in sprinting allows the athlete to bring the leg through easily and quickly.

technique where leg speed is important, but not so vital to middle-distance running techniques.

Task 35

Identify which of the following athletes has the smaller moment of inertia in the following sporting situations. Give reasons for your answers.

1　Two divers performing tucked back somersaults – one weighing 72kg and the other weighing 68kg.

2　Two gymnasts of the same height performing cartwheels – one with bent legs and one with fully extended legs.

3　Two trampolinists performing full twists – one with arms together stretched above head and the other with arms outstretched to the sides.

Angular momentum

Angular momentum refers to the amount of motion that a rotating body possesses. A high moment of inertia or a large angular velocity will create a large angular momentum.

$$\text{angular momentum} = \text{moment of inertia} \times \text{angular velocity}$$

In sports involving rotation it is often important for athletes to generate a large angular momentum at take off. In high diving, for example, a diver needs to create sufficient angular momentum at the start of the dive to allow him (or her) to perform the numerous somersaults and twists that occur later. This is why a diver ensures that his body is extended and spread out at take off, giving him a high moment of inertia and a large angular momentum with which to complete the dive.

Conservation of angular momentum

The angular momentum generated at take off is conserved during flight. For example, the angular momentum a diver generates at take off remains the same while the diver is in flight. This principle is also evident in a spinning ice skater, despite him or her being in contact with the ground, because the frictional force between the smooth surface of the blade and the ice is so small that it can be ignored.

The **law of the conservation of angular momentum** is a result of Newton's First Law. For a rotating athlete in flight or a skater spinning on ice, there is no change in the athlete's angular momentum until he or she lands, collides with another object or exerts a torque onto the ice with the edge of the blade.

HOT TIPS

For angular momentum to remain constant:

• if moment of inertia decreases, angular velocity increases – athletes pull their bodies in to rotate faster.

• if moment of inertia increases, angular velocity decreases – athletes spread their bodies out to rotate slower.

To be able to apply this law to sporting techniques, we need to remember two important considerations.

- Angular momentum = moment of inertia × angular velocity
- Once in flight, an athlete can manipulate his (or her) moment of inertia by changing body position – that is, bringing his mass closer to the principle axis of rotation lowers moment of inertia and taking his mass further away from the principle axis of rotation increases moment of inertia.

Let us consider two specific sporting examples where athletes make use of conservation of angular momentum to their advantage.

Diving

Consider a diver who takes off from the board to complete one and a half back somersaults about the transverse axis as shown in Figure 3.68.

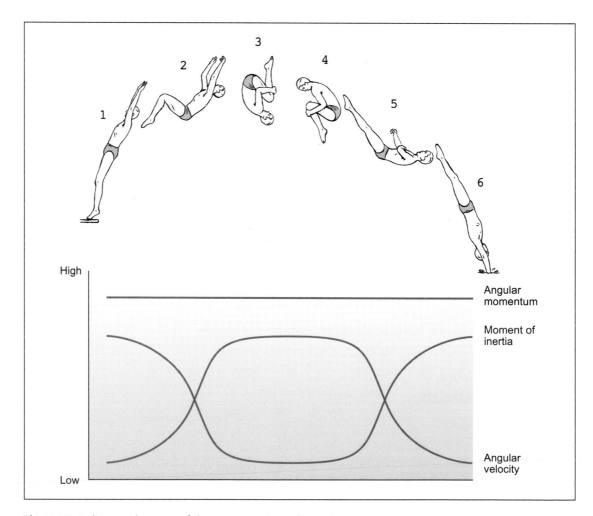

Fig. 3.68 A diver makes use of the conservation of angular momentum.

The amount of angular momentum generated at take off stays the same during flight until the diver hits the water on entry. At take off, the diver ensures a large moment of inertia by spreading his (or her) body away from the transverse axis. This gives him a large angular momentum to enable him to complete the dive. In positions 2, 3 and 4 the diver brings his arms, legs and head in towards the axis of rotation, thereby decreasing his moment of inertia. This causes angular velocity to increase and the diver spins quicker during this section of the dive. To control his entry into the water and avoid over-rotation, the diver needs to reduce his rate of spin towards the end of the dive. To do this he spreads his body as shown in positions 5 and 6. This increases his moment of inertia and decreases his angular velocity to ensure a controlled entry into the water.

Figure skating

Another example of an athlete manipulating their moment of inertia to increase or decrease rate of spin occurs when a figure skater performs a multiple spin about the longitudinal axis. During the spin, angular momentum is conserved. The skater's starting position is with both arms out to the side and one leg extended behind them. This makes them spread out from the axis rotation, giving them a large moment of inertia and a large angular momentum with which to start the spin. The skater then pulls the arms and leg inwards and will often cross the arms across their chest and cross their ankles. This greatly reduces moment of inertia, meaning that angular velocity is considerably increased and the skater spins very quickly. When the skater spreads their arms and legs out again, moment of inertia is increased once again and the rate of spin reduced.

Task 36

Working with a partner, help each other to explain how a slalom skier uses conservation of angular momentum to his/her advantage.

Revise as you go!

- How are levers classified? Define and give an example of a third class lever.
- Why are the majority of levers in the body third class levers?
- Define the moment of a force and state how it can be increased.
- Describe what is meant by a principle axis of the body.
- Name the three principle axes of the body.
- Give an example of a rotation that occurs about the longitudinal axis.
- Give the equation and units of measure for angular velocity and angular acceleration.
- Explain what is meant by the term moment of inertia.
- Define angular momentum and explain how a spinning skater makes use of the law of conservation of angular momentum.

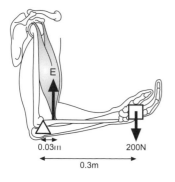

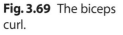

Fig. 3.69 The biceps curl.

Sharpen up your exam technique!

1 Explain how a sprinter's stability changes through the three phases of a sprint start: 'on your marks', 'set', 'bang'. (6 marks)

2 Physical Education students may carry out weight training as part of a fitness programme. One of the exercises used may be the biceps curl shown in Figure 3.69.

Assuming the arm is stationary, use the principle of moments to calculate the force E exerted by the biceps brachii. Show your working. (3 marks)

3 The diagram below shows a gymnast performing a tucked front somersault

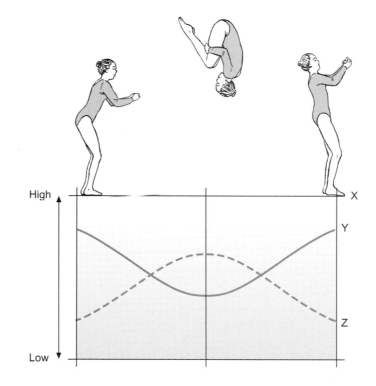

Fig. 3.70 A gymnast performing a tucked front somersault.

a) Identify the aspects of angular motion represented by the lines labelled X, Y and Z. State the principle that illustrates the relation between the three factors. (4 marks)

b) Use your understanding of this principle to explain why a gymnast is able to perform a greater number of tucked somersaults than straight somersaults during flight. (4 marks)

Chapter 4 **Sport psychology**

Section 1: *Personality*

Learning objectives

KEY WORDS

Perceptual

The interpretation of environmental information.

Cognitive

The process of thought.

Arousal

A physical and mental state of preparedness.

Activation

A condition that reflects the degree of physical readiness.

At the end of this section you should be able to:
- define personality
- understand the theories of personality
- have an awareness of links between personality and sports performance
- explain trait, social learning and interactionist perspectives
- justify the limitations of personality profiling in sport.

Introduction

Psychology of sport performance is an extension of the AS course entitled 'Acquiring and Performing Movement Skills'. The AS course focused upon how skills are learned and controlled. Sport psychology addresses the important role of the human mind in the production of optimal performance in sport. Strong links exist between the courses and they will be suggested throughout the text.

Fig. 4.01 The ideal level of arousal required for successful sports performance differs between each personality. Here, the tennis player controls her emotions to ensure maximum concentration is given to receiving service. She has made a commitment to improve her game and appears to be confident.

Athletes display their own unique patterns of behaviour in the course of sports performance and the notion that personality is related to sports behaviour is attractive to sport psychologists.

Confidence is one example of a behaviour pattern within personality, and this ultimately determines whether an individual has a strong commitment to participate and achieve in a sport-related activity. However, the study of personality in sport also includes **perceptual** and **cognitive** characteristics such as the individual's ability to concentrate and direct the focus of attention in a competitive situation when there is great pressure to succeed. The capacity to concentrate is influenced by emotional **arousal** and successful performance depends upon the control of this state of **activation**.

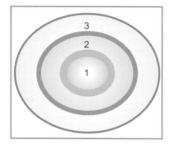

Fig. 4.02 Concentric ring theory.

KEY WORDS

Learned helplessness

A feeling that failure is bound to happen and is uncontrollable. This mode of behaviour is also associated with a loss of confidence and withdrawal of commitment.

KEY WORDS

Aggression

An action intended to bring about harm or injury. Aggressive behaviour is undesirable and dysfunctional in the context of sport.

What is personality?

' *Personality is the sum total of an individual's characteristics which make him unique.* '
(Hollander)

' *Personality is the more or less stable and enduring organisation of a person's character, temperament, intellect and physique, which determines the unique adjustment* [the individual makes] *to the environment.* '
(Eysenck)

It is significant to note that both definitions emphasise that the personality of each individual is unique.

Hollander (1967) believed a model comprising three concentric rings could represent the structure of personality. As one moves to the centre of the model, the boundary lines grow wider. This denotes that each new layer becomes progressively difficult to penetrate.

1 The psychological core

This is the 'real you'. It is almost impossible for the psychologist to reach this level for the purpose of research, as the individual will always protect this private centrepiece. The core stores the concept of true self and is not revealed.

2 Typical responses

This level represents the usual manner in which a response to an environmental situation is made. For example, one individual may perceive defeat as a positive learning experience and work harder in training to succeed next time. Another may suffer a different reaction that brings about a condition known as '**learned helplessness**' and withdraw his/her commitment. A typical response is learned and stored as experience. Such responses may indicate the nature of the core. For example, a player who consistently responds to pressure situations with feelings of fear and tension is likely to be a highly anxious person at core level.

3 Role-related behaviour

This is the surface of personality. Role-related behaviour is determined by our perception of the environment at any given moment in time. As perception is influenced by many factors, it can be changed at any time. In this way, the action of the individual may not be a typical response but an uncharacteristic action. For example, the usually calm athlete may for once be guilty of an act of **aggression** and in retrospect wonder how this one-off behaviour came about. Role-related behaviour might not be normal behaviour and not a true indicator of personality.

Psychodynamic theory

The first presenter of psychodynamic theory was the clinical psychologist Sigmund Freud in 1933. Freud believed that personality comprises three components, namely – id, ego and superego. These components interact to produce individual patterns of behaviour in sport.

- The id represents our basic instincts over which we have no conscious control. Eating when hungry is an example of such an instinct.
- The ego is our conscious link with the reality of the situation and seeks to satisfy the basic instincts. For example, a basic instinct is to eat when hungry. The ego will set out to satisfy the need. This would involve buying and cooking food, which is normal behaviour. However, if there is no money, the ego may instigate a motive to steal.
- The purpose of the superego is to be the 'moral arm' of the personality and this will judge whether behaviour is appropriate and acceptable. In other words, it is our social conscience.

According to this theory, personality is formed because of a permanent state of psychological conflict between seeking, releasing and inhibiting behaviour.

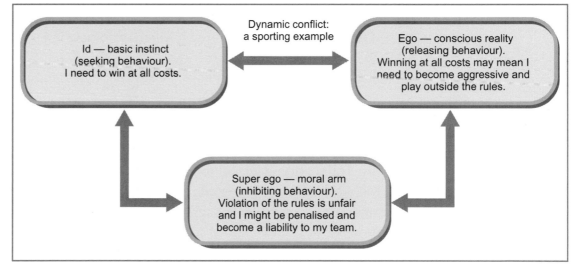

Fig. 4.03 Psychodynamic theory.

KEY WORDS

Nature

A product of the genes of our parents. A genetically inherited predisposition.

Nurture

A learned pattern of behaviour acquired through reinforcement, imitation of the behaviour of others and general environmental influences.

Interaction

When things combine together to influence each other.

Athletic aggression is a good example of this approach. Instinct theory provides one explanation for violence in sport. This will be seen in the section dealing with aggression.

A question extending through the entire Sport Psychology syllabus is whether behaviour is a product of **nature**, the result of **nurture**, or determined by the **interaction** of both of these factors.

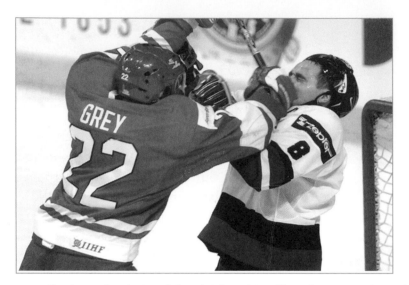

Fig. 4.04 The ego will release the desire of the id. Often this will result in an undesired response if the superego fails as a mechanism of control, as in this picture. The superego inhibits our basic intentions, and this can be developed to bring about productive and desirable behaviour in sport.

Trait theory of personality

TASK 1

By using an example from a sporting event in which you have recently taken part or watched, explain how the superego operated to control the behaviour of yourself or another player.

KEY WORDS

Trait theory

People are born with established personality characteristics. Behaviour = Function of Personality (B = F(P))

Trait

An indelible characteristic of personality. A trait is an instinct. Therefore, this theory links with the psychodynamic theory of personality.

A **trait** is a characteristic of personality, which is said to be inherited by a child at birth. Traits are considered to be natural forces or instincts causing an individual to act in a certain way. For example, one might be considered ambitious, competitive or aggressive. Traits are thought to be stable, enduring and consistent across all situations.

A psychologist named Cattell (1965) identified sixteen groups of traits, which he claimed were present within all people at varying degrees of intensity. Traits are arranged in hierarchical form with the primary or strongest overriding weaker or secondary traits.

A great strength of trait theory is that it allows easy and objective measurement to be put in place through questionnaires. A major drawback is that it is not a true predictor of behaviour, and it appears that no significant difference exists between sports performance and people with differing trait strengths. A further weakness is

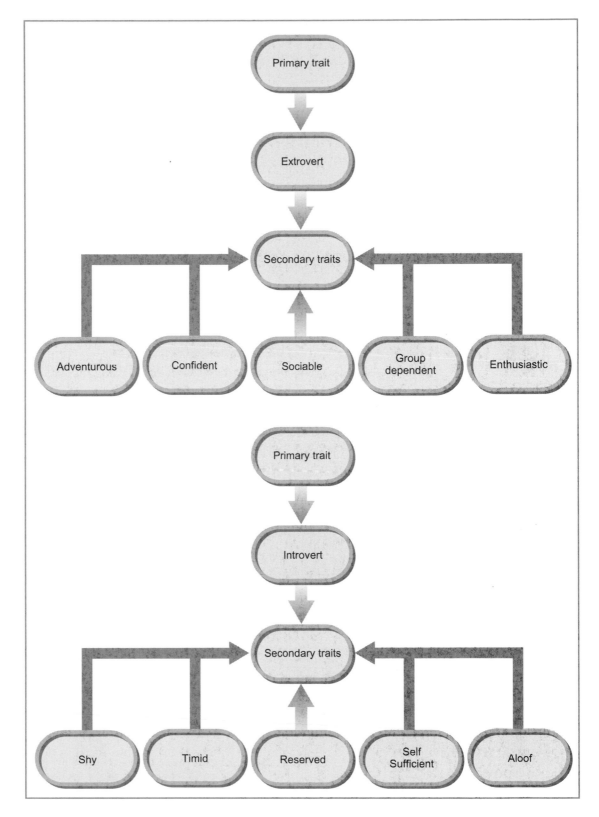

Fig. 4.05 Trait theory of personality. Note that the secondary traits of extrovert and introvert personalities are direct opposites.

that trait perspective does not take into account the influence of the environment in the formation of personality. In this way, trait theory conflicts directly with social learning views.

Cattell's work was supported by Eysenck (1968) but stated that the traits most likely to be displayed should be known as the personality type. Personality types are arranged on two dimensions and can be regarded as **continuums**.

Eysenck's personality types

Eysenck recognised four personality types (see Figure 4.06).

1   Neurotic (**unstable**) and **extroverted**.
2   Stable and extroverted.
3   **Stable** and **introverted**.
4   Neurotic and introverted.

Many studies have been undertaken in an attempt to prove the existence of the ideal sports personality and for many years it was said that the majority of sports performers had a personality profile, which registered in the stable and extroverted area. A sport psychologist named Ogilvie (1966) believed that one was born with a personality type to make prowess in sport easy. He recognised the traits thought to belong to elite performers such as endurance, aggression, ambition and dominance. Studies in the 1960s indicated that games players of a high standard were indeed extroverted and stable. Gondola(1968)found that although some marathon runners tended to be introverted and stable, many top performers had different personality profiles. However, Mischel (1973) strongly opposed the theory that an ideal athletic personality existed and claimed that no personality profile has been found to discriminate between athletes and non-athletes. Finally, Gould stated that personality type does not predict excellence or participation in sport.

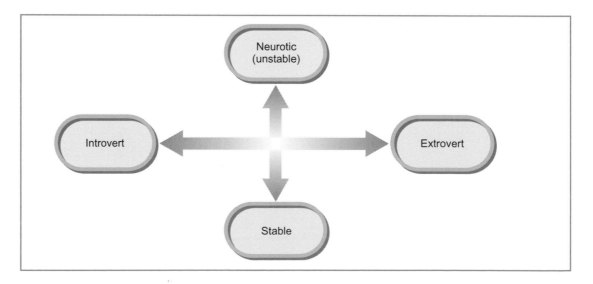

Fig. 4.06 Personality types.

Arising from the trait perspective is the 'narrow band approach' to the explanation of personality. This theory, presented by Girdano (1990), recognises two distinct personality types – type A and type B:

Type A characteristics:
- Highly competitive
- Strong desire to succeed
- Works fast
- Likes to control
- Prone to suffer stress

Type B characteristics:
- Non-competitive
- Unambitious
- Works more slowly
- Does not enjoy control
- Less prone to stress

KEY WORDS

Social Learning Theory

All behaviour is learned from environmental experience.
$B = F(E)$

Social learning theory

Behaviour = Function of Environment (B = F(E))

This theory suggests that all behaviour is learned through interaction with the environment and that inherited factors do not influence personality. Therefore the response made by an individual cannot be predicted. Bandura believed that learning takes place in two ways. First, we tend to imitate the behaviour of others through observation. This is referred to as modelling. Second, new behaviours are acquired when they are endorsed through social reinforcement. For example, a young footballer observes a professional player intimidating an opponent through hard and aggressive tackling. Using the senior player as his model, the young player adopts the same tactics and is rewarded for it by the coach. Therefore the coach has reinforced the player's behaviour. This example indicates that undesirable behaviour could be acquired through modelling and social reinforcement.

The weakness of social learning theory is that it takes little account of inherited behaviours.

KEY WORDS

Interactionist Theory

Behaviour occurs from the influence of inherited traits and learned experiences. $B = F(P)E$

Interactionist theory

Behaviour = Function of Personality × Environment (B = F(P) × E)

This approach considers both the inherited characteristics and the environmental influences in the development of personality. This theory combines trait and social learning theories and is generally accepted to be a more realistic explanation of personality.

A psychologist named Bowers (1978) went so far as to claim that 'interaction between the person and the situation explains twice as much as traits and situations alone'.

The sport psychologist aims to produce a personality profile. These are produced through testing. Tests are shown below.

KEY WORDS

Sceptical approach

This is an approach to personality study that questions the link between personality and sports performance.

Credulous approach

This is an approach to personality study supporting links between successful sports performance and a particular personality type.

Objective evidence

Evidence proven without question or doubt, usually as a result of statistical analysis.

HOT TIPS

• It is important to understand the nature, nurture and interactionist perspectives of behaviour.

• Review the strengths and weaknesses of each perspective.

• Be aware of the problems associated with the use of personality profiling in sport.

1 Observation is a widely used technique for assessing personality. The behaviour of a performer can be recorded in certain situations over an extended period. If response patterns are consistently repeated, a description of personality can be made.

2 Psychometric methods involve the administration of a self-report questionnaire, and the Sixteen Personality Factor Questionnaire (16PF test) designed by Cattell is used to predict personality in sport.

However, there are problems associated with the use of personality profiling in sport. Although the evidence gained from self-report inventories and observation studies are valid, it is not reliable due to the subjective nature of the conclusions. There is a danger that evidence can be too generalised and a view known as the '**sceptical approach**' claims that personality traits alone cannot predict behaviour. Finally, while the '**credulous approach**' believes there is a link between personality and performance in sport, **objective evidence** to support this claim is lacking.

Revise as you go! Test your knowledge and understanding

• Briefly define the term 'personality'.
• Identify and explain the components of the concentric ring theory of personality.
• Describe the psychodynamic approach to personality.
• How could the coach use a personality profile to change undesirable and abnormal behaviour in sport?
• Outline the differences between trait and social learning theories of personality.
• Identify and define the four personality types that were recognised by Eysenck.
• Outline the drawbacks of the trait and social learning perspectives of personality.
• Identify the methods used to assess personality.
• List the problems that have arisen when personality profiling has been used to predict competence in sport.

Fig. 4.07 Trait and social learning perspectives do not take into account the interaction between hereditary personality factors and the situation. The coach must be aware of how the individual will respond in a given situation before behaviour can be controlled.

Sharpen up your exam technique!

1   What is meant by the trait perspective in personality research and what problems are associated with this perspective? (4 marks)

2   What are the problems of linking personality characteristics with performance in physical activity? (4 marks)

3   Describe the interactionist approach to personality and use a practical example from physical education or sport to support your answer. (3 marks)

Section 2: *Attitudes*

Learning objectives

At the end of this section you should be able to:
- understand how attitudes are formed and influenced
- explain how attitudes can be changed
- understand the links between attitudes and behaviour in sport
- understand the meaning of the term 'achievement motivation'
- understand the link between personality and the motive to achieve.

Introduction

KEY WORDS

Attitude

A learned behavioural predisposition.

Attitude objects

The people, subject or situation towards which an attitude is directed.

A mode of behaviour that is often thought to be a typical reaction of an individual is termed an **attitude**. Attitude is invariably associated with personality and is frequently used to explain a pattern of behaviour or a response in a given situation. Moody (1980), a leading sport psychologist, describes attitude as:

> ❝ *a mental state of readiness organised through experience that influences the response of an individual towards any object or situation with which it is related.* ❞

An attitude is an enduring emotional and behavioural response, and although it can be established firmly, an attitude is unstable and can be changed and controlled. Attitudes are directed towards '**attitude objects**', which could include places, situations and the behaviour of other people. For example, a player may dislike training. The attitude object is the training and the player in this case may adopt a negative attitude during training. In this way an attitude would strongly influence the way individuals perceive and behave in sports situations.

Formation of attitudes

Attitudes are formed mainly through experiences. A pleasant experience in physical education brought about when positive reinforcement follows success is likely to promote a positive attitude towards physical activities and sport, whereas an unpleasant encounter such as the experience of failure, criticism or injury, would bring about a negative attitude and sport becomes an 'object' to be avoided in the future.

Several other agents shape our attitudes. In early childhood parents play the most significant role, whilst in teenage years the **peer group** has the most powerful influence. If a group of friends participate enthusiastically in the aerobics club, it is likely that in an effort to conform the reluctant individual may also join in. At this time, the teacher or coach may be a guiding figure in attitude formation by presenting new experiences and possibilities.

Furthermore, a role model can greatly influence the attitude of the individual, and Bandura believed that effective learning takes place by watching and imitating the behaviours of significant others. The whole process of interaction between individuals and groups of people is called **socialisation**. This process along with the accumulation of knowledge and the development of direct environmental experiences, does much to formulate attitudes.

Attitudes can bring about false perceptions, which influence our judgement inappropriately and bring about behaviour that is inconsistent and prejudiced. **Prejudice** is a prejudgement arising from an evaluation based on inadequate information. A second definition of attitude may be considered at this point:

> ❝ *An attitude is a predisposition to act in a certain way towards some aspect of a person's environment including other people.* ❞
> (Mednick)

For example, the teacher may regard a talented sports player as lazy and disinterested because the player chooses to opt out of practice. It may be that the player is keen to secure a place in the team but avoids practice because he or she is disliked by a group of established players. The behaviour of the player is not in accordance with an apparent attitude toward the practice but is based on a desire to avoid an unpleasant social experience. The teacher's attitude has by now been marked with prejudice. Research tends to focus on **negative prejudice,** although positive prejudices can also be formed. For example, the coach may favour a particular player. This is recognised as favouritism.

KEY WORDS

Peer group

An immediate group of friends or associates.

Socialisation

The process of mixing and relating to other people.

HOT TIPS

Review 'Observational Learning' pages 153–4 of *Advanced PE for OCR, AS*.

KEY WORDS

Prejudice

An unfounded biased judgement.

Negative prejudice

A biased judgement that forms an unwarranted negative attitude – for example, an illogical dislike of someone or something.

The components of attitude
The triadic model of attitudes

An attitude comprises three components.

1 The cognitive component

This is also known as the information component. This component also reflects beliefs and knowledge. For example, you believe that fitness training three times a week enhances the quality of life. Furthermore, you have the knowledge to support this opinion.

2 The affective component

This consists of feelings or an emotional response towards an attitude object and is also known as the emotional component. It is here that an evaluation of an attitude object is made. For example, training is enjoyable and I feel good when participating.

3 The behavioural component

This concerns how a person intends to behave towards an attitude object. For example, joining a fitness club to follow an organised fitness programme.

Changing attitudes
Cognitive dissonance theory

This theory was presented by a psychologist named Festinger and states that if a person holds two ideas that oppose and conflict with each other an element of discomfort arises. This emotional discomfort is called **dissonance**. For example:

- a player wishes to perform to a high standard, but does not want to dedicate more time to sport
- the coach wishes to pursue a youth policy, but is worried that in doing so the team could lose many games in the short term.

To reduce this feeling of dissonance, the impact of one of the conflicting ideas could be lessened and therefore an attitude would change. For example:

- the player rejects the opportunity to perform at a high standard and so there is no need to increase dedication
- the coach accepts that losses will be incurred if a youth policy is pursued.

Altering any one of the three components seen in the Triadic model can bring about a change in attitude.

- Updating knowledge or providing a person with new information can change the cognitive component. For example, a person seeking to improve fitness who decides against jogging for fear of injury may review this opinion as the latest research states that running in moderation actually prevents joint deterioration.

- Providing a person with new and positive experiences can modify the affective component. For example, a student who has a negative experience through excessive physical contact in rugby may enjoy the indoor 'tag' version of the game and in this way change his or her attitude towards participation.
- If a skill is simplified or if some form of guidance is used to make execution easier, the behavioural component of attitude can be changed. For example, fitting the novice skier with short skis would give more control and reduce apprehension; making use of the tumbling belt would provide assurance to the trampolinist when attempting an agility she or he had previously avoided. Applying reinforcement and punishment can make further behaviour modifications.

HOT TIPS

Changing undesired behaviour and negative attitudes in sport is a major purpose of sport psychology. Study the methods used to change an attitude as it is an area likely to be questioned.

TASK 2

By giving practical examples, discuss how cognitive dissonance theory could change a negative attitude towards exercise.

A change in popularity of an attitude object may also change behaviour towards it. For example, increasing numbers of women are attracted to track athletics partly due to the updated image of the prime role models.

Persuasive communication theory

As the name of the theory suggests, this method involves changing the attitude of a person through a process of persuasion. There are four elements to persuasive communication theory.

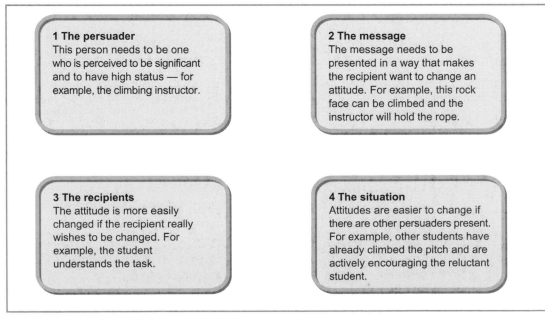

1 The persuader
This person needs to be one who is perceived to be significant and to have high status — for example, the climbing instructor.

2 The message
The message needs to be presented in a way that makes the recipient want to change an attitude. For example, this rock face can be climbed and the instructor will hold the rope.

3 The recipients
The attitude is more easily changed if the recipient really wishes to be changed. For example, the student understands the task.

4 The situation
Attitudes are easier to change if there are other persuaders present. For example, other students have already climbed the pitch and are actively encouraging the reluctant student.

Fig. 4.08 The four elements of persuasive communication theory.

HOT TIPS

An attitude cannot be relied on to predict behaviour.

> **TASK 3**
> Describe a practical situation in physical education when persuasive communication theory could be used to change an attitude.

Although it is assumed that attitudes direct an individual to behave positively or negatively towards an attitude object, attitudes in general are poor predictors of behaviour.

A person may have a very positive outlook on physical fitness, but this alone will not guarantee that he or she will attend circuit-training sessions three times a week. Both social and situational factors influence actual behaviour very strongly. Fishbein said that as attitudes become more specific they are more likely to predict behaviour. For example, the student who is positive about fitness activities but specifically enjoys circuit training is more likely to attend a session.

HOT TIPS

Behavioural intention is the strongest predictor of behaviour.

However, the most effective predictor of behaviour according to Fishbein (1974) is behavioural intention. This occurs when a declaration of the intended behaviour is made before the event. In this case, the student would state that he/she would definitely attend the circuit-training session.

Achievement motivation

Motivation has been described as the desire to fulfil a need. It functions on two levels both energising behaviour, so giving the drive to achieve a goal, and it also directs behaviour, enabling a person to focus or concentrate on a particular task or situation. Motivation links closely with arousal and this association will be discussed on page 252.

This section examines the topic of achievement motivation, which is a concept developed by sport psychologists to link personality with competitiveness. The major issue centres on the extent to which an individual is motivated to attain success. Inevitably, success in sport is measured against some competitive goal and therefore achievement motivation and competitiveness are inextricably linked.

HOT TIPS

Mastery goals are also called process goals. Ego goals are also called outcome goals.

Biddle, a leading sport psychologist, suggests that there are several types of goal against which success can judged.

- **Mastery or task goals.** These are associated with self-improvement – for example, striving to achieve a personal best in track and field or monitoring and improvement in shooting technique in netball. These goals are also called process goals.
- **Ego or ability goals.** These involve a comparison against one's rivals – for example, winning the club tennis championship would mean defeating all opponents. These goals are also referred to as performance or product goals.

- **Socially approved goals**. These involve seeking social reinforcement as a measure of success – for example, winning to earn approval from parents, peers or coaches.

KEY WORDS

Self-confidence

Confidence is global and applies to all situations because it is a stable personality characteristic.

The most competitive of individuals may strive to satisfy each of the three outcomes. A return to the issue goal types will be made on pages 247–8 in the context of goal setting and the raising of **self-confidence**.

Some psychologists believe that a competitive inclination is a product of nature. Murray (1938) indicated that it was natural for one individual to strive to surpass another. However, the social psychologist Bandura (1968) believed that a competitive orientation was a product of learning.

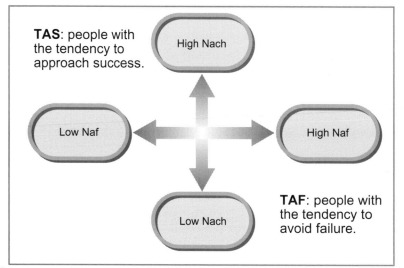

TAS: people with the tendency to approach success.

High Nach

Low Naf

High Naf

TAF: people with the tendency to avoid failure.

Low Nach

Fig. 4.09 Personality factors that determine competitiveness.

Atkinson and McClelland (1976) presented the interactionist view and stated that competitive motivation was generated through a combination of personality and the situational factors. Figure 4.09 indicates the personality factors that determine competitiveness. In any challenging situation everyone will have both a need to achieve and a need to avoid failure. Whichever feeling is the stronger will determine whether the task is accepted or declined.

The individuals marked as TAS have a high need to achieve (high Nach) and a low need to avoid failure (low Naf). They are regarded as people who are motivated to succeed and are not worried about the possibility of failure.

They are more competitive and tend to be stimulated by situations involving risk. TAF characteristics have a high need to avoid failure (high Naf) and are worried by the prospect and therefore lack a competitive edge. They have and a low need to achieve (low Nach) and are motivated to avoid failure. The situational factors that determine competitiveness involve the probability of success when a challenge is undertaken and the resulting incentive value if success is attained.

HOT TIPS

TAF = tendency to avoid failure
TAS = tendency to approach success.

TASK 4

Discuss two events in sport – one that would have resulted in a high incentive value and one in which the outcome would have given a low incentive value. Give reasons to suggest why these values are different.

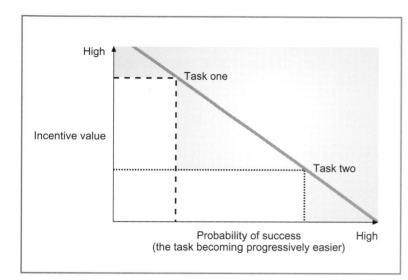

Fig. 4.10 The relationship between probability of success and incentive value.

Fig. 4.11 If the probability of success is low, the incentive value will be high. This swimmer has suceeded against high odds.

KEY WORDS

Incentive value

Relates to the degree of pleasure experienced when success is achieved.

KEY WORDS

Attributions

(In the context of sport) refers to the reasons given for success or failure.

HOT TIPS

• Link attribution (page 267) with achievement motivation.

• Consider how goal setting (page 248) could relate to achievement motivation and attribution.

The probability of success relates to the difficulty of the task. Incentive value is associated with the feelings an individual will have about the achievement if it came about. Task one (Figure 4.10) would be a relatively difficult task, but if success were achieved, the individual would experience a high degree of satisfaction and believe a considerable gain had been made. However, this type of task involves the risk of failure and would be taken on by a person with TAS personality characteristics. TAF personalities would tend to accept task two in Figure 4.10. This would be relatively easy and as little risk would be involved the incentive value would be low.

People who have a greater need to succeed (high Nach) rise to challenges and adopt what is known as 'approach behaviours'. People with a need to avoid failure (low Naf) avoid risk situations and this leads to 'avoidance behaviours'. The '**attributions**' for success or failure differ greatly between the two personality types.

The Atkinson and McClelland theory is best at predicting situations where there is a 50/50 chance of success. It is in these situations that the motive to achieve is strongest in those with TAS characteristics, as they enjoy competing against others of equal ability and being evaluated on the basis of ego or ability goals. Low achievers fear negative evaluation associated with failure and so a 50/50 chance of success causes maximum uncertainty and stress about performance. Because of this, high Naf (TAF) personalities tend to opt for easy tasks or those in which a successful outcome is impossible. Although failure is inevitable in the latter task, self-esteem is protected and the low achiever might emerge with credit for effort made against the odds. This is termed 'heroic failure syndrome'.

TASK 5

Discuss the strategies a coach could use to ensure that performers experience high incentive values during every training session.

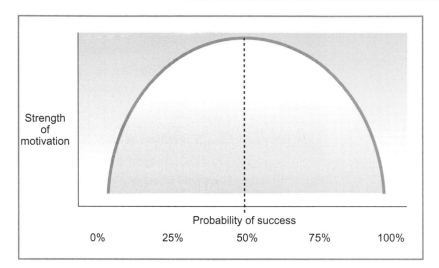

This interactionist model of achievement motivation predicts that in a situation in which the odds on attaining success stand at 50/50, personalities with a high need to achieve are at their highest point of motivation and are more likely to take the risk.

Fig. 4.12 Interactionist model of achievement.

HOT TIPS

There is no correlation between TAS and extrovert personalities.

Revise as you go! Test your knowledge and understanding

- Define the term 'attitude'.
- By using an example from physical education or sport, explain the meaning of the term 'attitude object'.
- Describe how an attitude might be formed.
- List the three components of an attitude.
- Name and describe two ways to change an attitude.
- Define the term 'prejudice' and describe how a prejudiced attitude may be formed in physical education or sport.
- How well do attitudes predict behaviour in the context of sport?
- What is meant by the term 'behavioural intention'?
- Define the term 'achievement motivation'.
- Explain what TAS and TAF is.
- Describe how the probability of success relates to incentive value.
- Explain why it might be easier to coach people with a high need to achieve as opposed to those with a high need to avoid failure.
- Describe how personality and the situation interact before a high need to achieve is developed.

Sharpen up your exam technique!

1 The attitudes and prejudices we bring to sport can have a significant impact on performance. Identify one prejudice in physical education or sport and explain what might have caused the formation of that prejudice.   (4 marks)

2 Use psychological theories to explain how a teacher of physical education could change the negative attitude that a pupil may have towards swimming. (3 marks)

3 A player with a positive attitude fails to attend additional training sessions. Explain why the coach would be ill-advised to trust the consistency of a 'good attitude'.   (4 marks)

4 A young person may decline to get involved in a particular sport and display a negative attitude. What may have influenced the attitude of this young person?   (3 marks)

5 Identify the characteristics of a young person who is motivated to achieve in sport.   (5 marks)

6 Outline the strategies that a coach could adopt to encourage all performers to have a high motive to succeed.   (4 marks)

7 By giving an example from sport, explain the meaning of the term 'high incentive value'.   (3 marks)

8 As a teacher, how would you change the approach of a student who has a low need to achieve in sport?   (4 marks)

Section 3: *Group dynamics of sport performance*

Learning objectives

At the end of this section you should be able to:
- define a group or team
- understand Steiner's model of group performance
- explain the Ringlemann effect and social loafing and how they damage the cohesiveness of the group or team
- explain the factors affecting the development of group cohesion and how breakdown can be prevented
- identify the characteristics of leaders
- understand the importance of effective leadership
- describe emergent and prescribed leaders
- understand trait, social learning and interactionist perspectives on leadership
- explain the theories of leadership.

KEY WORDS

Interactive sports

Sports in which team members work with and rely on each other – for example, netball, rugby and hockey.

Introduction

In the context of **interactive sports** it is said that a champion team will defeat a team of individual champions and therefore the study of how groups operate as a unit is important.

Although a group can be described as comprising three or more individuals, this is not an adequate definition. The important factor in the formation of a group is that individuals interact. Group members should be aware and relate to each other by having a shared objective, which will bring about interaction.

> ❛ *Groups are those social aggregates that involve mutual awareness and the potential for interaction.* ❜
> (McGrath)

According to Carron, a group will form a 'bond' if the following characteristics are in place:
- a collective identity
- a sense of shared purpose
- a clear structure for communication.

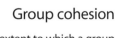

KEY WORDS

Group cohesion

The extent to which a group sticks together in pursuit of a common goal.

The term given to describe the degree of successful bonding or the strength of collective group co-operation is called **group cohesion**.

There are two dimensions in group cohesion and these are termed social and task cohesion. Although both are important, the nature of the game determines the contribution each makes towards collective group cohesion.

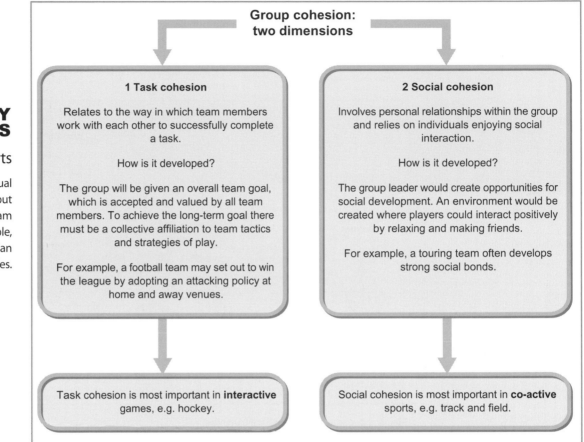

KEY WORDS

Co-active sports

Sports in which individual participation is required but aggregate into a team performance – for example, athletics and equestrian activities.

Fig. 4.13 Two dimensions of group cohesion.

TASK 6

Identify any successful sports team or organisation.

1 By applying the terms of McGrath and Carron, discuss how well the team operates as a unit.
2 Identify outstanding individuals, key pairings or sub-groups that operate in the context of the whole group.
3 Identify an occasion when the cohesiveness of the unit has broken down and suggest reasons for this breakdown.
4 Discuss how cohesiveness was restored.

KEY WORDS

Sub-groups

Small groups contained within the whole group.

Group dynamics

The social processes operating within the group between individual members.

Within a large group such as a county netball squad, there is the possibility that **sub-groups** will emerge.

Sub-groups damage the formation and development of a cohesive team and the coach should assess the **group dynamics** and, if necessary, adopt measures to unify it. One way to gather information about the dynamics of the group is to compile a socio-gram. In the socio-gram in Figure 4.14, each player was identified by a letter and asked to nominate three players with whom they could best work within a team situation.

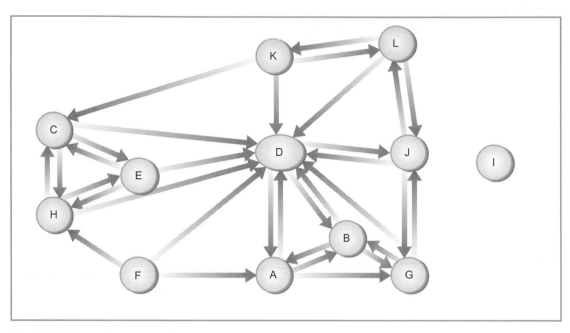

Fig. 4.14 Group dynamic socio-gram.

TASK 7

This socio-gram helped to select a starting five in basketball. The coach selected A, B, G, J and D. Why do you think this is?

There are several issues to observe within this socio-gram.

- D is the most popular and would possibly be the captain. Someone who is chosen by many is termed 'star'.
- C, E and H are an exclusive group. The term given to a sub-group of three would be triad or clique.
- K and L voted for each other and this pattern would constitute a reciprocal pair.
- F would be a reject as this person made three nominations but received none in return.
- I did not make choices and received no nominations. Such a figure is an isolate.

Fig. 4.15 The scrum is an interactive situation. There is the potential to lose cohesion through losses in co-ordination and motivation.

Rugby is an interactive game that relies on units within the team working closely together and individuals performing tasks that may remain unnoticed by spectators. The potential of the team to function as a cohesive unit is impeded when co-ordination between team players fails and the motivation of the individual drops. Steiner presented a model to explain the breakdown of cohesion.

Steiner's model

Actual Productivity = Potential Productivity – losses due to Faulty Processes (AP = PP–FP)

Actual productivity is the team performance at a given time during the game or event and refers to the extent of successful interaction. Potential productivity is the maximum capability of the group when cohesiveness is strongest. Faulty processes relate to the factors that can go wrong in team performance, which will impede or even prevent group cohesion and detract from the collective potential of the team.

There are two faulty processes that bring about losses in potential productivity.

1 Co-ordination losses

HOT TIPS

The causes of coordination breakdown and social loafing are popular questions.

These losses occur because the operational effectiveness of the group as a unit cannot be sustained for the duration of a match. Even the most carefully planned and rehearsed strategy may fail occasionally because of a positional error or because of an ill-timed move. Any breakdown in teamwork is regarded as a co-ordination loss and is termed the Ringlemann effect. Ringlemann stated that problems in team co-ordination are more likely to occur as the team numbers increase. For example, a basketball team is more likely to operate together successfully than a Rugby Union team. Research on co-ordination losses was based on studies into tug of war, where it was found that a team of eight did not pull eight times as hard as solo performers.

2 Motivation losses

These relate to an individual who suffers a reduction of motivation during performance causing the player to withdraw effort and 'coast' through a period of the game. This relaxation of effort is called 'social loafing' and this would detract from the cohesiveness of the team. A feeling that others in the team are not trying and when the efforts of the individual are not recognised cause social loafing. A player with low self-confidence or one who has suffered a negative experience will tend to be a loafer. A loss of motivation occurs if a task is perceived to be too difficult and can be linked with 'avoidance behaviour' mentioned in the last section. Loafing will also arise if a player feels that their performance is never watched or evaluated by the coach.

Group cohesion is the force that binds a group together, helping to prevent faulty processes. **Group locomotion** is the process that explains the reason why the group has formed and symbolises the activity of the team. For locomotion to be efficient there must be a leader to ensure the co-ordination of team members.

KEY WORDS

Group locomotion

The motivation that has brought about the existence of the group. It implies the drive to achieve group objectives.

TASK 9

1 Analyse a period of a game situation (preferably played by your school or college). Identify:

  (a) situations when group cohesion facilitated good play
  (b) circumstances when team play broke down due to the onset of faulty processes
  (c) the faulty processes.

2 Discuss how the coach would prevent the Ringlemann effect and social loafing from occurring.

Leadership

The importance of effective leadership

HOT TIPS

Consider the P.E. teacher as the leader of the class. Review the decisions made in order to teach a skill. Review 'Practice types' and 'Learning Skills' on pages 118 and 151 of *Advanced PE for OCR, AS*.

Most successful teams have strong leaders and the importance of this role is evident in all categories of sport. The performance of a leader is very clear in interactive games like hockey and football. However, although the leader's contribution in co-active team games like swimming and athletics is less obvious, the position remains influential.

Leadership may be considered as the behavioural process of influencing individuals and groups towards set goals. As such, a leader has the dual function of ensuring player satisfaction whilst steering the individual or group to success. In the pressured environment of modern-day sport, the leader's duties are becoming harder. At the higher levels there may be several positions of control. An outstanding example of effective leader behaviour is that of Martin Johnson, the England Rugby Union captain who led his team to World Cup success in 2003.

Characteristics of an effective leader

HOT TIPS

The characteristics of effective leadership are a popular examination question and are often overlooked. It is wrongly assumed that good players make good leaders.

An effective leader should have the following qualities:

- good communication skills
- highly developed perception skills
- good at making decisions
- empathy with team members
- understand the needs of others
- experience
- vision
- ambition
- determination.

A controversial issue arising in most sport psychology components is whether human behaviour is inherited or learned. This nature or nurture debate is also present in the topic of leadership. A key issue focuses on whether a good leader born or made.

Trait approach

HOT TIPS

Look back at the work you did on the trait theory of personality, page 224.

The presenters of trait theory believe that leaders are born with the skills necessary to take charge. They consider leadership traits to be stable personality dispositions such as intelligence, assertiveness and self-confidence. If this is true, a leader should be able to take control of any situation. This is highly unlikely. An early trait theory is the 'great man theory of leadership', which suggested that the necessary qualities are inherited by sons (not daughters) whose fathers have been successful in this field. This is not a popular theory. Like early trait personality research, leadership trait work has revealed few conclusive findings.

Although certain traits may be helpful in leadership, they are not essential and so trait theory is not a good predictor of behaviour. People who have dominant traits in tough mindedness and independent thinking are not guaranteed success in leadership.

Social learning theory

Proponents of this theory believe that all behaviours are learned and that learning comes about through contact with strong environmental forces. For example, when an aspiring captain judges a situation to have been handled well by an experienced leader, the method will be remembered and copied should a similar situation arise. The process of imitating the successful behaviour of role

Fig. 4.16 Watching, learning and copying from others changes the behaviour of the observer. Reinforcement occurs if behaviour is successful. This process strengthens the learning bond.

models is called 'vicarious reinforcement' – the skills of leadership can be acquired by imitation and developed through experience. The weakness in social learning theory is that it does not take into account the trait perspective.

Interactionist theory

According to this theory, leadership competencies emerge because of inherited abilities and learned skills. Gill (2000) indicates that interactionist theories give a more realistic explanation of human behaviours in sport.

Selection of a leader

A leader can be selected in one of two ways.

- An emergent leader already belongs to the group and selection to the position of authority is made formally – for example, by vote or interview – or the role is assumed and readily accepted by the group.
- A prescribed leader is selected from outside of the group and is known as an external appointment.

TASK 10

Identify an example of an emergent and a prescribed leader from a sporting context. Give three advantages and three disadvantages of the emergent and the prescribed leader's position when charge of a group is first taken.

Styles of leadership

Fiedler's contingency model

Fiedler identified two types of leadership in his contingency model.

- Task-orientated or autocratic leaders.
- Social- or person-orientated leaders, also referred to as democratic leaders.

HOT TIPS

In the exam you are often asked to match a leadership style with a situation.

The autocratic leader tends to make all of the decisions and is motivated to complete the task as quickly and effectively as possible. This leadership style is authoritarian and does not take into account the opinions or preferences of the group. The autocratic leader will not share responsibility and focuses on group performance and achieving goals. This style would be most effective when quick decisions are needed for large groups of people – for example, in interactive games. Furthermore, a task-orientated approach would be required in potentially dangerous situations that could be life threatening in outdoor pursuits.

Fig. 4.17

HOT TIPS

Note that the autocratic style of leadership is best for interactive gaames. Democratic is best for co-active games. Look back at page 237, task cohesion and social cohesion.

HOT TIPS

Be able to describe a highly favourable and a highly unfavourable situation in PE or sport. Be aware that the autocratic task-orientated leader would operate best in the most and least favourable situations.

TASK 11

Discuss why an autocratic style of leadership would be most effective in the situation in Figure 4.17.

The democratic leader will share the decisions with the group and is often ready to share responsibility. This type of leader believes in consultation and is interested in developing meaningful inter-personal relationships within the team. The belief is that by giving 'ownership' of the task to each individual, the group will work harder, develop unity and a common purpose. This style would be effective in a co-active game when time constraints are not as exacting and personal support may be required.

According to Fiedler, the correct style of leadership to adopt depends on the 'favourableness' of the situation.

A highly favourable situation	A highly unfavourable situation
Leader's position is strong	Leader's position is weak
Task is simple with clear structure	Task is complex with vague structure
Warm group and leader relations	Hostile group and leader relations

Fiedler states that autocratic task-orientated leaders are more effective in both the most favourable and the least favourable situations. Democratic person-orientated leaders are more effective in moderately favourable situations (see Figure 4.18 below).

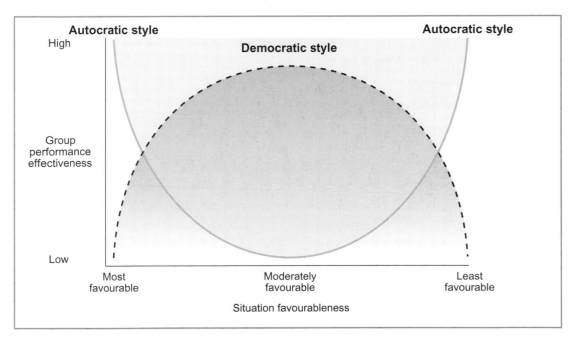

Fig. 4.18 Fiedler's leadership style and favourability of the situation.

Laissez-faire leadership style

In this style, the leader will stand aside and allow the group to make its own independent decisions. This style can be self-implementing if the leader is lacking confidence or motivation resulting in a loss of group direction. Lewin (1985) found that members of this type of group tended to be aggressive toward each other when mistakes occurred and they gave up easily.

The multidimensional model of sports leadership

Chellanduria believed that the effectiveness of leadership could be judged on the degree of success accomplished during a task and the extent to which the group experienced satisfaction while being led to the goal.

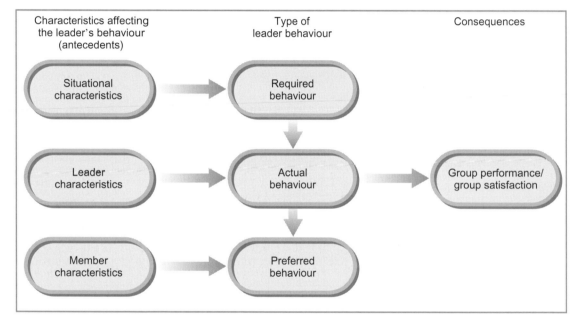

Fig. 4.19 Multidimensional model of sports leadership.

Chellanduria stated that three factors interact to determine the behaviour adopted by the leader. These initial factors are termed **antecedents**.

• **Situational characteristics.** Examples of these are environmental conditions such as whether the group is involved in interactive or co-active sports. The numbers involved in the team is another important factor, as would be the time constraints of the play or overall match. Considerations about the strengths of the opposition would also be part of the situation.

• **Leader characteristics.** This includes the skill, personality and experience of the leader. In addition, the inclination the leader has towards a person or a task-orientated style would be a significant characteristic.

• **Group member characteristics.** The factors relating to members would involve age, gender, motivation, competence and experience.

Next, Chellanduria recognises three types of leader behaviour that would be guided by the antecedents.

- **Required behaviour.** This involves what ought to be done by the leader in certain situations. The leader's behaviour may be dictated by a strategy or organisation system.
- **Actual behaviour** is what the leader chooses to do as the best course of action in the given situation. Actual behaviour is greatly influenced by the competence of the leader.
- **Preferred behaviour** concerns what the group or athlete wants the leader to do. The leadership style preferred by the group is usually determined by the member characteristics.

The important element of the theory is that if all three of the leader's behaviours are **congruent**, then member satisfaction and high group performance will result. In other words, effective leadership has taken place if the actual leader behaviour has surpassed the situational demands and the style has met with the approval of the group.

KEY WORDS

Congruent

Coincide exactly.

HOT TIPS

All three leader behaviours must coincide exactly before effective leadership can take place.

HOT TIPS

The key to understanding the multidimensional model of sports leadership is that optimal performance and group satisfaction occurs if the leader behaviour is appropriate for the situation and suits the preference of the group.

HOT TIPS

Link group cohesion with leadership.

TASK 12

Make two copies of the multidimensional model of sports leadership and consider the following examples:

1   the captain of a senior international team
2   the coach introducing youngsters to a gymnastics.

For each example, fill in the boxes relating to the characteristics affecting leader behaviour and the type of leader behaviour. Discuss how both leaders would attain high performance while ensuring group member satisfaction.

Revise as you go! Test your knowledge and understanding

- What do you understand by the term 'group'?
- Define the terms 'group cohesion' and 'group locomotion'.
- Name and describe the sub-groups that can operate within the main group.
- How could the coach prevent the formation of sub-groups?
- What is meant by Steiner's prediction $AP = PP - FP$?
- Identify two FPs and explain how FPs could be prevented.
- List five characteristics of an effective leader.
- Describe two leadership styles outlined in Fiedler's contingency model.
- List the factors that would cause both a highly favourable and a highly unfavourable leader situation to exist.
- Identify the leadership styles that suit unfavourable and moderately favourable situations.

- Outline the disadvantages of a laissez-faire approach to leadership.
- State what is meant by the term 'congruence of leader behaviour'.
- Why is congruence of leader behaviour important to the effectiveness of leadership?
- Outline the key prediction made by Chellanduria in the multidimensional model of sports leadership.

Sharpen up your exam technique!

1 What factors affect the cohesion of a group? (4 marks)

2 What does social loafing mean? What causes it? (4 marks)

3 As a team coach, how would you minimise the chances of social loafing occurring? (4 marks)

4 There may be co-ordination problems relating to team performance, which contribute to the faulty processes. What is the Ringlemann effect? Explain the strategies that a coach could use to minimise this effect. (6 marks)

5 Leadership is important in optimising team performance in sport. 'Leaders are born and not made' is a common view relating to the concept of leadership. Give some qualities of a good leader in the context of sport and discuss the view that a leader is a product of both nature and nurture. (7 marks)

6 How might a sports team select a leader? (2 marks)

7 With reference to the multidimensional model of sports leadership, explain how the optimal performance and satisfaction of a group of sports performers can be achieved. (6 marks)

8 By using a practical example to illustrate your answer, explain when an authoritarian style of leadership could be used. (4 marks)

Section 4: *Mental preparation for sport performance*

Learning objectives

At the end of this section you should be able to:
- understand the meanings and the links between the following terms: commitment, self-confidence, concentration and control of emotion
- explain each term in the context of mental preparation for sport performance
- identify and explain the relevant theories associated with each term.

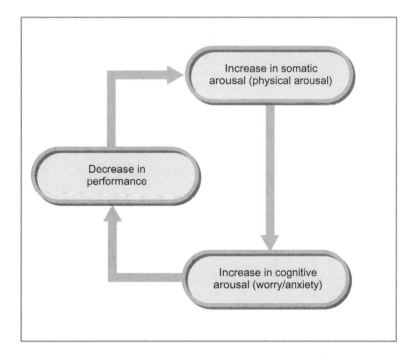

Fig. 4.20 Negative thought anxiety cycle (Ziegler).

HOT TIPS

Link commitment with achievement motivation by referring to approach and avoidance behaviours.

Introduction

A committed performer in sport will become involved in challenges and develop the capacity to persevere often in the face of adversity. Without commitment the aspirations of the individual will not be realised and potential will remain unfulfilled.

Commitment is readily displayed after a run of success. Success develops confidence and with it brings the expectation of higher attainment. On the other hand, failure would reduce confidence and cause an increase in anxiety to impede future performance. The relationship between increasing anxiety and sport performance operates on a downward spiral resulting in learned helplessness, avoidance behaviours and a withdrawal of commitment.

Measures can be put into place to increase the level of commitment and to address the issues of confidence, concentration and control of emotion in all circumstances. One such measure is goal setting.

SportscoachUK believes that the setting and successful attainment of goals helps to increase commitment, develop self-confidence, focus attention and reduce the anxiety of the practising athlete.

Goal setting

A goal could be described as a standard of excellence that the individual is trying to accomplish. Goals have three different lengths, long term, medium term and short term.

A long-term goal is a strong motivating force and could be described as the ultimate aim or dream. Such a goal could take years to be attained and the opportunity for attainment may arise only once – for example, competing in an Olympic Games.

HOT TIPS

Feedback is most effective when given alongside short-term goals.

Medium-term goals give the opportunity for achievement on a monthly or annual basis while a short-term goal can be awarded and reviewed on a daily or weekly basis. The short-term goals provide important feedback concerning the progress towards the final destination.

Types of goal

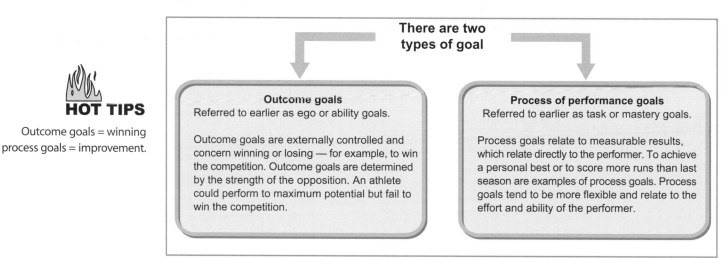

HOT TIPS

Outcome goals = winning process goals = improvement.

There are two types of goal

Outcome goals
Referred to earlier as ego or ability goals.

Outcome goals are externally controlled and concern winning or losing — for example, to win the competition. Outcome goals are determined by the strength of the opposition. An athlete could perform to maximum potential but fail to win the competition.

Process of performance goals
Referred to earlier as task or mastery goals.

Process goals relate to measurable results, which relate directly to the performer. To achieve a personal best or to score more runs than last season are examples of process goals. Process goals tend to be more flexible and relate to the effort and ability of the performer.

Fig. 4.21 The type of goal can directly influence confidence (see page 249).

> **TASK 13**
> Decide the type of goal that would be most effective to increase the confidence of the athlete. Give reasons for your answer.

HOT TIPS

A process goal is more likely to change TAF behaviours into TAS behaviours (see page 231–2).

It is safer to set process goals because the performer has some control over the attainment. The achievement of an outcome goal like winning can never be guaranteed in top-class sport and failure to reach this type of goal can have a negative effect on self-confidence. However, to reach a performance target against oneself is a more accurate reflection of progress and commitment.

Fig. 4.22 Outcome goals are measured by winning or losing.

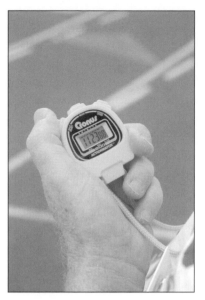

Fig. 4.23 Process or performance goals measure improvement.

Sport psychologist Gill (2000) noted that athletes who pursued process goals were less anxious and performed better than those seeking outcome goals. Furthermore, it is better to set specific and measurable goals rather than 'do your best goals' or no goals. When setting a goal to improve netball shooting, it is important to be specific – for example, improving from a 75 per cent to 85 per cent success rate.

It is important to be aware of the SMARTER principle of goal setting as identified by SportscoachUK. These principles describe the qualities required for the effective setting of process goals.

Specific to the event or skill.
Measurable targets ensure that progress can be compared with a standard.
Accepted by the coach and the performer.
Realistic goals should be set that are challenging but within reach.
Time limitations must be in place.
Exciting goals will inspire and reward the performer.
Recording progress provides feedback and motivation: 'Ink it, don't think it.'

Self-confidence

> *The most consistent difference between elite and less successful athletes is that elite athletes possess greater self-confidence.*
> (Gould *et al*)

KEY WORDS

Self-efficacy

Specific self-confidence. It relates to personal perception of competence in particular situations and so fluctuates greatly.

Micro approach

A narrow or specific approach.

Leading social psychologist Bandura put forward the notion that as people become competent in particular skills and situations they develop a feeling of **self-efficacy**.

Self-efficacy relates to specific situations only and is not the same as self-confidence, which is a far more general term. For example, a player may have high self-efficacy when involved in rugby, which would facilitate a confident and committed performance, but lack efficacy in racquet games. For this reason, self-efficacy is a **micro approach** to understanding self-confidence, but the terms are interchangeable.

It is significant that Bandura proposed that people with high self-efficacy tended to seek challenges, apply effort and persevere with tasks (TAS behaviour). They also tend to attribute success to factors that relate directly to themselves, such as ability and effort. These attributions would elevate confidence and increase the expectation of success in the next challenge.

HOT TIPS

Link self-efficacy with achievement motivation, attribution and attribution retraining.

On the other hand, those low in self-efficacy avoid challenges, become anxious when faced with difficulties and attributed failure to themselves (TAF behaviours).

The level of efficacy determines efficacy expectations, which directly influence the choice and commitment an individual makes regarding sporting activities. Most importantly, efficacy expectations can be changed by an input of four major types of information, which are the sub-processes in self-efficacy theory. By applying each of the four sub-processes, the coach can change the negative expectation and raise specific self-confidence of those lacking in self-belief.

HOT TIPS

Makr sure you can list and explain the four components of self-efficacy theory. They arise frequently in questions.

Self-efficacy theory

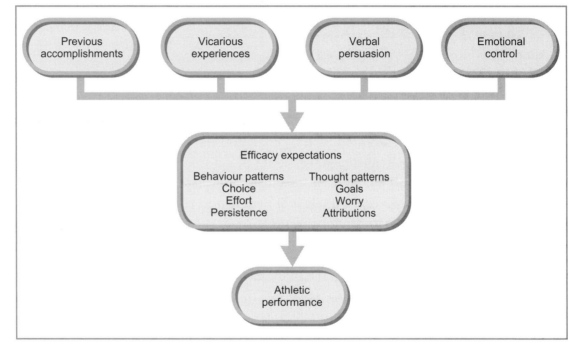

Fig. 4.24 Self-efficacy theory.

HOT TIPS

Look back at learned helplessness on page 220.

KEY WORDS

Creative imagery

Forming a picture of others performing the task. A cognitive process similar to mental rehearsal.

- **Previous accomplishments.** A performer who experiences learned helplessness or a loss of confidence could be reminded of previous successes in the related skill or situation. Reinforcement of past attainments represents the most powerful effects on self-efficacy as they are based on personal mastery experiences.
- **Vicarious experiences.** This process involves watching others perform the skill in question. The use of a demonstration or a model of the required behaviour reduces worry and develops confidence although it is less powerful than the use of previous accomplishments. '**Creative imagery**', or modelling, is also a useful vicarious process for highly experienced athletes who lack confidence due to a loss of form or are back in training after injury.

Fig. 4.25 Imagery played an important part in enhancing and maintaining Steve Backley's confidence: 'I practise imagery at all times – it is almost an obsession – I sometimes visualise myself throwing 90 metres.'

- **Verbal persuasion.** This involves convincing the athlete he or she has the ability to perform the skill in question. This positive talk or persuasion is an attempt to manipulate behaviour and is usually conveyed by the coach although many successful sports players reassure themselves through 'positive self-talk'.
- **Emotional control.** This refers to the evaluation the performer makes of a physiological state. For example, those lacking in efficacy may perceive increased heart and respiration rates as a symptom of apprehension and nervousness and not as a positive physiological preparation for action.

HOT TIPS

A lack of confidence results in high arousal levels. Refer to Figure 4.01 on page 219 and think about the links between confidence, control, concentration and commitment.

Sport specific model of sport confidence

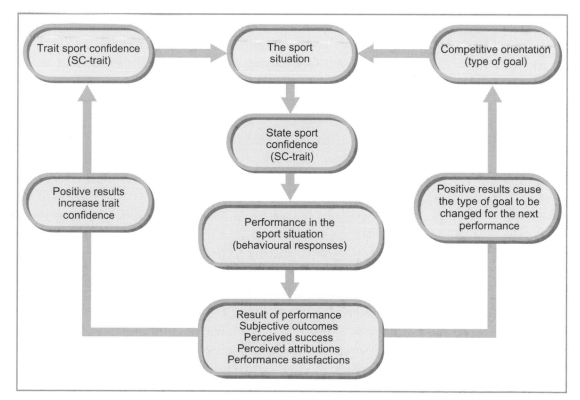

Fig. 4.26 Sport-specific model of sport confidence (Vealey).

The Vealey model relates directly to sports situations and she defines sport confidence as 'the belief or degree of certainty individuals possess about their ability to be successful in sport'.

Explanation of the model

1 The athlete confronts the objective sport situation (which can be general or specific – for example, the whole football match or the penalty shoot out) with a degree of **trait sport confidence**.
2 The athlete also has a competitive orientation. This refers to the type of goal used by the performer to judge success – for example, process or outcome goal.
3 The level of trait confidence and the type of goal to measure success interact with the sports situation. This interaction produces **state sport confidence**.
4 The degree of state sport confidence helps to predict the standard of sport performance in the given situation.
5 A subjective evaluation will follow performance. This will include how the performer has interpreted success (perception), the causes of success (attributions) and performance satisfaction.
6 These subjective outcomes modify trait confidence and the nature of the goal set to measure achievement, and this is reflected in other sports.

Vealey identified a number of sources of sports confidence.

- Mastery of skill. This occurs when a skill has been acquired and the performer perceives that progress has been made.
- Styling. Confidence will develop if the individual is able to demonstrate a highly skilled performance to significant others.
- Physical and mental preparation will increase the likelihood of successful performance.
- An accurate self-perception will help the individual to endorse the strengths and address the weaknesses in performance.
- Social reinforcement and a sense of belonging to a cohesive team unit will raise confidence.
- Effective leadership promotes confidence in team members.
- Vicarious experiences do much to convince the performer that success in a new situation is possible. Modelling takes place by copying others who have mastered the skill and by practising symbolic imagery.
- Environmental comfort emphasises that the apprehensive individual will be helped if the working conditions are suitable – for example, the novice should not be observed when learning a new skill.
- Situational favourableness. If practice is going well and desired results are forthcoming then confidence will increase.

Concentration

Concentration involves focusing attention onto the relevant environmental cues and maintaining attentional focus until the skill has been completed. Martens proposed that mistakes happen in top-level sport not because technique is suspect, but because of attentional errors.

Concentration can be drawn by external factors such as stimulus intensity, but internal processes such as cognition and the emotional condition of arousal are also determinants. This section is concerned with how internal processes control attention and concentration.

Arousal can be considered as the level of excitement or activation generated in the central nervous system. At low levels, arousal is associated with lethargic sleep-like states while at the highest levels it stimulates extremely alert states and frenetic behaviour often seen in life-threatening situations. The inverted U hypothesis predicts the influence that varying degrees of arousal have on the performance of motor skills.

Fig. 4.27 Concentration is vital to the information processing and decision-making systems. It is the key to successful execution of all sports skills.

KEY WORDS

Perceptual field

Attentional focus.

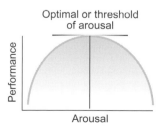

HOT TIPS

As arousal increases so does the quality of performance up to a critical or optimal point. After this threshold, if arousal continues to increase, performance will deteriorate.

It is straightforward to predict that poor performance occurs when the individual is either under- or over-aroused and that skills are produced to best effect at optimal levels of arousal. However, it is important to explain why this is the case.

When arousal is low, the **perceptual field** widens and an excessive number of environmental cues enter into the information processing system.

Selective attention is not in operation and concentration on relevant information is difficult.

As a consequence, a condition known as information overload occurs and the process of decision-making is seriously impeded causing mistakes in performance.

As arousal increases, the perceptual field will adjust to the ideal width enabling the performer to focus on the most relevant information. Selective attention is fully operational and the potential to concentrate is maximised. The theory, which predicts the selection of the most relevant environmental data at the optimal arousal level, is termed 'cue utilisation hypothesis'. This would account for efficient decision-making and effective performance.

Beyond the optimal threshold, the perceptual focus narrows excessively and the relevant cue may be missed. At this stage, the athlete may appear highly agitated and begin to panic in an effort to succeed. This condition is known as hyper-vigilance or panic.

Optimal or threshold of arousal

Performance

Arousal

Fig. 4.28 Inverted U hypothesis.

Attentional styles

Although adjustment of the perceptual field explains how attentional focus is maximised, it does not make clear what happens when the **width of attention** needs to change in response to varying situations in sport. For example, the goal attack in netball requires a narrower width of attention when shooting than the centre player in an open passage of play.

Nideffer (1976) identified four types of attentional style in sport and these have been arranged on two dimensions.

* Width (broad/narrow)
* Direction (internal/external).

Nideffer recognised four attentional styles:

* broad/external
* external/narrow
* narrow/internal
* internal/broad.

The broad and narrow dimension (width) represents an information continuum and refers to the number of environmental cues that require attention. The 'broad' extreme demands the performer to attend to many sensory cues while the 'narrow' extreme requires focus onto one cue.

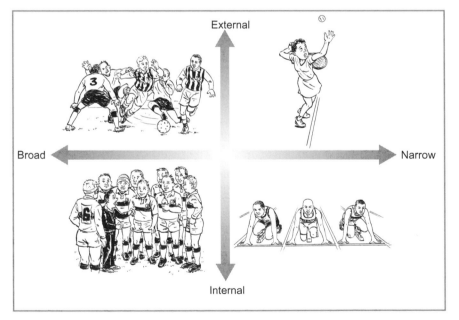

Fig. 4.29 Four attentional styles.

On the direction dimension, external attention relates to focus as being outward and directed onto an object such as the ball in basketball or the movement of an opponent in tennis. Internal attention refers to an inward focus onto thoughts or feelings. For example, a coach analysing strategies or a javelin thrower may use imagery techniques and mental rehearsal during preparation.

The external/internal dimension is not a continuum but represents a dichotomy, meaning it is either one or the other and there are no in-between states.

In activities in which the environment changes, it may be necessary to use all four styles when appropriate. This shift in attentional focus could happen in the preparation or the execution of the skill. For example, the hooker in Rugby Union will throw the ball into the line using a narrow and external focus while preparation for the throw would require an internal and narrow style. If the hooker should then run with the ball in open play, broad and external attention will be needed.

> ### TASK 14
> If the hooker in a rugby team was also the captain, discuss the attentional style required to work out a strategy of attack in a low-scoring match. Justify the placement of the activities in those particular quadrants shown in Figure 4.29 on page 254.

Emotional control

Nothing is attained in sport without a degree of motivation and so study of this area is of particular interest to the sport psychologist. The terms of arousal, activation, stress and anxiety relate to motivation, and although the terms are often used interchangeably, it is important that each is clearly defined.

- **Motivation** is a psychological drive to achieve a need or goal. It is divided into two dimensions. These are intensity of behaviour and direction of behaviour.
- **Arousal** is the intensity of behaviour. It ranges on a continuum from deep sleep to highly agitated and frenetic behaviour recognised as hyper-vigilance. Arousal has two forms, one being a physiological state termed somatic arousal, which can be measured objectively, and the second being cognitive arousal. Therefore, arousal can be viewed as being multidimensional. An increase in cognitive arousal eventually leads the performer into a state of worry or apprehension. In this way there is a close link with anxiety.
- **Anxiety** is an emotional state closely linked to cognitive arousal, and is characterised by feelings of worry, apprehension and psychological tension.
- **Stress** is an environmental stimulus like conflict, competition or frustration, that triggers arousal. Such stimuli are called stressors.
- **Activation** describes a state of physiological preparedness, which is directly associated with the degree of arousal – for example, fight or flight.

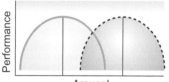

Fig. 4.30 Performance and arousal.

It has previously been established that arousal will improve the quality of performance up to an optimal point. However, this optimal threshold changes or 'shifts' for every individual and different situation.

Four factors necessitate the understanding of this 'shift' in optimal arousal.

- **Personality.** Extroverts perform best when arousal level is high. However, an introverted personality type would return full potential in conditions of low arousal. Introverts have a very sensitive reticular activation system (RAS), which increases the tendency towards anxiety. Extroverts tend to seek the stimulation of the RAS and so perform to maximum potential in stressful circumstances. RAS is involved in the process of selective attention.

- **Task type.** Simple tasks such as shot putting tend to be gross, habitual and have a wide margin for error. These skills are best performed in conditions of high arousal. Complex tasks are often more perceptual, manipulative and have less tolerance for error. An example of a complex task, which is performed best in conditions of low arousal, is spin bowling in cricket.
- **Stage of learning.** The athlete at the expert or autonomous stage of learning would find that high arousal would enhance performance, whereas those at the cognitive or associative stages have a greater need to concentrate on basic movements. They would learn and perform best when in a calmer emotional state.
- **Experience.** The highly experienced veteran player would find that performance improves when arousal is high. On the other hand, the novice performs best in conditions of low arousal.

Individual zone of optimal functioning (IZOF)

HOT TIPS

Mental preparation and arousal not only influence sports performance but also motor skill learning. This makes for good synoptic links between movement skills and sport psychology (see pages 151–6 of *Advanced PE for OCR: AS*).

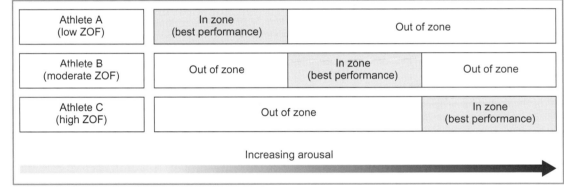

Fig. 4.31 Individual zone of optimal functioning (Hanin).

HOT TIPS

An athlete will enter the zone when arousal is at an optimal level and the situation matches the athlete's strongest attentional style.

Hanin found that top athletes have an individual zone of optimal arousal in which best performance occurs. Outside of this zone, poor performance occurs. Hanin's theory differs from the inverted U hypothesis in two ways.

- The optimal level of arousal does not always coincide with the mid point of the arousal continuum but varies in accordance to the individual and the situation.
- The optimal level of arousal is not a single point but a 'band width'. Both theories indicate that 'ideal' arousal states differ, and the implication is that teachers and coaches should guide the performer towards their personal 'optimal threshold' or 'individual zone of optimal functioning'.

The characteristics of being in the zone include: the performance appears effortless and automatic with the athlete feeling in full control; the attention and concentration of the performer is focused; the execution of the skill brings enjoyment and satisfaction.

Anxiety

Spielberger identified two sources of anxiety. Some people appear to be anxious at all times and in everything they undertake. This is recognised as trait anxiety and is genetically inherited. As an indelible characteristic of personality, trait anxiety tends to be permanent and relatively stable. The second source is state anxiety, which fluctuates in response to a given situation and is associated with arousal.

State anxiety is a learned behavioural response and as an unstable condition, it can be controlled and manipulated to facilitate optimal performance.

In competitive sports situations, anxiety is most frequently generated if the athlete feels that his or her ability is not up to coping with the situation. Martens proposes a three-way imbalance in perception.

> *Anxiety occurs when there is a substantial imbalance between the individual's perception of their ability and their perception of the demands and importance of the situation.*

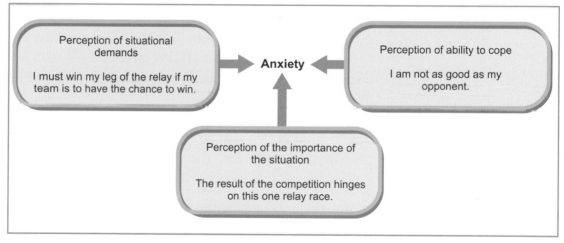

Fig. 4.32 Generation of anxiety.

- **Somatic response.** This type of response will follow the curve of performance as predicted in the inverted U hypothesis and refers to physiological changes. The athlete who is experiencing high anxiety will experience excesses in muscular tension, heart and respiration rates, resulting in impaired movement. Such a condition will not allow the performer to enter a '**peak flow**' state.
- **Cognitive response.** Reflects increasing worry about performance. If this remains unchecked, the athlete will become increasingly apprehensive and develop doubts and negative thoughts. Attentional changes occur and this will adversely influence the information processing system. If the athlete experiences worry, he or she will not attain a 'peak flow' state.

Fig. 4.33 An athlete engaged in mental rehearsal prior to performance.

Anxiety management to improve performance

The methods to control anxiety are listed as somatic or cognitive techniques.

Cognitive methods include the following.

- **Imagery.** The anxious person must withdraw from the situation and imagine him or herself to be in a peaceful and calm setting in which he or she has total control. This would be an excellent technique to use when complete relaxation is required when high somatic and cognitive arousal interact adversely. Imagery can also take the form of mental rehearsal. Mental rehearsal involves thinking through as vividly as possible prior to performance. Expert performers cannot only recall a visual image but also kinaesthetic imagery (that brings to mind the feel of the skill) can prevent negative thoughts and raise the confidence of the athlete. Finally, creative imagery has a positive effect on self-confidence and is a form of vicarious experience mentioned in self-efficacy theory.
- **Thought stopping.** This technique requires the athlete to refuse to think negatively. Any negative inclination should be stopped and substituted with a positive thought.
- **Positive talk.** This involves the athlete endorsing his or her own ability or progress by literally talking to him or herself. This is common practice amongst tennis players and batters facing confidence-threatening situations in cricket. Speaking aloud commits the athlete to the task and does much to raise confidence.
- **Rational thinking.** It has been said that anxiety grows from an imbalance of perception between ability and situational demands. Rational thinking involves focusing inwardly into the internal and narrow style of attention and evaluating the situation and its possible consequences logically.

Somatic methods include the following.

- **Progressive muscular relaxation.** This requires the athlete to increase the tension of the muscles throughout the body and gradually relax each group in turn. Jacobson devised this effective technique in 1938. However, the fact that it is time consuming is a major drawback.
- **Biofeedback.** This involves providing the athlete with immediate physiological feedback. For example, an ongoing reading from an electrocardiograph can help an anxious subject to control heart rate and reduce feelings of anxiety.

Peak flow experience in sport

This condition links together the whole section relating to mental preparation for sport. Peak flow was recognised by Csikzentmimalyi and described as an optimal experience that facilitates best performance and is intrinsically rewarding.

Factors that contribute to the peak flow experience

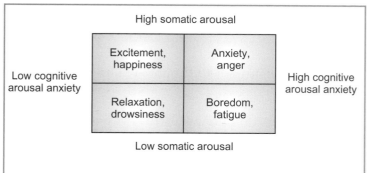

Fig. 4.34 Peak flow experience – the interaction of somatic and cognitive arousal.

- Peak flow occurs when somatic arousal has reached an appropriate threshold and cognitive arousal is low.
- Flow state is attained when the performer has a balanced perception of the demands of the situation and his/her ability to cope.
- A high incentive value is to be gained from a challenge that is both realistic and attainable.
- The focus of attention and concentration is maximised.
- There is a self-confident belief that nothing can go wrong.
- The situation suits the athlete's strongest attentional style.

During these rare moments in sport, the athlete assumes control over all internal and environmental variables and a time of greatest happiness and self-fulfilment is experienced.

Revise as you go! Test your knowledge and understanding

- What is the purpose of goal setting?
- Describe what short-, medium- and long-term goals are.
- Outline the difference between outcome and performance or process goals.
- Identify the type of goal that should be issued to an athlete lacking in confidence.
- Outline the principles of good goal setting.
- What is meant by 'self-efficacy'?
- Identify and explain the four sub-processes of self-efficacy theory.
- List five sources of sport confidence as identified by Vealey.
- Describe the prediction made by the inverted U hypothesis.
- Explain why maximum performance potential cannot be achieved in conditions of under- and over-arousal.
- Identify and explain Nideffer's four attentional styles.
- Describe the relationship of optimal arousal with personality, stage of learning, task type and experience.
- According to Hanin, what are the characteristics of being 'in the zone'?
- Explain why the construct of arousal is considered multidimensional.
- Describe the outcome of a combination of high somatic arousal and high cognitive arousal.
- Identify five techniques to managing anxiety.
- List five characteristics of peak flow experience.

Sharpen up your exam technique!

1   Define what is meant by 'stress' and in the context of physical activity give an example of a 'stressor'. What do the results of the Sports Competitive Anxiety Test (SCAT) indicate?   (4 marks)

2   Define state and trait anxiety and give examples to support your answer.
                                                                                (3 marks)

3   There are cognitive and somatic methods of managing stress in sport. Outline three methods of stress management and show how they can be applied to a situation in sport.   (4 marks)

4   What is meant by the term 'self-efficacy'? By using an example from sport, show how a coach could help a performer with low self-efficacy.   (5 marks)

5   Using the inverted U hypothesis, discuss the view that a high level of arousal is desirable for the performance of motor skills.   (4 marks)

6   Explain the cue utilisation hypothesis, its links to arousal and its effects on performance.   (6 marks)

7   By using practical examples to illustrate your answer, explain Vealey's model of sports confidence.   (4 marks)

8   Hanin identified what is termed as the 'zone of optimal functioning'. Explain the characteristics of being 'in the zone'.   (4 marks)

9   By giving an example of each, describe the four attentional styles identified by Nideffer.   (4 marks)

10 What strategies might the coach adopt to facilitate a 'peak flow' experience for the athlete?   (5 marks)

Section 5: *Competition effects on sport performance*

Learning objectives

At the end of this section you should be able to:
* distinguish between aggression, assertion and channelled aggression
* understand the major theories of aggression
* describe how aggressive tendencies can be eliminated
* explain social facilitation and social inhibition
* describe the major theories of social facilitation and link them to arousal
* understand the homefield advantage phenomenon
* prescribe strategies to combat social inhibition.

Aggression

Bull defined aggression as 'any behaviour that is intended to harm another individual by physical or verbal means', while Baron proposed that 'aggression is any form of behaviour directed toward the goal of harming or injuring another living being who is motivated to avoid such treatment'.

These definitions imply that aggression is socially unacceptable and so does not have a place in sport. While this is true, questions must be asked about actions like the crash tackle in rugby or the tia toshi throw in judo. Both these skills have the capacity to injure, but they are recognised as being a legitimate part of the sport. Baron gets closer to understanding the term by dividing aggression into three categories.

HOT TIPS

Give clear and unquestionable examples of hostile aggression, for example, a deliberate over the ball challenge in football.

HOT TIPS

Instrumental aggression is also known as channelled aggression.

- **Hostile (or reactive) aggression.** This is the type of aggression that needs to be eliminated from sport. The prime motive of such an act is to harm an opponent and the chief reinforcement of the aggressor is to inflict injury. Aggressive actions are outside the rules of any game, and discretions are dysfunctional in the context of sport and often detrimental to team performance. Parens describes aggression as 'hostile destructiveness'. Hostile aggression involves anger.
- **Instrumental (or channelled) aggression.** This describes an action that is within the rules and although the prime motive is the successful execution of the skill, there is still the intention to harm. The Rugby League player will run hard at the defence with the primary intention of breaking the tackles. However, the secondary intention is to inflict a painful experience so the defender may be reluctant to tackle next time. Anger is not evident.
- **Assertive behaviour.** This does not attempt to harm and is strictly within the rules and spirit of the game. For this reason it could be said that assertion is not a form of aggression. It involves robust but functional play, which is primarily focused on completing the skill successfully, and this is the major reinforcement. To drive through a group of players to score in basketball is assertive and not aggressive. Assertion was described by Parens in 1987 as 'non-hostile self-protective mastery behaviour'.

Antecedents of aggression in sport

An antecedent is a prior circumstance that could account for behaviour. In brief, an antecedent is a cause.

- The nature of the game (contact or non-contact).
- The wide division between the scores will increase the chance of aggression.
- Previous experience may have developed grudges or scores to settle.
- Frustration caused by poor form, opposition and referees' decisions.
- Hostile crowds.
- The venue. Away teams commit more fouls.

- Excessively high arousal levels.
- Extrinsic rewards.

Theories of aggression
Instinct theory – trait perspective

Freud initially proposed instinct theory but Lorenz later extended his work in 1966. This perspective states that aggression is genetically inherited and that a trait of violence lies within everyone due to a basic instinct to dominate. Freud called this innate characteristic the 'death instinct', the purpose of which is to seek aggressive destruction. Lorenz put forward the idea that aggressive energy is constantly building up and needs to be released.

Social learning theory – social learning perspective

Bandura presented social learning theory in 1966, which was later extended by Leakey. Supporters of this theory do not believe that aggression is a biologically based innate characteristic but is nurtured through environmental forces. Aggression is therefore learned by watching and copying from role models and becomes an accepted mode of behaviour if it is reinforced.

Frustration aggression hypothesis – interactionist perspective

HOT TIPS

Learning theories can be found on page 151 of *Advanced PE for OCR: AS*. Learning theories and aggression make for a good synoptic link.

This is an interactionist theory and was proposed by Dollard. Frustration develops when goal-directed behaviour or a need to achieve is blocked. Frustration could occur in situations involving defeat, good opposition and poor officiating. This is considered to be an interactionist theory because it is instinctive to fulfil the need to release frustration. However, frustration is environmentally generated and aggression is the result, whereas with instinct theory, aggression is the goal. If the aggressive act is successful, frustration is released and the aggressor feels good and

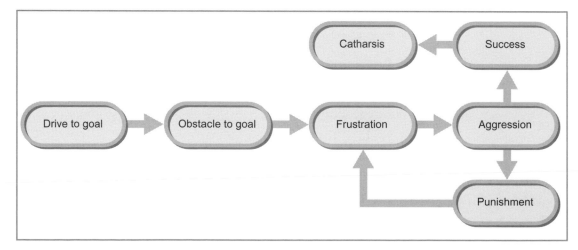

Fig. 4.35 Frustration aggression hypothesis.

learns that violent strategies are successful. Should aggression fail and result in punishment, further frustration is generated.

Aggression cue hypothesis (Berkowitz, 1969) – interactionist perspective

This theory pesents a second interactionist perspective and builds upon Dollard's work. However, Berkowitz believes that frustration leads to an increase in arousal which in some situations will result in aggression. Aggressive cues such as baseball bats, ice hockey sticks, the nature of the game, or if a violent act has been witnessed, will trigger aggression in sport if arousal among participants is high. However, the best players have the ability or temperament to control frustration and arousal.

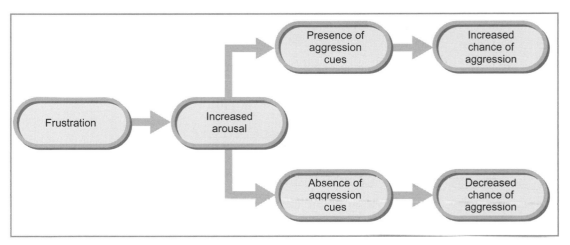

Fig. 4.36 Aggression cue hypothesis.

Methods to eliminate aggressive tendencies

HOT TIPS

Popular question topics include defining aggression, theories of aggression and controlling aggression.

- The coach must positively reinforce non-aggressive behaviour and negatively reinforce aggressive behaviour.
- Punish aggressive play.
- A player who is likely to be violent could be withdrawn from the situation.
- Misinterpretation of a situation could lead to an aggressive incident. By changing the athlete's perception of the situation, aggression will be avoided.
- Stress performance rather than outcome goals.
- Emphasise non-aggressive role models.
- Attribute successful performance to skilfulness and not to intimidation, and use attribution retraining to implement non-aggressive play.
- Make use of cognitive strategies such as rational thinking, self-talk and imagery to prevent aggressive behaviour.
- Implement stress management techniques.
- Lower arousal levels.

Social facilitation and audience effects

Most sports or physical activities take place in the company of other people either in the form of spectators or **co-actors**. It is well documented that the presence of others influences the performance of the individual.

The immediate effect of the presence of an audience is to increase the arousal level of the athlete. When this effect is positive and performance is enhanced, social facilitation has taken place. However, 'social inhibition' is the term given when a negitive effect on performance is experienced due to the attendance of spectators.

TASK 15

Using your knowledge of arousal theories, discuss the circumstances when performance was facilitated by the presence of others. Discuss the variables that are likely to result in social inhibition.

Triplett (1898) examined the possibility of social facilitation in what was arguably the first experiment in sport psychology. He found that the presence of others has the following effect on performance:

- arouses competitive drive
- releases energy
- increases the speed of performance.

Much of the current belief centres upon:

- Zajonc's drive theory of social facilitation
- Cottrell's evaluation apprehension.

Zajonc recognised different types of 'present others', which are outlined in Figure 4.37.

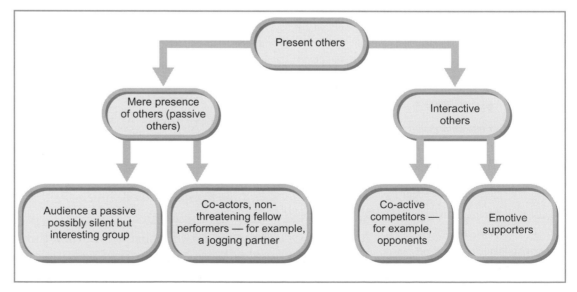

Fig. 4.37 Zajonc's drive theory of social facilitation.

HOT TIPS

Review pages 160–1 of *Advanced PE for OCR: AS* on motivation and arousal.

Our interest lies with 'passive others' as Zajonc believed that the 'mere presence' of other people is sufficient to increase the arousal level of the performer. He used drive theory to predict the effect of others on performance.

Drive theory indicates a relationship between arousal and performance. An increase in arousal is proportional to an increase in the quality of physical performance. However, the quality of performance depends on how well the skill has been learned.

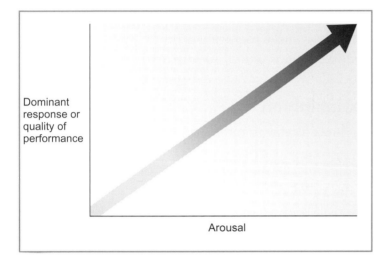

Fig. 4.38 Drive theory of social facilitation linking arousal with the emergence of the dominant response.

Actions that have already been learned or what are termed 'learned behaviours' tend to be our dominant responses. A dominant response is the behaviour most likely to occur when we are pressured to respond. Hull suggested that as arousal increases, as would happen in a situation where spectators were present, there is a greater likelihood of our dominant response occurring.

High arousal would be beneficial at the expert stage (autonomous phase of learning), because our dominant behaviour would tend towards the correct response. However, at the novice stage of performance (associative stage of learning), our dominant behaviour is likely to exhibit mistakes.

HOT TIPS

Zajonc's drive theory of social facilitation is supported by the belief that arousal caused by an audience is a natural (innate) reaction.

Martens confirmed Zajonc's predictions that the presence of an audience increased arousal and this impaired the learning of complex skills and facilitated tasks that had been over-learned (grooved). Obermeier found that co-actors helped the individual to run faster and caused improvement of simple muscular endurance tasks. Gymnast James May stated that increased arousal interfered with fine motor control required on the pommel horse, but improved the more explosive movement required on the vault.

Cottrell questioned the belief that the mere presence of others raised arousal levels. He proposed that an audience could have a calming effect in some circumstances. Increases in arousal were only evident when the performer perceived that the audience was assessing performance. Hence, Cottrell's theory was termed 'evaluation apprehension'.

HOT TIPS

A player in a sports representative trial would be assessed on outcome goals. This may evoke evaluation apprehension. Review the information on goal setting on page 248.

Homefield advantage

Large supportive home crowds are believed to provide the home team with an advantage and this is known as homefield advantage. This phenomenon is most evident in indoor sports such as ice hockey and basketball. It must be noted that the crowds in these sports are located very close to the action and, as proposed by

HOT TIPS

Research indicates that away teams tend to be more aggressive than home teams.

HOT TIPS

Information processing models can be found on page 129 of *Advanced PE for OCR: AS*.

HOT TIPS

Remember, best performance is achieved in the condition known as Peak Flow (see page 259).

Schwartz, the situation would increase audience influence. This theory is called the 'proximity effect'.

Distraction/conflict theory (Baron, 1986)

More recently, Baron indicated that the performers attentional capacity explains social facilitation. Study of information processing models, cue utilisation and attention styles reveal that an individual can attend only to a limited amount of environmental cues. Baron proposed that spectators demand the same amount of attention as would data from the sports situation. This added distraction is yet more competition for attentional space. He concludes that easy tasks requiring little attention are performed best in front of crowds while complex actions would be impaired.

Strategies to combat social inhibition

- Practise selective attention to direct attention onto the task and cut out the awareness of others.
- Make use of cognitive visualisation techniques such as imagery and mental rehearsal to further shut out the audience.
- Ensure that essential skills are over-learned and grooved because when over aroused, dominant responses are most likely to emerge.
- Introduce evaluative others into practice.
- Simulated crowd noises, which reinforce performance positively, have proved effective.
- Raise the athletes' awareness of the zone of optimal functioning (ZOF).
- Incorporate stress management into training.
- Appropriate use of attribution will raise confidence when the athlete is faced with an audience.

Revise as you go! Test your knowledge and understanding

- Define 'aggression', 'instrumental aggression' and 'assertive behaviour'.
- List five antecedents of aggression.
- Identify and explain four theories of aggression.
- Outline five methods to eliminate the aggressive tendencies of performers.
- Distinguish between social facilitation and social inhibition.
- Explain the circumstances under which the presence of others enhances performance.
- Explain the drive theory of social facilitation.
- Describe evaluation apprehension.
- Explain distraction/conflict theory.

Sharpen up your exam technique!

1 In the context of physical activity, show what is meant by the drive theory of social facilitation.

(4 marks)

2 By using a practical example from sport, explain the theory of 'evaluation apprehension'. (3 marks)

3 What measures might a coach take to prevent social inhibition? (4 marks)

4 An aggressive action is likely to impede performance. Identify the strategies that would prevent abnormal aggressive behaviour. (4 marks)

5 Discuss the view that aggressive behaviour is a product of nature rather than nurture. (5 marks)

Section 6: *Consequences of sport performance*

Learning objectives

At the end of this section you should be able to:
- identify the reasons for success and failure in sport
- demonstrate knowledge of Weiner's attribution model
- explain and justify the use of attribution retraining in the promotion of mastery orientation and avoidance of learned helplessness.

Attribution theory

The topic of attribution looks at the common reasons given by coaches and players to account for their successes and failures in sport. Weiner's attribution model will be the focus of this section.

Weiner's attribution model

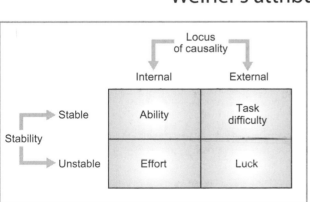

Fig. 4.39 Weiner's attribution model.

The locus of causality is the vertical dimension and refers to the 'place' in relation to the individual where success is thought to have occurred. The internal locus relates to factors within the domain of the individual (effort and ability). However, factors such as task difficulty and luck lie in the external dimension.

Stability relates to the horizontal dimension. A stable element is considered permanent while an unstable factor is temporary and can be changed.

Essentially, the coach should be looking to attribute defeat to external attributions in order to sustain confidence and to establish a winning expectation. Such factors take away the responsibility of the loss from the players. This would maintain self-esteem, sustain motivation and restore pride and confidence.

An example of external attributions would be to state that the task was too difficult on this occasion but winning is possible in the future, or to suggest the opposition were lucky and the losers were unlucky.

Internal attributions should reinforce victory, as this would elevate confidence and endorse a 'win' expectation.

People who are low achievers, recognised as those with a low need to achieve and a high need to avoid failure (TAF), tend to attribute a lack of success to internal factors. This would take away confidence and reduce expectation of future success. Learned helplessness would develop and avoidance behaviour would result. The same people tend to attribute success to external factors. Once again, confidence and expectation of attainment in the future would be minimal.

KEY WORDS

Mastery orientation

The strong motive to succeed found in the high achiever. This type of person will expect to succeed but will persist when failure is experienced.

On the other hand, high achievers (TAS) would attribute their success to internal factors and therefore seek more difficult challenges, while failures are put down to external variables. In this way, the high achiever is more persistent in the face of failure and develops **mastery orientation**.

Performers who relate mastery to outcome or ego goals tend to attribute success to internal and stable factors, while those who pursue task or process goals are inclined to attribute success to internal and unstable reasons.

Attribution retraining

KEY WORDS

Attribution retraining

The coach changes the usual external attributions for failure into internal, unstable controllable factors.

Controllability is a third dimension to the attribution model. The athlete has little control over ability, luck or the difficulty of the task but has complete control over effort. Effort attributions are classified as internal and unstable and they can be changed by the performer. For example, after failure the coach may say, 'With sustained effort you can succeed.' This would give the athlete control over the situation and provide the possibility of working through to success. Several other attributions would sit in this 'box of control'; here are some to think about.

- Concentration.
- Commitment.
- Control of arousal (somatic and cognitive).
- Confidence.
- Attitude.
- Attention.
- Mental preparation.
- Physical preparation.

The control given to the failing performer by attributing a lack of success to internal and unstable factors will help to prevent learned helplessness.

Sharpen up your exam technique!

1   Outline the reasons a coach might give for the loss of an important game.
(4 marks)

2   How might the same coach use the result of this last game to re-motivate the players for the next match? (4 marks)

3   As the coach, how would you use the model of attribution to decide what to say to your team if they had just lost but played well? (4 marks)

4   Describe how you would use the attribution model to develop mastery orientation and prevent the onset of learned helplessness. (4 marks)

5   Use Figure 4.40 to identify why an athlete might decide to continue to compete after failure. (4 marks)

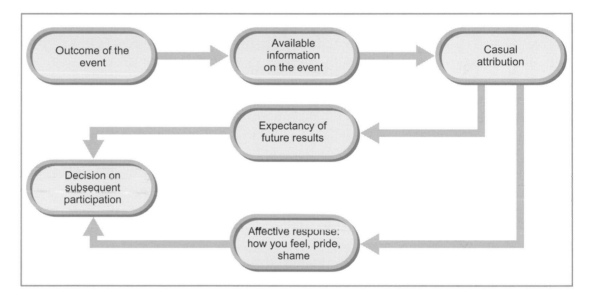

Fig. 4.40 The type of attribution given by the coach directly influences the commitment of the performer.

6   Those who achieve little in sport often attribute their failure to factors outside of their control and learned helplessness can result. Using examples from sport, explain what is meant by 'learned helplessness' and identify how attribution retraining can help to limit its effects. (6 marks)

Chapter 5 **Exercise and sport physiology**

Section 1: *Energy*

Learning objectives

At the end of this section you should be able to:
- define the terms 'energy', 'work' and 'power' using the correct units
- identify examples of potential, chemical and kinetic energy within the body
- describe the role of ATP within the body and explain how energy is made available for muscle contraction
- describe the three energy systems for ATP re-synthesis
- identify the thresholds of each of these systems
- explain the term 'OBLA'
- explain the factors that determine how these systems combine to provide energy for different sporting activities.

Energy concepts
What is energy?

Energy is the ability to perform work.

Often the amount of 'energy' is displayed on the side of food items and is measured in joules (J). Energy is also measured in calories, where one calorie is equal to 4.18 joules.

KEY WORDS

Energy

The ability to perform work. Usually measured in joules (J).

Force

A push or pull that alters, or tends to alter, the state of motion of a body. Force is measured in newtons (N).

Power

The rate at which we can work or work/time. Power is measured in watts (W).

What is work?

Work = **force** × distance

How much work would you perform if you had to push a scrummaging machine weighing 7200N back three metres?

$$7200 \times 3 = 21{,}600\text{Nm or } 21{,}600\text{J}$$

What is power?

Power = work/time

Power is considered to be a combination of strength and speed. Consider the scrummage machine example above. The first XV move the machine in four seconds, whereas it takes the second XV pack six seconds. Which is most powerful?

First XV	Second XV
21,6000/4	21,6000/6
= 54,000w	= 36,000w

The first XV scrum is more powerful. Power is measured in watts (W).

TASK 1

1 Get all your classmates to perform a 30m sprint and record the time taken.
2 Weigh all your classmates, remembering to convert kgs into Newtons if necessary.
3 Complete the following table by calculating work done and power.

Name	Weight (N)	30m sprint (s)	Work (J)	Power (W)

Energy can exist in different forms. You may remember seven different forms of energy from GCSE science, but you only need to be concerned with three different forms.

KEY WORDS

ATPase

Adenosine triphosphate (ATP), the enzyme that helps break down ATP to release energy.

Adenosine triphosphate (ATP)

ATP is the only immediately usable source of energy in our bodies. It can be referred to as our 'energy currency'.

- **Kinetic.** Energy seen as muscle movement – for example, running, hitting and so on.
- **Chemical.** Energy stored in compounds in our bodies – for example, ATP, phosphocreatine, carbohydrates and fats.
- **Potential.** Stored energy waiting to happen –for example, ATP does nothing until the phosphate group is released with the help of **ATPase**.

ATP is **adenosine triphosphate**. This compound is the only immediately usable form of energy stored in our bodies. Although we have other energy rich compounds such as phosphocreatine and glycogen, ATP is the only one that can be utilised by the muscles to create movement.

This energy is so readily available because ATP is stored within the muscle cell. The only problem with this arrangement is that only a very small amount of ATP can be stored in our bodies. The total mass of ATP in the whole body is only 85g – enough to last for about two seconds of exercise. To maintain exercise beyond two seconds, ATP has to be re-synthesised from adenosine diphosphate (ADP) and a phosphate group ('P' or 'Pi' as it is sometimes referred to).

The energy is stored in the bond between the last two phosphate groups. When this bond is broken by the action of the enzyme ATPase, energy is released that can be used by the muscle cell to contract (think back to the sliding filament theory).

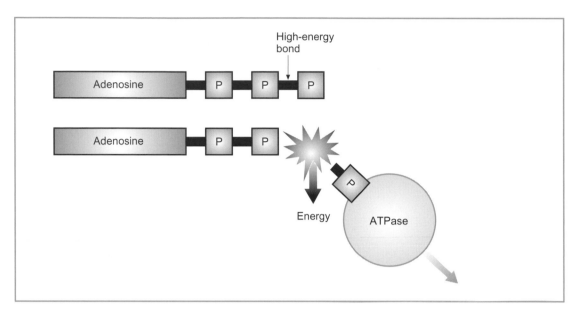

Fig. 5.01 ATP.

Remember that chemical reactions that give out energy or heat, such as the breakdown of ATP, are known as **exothermic** reactions, while those that need energy to proceed (that is, use energy) are known as **endothermic**.

$$ATP \rightarrow ADP + P + energy \quad (exothermic)$$
$$ADP + P + energy \rightarrow ATP \quad (endothermic)$$

ATP re-synthesis

ATP stores are low in our bodies and so ATP has to be re-synthesised to keep exercising. Depending on the intensity of the exercise, this is achieved by three **energy systems**. It is important to realise that these systems do not work in isolation. The amount of ATP re-synthesis done by each system will depend purely on the intensity of the exercise and two systems can be working at the same time to re-synthesise ATP. The following text will look at each system and its way of providing ATP before looking at how the systems combine to provide a constant supply of ATP for working muscles.

Anaerobic

A reaction that can occur without the presence of oxygen.

Coupled reactions

The products of one reaction are then used in another reaction.

Sarcoplasm

The gel-like content of a muscle that contains all the organelles of the cell.

HOT TIPS

All anaerobic processes take place in the sarcoplasm of the muscle cell and all aerobic processes take place in the **mitochondria**.

KEY WORDS

Mitrochondria

The 'powerhouse' of the cell where all aerobic processes take place.

Anaerobic glycolysis

The process of breaking down glucose into pyruvic acid.

Pyruvic acid

Product of the partial breakdown of glucose during anaerobic glycosis.

The phosphocreatine system

Also known as the creatine phosphate or alacticacid system, this system uses another high-energy compound known as phosphocreatine to provide the necessary energy to combine ADP and P.

$$PC = P + C + energy \qquad (exothermic)$$
$$energy + ADP + P = ATP \qquad (endothermic)$$

These chemical reactions take place in the **sarcoplasm** of the muscle cell and do not need oxygen to proceed. This system is known as an **anaerobic** system. Because the energy produced by one reaction is used by another reaction, these are known as **coupled reactions**.

Advantages	Disadvantages
It provides ATP re-synthesis very quickly because the PC is stored in the muscle cell and there are very few steps in the reaction	There is only a small amount of PC stored in the muscle cells – remember, there is not much space
Because oxygen is not required, there is no delay to wait for oxygen to be supplied from the lungs	Only one mole of ATP is re-synthesised from one mole of PC
It can provide energy for very high-intensity exercise such as high jumping, kicking a ball, or hitting a powerful tennis serve	It will only provide energy for a maximum of ten seconds
PC will re-synthesise quite quickly and so recovery times for this system are very quick. (See Section 2 in this chapter on recovery for further information)	
There are no harmful by-products that will cause fatigue	

Fig. 5.02 The advantages and disadvantages of the phosphocreatine system.

Lactic acid system

The lactic acid system is another anaerobic system that does not require oxygen to function. This time the fuel used is carbohydrate – a compound made of carbon, hydrogen and oxygen that is found in foods. Carbohydrate, stored in the muscles and liver as glycogen, is converted to glucose by the enzyme glycogen phoshorylase and undergoes a series of reactions known as **anaerobic glycolysis** started by the enzyme phosphofructokinase (PFK) until eventually it is converted to **pyruvic acid**. During this process, two moles of ATP are re-synthesised. Due to the lack of oxygen, the pyruvic acid is converted to lactic acid by the enzyme lactate dehydrogenase. All of the above reactions take place in the sarcoplasm.

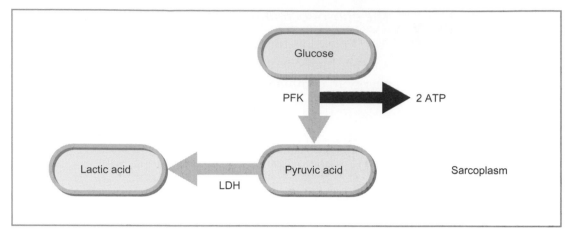

Fig. 5.03 Anaerobic glycolysis.

Advantages	Disadvantages
There is a relatively large amount of glycogen stored in our bodies and so this system can provide more ATP than the PC system	The by-product, lactic acid, reduces the pH of the muscle cell, making it more acidic; this prevents the enzymes from functioning properly, causing muscle fatigue
There are still relatively few chemical reactions taking place and so ATP can be provided quickly for high-intensity activities that last anywhere from 15–180 seconds, such as a 400m race	
Because oxygen is not required, there is no delay in oxygen being supplied from the lungs	

Fig. 5.04 The advantages and disadvantages of the lactic acid system.

Aerobic system

As the name implies, this system requires oxygen as a fuel alongside glycogen or fat to re-synthesise ATP. The first part of the system is identical to the lactic acid system. The only difference is, when oxygen is readily available, and the intensity of exercise allows, the pyruvic acid is moved into another set of chemical reactions instead of being converted into lactic acid.

Think of the difference between the aerobic system and the lactic acid system as burning wood. If you have plenty of oxygen available, you can burn the wood well; all the heat is given off and you are left with just ash. If there is not enough oxygen available, the wood just blackens; a little heat is given off and you are left with charcoal. Eventually, carbohydrate will be completely 'burned', and the harmless waste products of carbon dioxide and water are produced and removed from the

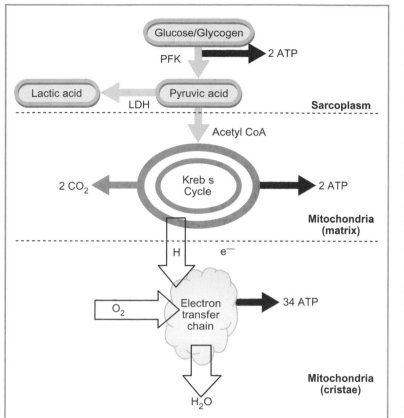

Fig. 5.05 The aerobic system.

body, liberating a huge amount of energy. If fat was used, the amount of energy is even greater even though more oxygen is required to complete this process.

The pyruvic acid is taken by the coenzyme acetyl CoA into the **Kreb's Cycle** (also known as the tricarboxcylic acid cycle or the citric acid cycle). Here, a series of chemical reactions occurs, further breaking down the carbohydrate compound. This takes place in the matrix of the mitochondria. Once this series of reactions is completed, carbon dioxide and hydrogen ions are produced. Two moles of ATP are also re-synthesised at this time. If fat is being used as a fuel, it enters the Kreb's Cycle as fatty acids and a process known as beta-oxidation occurs. The CO_2 is removed via the lungs and the hydrogen atoms enter the next series of reactions known as the **electron transfer chain**. This occurs in the cristae of the mitochondria, and here electrons are removed from hydrogen and passed down the electron chain providing energy to resynthesise 34 moles of ATP. The hydrogen is combined with oxygen to produce water.

$$C_6H_{12}O_6 + 6O_2 = 6CO_2 + 6H_2O + energy \quad \text{(exothermic)}$$

KEY WORDS

Kreb's Cycle

The cyclical process of breaking down pyruvic acid in CO_2, H^+ and e^- whilst providing the energy for the resynthesis of 2ATP.

Electrons

A negatively charged particle of an atom (e^-).

Electron transfer chain

The process of combining H^+, e^- and O_2 to produce water and provide energy for the resynthesis of 34ATP.

Advantages	Disadvantages
A large amount of ATP can be re-synthesised. 36 to 38 moles can be produced from one mole of glycogen – even more from fat	Due to the need for oxygen, the system cannot re-synthesise ATP immediately; there is a delay while oxygen is transported from the lungs to the working muscles
Activity can last for hours	This system cannot provide ATP while working at higher intensities, again due to the time taken to provide oxygen to the working muscles
There are no harmful by-products of the chemical reactions	

Fig. 5.06 The advantages and disadvantages of the aerobic system.

KEY WORDS

Energy continuum

The relative contribution of each energy system to ATP resynthesis determined by the intensity and duration of exercise.

Energy continuum

In any given situation our energy systems rarely work in isolation. Consider the games player in netball, football or hockey, for example. There is a general amount of movement at low intensity while jogging back into position, but there is also a fast break – the sprint down the wing, the sudden dodge. Energy is provided by all three energy systems, and the contribution of each is determined by the intensity of exercise and the duration of the exercise.

The extreme examples are easy. Consider the marathon runner Paula Radcliffe. For her activity, lasting some two hours and fifteen minutes, the aerobic system provides

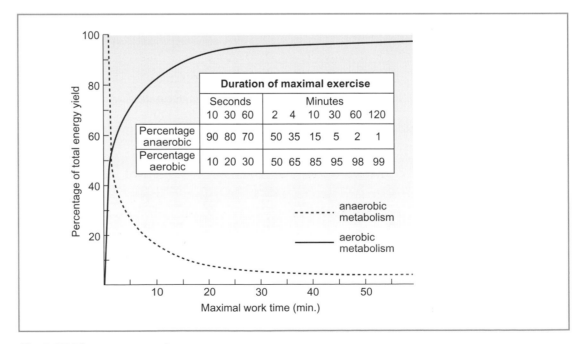

Duration of maximal exercise								
	Seconds			Minutes				
	10	30	60	2	4	10	30	60	120
Percentage anaerobic	90	80	70	50	35	15	5	2	1
Percentage aerobic	10	20	30	50	65	85	95	98	99

Fig. 5.07 The energy continuum.

the majority of the energy. For the shot putter, it is the PC system. What about the 800m runner or the tennis player?

The position of each activity is governed by the intensity of the sport – that is, how quickly the energy needs to be supplied and the duration of the activity. An easy indication of the intensity of exercise is to look at the heart rate and calculate a percentage of the performer's maximum heart rate. A more accurate assessment of the intensity is to measure the percentage of his or her **VO$_2$ max** (see pages 290–96 for a more detailed explanation of this value).

KEY WORDS

VO$_2$ max

The maximum amount of oxygen that can be taken into the body and utilised.

TASK 3

1 Consider the following activities and state what percentage of energy will be provided by each of the three systems.

Activity	% PC	% lactic	% aerobic
Shot putter			
Marathon runner			
800m runner			
Tennis player			
Netball centre			

2 Justify your answer for each activity.

Thresholds

The threshold of any system is the point at which that energy system is unable to provide energy. For example, the threshold of the PC system is the point at which PC can no longer provide energy for the working muscles. This threshold is about ten seconds.

KEY WORDS

Onset of blood lactate accumulation (OBLA)

The point at which the concentration of lactic acid in the blood rapidly increases.

The threshold of the aerobic system has been studied in some depth, well beyond the level of this textbook. The idea that there is a certain point where the aerobic system cannot supply the energy quickly enough and our body has to switch to anaerobic processes has been studied. Taking a blood sample and measuring the concentration of lactic acid can readily measure this point. A normal value during rest or aerobic exercise would be anywhere between 1–2mmol of lactic acid per litre of blood. Once this value goes above 4mmol (according to some researchers) or the point at which there is a rapid increase in this value, the **onset of blood lactate accumulation** (OBLA) has been reached. This point will vary depending on the aerobic fitness of the performer. In untrained individuals, this may occur at about 50 per cent of their VO₂ max, whereas in highly trained individuals, this may occur at about 85 per cent of VO₂ max. This is due to their increased ability to remove waste products and supply oxygen to working muscles.

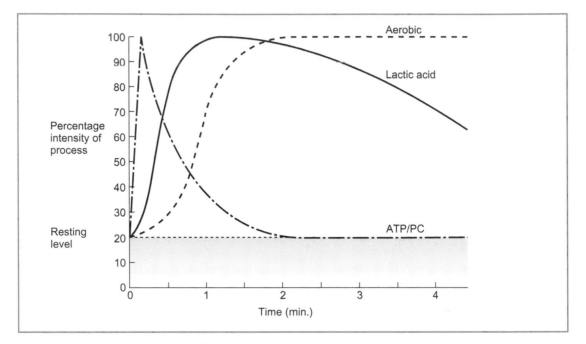

Fig. 5.08 Energy system thresholds.

The supply of oxygen could be a factor in determining which energy system is being used. Other factors to consider are the activation levels of the various enzymes and the food fuels being used. Figure 5.9 shows the activation for each system.

Energy system	Controlling enzymes	Activator
PC system	Creatine kinase	Increase in ADP
Lactic acid system	Phosphofructokinase	Decrease in PC
Aerobic system	Phosphofructokinase	Increase in adrenalin/decrease in insulin levels

Fig. 5.09 Activators for energy systems.

One final factor that will determine the energy system used is the food fuel available. Again, the stores of these available to the performer will vary according to his or her fitness levels (see adaptations to training, pages 294–96).

Revise as you go! Test your knowledge and understanding

- Define 'energy', 'work' and 'power', giving the correct units for each.
- Identify examples of kinetic, chemical and potential energy in our bodies.
- What is ATP and why is it so useful?

- What is the difference between an exothermic and endothermic reaction?
- What is the energy yield, in terms of ATP, of each of the three energy systems?
- Identify a key enzyme in each of the three energy systems.
- Why is the energy continuum a useful concept for coaches and performers?
- What is OBLA?

Sharpen up your exam technique!

1   Define the term 'energy' and explain the role of ATP within the body. (3 marks)

2   Powerful athletes are usually suited to short duration, high-intensity activities such as the 100m sprint. Define the term 'power', giving units of measurement, and describe a test used to measure power.   (4 marks)

3   Describe the energy system that provides the greatest percentage of energy required for a 100m sprint. Explain why this is the predominant energy system.   (7 marks)

4   Describe the lactic acid system of ATP production and give an example within a team game when this energy system is predominantly used.   (6 marks)

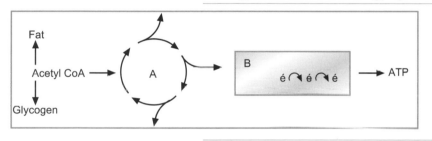

5   Both fats and acids can be broken down aerobically to release energy for ATP resynthesis. Outline the processes that take place during stages A and B of fat and glycogen metabolism, highlighted in the figure opposite.   (6 marks)

6   Athletes often use a mix of three energy systems to resynthesise ATP during an activity. Explain the term energy continuum and, using examples from Physical Education or Sport, illustrate when and why an athlete would switch from one energy system to another.   (4 marks)

Section 2: *The recovery process*

Learning objectives

At the end of this section you should be able to:
- explain how the body returns to its pre-exercise state
- define oxygen debt and EPOC
- identify the two components of EPOC
- outline the processes that replenish fuel stores during recovery
- explain how myoglobin stores are replenished
- describe the removal of CO_2 from the body
- discuss practical implications of recovery for planning training sessions.

TASK 4

Using the investigation on the heart rate response to exercise undertaken in your anatomy and physiology work as an example:

- exercise sub-maximally for ten minutes at a steady rate – for example, on a treadmill or cycle ergometer
- monitor your heart rate every minute during the exercise and continue to record your heart rate every 30 seconds after the ten minutes have ended
- do this for approximately fifteen minutes after you have finished your exercise or until your heart rate is back down to its normal resting value
- draw a graph of your results.

When you look at your graph, it should be clear that your heart rate does not return immediately to its normal resting value. The heart rate is elevated to help the body return to its pre-exercise state and this process is known as recovery.

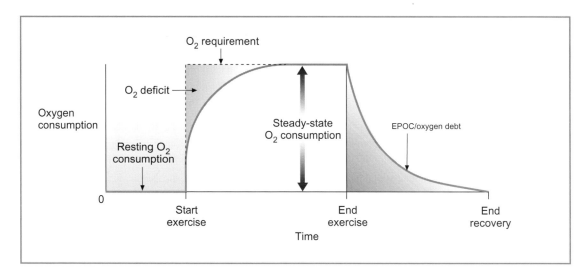

Fig. 5.10 Oxygen debt and deficit.

The old term for this elevated heart rate was oxygen debt, as it was thought that you had to pay back the oxygen that you borrowed (paying back the debt). The analogy was not quite accurate and more up-to-date terminology is required to explain the process of recovery. However, the term 'debt' will continue to arise from time to time.

A note on oxygen deficit

Although not stated in the specification, oxygen deficit is a useful concept to know. It takes the aerobic system a little while to provide energy for muscular work, even at low intensities. During this time, the anaerobic processes must provide the energy. Oxygen deficit can be thought of as the extra amount of oxygen that would be needed to complete the entire activity aerobically.

After exercise, heart rate and ventilation rates are elevated. You are providing your body with more oxygen than it needs for your activity levels. Why?

HOT TIPS

Both the restoration of PC and the removal of lactic acid require energy from the aerobic system.

KEY WORDS

Excessive post-exercise oxygen consumption (EPOC)

The amount of oxygen above the amount normally required to return the body to its pre-exercise state.

TASK 5

Make a list of all the things you think you have used during your exercise period. Think about:

- the energy systems that you have been using and the fuels that are used
- the possible waste products that are produced by your body as you exercise.

The extra oxygen that the body takes in after exercise is known as **excessive post-exercise oxygen consumption** (**EPOC**). When you look at the graph you drew for Task 4, you will see that your heart rate begins to drop very quickly immediately when you stop exercising, but its recovery begins to slow down gradually. This gave researchers the idea that recovery takes place in two stages: the fast immediate stage and a slower longer stage.

Alactacid debt (the fast stage)

During this stage of the recovery process, the energy provided by the elevated metabolism is used to help the PC system recover. It takes approximately three minutes for the PC stores to fully recover and about 30 seconds for 50 per cent recovery. The process requires approximately four litres of oxygen.

Myoglobin

Myoglobin is a protein molecule that, similar to haemoglobin, helps with the transport of oxygen. Myoglobin is found within the muscle sarcoplasm and helps to transfer the oxygen from the blood supply to the mitochondria, where it is needed to fuel aerobic metabolism.

During recovery, the oxygen used needs to be replaced. It takes about 0.51 seconds to replace the oxygen stored in myoglobin and the process takes one to two minutes. During recovery, with elevated ventilation and heart rates, there is a surplus of oxygen available for this to occur.

Lactacid debt (the slow stage)

During this stage, as the name implies, lactic acid is removed from the body. It can take as long as an hour for all of it to be removed. Lactic acid can be removed in four ways:

- 60 per cent is converted back to pyruvic acid and enters the Kreb's Cycle; it is used in aerobic metabolism
- it can be converted back to glucose (a process known as gluconeogenesis that takes place in the Cori Cycle)
- it can be converted into proteins
- it can be removed via sweating and in urine.

Removal of CO_2

The increased concentration of CO_2 formed as a waste product from the aerobic system has to be removed from the body. The majority of the CO_2 (70 per cent) is removed in the plasma of the blood by forming carbonic acid. Chemoreceptors would detect elevated levels of CO_2/low pH and would stimulate the cardiac and respiratory control centres. Hence, both cardiac output and respiratory rate remain higher during recovery to expel the CO_2 from the lungs.

Replenishment of glycogen stores

After exercise, glycogen stores in the liver and muscles will be depleted. The only way to replenish these stores is through ingestion of carbohydrate. Often this is through eating, but some athletes (particularly long-duration athletes – for example, Tour de France cyclists) have to take glucose solutions intravenously to replace it more quickly. It can take about 48 hours with a high carbohydrate meal to totally restore glycogen after a heavy bout of training (see Section 5 in this chapter on nutritional ergogenic aids).

Implications of recovery for planning training sessions

- The restoration of PC is very rapid and full recovery only takes three minutes. If speed work is the specific objective of the training session, sufficient time should be allowed to ensure full recovery. Sufficient recovery time is vital in maximal/high-intensity training and is often overlooked.
- Use an active cool down during recovery time. Research has proved that the removal of lactic acid is considerably quicker if an active cool down is followed. Although the level of exercise is very specific to the individual, moderate intensity (around 35 per cent of VO_2 max) seems to be most beneficial.

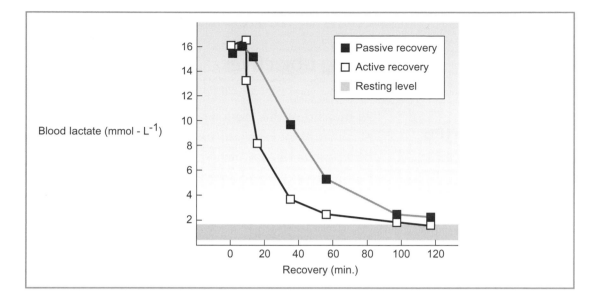

Fig. 5.11 The effects of active recovery on lactic acid.

- Monitor training intensities carefully; this way OBLA can be avoided and the quality of training maintained.
- Warm up thoroughly before training. This will help to reduce oxygen deficit by increasing the oxygen supply to the working muscles and ensure myoglobin stores are full.

Revise as you go! Test your knowledge and understanding

- Define oxygen debt/EPOC.
- Identify two components of oxygen debt/EPOC.
- Outline the processes that occur in each stage.
- Why is it important to replenish myoglobin stores with oxygen?
- How long does it take a triathlete to restore glycogen levels after an event?
- How is CO_2 removed from the working muscles?
- How would knowledge of recovery help a coach to plan a training session?

Sharpen up your exam technique!

1 The recovery process, shown in Figure 5.11, is concerned with returning the body to its pre-exercise state. Identify and describe the processes that take place during oxygen debt/EPOC. (6 marks)

2 Using examples from physical education or sport, show how knowledge of the recovery process can be put into practice to aid the performer. (3 marks)

3 After 60 minutes of exercise, the athlete rests and enters the recovery period/EPOC. Outline the two main physiological processes that will take place during this time. (5 marks)

Section 3: *Principles of training*

Learning objectives

At the end of this section you should be able to:
- identify and explain six principles of training – namely overload, progression, specificity, reversibility, moderation and variance
- discuss the physiological implications of warm up and cool down
- explain the cause of DOMS
- explain and give examples of the process of periodisation
- describe the characteristics of macro-, meso- and micro-cycles using practical examples from your sport.

Introduction

There are many different types and variations of training methods used by sports people and it would be impossible to have knowledge of all of them. However, there are certain rules that govern the use of all training methods and these are known as the principles of training. For the OCR specification, you need to know about six of them.

Fig. 5.12 Training should always be specific to the event.

Specificity

To get the best results from training, it must be geared towards the demands of the activity. These demands could be the energy system that is predominantly used, the muscle groups that are being used or the components of fitness that are crucial – for example, maximum strength for a weightlifter. The training also has to be specific to the individual who is doing it, his or her age, ability, current fitness level and so on.

Progression

Our bodies adapt to the stresses and loads put on them. After a while, the body will have adapted fully and no other changes will occur unless the training is made harder. Progression is important to keep making the body adapt and improve. This progression needs to be steady and consistent. It is often said that the quicker you gain fitness, the quicker you will lose it. When you consider the chances of injury or anything else that stops training, a steady progression is vital to allow for a period when you cannot train.

Overload (FIT)

To make the body adapt, it must be made to work harder than it normally does. This is known as overload. The body can be overloaded by manipulating three factors of training:

- frequency – how many units per week, per phase or per year
- intensity – how fast, higher weights and so on
- time – how long you train for within each unit.

Reversibility

Fitness levels quickly drop when periods of inactivity occur. It is vital that training programmes avoid any long periods of inactivity, even during the off-season time. The loss of fitness will be reduced if steady progression has been made throughout training.

Moderation

Although overload is vital for the body to adapt, caution must be taken not to overload too much. Overuse injuries will occur and, particularly for younger performers, burn out can occur. Not only does the body get too tired but also, psychologically, the performer has had enough.

Variance

To make the body adapt, a long period of training must take place (remember progression and moderation). During this time, boredom can become an issue. A variety of different trainings sessions, which are carefully planned to avoid repetition, are vital to keep up concentration and commitment. Variety also helps prevent overuse injuries of specific areas of the body and helps to maintain moderation.

Physiological implications of the warm-up

TASK 6

Look back to when you planned a warm up for your work on the Personal Performance Portfolio.

- Plan a short warm up specific to your activity.
- State what you think the benefits of a warm up are – for example, the possible effects on skeletal muscle tissue and on the cardio-vascular system.

Much research has gone into the advantages of warming up and there has been recent speculation as to its effectiveness in preventing injury, but this topic is beyond the scope of this textbook. We are only concerned with the physiological responses to warm up and what advantages these may give the performer.

- Reduction of injury (some mixed views at the moment, but still worth an exam mark) due to improvement of the flexibility of muscles and connective tissues.
- The greater elasticity of muscles that helps prevent injury will also help give a greater speed and strength of contraction.
- The co-ordination between antagonistic pairs is improved, again helping the speed of contraction and relaxation.
- The increased temperature helps enzymes function more efficiently.
- Increased cardiac output due to a greater venous return from the already working muscles.
- Vasoconstriction to non-essential areas of the body and vasodilation to the working muscles. The resultant vascular shunt increases blood flow and therefore oxygen to the working muscles.
- The increased blood flow will help prevent OBLA occurring. This is due to less lactic acid being produced, as an anaerobic system will not have to supply as much energy at the start of exercise, and improved aerobic respiration to remove any that is formed.

KEY WORDS

DOMS

Delayed onset of muscle soreness that occurs 24 to 48 hours after exercise.

Delayed onset of muscle soreness (DOMS)

How often have you felt pain in your muscles 24 to 48 hours after training or competing? Lactic acid has been removed within an hour or so of training, so something else must be causing this pain. After training, muscles can have slight tissue damage. This can be caused by excessive forces acting on the muscles and particularly by the use of excessive eccentric muscle contractions.

To prevent the onset of **DOMS**, make sure you are thoroughly warmed up before the training unit. It is advisable to avoid eccentric contractions at the start of any training programme. Make sure the principles of progression, moderation and variability are used to avoid excessive overload, and allow time for recovery. Some performers have been known to use massage, hot baths and ice therapy to reduce DOMS. Other performers and coaches advocate the use of a particularly strenuous session right at the start of the training. Once the athlete has recovered from the initial soreness, subsequent pain will be less.

Fig. 5.13 Eccentric forces are often used under braking situations – For example, the deep knee bend after a gymnastic vault. Imagine the force the muscles have to endure when landing.

Physiological implications of a cool down

The main benefits of a cool down are to speed up the recovery process already described in Section 2 of this chapter. To help the body remove all the waste products that build up during exercise – that is, lactic acid and carbon dioxide – the capillaries need to be constantly flushed with oxygenated blood. This will help to metabolise lactic acid into CO_2 and H_2O.

Avoiding 'blood pooling' is one of the most important purposes of a cool down. The mechanism in which venous return is maintained in the body means that the muscle pump squeezes the blood back to the heart. After strenuous exercise, cardiac output is very large and most of our blood is circulated to the working muscles. If exercise suddenly stops, there is no mechanism for returning the blood with all the waste products to the heart. Light aerobic work during recovery will help to maintain a good level of venous return and prevent the blood pooling in the muscles.

A cool down also allows our muscles to cool down slowly, which may be helpful in reducing the amount of muscle cell damage that could occur. Many people will often use this time to work on flexibility. Muscles are at their most elastic and pliable when they are warm. This then proves to be an ideal time to stretch and generally calm down after a vigorous training session.

Cool down will help to prevent immediate soreness after training, but delayed onset of muscle soreness is due to actual damage to the muscle tissue, not lactic acid.

Periodisation of training

In order to apply the principles of training in an effective manner, all training must be well planned. The aim of any training is to improve performance but equally important is the aim to improve performance for a specific event – for example, the Olympic Games.

KEY WORDS

Periodisation

Breaking the training programme into periods of time that will help the athlete reach their peak performance at a certain time – for example, the Olympic Games.

Macro-cycle

The year (at least).

Meso-cycle

Approximately six weeks.

With this in mind, athletes and coaches must direct their training to allow the performer to 'peak'. The process of doing this is known as **periodisation** – that is, breaking the training programme up into manageable sections, each with its own aims and objectives. In the early days of sports training, splitting the year into pre-season, competition and recovery (or transition) was enough. As training methods have developed, many sophisticated systems have been used. A huge amount of detail does not need to be known, but the following terms are well used.

A **macro-cycle** is the whole training programme. Often the calendar year is used, but if you consider an Olympic athlete, it may be four years. This is broken into meso-cycles.

A **meso-cycle** is a phase of training, often about a month or six weeks. The length of each meso-cycle will depend on its aim. Many performers will use six meso-cycles or phases.

- Phase 1 will be general fitness work leading towards more specific fitness requirements. This stage can be thought of as training to train.
- Phase 2 is more specific to the sport and will deal with specific fitness issues such as speed, strength, skills and techniques. Intensity of training increases considerably and the idea is to bring the new levels of fitness and skill together. It might be thought of as training to compete.
- Phase 3 is the start of the competitive season and general training is reduced and replaced by competition work. For example, this would be the start of the netball season, where you want to get off to a good start to the league, or it may contain the qualifying competition for the county athletics championships.
- If the season is long, there may be a phase 4, where training and competition is reduced (if possible) to allow the body to recover and prevent overuse injuries.
- This will be followed by phase 5, which is the culmination of competition – for example, the county championships or the cup final.
- Phase 6 is the recovery or transition phase during which the body is allowed to recover from the vigour of the previous season.

KEY WORDS

Micro-cycle

Often a week.

Unit

A period of training with a specific aim.

Each meso-cycle is broken into **micro-cycles**. A micro-cycle, more often than not, is a typical week that is broken down into training units. A **unit** is a period of training with a specific aim – for example, six times 60m sprints for developing speed.

Any training 'session' may contain one or more units. For example, time may be spent on stretching and mobility work before doing some skills work on shooting, then finishing with a 30-minute run for aerobic fitness (this would have been three units in one session).

Fig. 5.14 Imagine planning training programmes for these athletes.

TASK 7

Devise your own training plan for your own activity.

1 Define the length of your macro-cycle (use a year if there is not a specific event you can think of).

2 Divide your macro-cycle into meso-cycles. Think carefully about the number of your meso-cycles, as you may not need the six highlighted above.

3 Design a micro-cycle from each of your meso-cycles, demonstrating the difference in content depending on the time of year. Remember to apply the principles of training.

4 After planning your micro-cycle, highlight the key guidelines you would give to a coach to help him or her plan effective micro-cycles.

HOT TIPS

Examiners use the term 'guidelines' when they are looking for the main considerations when designing a training programme. They are not the same as principles but are often based on them.

Having seen how a training year can be arranged, consider what needs to be done in each of these training units to maximise performance.

Revise as you go! Test your knowledge and understanding

- Identify the six principles of training and give a practical example for each one.
- Explain the key benefits of a warm up.
- Explain the importance of a cool down.
- What is DOMS?
- What does periodisation mean?
- How long, generally, do a macro-cycle, meso-cycle and micro-cycle last?

Sharpen up your exam technique!

1 Overload, progression, specificity and reversibility are commonly referred to as the four principles of training. Using an example from physical education and sport, show how you would incorporate these principles into your training programme.

(6 marks)

2 After a particularly strenuous weight-training session, the shot putter may experience soreness immediately after the session and the following day. Explain the reasons for this during both these times and identify strategies that could be used to keep the pain to a minimum.

(6 marks)

3 During a macro-cycle, a number of physiological adaptations will occur. The following graph shows the effect of a particular type of training on skeletal muscle.

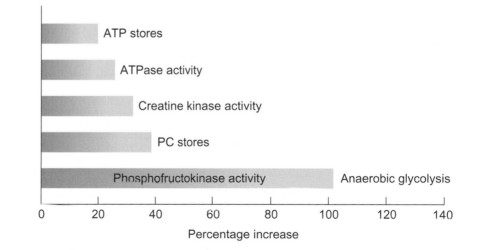

Fig. 5.15 A graph to show physiological adaptations.

What type of athlete might benefit from such training effects? If you were this athlete's coach, describe the guidelines you would follow when designing a micro-cycle training regime.

(7 marks)

Section 4: *Components of fitness and improving performance*

Learning objectives

At the end of this section you should be able to:
- provide definitions of the components and explain the factors that affect their values
- identify and briefly describe methods of evaluating the components
- identify and explain different types of training to develop the components
- identify the energy systems and food/chemicals used
- identify and explain the physiological adaptations that take place after training.

Aerobic capacity

Often known as VO_2 max, this is the maximum amount of oxygen that can be taken into the body and utilised. It is often expressed as millilitres per kilogram of body mass per minute (ml kg^{-1} min^{-1}).

It is important to remember this definition, as not all the oxygen that enters the body is utilised. Resuscitation would be a pointless exercise if it did.

VO_2 max has undergone considerable research in sports science and one of the most researched questions is 'what limits VO_2 max?' There is probably still no single definitive answer to this question, but its study helps us understand VO_2 max and the adaptations that occur due to training (see pages 291–96).

Four areas can affect VO_2 max and four questions need answering.

- **External respiration.** Can training help get more oxygen into our bodies in the first place?
- **Transport of oxygen around the body.** Can training increase the amount of oxygen delivered to the working muscles?
- **Internal respiration.** Can training increase the amount of oxygen removed from the blood and into the muscle?
- **Utilisation of oxygen.** Can we use the oxygen once inside the muscle cell?

These questions will be answered on the following pages.

Studies show that training can improve VO_2 max by as much as 20 per cent, but many factors that control VO_2 max are genetically determined and governed by age and sex.

Age (years)	Very poor	Poor	Average	Good	Very good
20–29	38	39–43	44–51	52–56	57+
30–39	34	35–39	40–47	48–51	52+
40–49	30	31–35	36–43	44–47	48+
50–59	25	26–31	32–39	40–43	44+
60–69	21	22–26	27–35	36–39	40+

Fig. 5.16 VO_2 max values for men (ml/min/kg body weight).

Age (years)	Very poor	Poor	Average	Good	Very good
20–29	28	29–34	35–43	44–48	49+
30–39	27	28–33	34–41	42–47	48+
40–49	25	26–31	32–40	41–45	46+
50–65	21	22–28	29–35	37–41	42+

Fig. 5.17 VO_2 max values for women (ml/min/kg body weight).

HOT TIPS

For each fitness component in this book, know the name of a test, brief methodology, and how the result is evaluated. Often, 'compare to standardised table' will secure a mark.

Test

Many tests are available for predicting VO_2 max. The most commonly used one is the multistage fitness test. Using a progressive and maximal 20m shuttle run test, researchers at Loughborough University created a standardised scoring table to predict VO_2 max.

One of the limitations of such a test is the danger involved in completing a maximal test. An alternative is the PWC170 test that looks at the relationship between heart rate (HR) and VO_2 max at sub-maximal intensities. This is much safer than using maximal tests and can give quite accurate results. Other tests such as Cooper's Run and various step tests are also sub-maximal predictors of VO_2 max.

Analysing the content of expired air while exercising is the most accurate way of calculating VO_2 max. The equipment required for such tests is seldom found in schools and sixth form colleges, but you may have the opportunity to see this equipment in a local university or college.

HOT TIPS

Use the FIT principle of overload (frequency, intensity, time) for each fitness component. For example, for aerobic training:

F = three to five days a week
I = 55–90 per cent maximal heart rate
T = 20–60 minutes of continuous or intermittent exercise.

Training

There are three distinct types of training:

- continuous training
- fartlek training
- repetition training (interval training being the most common form).

The variations on these are massive and well beyond the scope of this textbook. You will already know specific examples for your activity or your teacher will be able to give you more examples.

Continuous training

This is running, cycling, swimming and so on, at a steady intensity from anything above 30 minutes. It is suited to long-distance endurance athletes. Observing heart rate easily monitors the intensity of such a training method. Various people give many different values for the ideal target heart rate.

Some people consider 70 per cent of maximum heart rate to be the level that must be achieved for aerobic training to make any adaptations. The American College of Sports Medicine (ACSM) considers that any activity that increases heart rate above 55 per cent of maximum will cause adaptations in our bodies. This figure is particularly low to allow for very unfit people at the start of any training.

Maximum heart rate can be estimated by using the equation: 220 – age.

Maybe a more accurate but harder way of monitoring intensity is to consider the percentage of VO_2 max that is being utilised. Figure 5.18 compares these two sets of values.

% max. heart rate (HR)	% VO_2 max
50	28
60	42
70	56
80	70
90	83
100	100

Fig. 5.18 Comparison of % maximum heart rate with % VO_2 maximum.

Very few athletes have the opportunity to measure accurately their VO_2 max, so a Finnish physiologist, Karvonen, attempted to make a more accurate link between heart rate and VO_2 max. By taking into account the heart rate reserve (maximal heart rate – resting heart rate) and using the equation below, a heart rate threshold can be calculated that relates well to the percentage of VO_2 max.

$$HR_{threshold} = HR_{rest} + 0.75 \, (HR_{max} - HR_{rest})$$

This is known as Karvonen's Principle.

Fartlek

Fartlek, the Swedish for speed play, is another type of continuous training but builds in variables to prevent boredom and can often simulate game situations. This system combines variety by including changes in pace, incline (downhill as well as uphill) and terrains, such as sand and grass. The advantages of this style of training, as well as creating variety, are that it can push the performer to the edge of his or her anaerobic threshold. This helps to bring about increases in VO_2 max. The different terrains may also bring about gains in the strength of soft tissues, such as ligaments and tendons, and help develop dynamic balance.

TASK 8

1 Construct a fartlek run around your home or college. Try to think about change of pace, change of incline and change of surface.
2 Identify these on a plan of your route and, if possible, monitor your heart rate throughout the route and identify the periods of high and low intensity.

Interval training (repetition training)

Interval training is periods of work dispersed by periods of rest or recovery. Altering a number of components can control the intensity of the session and its specificity.

Interval training can be used for both aerobic and strength training. Compare how these components are manipulated for each type of training.

Component	Examples	
Work period	Distance or time	400m run
Rest period	Distance or time	400m jog
Intensity of work period	Speed, VO_2 max, HR, time, and so on	HR of 180
Activity of rest period	Jogging, walking, stretching and so on	Jog to bring HR back to 120
Number of sets and repetitions		$2 \times 4 \times 400m$
work:relief ratio	1:1 or 1:2	90s run:180s jog

Fig. 5.19 Components of interval training.

Interval training allows training at higher intensities without the associated fatigue. Training around an anaerobic threshold has been proved to create quicker gains in aerobic capacity than continuous training. However, the quicker the type of fitness gained, the quicker the adaptations are lost in times of little or no training (look back to the principles of reversibility and progression – pages 284–85).

TASK 9

1   Design an aerobic-based interval session for a performer of your choice.
2   How could you apply progression and overload to this session?

Interval training gives games players a good opportunity to incorporate sports-specific skills into aerobic work. This will increase the specificity of training.

TASK 10

Incorporate some sports skills into your interval training session from Task 9. For example, instead of just running 200m, in pairs, complete fifteen rugby passes.

Energy system

The aerobic energy system is the key provider of energy for this fitness component. However, the systems do not work in isolation and even extreme aerobic events such as the Tour de France will need energy from the lactic acid system. A very effective way of training for aerobic activities is to work around the anaerobic threshold. This will increase the amount of activity the performer can sustain without crossing the threshold or initiating OBLA. A highly trained marathon runner can work at 85–90 per cent of his or her VO_2 max for the whole marathon. Untrained performers could perhaps work at 65 per cent. The percentage of the VO_2 max at which a performer can work is probably a better predictor of VO_2 max than his/her VO_2 max value.

Adaptations

After a prolonged period of aerobic training, a large number of long-term responses or adaptations will take place. Figure 5.20 summarises these adaptations and their effects.

Where	What changes	Effect
Lungs	Respiratory muscles become stronger	Efficiency of respiration increases
	Lung volume increases due to utilising more of the available alveoli	Diffusion of gases is increased due to greater surface area

KEY WORDS

Hypertrophy

The increase in the size of a muscle.

Where	What changes	Effect
	Maximum pulmonary ventilation is increased due to greater tidal volume and increase in breathing rate	Greater diffusion rate, which might not be that important in getting oxygen in but will certainly help in getting carbon dioxide out
Heart	Myocardial **hypertrophy** (heart gets bigger – both size of left ventricle and thickness of muscle)	Stroke volume increases thus increasing maximal cardiac output
	Resting heart rate decreases (bradycardia)	Heart is more efficient due to increased SV and fewer beats are needed to supply the same amount of oxygen
Vascular system	Arterial walls become more elastic	Enables greater blood pressures to be dealt with and maintain blood flow
	Increased number of capillaries at muscle and lungs	Greater surface area and therefore greater gaseous exchange
Blood	Blood plasma volume increases	Increased blood plasma volume decreases the viscosity of the blood and allows a greater flow through capillaries; greater blood volume will increase stroke volume
	Red blood cell and haemoglobin increase	Greater amount of haemoglobin for oxygen transport
Muscle	Mitochondria increase in size and number	Increased aerobic metabolism
	Myoglobin levels increase	Helps transport the oxygen from the capillaries to the muscle cells
	Increased enzyme activity	Increases the efficiency of the aerobic energy system
	Muscle stores of glycogen increased and utilisation of fats as a fuel increase	Increases amount of aerobic energy produced; fats provide a large amount of energy and allow glycogen to be saved (known as the glycogen sparing effect)

Fig. 5.20 Adaptation to aerobic training.

HOT TIPS

Make sure your exam answers in this area are specific to the question. If cardiac changes are asked for, give cardiac changes.

Possible answers to aerobic training effects and VO_2 max limitations include the following.

- Training will increase the amount of oxygen that is provided by the respiratory system, but tests have shown that our bodies receive more than enough oxygen anyway and this is not the limiting factor for healthy individuals. This could be a factor for someone with a respiratory ailment such as asthma. Some studies have proved that it may be a limiting factor for some extremely well-trained endurance athletes. If all the adaptations described later on in this section are developed to their maximum, external respiration may be a limiting factor, although this would be very rare.

- Studies have shown a direct link between aerobic training, cardiac output and VO_2 max. It is also possible to increase the oxygen-carrying capacity of the blood to improve aerobic performance. Performers train at altitude (legal) and use substances such as recumbinant erythropoietin (illegal) to increase the amount of oxygen carrying haemoglobin. Supply of oxygen to the working muscle is thought to be the major limitation of VO_2 max.

- Training can help to increase the extraction of oxygen from the blood. This increases what is known as the arteriovenous oxygen difference (a-v O_2 diff). This is the amount of oxygen that is taken out of the blood, and is calculated by measuring how much oxygen is in arterial blood and how much is left in venous blood. This value increases after training, partially due to improved distribution of blood to working muscles.

- Once in the muscle cell, the use of oxygen can be increased. Our bodies, after prolonged training, increase the levels of myoglobin and mitochondria. These increases, alongside the increases in enzyme activity, help to improve VO_2 max. However, the muscle fibre type will play a large part and this is determined genetically and will not alter much through training.

It can be seen that numerous adaptations occur and any number of variables could limit VO_2 max although delivery of oxygen to the working muscles is probably the single greatest limiting factor.

Strength

There are three different types of strength.

- **Maximal strength** – the maximum force that can be produced in a single voluntary contraction. This would be crucial for a weightlifter, for example.

- **Explosive strength or power** – a combination of speed and strength or the ability to overcome resistance with a high speed of contraction. The shot putter is a good example of this type of strength.

- **Strength endurance** – the ability to sustain a number of muscular contractions for a period of time. A good example would be an Olympic rower.

The strength of a muscle will be determined by the following two factors.

- **Muscle fibre type.** Your body contains different types of muscle fibre: Type I and Type II (a and b). Type IIb are the strongest fibres, and can also contract and relax very quickly. This makes them important for explosive strength as well as maximal strength. The percentage of each of these fibres is mostly genetically determined.

- **Cross-sectional area.** The cross-sectional size of the muscle determines the strength it can produce. Human muscle can produce three to eight kilograms of force per cm^2 of muscle cross-section. The exact value will depend on the lever system being used by the joint.

Tests

Strength	Test
Maximal strength	Hand grip dynamometer/1RM maximum lift
Elastic strength	Sergeant jump/Wingate test
Strength endurance	National Coaching Foundation sit-up test

Fig. 5.21 Standard tests for strength.

HOT TIPS

For strength training:

F = at least twice a week
I = 80–90 per cent for maximum strength; 40–80 per cent for strength endurance
T = one to seven repetitions for maximum strength; twelve or more for strength endurance.

Training

There are many different types of strength training and many different methods within each type. Some of the key principles of each type will be looked at with a few examples. Look at specific strength training books or ask your teachers and coaches for more examples.

Weight training is using a resistance, either in the form of free weights or a machine to overload the body. Resistance training is a slightly broader term, as the resistance can be provided by a number of different pieces of equipment such as a bungee cord or your own body weight as in a push up. Plyometrics are techniques used to develop power, and circuit training is another common method to increase general strength.

General guidelines

In order to be able to control overload, three concepts must be understood: repetitions, sets and resistance, which is often described as a percentage of repetition maximum (RM).

Repetitions	The number of times the exercise is to be performed without stopping
Sets	A specified number of repetitions of an exercise followed by a period of rest (at least for that muscle group)
Resistance (repetition maximum)	The maximum load a muscle group can lift a given number of times without fatiguing – for example, a ten repetition maximum or 10RM is the weight or load a person can lift ten times and ten times only

Each of these components can be manipulated to bring about the correct overload for the type of strength to be developed.

The only other factor to consider is the speed at which the resistance is moved. Generally, the quicker the resistance is moved, the less strength gains occur.

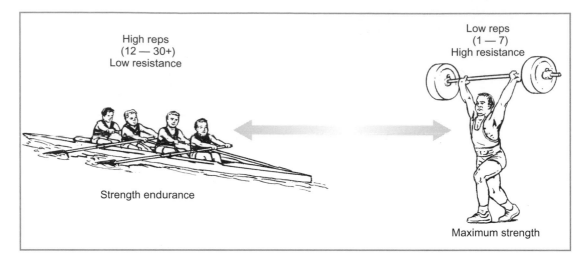

High reps
(12 — 30+)
Low resistance

Low reps
(1 — 7)
High resistance

Strength endurance

Maximum strength

Fig. 5.22 The relationship between number of repetitions and resistance.

However, if elastic strength or power is the main concern, the exercises should be undertaken at the relevant speed. If done slowly, most of the adaptations that occur will be within the muscle cell (myogenic), whereas quick actions are more likely to bring about neural adaptations (see page 301).

Weight training

Many different systems of weight training are used and a full discussion of them is beyond this textbook, but there are some simple systems that could be tried.

Simple set	Select a number of exercises that overload different parts of the body – for example, bench press, leg extension, lat pull down, bicep curl and so on, and complete ten repetitions at a weight you are confident in lifting (approx 10RM). When you are more confident and can lift this weight, say, fifteen times, increase the weight to ensure progression. To maintain the overload you could increase the weight being lifted or increase the number of sets being done – that is, do two sets of ten instead of just one. The method of increasing the overload will depend on the type of strength you are trying to develop (remember Figure 5.22).
Pyramid system	Repetitions are reduced as the load increases. Often the last set will consist of only two lifts.
Inverse pyramid or Oxford	Repetitions increase as the load is reduced.
Super set	Exercise two antagonist muscle groups without rest between sets.
Multi-poundage	Select your 10RM and complete a set of ten. Then remove 5kg and complete as many repetitions as possible and again remove 5kg.

Fig. 5.23 Examples of weight-training systems.

> ## TASK 11
> Plan a strength training session for a performer of your choice. Make sure you are specific in the type of strength that is required and that you apply the principles of training, particularly overload (sets, repetitions and resistance).

Plyometrics

KEY WORDS

Stretch reflex

Also called myotatic reflex. Prevents muscle damage by making the muscle contract before it is overstretched.

Plyometric training is a method of training to help performers who require a large degree of power. Consider a long jumper: it would not be worth his (or her) while developing huge amounts of maximum strength if they could not apply it quickly enough in the take off phase of his event. Plyometrics takes advantage of the elastic nature of the muscle and the **stretch reflex**. This reflex stops the muscle stretching too far and causing injury by making it contract.

The basis of plyometrics is to make the muscle undergo an eccentric muscle contraction before completing the concentric phase. Examples of these types of exercises are double-footed hurdle jumps, depth jumps, alternate leg bounds and so on.

Fig. 5.24 Plyometric techniques.

Circuit training

A common form of strength training, a typical circuit would include eight to ten stations where different activities were performed. These may be free weights or other resistance activities such as push-ups, sit ups and so on. The activities should mainly be arranged so that consecutive stations do not stress the same part of the body.

Performers usually work for a set period of time – for example, 30 seconds or one minute – before rotating to the next station. The time on the exercise and the recovery between stations can be manipulated to control overload and progression. Circuit training is usually used for general fitness and is an ideal way of keeping large numbers of performers working in a relatively small space.

TASK 12

Design a circuit training session for your sport. Outline in your plan the following components:

- the exercises to be completed
- the order
- work:relief ratio.

Interval training

As in aerobic training, interval training can be used for strength gains. Due to the fact that the nature of the work will be high intensity, the work:relief ratio needs to be much greater. For maximum intensity work, it would be as much as 1:10. This is a feature of high-intensity interval training often overlooked by coaches. By not allowing enough rest time, the quality of the session begins to drop and endurance starts to be the component of fitness developed, not strength or power.

Energy systems

The predominant energy systems used will depend on the type of strength being utilised. For maximal and elastic strength, the ATP/PC system will be predominant and the limited ATP stores and phosphocreatine are the fuels for such types of strength. Strength endurance will use the lactic acid system and glycogen will become the predominant fuel.

Adaptations

Adaptations take place in the muscle cell itself and in the neural system that controls the muscle.

Muscular adaptations

The most common adaptation is for muscle hypertrophy to occur. The myofibrils become thicker due to increased protein synthesis. Remember, proteins are responsible for forming many of the structures in the body. What is less clear is if new muscle fibres are created. One theory is that muscle fibres may split, a process known as **hyperplasia,** and develop into two new fibres. Although this has been found in animal studies, little research is available for humans. Even if it does occur, studies have shown that the greatest contribution to muscle size through resistance training is hypertrophy of existing cells, not the creation of new ones.

Energy stores within the muscle cells increase. ATP, phosphocreatine and glycogen are all found to increase. This provides more fuel for anaerobic energy systems. Additionally, the body's tolerance to lactic acid seems to increase, allowing it to work longer at higher intensities. Resistance training has also been found to increase the strength of ligaments and tendons, and increase the deposit of calcium onto bones, making them stronger.

Neural adaptations

It has been found that after resistance training, the total number of motor units recruited is increased. Not only is the total number greater, but also the synchronisation of contraction is improved. That is, all the motor units recruited contract at the same time, again increasing strength.

It would also seem that the **golgi tendon** is inhibited. This is the system responsible for limiting muscle contraction so no damage occurs to it or its surrounding tissues. With this system inhibited, the muscle can create more force.

Flexibility

There are two main types of flexibility.

- **Static flexibility** – the range of movement about a joint with no emphasis on speed. An example of this may be the gymnast performing the splits.
- **Dynamic flexibility** – the ability to use a range of joint movement in the performance of a physical activity at either a normal or rapid speed. The gymnast performing a straddle vault would be an example.

The type of joint will limit the range of movement (ROM) available. Freely moving ball-and-socket joints will provide a far greater ROM than a condyloid joint. The nature of the bones – for example, the presence of any bony features such as processes – will limit movement. Other limiting factors are:

- length and elasticity of muscle tissue
- length of tendons and ligaments
- the elasticity of the skin and amount of fat around the moving area
- the temperature of all soft tissues
- the age of the performer
- the sex of the performer.

Flexibility is a very specific component of fitness and the fact that a performer is flexible around the hip joint does not mean he or she will be as flexible around the shoulder joint.

HOT TIPS

For flexibility:

F = two to three times per week

I = mild tension but no pain

T = hold each stretch for ten to 30 seconds; repeat three to five times.

Test

The most used test of flexibility is the sit and reach test. Using a sit and reach box (or normal school bench and metre rule), the subject places his (or her) feet against the flat edge with his legs straight and knees locked. The subject then reaches high and stretches as far past (towards) his toes as possible. This position should be held for at least two seconds and the score recorded. When measuring the stretch, the toe line should be at 15cm on the ruler with the 0 facing towards the subject.

Other tests include the use of goniometers, which often look like large protractors, to measure the angle at various joints.

KEY WORDS

Proprioceptive neuromuscular facilitation (PNF)

Uses the principle of reciprocal innovation to allow the muscle to relax and stretch further.

Active stretches

Ones in which the muscles create the force for the movement.

Passive stretches

Ones in which the body is moved by an external agent, such as a partner, device or gravity.

Training

Flexibility training is often categorised under three headings: static stretches, ballistic stretching and **proprioceptive neuromuscular facilitation**.

Static stretches are the traditional types of stretch we have all done as part of a warm-up routine. Within this category, there are **active stretches** and **passive stretches**. Active stretches are ones in which the agonist or prime mover muscles create the force to stretch the antagonist muscle. Passive stretches are ones in which the joints are moved to the end of their ROM by an external agent – often a training partner, device or gravity. These are thought to be more effective in developing flexibility than active stretching because of two reasons. The first is that

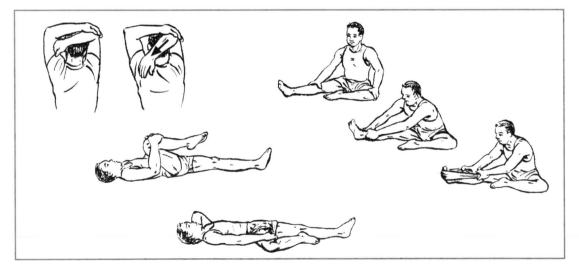

Fig. 5.25 Active stretches.

the stretch is not dependent on the force produced by the prime mover, which could be a limiting factor, and the second is that with the whole area relaxed, there is likely to be a greater range of movement.

Fig. 5.26 Passive stretches.

TASK 13

Produce a poster that would be suitable for displaying in a gym. It should include information on how to stretch all the major areas of the body, how long to hold the stretch for, and any other safety considerations you think are important. Try to include both active and passive stretching techniques.

Ballistic stretching often involves dynamic movements such as arm or leg swings. Due to the nature of these activities, they are associated with dangerous practice. However, these movements often mimic those used in sport and, if done in a safe and progressive manner, should not be discounted. One of the problems with ballistic stretching is the activation of the stretch reflex. As the muscle reaches the end of its ROM, the stretch reflex will make the antagonist contract to limit the stretch. This action is heightened at the end of a ballistic movement.

Activities requiring a large degree of flexibility, such as gymnastics and dance, often use ballistic methods effectively and safely.

Proprioceptive neuromuscular facilitation (PNF)

PNF stretching is a complex theory of stretching that many think is one of the most effective forms of flexibility training. Although there are many techniques, the general idea is based on reciprocal innovation. If, during a stretch, the agonist muscle contracts, the antagonist is made to relax through the process of reciprocal innovation – that is, nerve stimulation to that muscle is inhibited automatically. This allows the muscle to relax and stretch further. A common method is the hold-relax technique. A muscle is stretched to its maximum and then made to perform an isometric contraction (often against a partner) for a couple of seconds before stretching again. An increase in ROM is usually witnessed.

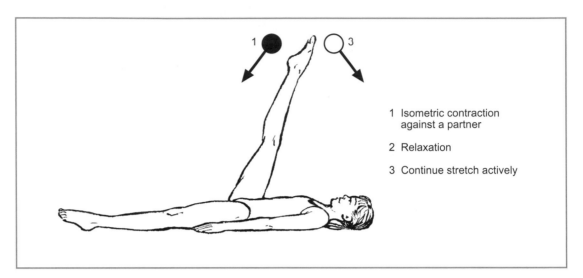

1 Isometric contraction against a partner

2 Relaxation

3 Continue stretch actively

Fig. 5.27 PNF stretch (hold-relax).

Adaptations

If you look at the list of limiting factors for flexibility on page 301, you will see that the only possible adaptations that occur are an increase in the length of the muscle and connective tissues (ligaments and tendons). If the change is a temporary one – after a warm up, for example – it is known as an elastic change. If the change in length is permanent after a long period of sustained stretching, it is known as a plastic change.

These adaptations are beneficial to the performer, as they allow the muscle to work more efficiently throughout the sports skill. It is also reported that increased flexibility may help in the prevention of and recovery from injury.

Other fitness components

	Definition	Test
Body composition	The percentage of muscle fat and bone in the body	Skin fold callipers (Jackson and Pollock) or hydrostatic weighing
Balance	The ability to maintain the centre of mass above the base of support; can be static (handstand) or dynamic (landing after catching a netball)	Stalk balance

	Definition	Test
Co-ordination	The ability to put a number of body systems into action simultaneously – for example, hand and eyes	Ball toss test
Agility	The ability to change body position in a precise and balanced manner	Illinois agility run
Reaction time	The length of time between the reception of a stimulus and the initiation of a response	Ruler drop test, various computer reaction time tests
Speed	The ability to move body parts quickly	Rolling 30m sprint

Revise as you go! Test your knowledge and understanding

- Define VO_2 max.
- What are typical values for VO_2 max for a healthy twenty year old?
- What factors could limit VO_2 max?
- Describe two ways of approving VO_2 max.
- Outline the adaptations that occur after a period of aerobic training.
- Define the three types of strength.
- Give outlines for FIT for each type of strength.
- What is plyometrics?
- Outline a quick circuit training plan.
- Identify both muscular and neural adaptations that occur after a period of strength training.
- Why is flexibility so specific?
- What is the difference between active and passive stretching?
- Why does PNF allow the muscle to stretch further?

Sharpen up your exam technique!

1 VO_2 max is a measure of aerobic capacity. Give reasons why the values of VO_2 max are lower for females than males. (3 marks)

2 Comment on the use of VO_2 max to predict athletic performance. (3 marks)

3 If an athlete completed a twelve-week programme of intense aerobic training, what physiological adaptations would you expect to take place within the cardio-vascular system? (5 marks)

4 Although strength is identified as a component of fitness, there are different types of strength. Provide a definition and method of evaluation for strength endurance and maximum strength. (4 marks)

5 How can performers improve their strength endurance? (3 marks)

6   What adaptations would you expect to take place within the muscle as a result of strength endurance training? (3 marks)

7   Circuit training is a popular method of strength training for many activities. Identify the main characteristics of circuit training and the general guidelines you would follow when planning a circuit. (4 marks)

8   The purpose of flexibility training is to improve or maintain the range of movement over which a muscle can act and joints can operate. Describe the types of training that can be used to increase the range of movement in a joint. (5 marks)

Section 5: *Ergogenic aids*

Learning objectives

HOT TIPS

Know an example of an ergogenic aid for both aerobic and anaerobic performers. Make sure you know what the effects are.

At the end of this section you should be able to:
*   understand how dietary manipulation, such as carbohydrate loading, pre- and post-event meals, and food/fluid intake during exercise can influence performance
*   describe the effects of creatine supplementation on performance
*   explain the use of blood doping and EPO as an aid to endurance athletes
*   identify the possible effects of alcohol, caffeine and anabolic steroids on sports performance.

Introduction

An ergogenic aid is any substance that aids performance. You may think it is a relatively new concept, but athletes have been taking substances to improve their performance from the very first days of sport. Ancient Greeks ate mushrooms and the Aztecs ate human hearts. Ergogenic aids are now big business.

Nutritional aids
Carbohydrate loading

This process involves the muscles 'super-compensating' and increasing glycogen stores. Stores are depleted by heavy training seven days prior to competition. The athlete consumes a diet high in fats and proteins but low in carbohydrate. After about three days, training is tapered down and the athlete consumes a high carbohydrate diet (at least 70 per cent carbohydrate). The body super-compensates for the previous lack of glycogen and stores more than before, thus increasing muscle glycogen levels.

Who benefits?

Performers who take part in long duration aerobic events – for example, marathon runners.

Potential risks

Training without sufficient glycogen stores is very difficult and quality may well be lost in the run up to a competition. There is also the danger of having depleted glycogen stores if you do not follow the correct diet prior to competition. Additionally, the athlete may gain weight because of water retention.

Pre-event meals

Meals high in carbohydrate should be eaten three days before competition to ensure muscle glycogen levels. Pre-event meals eaten two to four hours before will ensure that liver glycogen stores are high. Glucose can be eaten just prior to exercise (five minutes) if the athlete is comfortable doing so.

Who benefits?

Performers who rely on the breakdown of glucose for energy, such as games players and any aerobic athletes.

Potential risks

If the pre-event meal is consumed between fifteen and 45 minutes before exercise, it can have a detrimental effect. The large amount of blood glucose stimulates insulin to remove the glucose and a condition known as hypoglycaemia can occur, causing early exhaustion.

Post-event meals

Liver glycogen stores are readily replaced within hours after a carbohydrate-rich meal. Muscle glycogen stores are much harder to replace and can take several days after a long-duration activity such as a marathon. The best time to consume a post-event meal is as soon as is practical after the event. The rate of muscle glycogen replacement is significantly quicker during the first two hours after exercise.

Who benefits?

Performers who have taken part in activities that have utilised carbohydrate as an energy source.

Potential risks

There are no potential risks with post-event meals.

Food/fluid intake during exercise

Research in this area has found that consuming small amounts of carbohydrate while completing events that are greater than 45 minutes can have a beneficial effect by maintaining blood glucose levels.

Much research has been done into the replacement of water and 'sports drinks'. Dehydration is one of the greatest causes of fatigue and so every athlete should replace fluid at every opportunity. Unfortunately, the body's sense of thirst is a poor indicator of levels of dehydration. It only becomes thirsty *after* dehydration has begun. So, what is best: water or a 'sports drink'?

Sports drinks often claim to be one of three types. Hypertonic drinks contain relatively large amounts of carbohydrate to provide energy; isotonic drinks contain approximately the same amount of carbohydrate as contained in blood; and hypotonic drinks contain less carbohydrate. It has been found that large quantities of carbohydrate in the solution can help prevent fatigue in long duration events but it may feel quite uncomfortable in the stomach. It may also increase dehydration by diverting the water to the intestines. Water is excellent for preventing/reducing dehydration, but the addition of a small amount of carbohydrate may improve the uptake of water by the body from the intestine. One thing is sure, the flavour of the drink is vital in encouraging the performer to drink it and this is where many brands fall short.

A detailed description about this area is beyond the scope of this textbook but, due to the competitive nature of the sports drink industry, this area of sports research will never be far from the public eye.

Who benefits?

Performers in any event that lasts longer than 45 minutes – for example, footballers and triathletes.

Potential risks

Not all people are comfortable eating while exercising. Gastro problems can occur – particularly if the food is high in protein, fibre or very high in carbohydrate.

TASK 14

Using an activity of your choice, design an information leaflet identifying and explaining the guidelines for pre- and post-competition meals and eating/drinking during exercise. Your leaflet should inform the athlete when to eat and drink, what to eat and drink, and the benefit of such actions. Remember to make your leaflet specific for your activity. The requirements of a long endurance event, such as triathlon, may be completely different to a racquet sportsperson playing in a tournament.

Other aids to performance

Creatine

Creatine supplements have been available for many years in different forms. By increasing the amount of creatine in the diet, the performer can maximise the amount of phosphocreatine stored in the muscles.

Who benefits?

High-intensity athletes such as 100m sprinters. A greater amount of phosphocreatine allows the athlete to perform for longer on the PC system and maintains high power output.

Potential risks

The increase in creatine has been seen to put strain on organs such as the liver. Some studies have also found that it had a negative effect by increasing dehydration in performers.

Blood doping and erythropoietin (EPO)

KEY WORDS

Erythropoietin (EPO)

A naturally occurring hormone that increases the body's ability to manufacture red blood cells.

Although different processes, the theory behind these methods is the same. Both increase red blood cell concentration and haemoglobin levels, and increase the amount of oxygen reaching the working muscles. Blood doping works by removing red blood cells from the body, storing them and allowing the body to replace the cells. This process will take about five weeks, after which the original red blood cells can be reintroduced to the body. **Erythropoietin (EPO)** is a hormone that stimulates the body to create more red blood cells itself.

Who benefits?

All endurance athletes.

Potential risks

The increase in blood viscosity can put a huge strain on the heart, and blood clots and heart failure have been reported. Removing and storing blood has problems with contamination. Although EPO may appear safer, no one can predict how the body will react to a certain dose and so the dangers of clotting are even more serious.

Nasal strips

Nasal strips were originally designed to help prevent snoring and have absolutely no beneficial physiological effects for sports performers at all. Aerobic capacity is not usually limited by the supply of oxygen from the lungs, so even if the strips did increase air intake, no increased performance could arise.

Caffeine

Caffeine can help improve mental alertness, concentration and reaction time, and it has been proven to reduce the feeling of fatigue, allowing exercise at higher intensities for longer. It is also proven to increase ability to utilise fat as a fuel and increase aerobic capacity.

Who benefits?

Many endurance athletes due to the potential increase in fat metabolism.

Potential risks

Caffeine can increase the sensation of nervousness, anxiety and restlessness. Sleep can become disturbed and the risk of dehydration is increased. Caffeine is also addictive.

Alcohol

Alcohol is thought to have no beneficial effects on sports performance. Although it might make the performer feel more relaxed and self-confident, most research shows that it actually impairs psychomotor performance – it is just that the performer does not notice. Alcohol can also speed up dehydration, which again will inhibit performance.

Hormones and anabolic steroids

Anabolic (building) steroids (such as Nandralone) are thought to increase muscle mass and strength and help with the recovery from high-intensity training. The first two are proven; the increased recovery from exercise has yet to have any sound medical research to back up this claim.

Human growth hormone (HGH) can also increase the amount of glucose in the blood and increase the body's healing capability.

Who benefits?

High-intensity/short-duration athletes, such as weight lifters and sprinters. HGH has been found to be useful for endurance athletes due to the increase in glucose levels.

Potential risks

These steroids should be correctly called androgenic anabolic steroids. This is because they affect the balance of our sex hormones, testosterone and oestrogen. Women who take them often have a reduction in breast size, hair growth and develop a deeper voice, while men have breast enlargement, reduction in the size of their penis and so on. Other side effects include acne, weak joints and aggressive tendencies or 'roid rage'.

Human growth hormone (HGH) is similar in effect, although in developed adults it can make the bones thicken and deform, and cause internal organs to increase dangerously in size. The onset of diabetes and high blood pressure is also a common side effect.

A final word on ergogenic aids

The aids covered in this section are by no means exhaustive. Athletes and sports scientists will always be looking for ways in which the body can go faster, further, higher and stronger. As yet, there is no shortcut to top performance apart from hard work and dedication. The risks involved in most of these aids far outweigh the potential gains. The full impact of taking creatine supplements and the like is still unknown. Do not take the risk; do the work.

TASK 15

Produce an information poster on a number of commonly used ergogenic aids. Your poster should inform the audience of the name of the aids, the benefits and possible risks involved in their use, and the type of sportsperson who would benefit from their use.

Revise as you go! Test your knowledge and understanding

- Name three ergogenic aids that can help an endurance athlete improve his or her performance.
- For each aid, state two beneficial effects.
- For each aid, state two harmful side effects.
- Name two ergogenic aids that would help the high-intensity/power athlete improve his or her performance.
- For each aid, state two beneficial effects.
- For each aid, state two harmful side effects.

Sharpen up your exam technique!

1 Carbohydrates are used as an energy source during both aerobic and anaerobic conditions. It is therefore beneficial that an athlete's stores of carbohydrate are at a maximum before competition day. Discuss the advantages and disadvantages of carbohydrate loading.   (3 marks)

2 To gain the edge over rivals, aerobic athletes may be tempted to use an illegal ergogenic aid. Explain the ways in which such aids physiologically enhance performance. What are the long-term negative physiological effects?   (5 marks)

Chapter 6 **Improvement of effective performance**

Learning objectives

At the end of this chapter you should be able to:
- understand which practical activities you can choose to be assessed in
- understand how you will be assessed
- understand the terms 'standardisation' and 'moderation'
- appreciate how you can improve your performances
- understand the Evaluation and Appreciation of Performance aspect of your assessment
- appreciate how you can improve your Evaluation and Appreciation of Performance.

Introduction

Advanced level PE has as its central aim the linking of theory to practical and practical to theory. This enables you to gain not only knowledge of theoretical concepts but also an understanding and appreciation of them. You can also apply these concepts to your practical performances in order to improve your standards. Advanced level PE recognises that students should be able to capitalise on their practical talents by being assessed in practical activities, with these assessments contributing to the examination grade.

In your AS PE studies you would have been informed of the opportunities for assessment in practical activities, so you should be aware of the activities available. This chapter will identify ways in which you can improve the marks when you are assessed. Linked to one of the activities you are assessed in will be the Evaluation and Appreciation of Performance, in which you are required to observe a fellow student, comment on the strengths and weaknesses of his or her performance, then create an action plan to improve that performance.

Performing your practical activities should help you to understand your theoretical work while the Evaluation and Appreciation of Performance will help you in your synoptic assessment, for which you will be asked to apply to practical activities theory from areas in AS and A2. As was indicated in your AS PE studies, you will find useful information in this chapter, but to improve both your practical performance and your Evaluation and Appreciation of Performance there is no substitute for actual practice.

The chapter is divided into two sections: the practical activities and the Evaluation and Appreciation of Performance.

Your practical performance, knowledge and understanding will be assessed by your performance in two practical activities together with your spoken comments on a fellow student's performance, the Evaluation and Appreciation of Performance. In each of these three components you will be assessed out of 30 marks, which enables you to score a maximum of 90 marks.

Section 1: *The selection, application and improved performance of skills in an open environment (practical activities)*

Module content

Fig. 6.01 A singles game of badminton.

The activities are grouped together into ten categories. You must choose two activities, each from a different category. For example, you could choose swimming and badminton but not tennis and badminton. It is likely that you will continue with the two activities that you were assessed in for your AS PE studies but you may choose one or two different activities if you wish.

If you decide to change the activities from those you were assessed in at AS level, you should ensure that you can score more marks in them than you would if you did not change.

There are ten activity categories as shown on the following page. These are the activities that appear in the specification, but there are also some additional activities in which your centre may allow you to take part and be assessed. You can find a list of these on the OCR website: www.ocr.org.uk/develop/phys_ed/physedua.htm

Assessment

Your teacher will assess you throughout your practical activity course. This will enable your teachers to accurately assess you rather than have just one assessment session towards the end of the course (when you may have an 'off' day). This will ensure that if you are injured they have some marks on which to base their assessment. The final assessed marks have to be sent to the exam board by 31 March. If your practical activities are done in modular blocks, you will probably be assessed at the end of the module, whenever that is. For some 'summer' activities, this may be very early in your course. You may have to be videoed doing your practical activity.

Activity category	Activity
1 Athletic activities	Track and field athletics
2 Combat activities	Judo
3 Dance activities	Educational dance
4 Invasion game activities	Association Football
	Basketball
	Field hockey
	Gaelic Football
	Hurling
	Netball
	Rugby League
	Rugby Union
5 Net/wall game activities	Badminton
	Squash
	Tennis
	Volleyball
6 Striking/fielding game activities	Cricket
7 Target games activities	Golf
8 Gymnastic activities	Gymnastics
Trampolining	
9 Outdoor and adventurous activities	Canoeing
	Mountain walking
	Sailing
	Skiing
10 Swimming activities	Competitive swimming

Fig. 6.02 Activities and their categories.

The teachers in your centre will consult with each other to check that different activities assessed by different teachers or coaches in your centre are all at the same standard.

Standardisation is particularly important for many activities that cannot be done in your centre and are sometimes taught by coaches who are based at clubs. In cases such as these, the physical education teacher responsible for A level will liase with the coach to ensure that he or she is aware of what you need to do in your activity. This teacher will assess you with the help and advice of the coach.

Sometime between Easter and Whitsuntide, some students in your centre will be chosen to perform their practical activities alongside students from other centres in your area at a moderation. A moderator from the exam board will look at all these students' performances to check they have been assessed correctly and that marks awarded by the different centres are all at the same level. The moderator knows the correct levels and standards of performance and ensures that all candidates have been treated fairly.

Content of the practical activities

The OCR specification indicates that the focus of your activities will be on the 'the selection, application and improved performance of skills in an open environment'. These skills will be performed in the situation in which the activity normally takes place. The 'normal' situation will allow you to:

- show your knowledge of the activity's rules, regulations and code of practice
- perform to the best of your ability
- select the correct skill for a particular situation – for example, choose the correct stroke when batting in cricket
- repeat skills consistently – for example, get the skill right each time you perform it
- adapt skills where and when required – for example, adjust your pass in netball to avoid the opponent marking you from intercepting it
- show your tactical awareness – for example, putting simple agilities you can perform well in your gymnastics routine rather than complex ones in which you may not do well
- demonstrate the principles of fair play and sportsmanship – for example, accepting the officials' decisions without question; not using gamesmanship
- perform all of the above when under pressure.

The 'normal' situation in which the activity takes part is obviously not the same for all the activities. Examples of the 'normal' situation are as follows.

- Athletic activities: athletics, sprinting – sprint starts, sprint action, finishes together with a timed sprint.
- Combat activities: judo – formal contest.
- Dance activities: educational dance – choreograph and perform a solo dance routine lasting four minutes containing jumps, leaps, balances, rolls and turns.
- Invasion games: Association Football (soccer) – full game.
- Striking/fielding games: cricket – full game in which you will be assessed in fielding and either batting or bowling.
- Net/wall games: netball – full game.
- Target games: golf – full round.

- Gymnastic activities: trampolining – a ten-contact sequence to include a jump, a twist, a drop and a somersault.
- Outdoor and adventurous activities: canoeing – two-day expedition on appropriate water.
- Swimming activities: competitive swimming – racing starts, stroke technique in short race, racing finish together with a timed swim.

These 'formal' situations allow you to display the range of skills you have developed while also encouraging you to adapt them to meet the demands made on you. Because it is the 'normal' open environment, tactics and strategies will play a much bigger part than in the conditioned competitive situations you experienced at AS level. For instance, in mountain walking you will need to camp for two nights, which will necessitate you being much more aware of your nutritional needs and camping skills.

If you are to be successful in this open environment, then you will need to have perfected your skills with lots of practice so that they come to you automatically. This will enable you to concentrate on your tactics and strategies.

TASK 1

Find out what the 'normal' open situations are for the two activities in which you will be assessed.

What are the assessment criteria?

There are several key areas that your teacher will be looking at.

- How good your skills are, and the accuracy, control and fluency with which you perform them.
- Your use of advanced skills when appropriate, and their accuracy, control and fluency.
- Your understanding and use of strategies and tactics.
- Your overall standard of performance.
- Your level of physical endeavour, sportsmanship and flair.

Your teacher will use these criteria to put you into one of five bands (25–30, 19–24, 13–18, 7–12, 0–6) before he or she finally decides the exact mark to give you. Your teacher may also use the representative level at which you perform your activity to check that you are in the correct band.

Your teacher will do this assessment over a period of time but might have one final assessment session to finalise your mark.

What will I be required to do for my assessment?

How you will be assessed and what the focus of the assessment will be has been identified for each practical activity. Formal situations are used for your assessment and the list that follows shows the focus of assessment for each specific activity or the focus for all activities in a category where this is more appropriate.

- Track and field athletics: one event from one of the following areas – track, jumps, throws.
- Educational dance: jumps, leaps, balances, rolls and turns.
- Invasion games: techniques, tactical awareness and behaviour.
- Golf: club selection and distance. Stroke action and target accuracy.
- Gymnastics: an agility sequence containing three rolls, three jumps, three balances and three agilities together with at least two linking movements.
- Trampolining: a ten-contact sequence, which must contain a jump, a twist, a drop and a somersault.
- Mountain walking: use and interpretation of maps and their symbols, navigation using map and compass, hill-walking skills, organisation and use of equipment, application of safety principles, conservation practices and respect for others, wild camping.
- Competitive swimming: one stroke from front crawl, backstroke, breaststroke, butterfly.

These can be found in more detail in the 'Teacher support – coursework guidance' booklet, which can be found on the OCR website at: www.ocr.org.uk/develop/phys_ed/physedua.htm

Details of the focus for additional activities can also be found on this website.

Fig. 6.03 Practical activities being performed.

TASK 2
Access the OCR website and identify the assessment focus for each of your two assessed activities.

How can I improve my Practical Activity Performances?

You should now be aware of how and when you will be assessed as well as the focus for your assessment. This knowledge and understanding should help you to plan how to use your time to improve your performances in your practical activities and thereby increase the marks you are awarded.

If you are carrying on with the activities in which you were assessed in your AS PE studies, you will be aware of some of your strengths and weaknesses, particularly in the activity on which your Personal Performance Portfolio (PPP) focused. The first thing you should do is to evaluate your performance in your two activities, identify your strengths and weaknesses, then create action plans aimed at improving your performances.

Specific information in relation to improving performance in your activities can be found in coaching books, usually published by the governing or organising body. A good source of information for books of this type is www.1st4sport.com

When you are looking to evaluate your performance with a view to creating action plans, you should bear in mind the following questions.

- How consistent are you in using your skills accurately, with control and fluency?
- Do you have advanced skills, and can you use them appropriately and successfully?
- How well do you understand and apply strategies and tactics?
- How much effort and commitment do you put into your activity?
- Do you always display good sportsmanship, playing by the rules of the activity?
- In your activity, do you try to be creative and use your initiative?
- Are your levels of physical fitness appropriate for the activity?

TASK 3

1 Find the websites of the governing or organising bodies of your two activities to see which coaching manuals are available to help you to develop your skills. Alternatively you could access the 1st4sport website.

2 Check in the library of your school or centre to see if these coaching manuals are there for you to use.

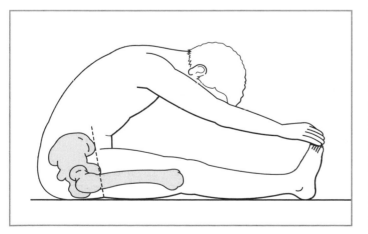

Fig. 6.04 Objective tests can be used to measure fitness.

Physical fitness

Your knowledge of this aspect of your activities should be improving now through your studies in Exercise Physiology, where you will be gaining an understanding of how training affects you. As you will be taking part in the 'normal' situation in which the activity is performed, your level of physical fitness will be very important. You should use a standardised test for each of the four main components of physical fitness to identify your level and, if you work on it, any improvement you make. You should look at strength, speed, stamina and suppleness.

Through your study of Exercise Physiology you will be able to be more specific about the aspects that are important to you and how to go about improving them. However, you should also seek advice from your teacher and coach. If you can improve your fitness, it will help your all-round performance and also help to improve the mark you get for 'physical endeavour'.

TASK 4

1 For each of your activities, consult your teacher or coach, together with the coaching manuals, to establish the important components of physical fitness.

2 Identify and describe a standard test for each of the fitness components important to your activities and test yourself.

3 Construct a training programme designed to improve your physical fitness for your activities.

Improving the quality and range of your skills

If you are following the same activities at A2 that you were assessed in at AS, you will have looked at the level of your skills. If you feel there is still room for improving them and even learning new ones, then:

- consult your teacher or coach and the coaching manuals to identify drills or practices that you can use
- consult the coaching manuals to identify the coaching points on which you need to focus
- remember that you will be assessed using these skills in the 'normal' activity situation; your aim therefore should be to be able to perform them in that situation
- listen to feedback given by your teacher or coach; this will help you to improve
- refer back to practices you did in your AS studies, if you are doing the same activities.

You should also refer to OCR's coursework guidance booklet, which identifies the movement phases into which the skills will be analysed for assessment purposes. These phases may also help you in improving and extending your range of skills. Some examples of these movement phases are identified below.

- **Track and field athletics**   Track events: Posture
  Leg action
  Arm action
  Head carriage
  Overall efficiency

Jumping events:	Approach
	Take off
	Flight
	Landing
	Overall efficiency
Throwing events:	Initial stance, grip and preparation
	Travel and trunk position
	Throwing action
	Release
	Overall efficiency

- **Games**
  - Preparation
  - Execution
  - Recovery
  - Results
  - Overall efficiency

- **Competitive swimming**
  - Arm action
  - Leg action
  - Body position
  - Breathing
  - Overall efficiency

TASK 5

For each of your practical activities, identify the movement phases that are used to analyse the activity and its skills.

In order to improve both your skills and your performance in general, it is important that you receive, listen and respond to feedback that is given by teachers and coaches.

Strategies and tactics

As you are now being assessed in the 'normal' situation in which the activity occurs, strategies and tactics will play a much bigger part in your performance and assessment. While you can only gain experience of strategies and tactics by taking part in the activity, you can improve your knowledge of this aspect by referring to the coaching manuals. You will need to gain experience by taking part in the activity regularly and you will need to adopt a strategy to enable you to achieve this. It may be that you can gain this within your school or college, but you may also wish to increase or widen this by joining a club in the local community. If this is the case, you should ensure that the coach or organiser is made aware of what you need to do to improve your assessment.

Section 2: *Evaluation and Appreciation of Performance*

In your AS PE studies you had to complete a Personal Performance Portfolio (PPP), which was based on your own performance in one of your practical activities. In A2 you have to do a similar piece of work, this time orally, when you will be asked to comment on one of your fellow student's performances.

This element of your practical assessment represents 5 per cent of your synoptic assessment, the remainder of which you do in Unit 5. As you will know, synoptic assessment requires you to link theoretical areas together and apply them to practical activities. You will be expected to do this in your Evaluation and Appreciation of Performance.

What do I have to do in my Evaluation and Appreciation of Performance?

You will choose one of the two activities in which you are being assessed and on which you wish to focus for this aspect of your assessment. You will then:

- watch a fellow student performing the activity
- evaluate the performance, identifying the strengths and weaknesses
- select a major weakness and create an action plan to rectify/improve it
- apply theory to justify/support your evaluation and action plan.

You will do this by talking to your teacher.

How do I do this?

Evaluation. You have already experienced the process of evaluation when you identified the strengths and weaknesses of your own performance for your PPP. This time you are going to carry out the same process, but instead observe a fellow student. You are going to identify what is:

- good about the performance – the strengths
- poor about the performance – the weaknesses.

As you did in your PPP, you can focus on the following areas:

- skills
- tactics/strategies
- fitness.

To help you do this you will refer to the phases that are used to analyse the activity and its skills (see pages 320–1).

Action planning. Initially, you have to select one of the major weaknesses identified in your evaluation to be the focus of your action plan. Having selected the focus, your action plan should have the following:

- a clear realistic goal – the major weakness you have identified
- a timescale
- a method for achieving the goal – detailed coaching points and practices.

Apply theory to support your evaluation and action plan. This should cover topics from the three main theory areas:

- anatomical and physiological aspects
- psychological aspects
- socio-cultural aspects.

You now have a clear structure or plan of what it is that you have to do. This can be identified as follows.

- Identify the movement phases that are used to analyse the activity.
- Accurately identify the major strengths of the performance.
- Accurately identify the major weaknesses of the performance.
- Construct a viable action plan to remedy a major weakness.
- Apply theory from physiological, psychological and socio-cultural aspects to support the evaluation and action plan.

TASK 6

Write out your check sheet for your Evaluation and Appreciation of Performance oral response. It should have the five points identified above. You should use this check sheet when you start to practise your observation and oral response.

How can I improve my Evaluation and Appreciation of Performance?

Like your practical performance, this aspect of your assessment is a skill and to improve it you need to practise it and receive feedback. Like other skills, it can be broken down into parts for you to practise.

Analytical phases

You need to know the movement phases that are used to analyse the activity. These can be found in the coursework guidance booklet issued by OCR.

Earlier in this chapter it was suggested that in order to improve your performance it would be helpful for you to make yourself aware of these phases. Some examples of these phases were given on pages 320 and 321.

You will be expected to know and use these phases for your Evaluation and Appreciation of Performance.

> ## TASK 7
>
> If you have not already done so, access the coursework guidance booklet and identify the movement phases for the activity on which you will focus for your Evaluation and Appreciation of Performance.

Identification of strengths

You should start by splitting the activity into the analytical movement phases and identifying strengths in each of these phases. It is suggested that you focus on the following three aspects.

1 Skills

These skills will be being performed under pressure. It is important that you are aware of the 'technical' models to which you are comparing the performance you are observing. As previously suggested, these 'technical' models can be found in the relevant governing or organising body coaching manuals. Knowledge of how the skill should be performed enables you to judge how good it is and to justify your evaluation by identifying why it is good. You will also use this knowledge when you are identifying weaknesses and constructing your action plan.

Fig. 6.05 A skill being performed under pressure.

2 Tactics and strategies

As performers gain a greater grasp of the skills within the activity, they are able to devote more attention to the tactics and strategies involved. They show an increased perceptual awareness accompanied by an increased capacity for decision-making. The majority of these increased capacities will be devoted to the performer attempting to influence the outcome of the activity through their use of tactics and strategies. Sometimes this will be shown through better teamwork. You will need to have a good understanding of the major tactics and strategies used in the activity to be able to evaluate the performer you are observing. This understanding will be gained from your own involvement in the activity but should be further improved by reading the appropriate coaching manuals and talking to coaches. You will be comparing the performer you are looking at to what you know he (or she) should be doing. This will enable you to identify what he is doing correctly. If he is part of a team, you will probably want to comment on the team's effective use of strategies as well as the individual's contribution.

3 Fitness

In the PPP, which you completed in your AS studies, you were asked to identify the components of physical fitness important in the activity on which you were focusing. This identification will be further developed by your studies in Exercise Physiology. You should apply this knowledge to your activity, which should enable you to identify and evaluate accurately the components of physical fitness appropriate to the performance you are evaluating. You should evaluate the fitness of the performer you are observing under the following headings as appropriate:

- Strength/power
- Stamina
- Suppleness/flexibility
- Speed.

You will be focusing on the aspects of fitness you know are important in the activity to assess whether or not the performer you are observing has good levels in these areas.

Some of the areas suggested above will be more relevant in some activities than others and you need to adapt them to suit the activity you are observing. Not only will you comment on the fitness aspects for which the performer has good levels, but also on his or her application of these strengths.

Identification of weaknesses

You should start again, by splitting the activity into the analytical movement phases and identifying weaknesses in each of these phases.

This aspect will follow the same path as the identification of strengths. You are identifying major weaknesses and those for which you can construct a viable action plan. You do not want to be too negative by identifying every small weakness, particularly those that do not significantly affect the performance.

The areas to focus on should be the same as those looked at when identifying strengths: skills, tactics and strategies, and fitness.

1 Skills

You will need to focus on the skills in which, when under pressure, the performer either performs poorly or chooses not to use at all. You will be able to identify those performed poorly by comparing them to the correct technical models and the coaching points as well as the level of success. When under pressure, some performers will be very inconsistent in some aspects of their skill production. This means they will be successful on one occasion and unsuccessful the next time. When under pressure, do they choose not to perform advanced skills indicating they are unsure or lack confidence in them?

2 Tactics and strategies

These will vary a great deal from activity to activity. They will focus on attempting to outwit the opposition or the environment and in team activities they will also include teamwork. Again, you will be comparing what your performer does against what you know to be good tactics and strategies. This will enable you to identify where he or she is going wrong. This may be focused on the individual you are observing or the team in general.

3 Fitness

Using the areas of fitness you have determined are important for the activity, you will identify those areas in which, in your opinion, the performer has weaknesses or in which you consider he or she could perform better by having increased levels of fitness.

It should have become apparent to you by now that in identifying strengths and weaknesses you are using the same information to determine both aspects. You should, however, ensure that you identify the strengths before the weaknesses, as it is easy to overlook them!

Construct a viable action plan to improve a major weakness

This is where you will select one of the major weaknesses you have identified and create a plan to remedy it, thereby improving the performance as a whole.

You will remember from your AS PPP that your action plan had to include the following aspects:

*   clear, achievable, realistic goals
*   timescale
*   method for achieving the goals – detailed coaching points and practices.

These must appear in your action plan.

Clear, realistic goals

This will, in fact, be to remedy the major fault you have identified and thereby improve the performance. All you have to do is select one of the major faults you have identified. You may, in addition, identify more specific goals – for example, to achieve Level 12 on the multi-stage fitness test rather than just to improve stamina.

When choosing the fault you should ensure you are able to suggest ways in which you will be able to remedy it – that is, to construct an action plan. Sometimes it is easier to focus on weaknesses within a skill or fitness area, as these are easier for creating action plans.

Timescale

You need to identify how long your action plan is designed to take, how often the practices or training will be and so on. Different action plans will have different timescales. Those designed to develop aspects of fitness will usually be over a longer period than those to develop skills.

You should give an indication of the overall length of the action plan – that is, the number of weeks or months – together with the frequency of the sessions (for example, number of times a week).

Method for achieving the goals

Here you will outline the practices and drills you will suggest that the performer does to remedy the weakness. This should be done in detail, identifying the coaching points for the skills you wish to be improved as well as each of the practices you will use. Remember that, as in your AS PPP, the practices you identify should show progression going from simple to complex and closed to open. You should, however, be realistic, starting the practices at a level that is appropriate to the performer you are observing.

You should demonstrate your knowledge of training by identifying exactly the aspects of fitness you are going to focus on together with their relevance and application in the activity.

Method for evaluating achievement of goals

In this section you will identify how you will determine how successful you have been in achieving your goals.

If you have been working on stamina, you may decide that you will use the multi stage fitness test. You would apply the test before the action plan is started to establish the performer's level of fitness and then again at various intervals to establish his or her progress. You may well use your method of evaluation as a 'goal' – in other words, if you are setting out to improve stamina then your goal may be to improve it from Level 6 to Level 10.

If your goal is to improve a skill, then you may well need to devise your own evaluative test. This may involve a field test where the performer applies the skill under pressure and you record his or her success rate. Again, the test results may be one of your goals – to achieve a success rate of 60 per cent in the field test.

Application of theoretical knowledge

You are also required to explain or justify your evaluative comments and your action plan by applying theory from the physiological, psychological and socio-cultural subject areas. This is not as difficult as it first appears but needs to be practised. You should identify theory areas from each of the three subject areas, which you can apply to your activity. Start off with a small list and see how you can apply these to your activity. You could begin with the following.

Physiological

- Important joints and their movements involved in the activity/skill.
- Major muscles involved – what are the important muscle groups involved?
- Physical fitness requirements of the activity – which aspects of fitness are important to the activity?

Psychological

- Classification of the skills involved – is the activity gross/fine, closed/open and so on?
- Identification of the underpinning abilities – what abilities are important to the activity/skill?
- Information processing demands – is there a lot of interpretation of information and are there decisions to be made?

Socio-cultural

- Performer's position on performance pyramid – what level is the performer at?
- Local support for the activity from the governing or organising body – what facilities or opportunities are there for those involved in the activity?
- Role of the media in the activity – is there good coverage of the activity? Are there role models to relate to?

You should write these down and use your list to remind you when you practise. (You will not be able to use a list when you are finally assessed!)

Once you are able to apply these theory areas to your activity, you should add to the list, gradually building up the theory you are able to apply to support your observations. You should be able to identify other theory areas from your course notes. By doing this you will build up your 'bank' of theory areas you know how to apply. When you are being assessed in your Evaluation and Appreciation of Performance, you may not be able to apply all the theory areas you have learned and practised in the performance you are observing, as they may not be relevant to that particular performance.

Some students will apply their theory, as they go through their plan – that is, they will apply theory to the strengths and weaknesses they identify and when they introduce their action plan. Others will wait until they have reached the end of their observations, then apply theory to support what they have said. You should try both methods and see which works best for you.

You should refer to pages 80–2 of OCR's coursework guidance booklet for examples of other theory areas that are suggested as being relevant to apply to your observations. They are only suggestions and you should not think that you will be able or required to apply them all!

> ## TASK 8
> Create a list of two or three theoretical concepts that you can apply to support your observations. Add these to your check sheet, identifying the outline structure of your response.

You should practise your Evaluation and Appreciation of Performance as many times as you can. Like any skill, you should break it down to its simplest form, practice this, then move on to practice the next stage until you have mastered the complete skill. At each stage you should add that stage on to those you have already mastered.

The following stages would be appropriate for you to practise.

- Identifying the strengths in each of the movement phases.
- Identifying the weaknesses in each of the movement phases.
- Identifying a major weakness, and creating a viable action plan to remedy it and improve the performance.
- Applying two to three concepts from each of the three theoretical areas.
- Increasing the number of concepts applied.

It may be that you can practise by looking at a video of the activity you are focusing on and you can record your response on tape so that you can listen to it and evaluate it yourself.

What will happen when I am assessed?

Your teacher will ask you to watch one of your fellow students performing the activity. They may ask you to focus on particular aspects of the performance or particular performers. They may allow you to select the aspects on which you wish to focus. After you have watched the performance for some time, they will ask you to comment on it. When you have started your response, you may well be able to look at the performance again to refresh your memory.

When you have observed the performance, the teacher will say something like, 'You have just observed the effective performance of Alex. Describe the strengths and weaknesses of the performance and create an action plan to improve a major weakness of the performance. You should apply your knowledge from physiology, psychology and socio-cultural areas to support your comments and action plan.'

The teacher will expect you to go through the stages you have already identified (as follows).

1 Identify the movement phases.
2 Identify the strengths of the performance.

3 Identify the weaknesses of the performance.
4 Select the major weakness.
5 Create a viable action plan on which you:
   (a) have clear, realistic, achievable goals
   (b) identify a timescale
   (c) identify the detailed coaching points you will use
   (d) identify the detailed practices you will use.
6 Apply theory to support your observations from:
   (a) physiological areas
   (b) psychological areas
   (c) socio-cultural areas.

If you get stuck or miss out a stage, the teacher will probably ask questions to help direct you. These questions should be the type that will guide you to think about a particular stage or area rather than needing a specific answer. Examples of these questions could include the following.

* 'What were the good elements of the performance you have just seen?'
* 'What are the causes of the faults/weaknesses?'
* 'If you were Alex's coach, what would you do in order to improve one of the major weaknesses which you have identified?'

Remember, this is your opportunity to tell your teacher how much you know and understand by applying it to the performance you observe. Ideally, once your teacher has asked you the starting question you should be able to keep talking about what you have seen until he or she wants you to stop!

Revise as you go! Test your knowledge and understanding

* Identify the two activities you are going to be assessed in together with the activity categories they are in.
* What are the performance situations in which you will be assessed in each of your two activities?
* Identify the movement phases that are used to assess each of your activities.
* Identify the coaching points for the skills in each of your activities.
* Identify progressive practices for each of the important skills in your activities.
* What are the important aspects of physical fitness for each of your two activities?
* Describe the major strategies in your activities.
* Name the activity you have selected on which to do your Evaluation and Appreciation of Performance oral response.
* Write out the six components you will cover when you do your Evaluation and Appreciation of Performance.
* List six concepts from each of the three theory areas, which you can apply in your oral response.

Chapter 7 **Synoptic application**

Learning objectives

At the end of this section you should be able to:
- understand what is meant by synoptic assessment
- understand how your exam question will be marked
- appreciate the importance of planning a synoptic answer
- understand the exact requirements of the synoptic paper
- know the characteristics of a high quality synoptic answer
- understand how to make links within and between areas of study
- identify the key dos and don'ts for synoptic success.

What is synoptic assessment?

Synoptic assessment is a form of assessment which tests understanding of the inter-relationship between different parts of a subject at the end of a course. It requires students to have a grasp of their subjects as a whole rather than as disjointed, unrelated parts.

As with all subjects, synoptic assessment in PE is worth 20 per cent of the overall mark.

- five per cent is awarded for evaluation and appreciation in coursework
- the remaining 15 per cent is given for a written synoptic question.

The following table should help put this weighting into context as it shows the relative weightings of the OCR Physical Education course.

Unit	Level		
2562	AS	Application of anatomical and physiological knowledge to improve performance	10%
		Acquiring and performing movement skills	10%
2563	AS	Contemporary studies in Physical Education	15%
2564	AS	Coursework (practical and PPP)	15%
2565	A2	Option 1: e.g. Historical studies, Comparative studies	7.5%
		Option 2: e.g. Sport psychology, Biomechanical analysis	7.5%
2566	A2	Exercise and sport physiology	5%
		Synoptic assessment	15%
2567	A2	Coursework (practical evaluation and appreciation)	15%

For synoptic assessment in PE one question is answered. This question does not need integration of knowledge from all six areas studied. Instead, there is a choice of:

- either a scientific question (both physiological work and psychological work are included in the scientific category)
- or a socio-cultural question.

The synoptic question is made up of two parts. Part One is based on AS work and Part Two is based on A2 work. Each could be made up of two or three sub questions. When selecting the question to be answered, choices need to be made within the scientific area and also (if you have studied both the historical and comparative option) within the socio-cultural area.

So, if you favour the scientific areas, you will choose one of the following six possible 'routes'.

- Route 1: AS Anatomy and physiology → A2 Exercise physiology
- Route 2: AS Anatomy and physiology → Biomechanics (only if the course has been studied)
- Route 3: AS Acquiring and performing movement skills → A2 Sport psychology (only if the course has been studied)
- Route 4: AS Acquiring and performing movement skills → A2 Exercise physiology
- Route 5: AS Acquiring and performing movement skills → A2 Biomechanics (only if the course has been studied)
- Route 6: AS Anatomy & physiology → A2 Sport psychology (only if the course has been studied).

Routes 1, 2 and 3 offer the greater scope for making links between AS and A2. Routes 4, 5 and 6 still have a scientific focus but combine both physiological and psychological studies. While routes 4–6 are allowed, they may not be the most sensible ones to choose, as they provide fewer opportunities for making strong linking statements (for which you will be given credit).

If on the other hand the socio-cultural area is favoured, one of the following two routes may be chosen.

- Route 1: AS Contemporary studies → A2 Historical studies (only if the course has been studied)
- Route 2: AS Contemporary studies → A2 Comparative studies (only if the course has been studied).

TASK 1

Discuss with your teacher the pros and cons of choosing a route that combines the physiological with psychological areas. For example, if you combine them you may get maximum knowledge marks, write fluently and consistently use technical language, but linking comments are likely to be more difficult to make and may be vague.

HOT TIPS

Use a pencil to cross through the question parts that you eliminate. It should help you to focus more directly on what you have to do.

The examination paper for Unit 2566 (Exercise and sport physiology and Synoptic application).

The exam paper for Unit 2566 will comprise a multi-page booklet including:

- the compulsory Exercise and sport physiology question in Section A
- two synoptic questions in Section B from which you choose one. You then need to answer from Part One and Part Two of the question you have chosen.

The examination is $1\frac{1}{2}$ hours long. It is advisable to spend no longer than 30 minutes on Section A to ensure adequate time for the synoptic question. You might then divide the remaining time as follows:

15 minutes	Choosing question and planning answer
20 minutes	Writing up Part 1 (AS)
20 minutes	Writing up Part 2 (A2)
5 minutes	Proofreading/checking your answer.

Planning the synoptic answer

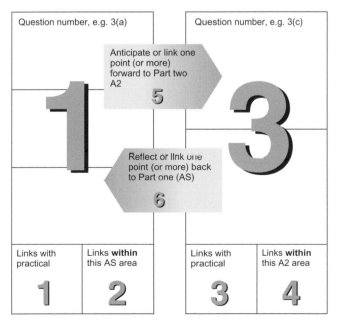

Fig. 7.01 A possible planning grid for the synoptic answer.

Planning the synoptic answer is absolutely essential! However, there is not a right or wrong way to plan, so rigid guidance cannot be given. The blank grid (Fig. 7.01) is just one possible format for ensuring that the key features of a high scoring synoptic answer are included. It should not be seen as a universal or foolproof planning method.

This model or grid is for a three part question in AS and a two part question in A2. The numbers indicate the order in which some candidates might plan their answer.

How is the synoptic question marked?

The total number of marks for the paper is 60. Fifteen of these are for the compulsory Exercise and sport

333

physiology question and 45 are for the synoptic question (representing 15 per cent of your final grade).

26 of the 45 marks are awarded for subject specific knowledge
19 of the 45 marks are awarded for 'synoptic' skills.

The synoptic question is therefore marked in two ways:

1. for subject knowledge
2. for other skills and related knowledge (see below).

You will score highly for knowledge marks (13 marks at AS plus 13 marks at A2) if you have learned and understood your work over the two years and revised well for the examination.

What makes a good synoptic answer?

When practising, planning and proofreading synoptic questions consider the following.

*   Does the introduction show that the question has been understood?
*   Have practical examples been given throughout?
*   When answering Part 1 – AS, and Part 2 – A2, have internal links been made?
*   Has at least one link been made from AS to A2 or vice versa?
*   Has every opportunity been taken to make a personal opinion or judgement (particularly in the socio-cultural question)? One way of doing this is by developing key points that you have already made.
*   Has technical language been used consistently and accurately? (particularly in the scientific question). For example, give all anatomical features their correct academic names.
*   Does each paragraph have a clear point and purpose?
*   Has each sub-question in Part 1 (AS) and each sub-question in Part 2 (A2) been addressed?

Subject specific information

The chart below shows specification areas that have appeared on past synoptic papers.

Scientific focus: Physiological route

(Question 2 on the exam paper)

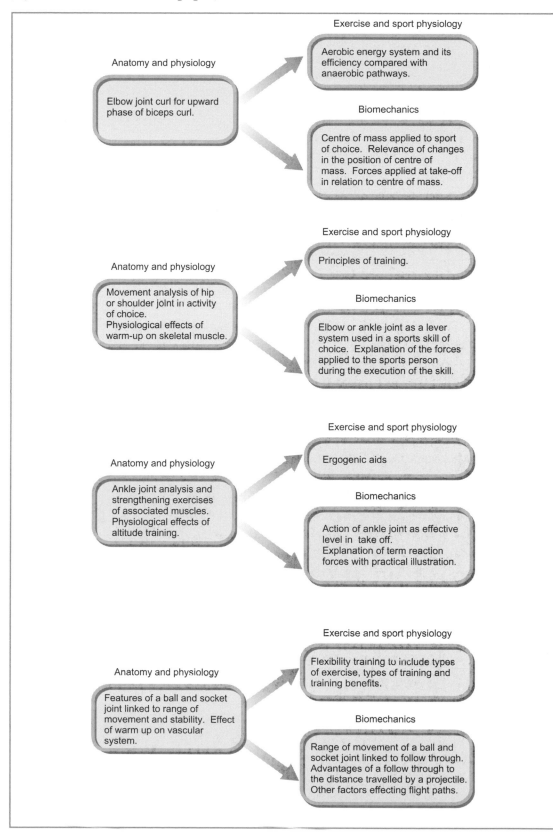

Scientific focus: Psychological route

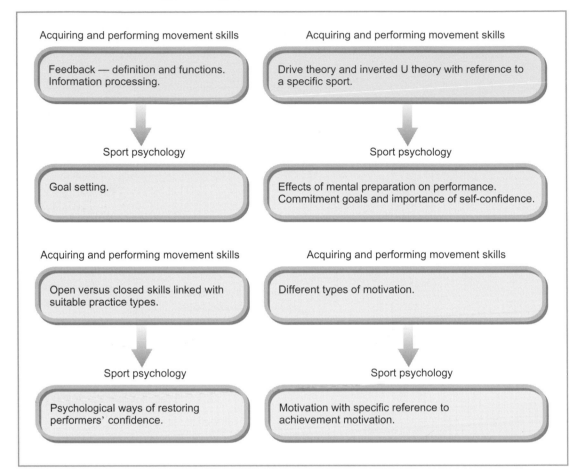

Socio-cultural focus

(Question 3 on the exam paper)

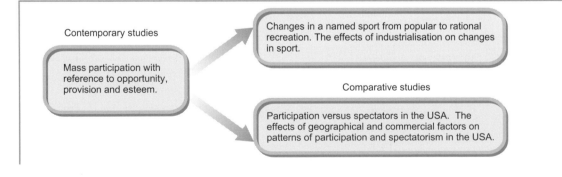

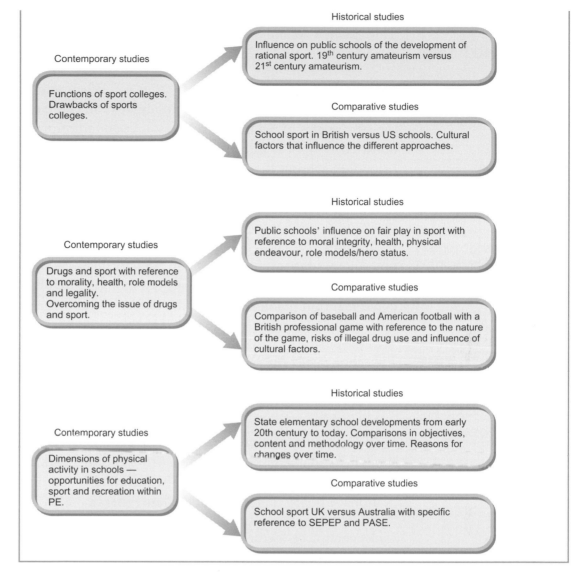

Making links within and between specification areas

Linking is very important, but it is just one characteristic of a good answer. Linking to practical performance is as important as linking within and between theoretical work.

Some examples of practical and theoretical links.

Practical links.

This is where a candidate illustrates a knowledge mark with a relevant practical example.

Example.

When answering a 'skill' question on different types of motivation and mentioning self satisfaction (for which a knowledge mark is gained), a candidate could then make the practical link that satisfaction is felt when completing a round of golf with a score below handicap.

Theoretical links.

This is when a candidate makes a link between a knowledge mark and another relevant theoretical area. Remember, there are two types of theoretical links.

Example 1, linking within AS or within A2. When answering a Contemporary studies question on Top Sport as an initiative in primary schools and mentioning the advantages of equipment and resources that are provided (for which a knowledge mark is gained) a candidate could then make the comment that in secondary schools the Sports College initiative also allows institutions to benefit from increased equipment, resources and facilities.

Example 2, linking forward from AS to A2 and/or back from A2 to AS. Anticipating forward. This example is for a candidate going down the pure physiology route and answering an AS part question on the effects of warm-up on the vascular system and an A2 part question on flexibility training. Here candidates could mention the link between the effects of the warm-up on the vascular system and how this benefits a flexibility training session.

Reflecting back. Another example would be for a candidate going down one of the two socio-cultural routes (Contemporary studies to Historical studies), and answering a Part 1 AS question on sporting excellence in the UK which linked with a Part 2 A2 question on factors affecting the development of excellence in nineteenth-century English public schools. Here, a candidate could mention the funding available in public schools (from endowments and school fees) and link this back to AS Contemporary studies by mentioning funding available through the National Lottery (and the World Class Programme).

Links cannot be learned ahead of the exam. The quality and quantity of links depends on knowledge and understanding of the specification as a whole and skilfulness at connecting related parts together. It also depends on the question set. The tables below are suggestions of parts of the specification that lend themselves to being linked. They are not exhaustive.

HOT TIPS

The keys to making good links are:

- knowledge and understanding of the subject as a whole
- careful thought and planning
- practice
- the nature of the question.

AS **Anatomy and physiology**	**A2** **Exercise and sport physiology**
Joints	Energy concepts and ATP Principles of training and components of fitness Aerobic capacity Strength Flexibility Performance enhancement
Motion and movement	Principles of training and components of fitness
Heart	Energy concepts and ATP Recovery process Aerobic capacity Performance enhancement
Vascular	Recovery process Principles of training and components of fitness Aerobic capacity Performance enhancement
Respiratory	Recovery process Principles of training and components of fitness Aerobic capacity Performance enhancement

Fig. 7.02 Some links between Anatomy and physiology (AS) and Exercise and sport physiology (A2)

AS **Anatomy and physiology**	**A2** **Biomechanics**
Joints	Levers Angular motion
Motion and movement	Newton's Laws Linear motion Force Work and power Projectile motion Centre of mass Levers Angular motion
Heart	
Vascular	Projectile motion
Respiratory	Projectile motion

Fig. 7.03 Some links between Anatomy and physiology (AS) and Biomechanics (A2)

AS Acquiring and performing movement skills	A2 Sport psychology
Theories relating to the learning of movement skills Motivation and arousal	Personality
Learning Skills in Physical Education	Aggression
Motivation and arousal Information processing	Arousal Attentional styles
Motivation and arousal Information processing Learning skills in Physical Education	Audience effects Stress anxiety
Motivation and arousal Abilities and motor skill development	Achievement motivation
Motor control Feedback	Attribution
Theories related to the learning of movement skills	Learned helplessness
Motor control of skills Theories relating to the learning of movement skills	Confidence theories Attribution retraining
Motivation and arousal	Goal setting
Motivation and arousal Reinforcement	Attitudes
Theories relating to the learning of movement skills Motivation and arousal	Group processes
Theories relating to the learning of movement skills Motivation and arousal	Leadership

Fig. 7.04 Some links between acquiring and performing movement skills (AS) and Sport psychology (A2)

AS **Contemporary studies**	A2 **Historical studies**
Leisure, physical recreation, outdoor recreation, sport	Popular recreation Rational recreation
Play, Physical Education, outdoor education	Public school athleticism State elementary education
Sport in schools	Public school athleticism State elementary education
Surviving ethnic sports Tribal and emergent cultures	Popular recreation
Sport and commercialism	Rational recreation
Excellence in UK sport	Public school athleticism Rational recreation
Mass participation	Popular recreation Rational recreation
Minority groups e.g. women	Women in sport in pre-industrial versus post-industrial times Public school athleticism Rational recreation

Fig. 7.05 Some links between Contemporary studies (AS) and Historical studies (A2)

AS **Contemporary studies**	A2 **Comparative studies**
Leisure, physical recreation, outdoor recreation, sport	Mass participation and excellence in France, USA and Australia
Play, Physical Education, outdoor education	Physical and outdoor education in France, USA and Australia
Sport in schools	School sport in France, USA and Australia
Surviving ethnic sports Tribal and emergent cultures	Ethnic sports in France, USA and Australia
Sport and commercialism	Commercialism, particularly in the USA
Excellence in UK sport	Excellence in France, USA and Australia
Mass participation	Mass participation in France, USA and Australia
Minority groups	Minority groups in France, USA and Australia

Fig. 7.06 Some links between Contemporary studies (AS) and Comparative studies (A2).

Do...	Don't...
revise your AS work well.	worry, the synoptic question for PE is more straightforward than it first appears!
answer one question (with an AS part and an A2 part).	attempt more than one question.
choose either a scientific or a socio-cultural question.	combine a scientific and socio-cultural question.
stick to what you have studied.	try questions on routes you have not studied!
focus on knowledge (26 marks).	be vague or go off the point.
focus also on synoptic skills, especially linking, analysis, judgement, use of specialist vocabulary and good quality written communication (19 marks).	restrict your AS revision to one area – you may not like the question that comes up in that area.
plan your answer with key words and bullet points – remember, key words mean you will get more marks!	over plan! you may run out of time to write up the question.
take care to answer all sub-parts of the AS question and the A2 question.	write down all the information you can recall without specific reference to the question.
answer the AS part question and then the A2 part question.	try to merge the two parts into one essay-style answer.

Fig. 7.07 A Do and Don't chart for answering the synoptic question.

Revise as you go! Test your knowledge and understanding

- How many synoptic questions must be answered?
- Which other question is on the same paper?
- How many parts to the synoptic question?
- How important is knowledge to the synoptic answer?
- How important are other features such as linking?
- What other skills are examined other than the ability to link?
- Identify three different types of linking for which credit can be given.

HOT TIPS

Remember, only one full question should be answered: Part 1 (AS) plus Part 2 (A2).

Sharpen up your exam technique!

Scientific focus

You must answer from both Part 1 *and* Part 2.

Part 1: Answer either (a) or (b).

HOT TIPS

Remember, the synoptic question is out of 45 marks: 26 for subject specific knowledge, and 19 for synoptic skills.

a) Application of anatomical and physiological knowledge to improve performance Flexibility is affected by the type of joint and the muscle attachments. With the aid of a diagram, identify the features of the hip or shoulder joint. Explain how some of these features affect the range of movement and stability of your chosen joint.

The range of movement of a joint can be affected by increased blood flow to the joint. One way of achieving this is through an effective warm up. Explain how a warm up affects the vascular system.

b) Acquiring and performing movement skills
Describe how information is processed in order to produce a skilful performance. Explain how an understanding of information processing can help the teaching of sports skills.

Part 2: Answer (c) or (d) or (e).

c) Exercise and sport physiology
The purpose of flexibility training is to improve or maintain the range of movement over which muscles can act and joints can operate. Electing either the hip or shoulder joint, give examples of types of flexibility exercises in an activity of your choice.
Describe the types of training that can be used to increase the range of movement in that joint. What are the benefits of flexibility training to a performer?

d) Biomechanical analysis of human movement
An increase in the range of movement of the hip or shoulder joint will enable a greater follow-through in a variety of sporting activities. Using a technique of your choice, explain how this would increase the distance travelled by a projectile. Describe the other factors that affect the flight path of an object.

e) Psychology of sport performance
Explain why the degree of arousal experienced by a performer will influence the quality of performance in a sports situation.
Outline strategies that could be used by the coach to control the athlete's concentration before a sports event.

Socio-cultural focus
You must answer from both Part 1 and Part 2.

Part 1

a) Identify current initiatives in UK schools, and in the UK as a whole, which should increase sporting excellence in the UK.

Part 2: Answer either (b) or (c)

HOT TIPS

Not all questions will have sub-sections. Sometimes broader questions will be asked (as in these socio-cultural examples).

b) Historical studies in Physical Education
Explain how nineteenth-century English public schools promoted and achieved sporting excellence.

c) Comparative studies in Physical Education
Identify an initiative in Australian schools that promotes sporting excellence. Compare cultural factors in the UK with those in Australia that might influence each country's view of sporting excellence.

Index